THE STACKPOLE SOCIAL SCIENCE SERIES

LAURENCE FOSTER, EDITOR

DYNAMIC URBAN SOCIOLOGY

Edited by

WILLIAM E. COLE
Head, Department of Sociology
University of Tennessee

THE STACKPOLE COMPANY
HARRISBURG, PA.

Printed in the U. S. A.
by
The Telegraph Press
Established 1831
HARRISBURG, PENNSYLVANIA

Authors of Chapters

SAMUEL W. BLIZZARD: 18
Pennsylvania State University
State College, Pennsylvania

CLARENCE E. BOEBEL: 16
Dale Avenue Settlement
Knoxville, Tennessee

WILLIAM E. COLE: 1, 4, 12, 13,
    14, 15, 19, 20
University of Tennessee
Knoxville, Tennessee

JERRY WALKER COMBS: 2, 3
Emory University
Emory, Georgia

RUSSELL R. DYNES: 7, 10
Ohio State University
Columbus, Ohio

LUKE EBERSOLE: 17
University of Tennessee
Knoxville, Tennessee

LLOYD H. ELLIOTT: 9
Cornell University
Ithaca, New York

PAUL M. AND LEAH G. HOUSER: 5
Kent State University
Kent, Ohio

EDWIN L. LIVELY: 6
Kent State University
Kent, Ohio

VIRGIL E. LONG: 8
University of Tennessee
Knoxville, Tennessee

ROBERT R. WESTON: 11
United Fund and Council
Knoxville, Tennessee

Preface

DYNAMIC URBAN SOCIOLOGY has been prepared as a basic text in urban sociology for college students. The book is designed for junior and senior levels.

In the structuring and preparation of the book several interesting features were stressed. We believe the volume is comprehensive enough to serve both courses in urban society and urban problems. To give added meaning and significance to the urban materials, emphasis is placed upon rural-urban contrasts. Both the general editor of the series and the editor of the volume desired a book which, in addition to a rich volume of knowledge of urban society, would give the student something he could apply as he lives and works in urban and rural-urban situations after his college days are over. Finally, in addition to sociologists who have written in their special fields, we desired that some chapters be prepared by specialists in other fields. For example, Professor Elliott works in the field of educational administration; Mr. Boebel is director of a settlement house, while Mr. Weston has headed Community Chests and Councils in Salt Lake City, Utah, and Knoxville, Tennessee.

Workshop suggestions and problems have been included at the end of each chapter. Ample bibliographies have also been included.

The editor wishes to thank Professor Laurence Foster, editor of the Stackpole Social Science Series, for his many suggestions, and wishes to thank Mrs. Margaret Garrett, Mrs. Billie Lewis, and Mr. Roy Cox for their aid in preparing the manuscript for publication.

WILLIAM E. COLE

Knoxville, Tennessee
March 15, 1954

Table of Contents

CHAPTER 1

Historical Perspectives In Urban Development

By WILLIAM E. COLE

The human race has lived most of its "life" under rural conditions. Indeed, as Professor Combs shows in Chapter 2, roughly 75 percent of the world's population today live in countries that are more than half rural.[1] At the same time, the urbanizing of populations constitutes one of the more marked social trends in both Western cultures and Eastern cultures.

In terms of historical time and archaeological time, cities are quite old. In terms of anthropological time they are of recent origin. One must hasten to add, however, that any datings on the beginnings of cities are subject to new archaeological excavations and explanations which may, at any time, push back the curtain of urban archaeological research to the remains of earlier cities than have to date been catalogued.

Back to Neolithic Time. There is considerable evidence that the earliest villages, towns and cities in Egypt, in the Euphrates Valley, in Greece, and in Northern Europe have their foundations in the Neolithic or New Stone Age culture. Besides the artifacts of this period, among them polished stone weapons and implements and pottery, two key elements in the culture of the Neolithic period were settled agriculture and the husbandry of domesticated animals—the dog, the pig, the horse, and the ox. Agriculture and the domestication of herds tended to demobilize nomadic people, at least for certain seasons of the year, and thus to develop village settlements. Upon Neolithic village foundations many cities were built, possibly in part because the villages were located at strategic localities. Cooper Cole cites evidence to support this claim:

> On the Islands of Crete are the ruins of the city of Knossos, the seat of the great Minoan Kingdom. The city surmounts a hill which was long considered a natural elevation. But as the work of excavation progressed it was found that one city was built on the ruins of another and that these continued downward to the base of the hill. There in the lowest levels, ninety feet below the surface, were found the remains of a Neolithic settlement . . .

[1] Chapter 2, p. 16.

Excavations at Susa, the capital of King Darius, reveal a Neo-lithic lower stratum. The same is true of Anau in Russian Turke-stan and at Alishar in Anatolia . . .

It appears then that the cultures of the Near East, of Egypt, of Greece and Rome and all central and Southern Europe rest defi-nitely on this Neolithic foundation, and that the two chief stones in the structure are agriculture and animal husbandry . . .[2]

We are told that as early as 5000 and 3500 B.C. stone age villages in South West Asia and North East Africa overshot in size the villages with a customary eight to thirty-five individual huts.[3] One lake dwelling village at Parma, Italy, constructed during the New Stone Age period, is estimated to have had a population of from 3,000 to 5,000 B.C.[4] Later, the metal ages, beginning with the Bronze Age (e.g., 2500 B.C.) gave many improved cultural items which added to the utility, conveni-ence and protection of centralized populations. Among these items were ornaments, improved tools and weapons, vessels, the wheel, and a group of occupations growing out of the smelting and fabrication of metal. Ac-cording to Walker: "There are clear records of Egyptian and Mesopo-tamian cities whose streets were laid out on the familiar rectangular pattern over five thousand years ago."[5]

The Greek City. The manifold contributions of Greece to the culture of the world make it imperative that the urban sociologist give some attention to the Greek city and its contributions. Brevity is necessary in a general text; however, the serious student may want to explore the detailed studies having to do with the Greek city[6] and Grecian civiliza-tion.

"The ancient Greeks called themselves Hellenes and their land Hellas."[7] The earliest inhabitants to arrive in Greece were semi-no-madic peoples from the Balkan peninsula. Clan elements apparently held the nomads together as well as did common hearths. These migra-tions were very active as early as 1300 B.C.

Aristotle in his *Politics* indicates that the Greek city passed through three stages in its development. The first stage was the community, or

---

[2] Fay Cooper Cole, *The Long Road From Savagery to Civilization* (Balti-more: The Williams Wilkins Co., 1933), pp. 50-51.

[3] Svend Riemer, *The Modern City* (New York: Prentice-Hall, Inc., 1952), p. 3.

[4] Noel P. Gist and L. A. Halbert, *Urban Society*, third edition (New York: Thomas Y. Crowell Co., 1948), p. 16.

[5] Robert Averill Walker, *Urban Planning* (Chicago: University of Chicago Press, 1949), pp. 3-46.

[6] Such as Gustave Glotz, *The Greek City and Its Institutions* (London: Routledge and Kegan Paul Ltd., 1950). Ralph Turner, *The Great Cultural Traditions* (New York: McGraw-Hill Book Company, 1941). Gordon Childe, *What Happened In History* (New York: Penguin Books Inc., 1946). Albert A. Trever, *History of Ancient Civilization*, Vol. I (New York: Harcourt, Brace & Company, 1936).

[7] Trever, *op. cit.*, p. 141.

oikia, a family structure involving all who ate at a common table and worshipped at a common altar, whether they were kin or non-kin, slave or master. Out of this social system developed the village, or kome, a larger grouping of families, where the oldest heads of the households exercised great powers. The third stage was an association of villages called the complete state and looked upon by Aristotle as the perfect community or polis. In these lay both fundamental strengths and fundamental weaknesses.[8]

The geographical features of Greece were especially favorable to the establishment of federated villages, although the determining factors

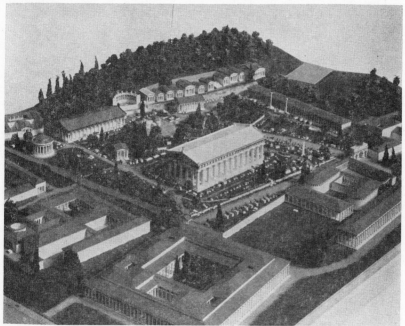

Courtesy of the American Museum of Natural History

FIGURE 1. Model of the Greek City of Olympia about 150 A.D.

which went into the formation of city states were as much ideological as geographical. There is some evidence that the concept of the city state was conceived as early as 1000 B.C.[9]

The coast of Greece offered fine harbors and fresh water supplies conducive to the growth of navigation, commerce and communication with other countries. The ancient Phratries had their gods, ancestral worship was common, so the altar and the temple became a nucleus around which centers of population were to grow. As Professor Glotz indicates: "Just as the kinsmen gathered before the altar of the family

[8] Glotz, op. cit., p. 1.
[9] Ibid., p. 12.

hearth, so the citizens celebrated the religion of the city before the common hearth.' "[10] The worship of Athena was a case in point and around the Acropolis Athens grew to a glorious position in Greece. Usually the Acropolis was on a hill which gave protection to the population. Around the lower reaches of these hills were frequently found walls, interspersed with towers which served as lookouts and housing for the defenders of the city. Entrance to the city when it was under siege was difficult, thus the place of ocean transport, water supply, worship, and protection were all important factors in the growth of the Greek city.

One other factor, the market, was important in the development of the Greek city. The market became a gathering place for people, and around it permanent settlements frequently grew. The Greek's love for sports and dramatic arts was so great that gymnasia, stadia and theatres were standard equipment of cities.

Greek leaders had varying conceptions of the ideal city. Hippodamus of Miletus held that the ideal city should have 10,000 inhabitants but Plato arrived at 5,040 as the ideal size. This number he obtained by applying the Pythagorean formula $1x2x3x4x5x6x7=5,040$.[11] Plato felt that this number was adequate for defense, was small enough to encourage mutual aid of the people to each other and to other communities, and also small enough that the citizens could select their magistrates with knowledge of their fitness.

Some Greek cities greatly exceeded the "ideal size." The city state of Athens in the Periclean Age had a population of between 40,000 and 50,000 adult males.

The contributions of Greece belong to both history and to sociology. Aside from their contribution to art, architecture, public works, and city planning, the Greek City State made many contributions to democratic ideology, to liberty and equality of its citizens. The Assembly of the People, the City Council, the rule of the Magistrates and the experiences, good and bad, in the unification of the city states constitute major cultural contributions stemming from the Greek city.[12]

Rome. Without a doubt Fustel de Coulanges over-simplified the development of the ancient city. He said:

> We should not have the idea of ancient cities that we have of those we see built in our day. A few houses are erected and that is a village; the number of houses is gradually increased and it becomes a city and we finish it, if there is room, by surrounding it with a moat and wall. Among the ancients a city was not formed in course of time by a slow increase in the number of inhabitants and buildings, but they constructed it at once, complete almost in a day.[13]

---

[10] *Ibid.*
[11] *Ibid.*, p. 26.
[12] For more detail see Turner, *op. cit.*
[13] Fustel de Coulanges, *La Cité Antique* (Paris: Hachette, 1900), p. 151.

There is some evidence that Rome was founded in this manner as village populations pushed southward from the Alps.[14] Rome reached a population of perhaps 800,000[15] during the time of Augustus (475-476), the last Roman ruler of the Western Empire. This population was achieved largely through the migration of conquered peoples to Rome.

The Roman State spanned the period 754 B.C. to the death of Justinian I in 565 A.D. and during that time had at least six different forms of government.

Roman urban architecture was on the whole on a grander scale than much of Greek architecture, perhaps due in part to improved methods of building and, secondly, to great emphasis upon architecture and buildings as an expression of power and strength. The public forum, with its auxiliary buildings, was the architectural center of the city as well as the center of trade, governmental activity, and amusement. Great stress was laid upon the erection of triumphal arches dedicated to the exploits of the emperors. The Etruscan arch was a central feature in buildings where great supporting strength was needed.

The Roman road system was one of the great achievements of ancient construction. Buildings were profusely ornamented. Some of the aqueducts and sewers were so well built that they are in fair state of preservation today. Excellent port facilities were maintained. Theatres, markets, and public baths reflected pride and public interest. Beyond this ostentation were the crowded slums where festered disease and discontent which at times were the undoing of the city itself. Beyond the slums toward the open country were the palatial homes of the landed classes.

The planners would say that Rome did not exemplify comprehensive master planning, and the political scientists and sociologists would agree that "Classic Rome, even more than Athens, was a city built by and for the few."[16]

The Cities of the Mayas. The cities of the Mayas have been inadequately recognized by urban sociologists. In view of the amount of excellent research which has been done on the Mayan cultures, this neglect must be due in large measure to the fact that Mayan cities are looked upon as monument structures or temples of worship.

The Mayan cultures reached high points in development in Yucatan Peninsula, in Guatamala, and British Honduras. The early period of the Old Empire began about 300 A.D. and extended to the "period

---

[14] See Pierre Clerget, "Urbanism: A Historic, Geographic and Economic Study," *Annual Report of the Board of Regents of The Smithsonian Institution, 1912* (Washington: The Government Printing Office, 1913), pp. 653-659.

[15] *Ibid.,* p. 653.

[16] Theodore T. McCrosky, et al., *Surging Cities* (Boston: Greater Boston Development Committee, 1944).

of disintegration" which was from 1400 to slightly after 1700 A.D.,[17] the Spaniards having arrived in 1559. Morley, in quoting Londa, describes an ancient Maya town as follows:

> Before the Spaniards had conquered that country (Yucatan) the natives lived together in towns in a very civilized fashion. They kept the land well cleared and free from weeds, and planted very good trees. Their dwelling place was as follows—in the middle of the town were their temples with beautiful plazas, and all around the temples stood the houses of the lords and priests and then (those of) the most important people. Then came the houses of the richest, and of those who were held in the highest estimation nearest to these, and at the outskirts of the town were the houses of the lowest class.[18]

Population estimates[19] of individual cities like Uaxactun, center of the Old Empire, have been made, with estimates exceeding 1,000 individuals per square mile of habitable land or about 50,000 population. Applying density study figures to the whole of Yucatan Peninsula population estimates ranging from 13,000,000 to 53,000,000 are obtained.[20]

On the basis of excavations and surface studies, Morley indicates four sites of Class I cities, nineteen Class II cities, thirty-nine sites in Class III, and fifty-four Class IV sites. Classification is based on size, the extent of architectural remains and the excellence of the sculptured monuments.[21]

Tikal, the largest city of the Maya civilization, has been described by Morley.[22] This city was located at Peten, Guatemala, at the head of the Holmul Valley. The civic and ceremonial heart of the city covered about one square mile. Smaller courts and plazas flanked by buildings extended outward in decreasing frequency for another two or three miles. Five great pyramid-temples, one of them 229 feet in height, gave the city its most outstanding architectural characteristic. Elaborate wood carvings graced the doorways, and elaborate carvings were made on all buildings. Lengthy causeways built of hand-placed and filled stone spanned the ravines to connect one group of temples and plazas with another.

Nature combined with the efforts of men to build a great Maya culture. As Morley says:

"The Yucatan peninsula furnished everything the ancient Maya manner of living required, and indeed in the greatest abundance—

---

[17] For interesting stages and development of Maya history see Sylvanus Griswold Morley, *The Ancient Maya* (Stanford University, California: Stanford University Press, 1947), pp. 80-81.
[18] *Ibid*, pp. 312-313.
[19] *Ibid.*, p. 314.
[20] *Ibid.*, p. 316.
[21] *Ibid.*, pp. 317-318.
[22] *Ibid.*, pp. 320-321.

building stone, lime and gravel for their religious and governmental buildings, timber and thatch for the houses of the common people, and exceedingly rich and varied flora, which supplied every kind of non-flesh food, seasonings, kitchen utensils, medicines, fibers for tex-

Courtesy of the American Museum of Natural History

FIGURE 2. Model of Maya Temple at Tikal, Guatemala.

tiles, and basketry. The forest also supplied game of all kinds; the jaguar and deer were especially hunted, their pelts being made into cloaks and sandals for the rulers and priest; finally, there were many birds of beautiful plumage.

"But amidst all this abundance, nature's richest gift to man was maize—the Maya staff of life—without which they never could have developed their highly distinctive culture, the most brilliant aboriginal civilization of the new world. And if we bear constantly in mind the fact that from three-fourths to five-sixths of everything the ancient

Maya eats, even today, is corn in one form or another, and that their culture was based directly upon, and derives straight from, agriculture as applied to the cultivation of corn, we shall have learned the most basic fact about the Maya civilization."[23]

The Medieval Town. In his classical and scholarly work on *The West European City,* Dickinson indicates three phases of development of the West European city—the Medieval covering the period 1000 to 1500; the Renaissance and Baroque covering the period 1500 to the middle of the nineteenth century; and the Modern phase following 1850.[24]

Many medieval cities had their beginnings in tribal settlements which grew out of trade, religion, tribal administration, or defense. Many medieval towns were castle strongholds surrounded by feudal lands, and many of them had cathedrals as their nucleus.[25] Others had their beginnings in the market place, some of which were planned street markets. Market places were frequently located in villages, where they were patronized by farmers of the surrounding countryside. As the markets grew in importance the villages grew and larger towns resulted. The real symbols of the medieval town and city, however, were the castle and the church.[26] On the continent of Europe the town wall was also an invariable development of the town.

Due to great epidemics in the fourteenth century, little growth was noticed in many of the medieval towns and cities. In 1348 the Black Death killed an estimated 25,000,000 persons in Europe, including 2,000,000 persons in England alone. In 1603 and 1625 it returned to kill an estimated 15 per cent of the population.

The Industrial Revolution. The next epoch in the stirring of the world, especially Europe, was the Industrial Revolution, which brought many changes affecting urbanization of populations.

Industrial development was a centralizing process especially where water power or steam power processes were involved. Improved transport—river, ocean, and land—developed with the Industrial Revolution. Improved ocean and river transport brought the growth of river and sea coast towns. At breaks in overland transportation along caravan and railroad routes settlements developed. Along with improved transport went improved storage of food and, finally, along with industrial development came improved agriculture, making it possible to free people from agriculture and to feed people in towns and cities with the surpluses grown on the lands.

As the Industrial Revolution proceeded in Europe, accompanying changes took place, making it possible for large areas of concentrated populations to exist with greater security against famine and disease.

---

[23] *Ibid.,* p. 158.
[24] Robert E. Dickinson, *The West European City* (London: Routledge & Kegan Paul, Ltd., 1951), p. 301.
[25] *Ibid.,* p. 311.
[26] *Ibid.*

Smallpox vaccination was introduced in 1798. In 1746 iron pipe was introduced in England and improved water supplies were on their way in the cities. Sanitary sewage systems began to replace cesspools. Later, e.g., 1850, refuse removal began to become common in European cities thus greatly improving environmental sanitation in cities twenty-five years before water filtration began on any considerable scale. Thus the conditions of life in large cities was made safer and large scale urbanization, as we shall see in the next chapter, was on its way.

WORKSHOP AND PROBLEMS

1. Characterize the neolithic period, giving the peculiar contributions which led to the centralization of people into villages.
2. What were some of the leading characteristics of Greek cities?
3. What forces in the history of Greece led to the growth of cities?
4. What were the greatest urban achievements made by the Romans?
5. What forces in the Maya civilization led to urbanization?
6. What factors during the medieval period kept city growth alive?
7. Collect a display of reproductions and exhibits of Mayan art.
8. Why did the Industrial Revolution accelerate urban growth?

BIBLIOGRAPHY

Childe, Gordon, *What Happened in History* (New York: Penguin Books, Inc., 1946).

Clerget, Pierre, "Urbanism: A Historic, Geographic and Economic Study," *Annual Report of the Board of Regents of Smithsonian Institution, 1912* (Washington, D. C.: The Government Printing Office, 1913).

Cole, Fay Cooper, *The Long Road From Savagery to Civilization* (Baltimore: The Williams Wilkins Co., 1933).

Coulanges, Fustel de., *La Cité Antique* (Paris: Hatchette, 1900).

Dickinson, Robert E., *The West European City* (London: Routledge and Kegan Paul, Ltd., 1951).

Gist, Noel P., and Halbert, L. A., *Urban Society*, third edition (New York: Thomas Y. Crowell Co., 1948).

Glotz, Gustave, *The Greek City and Its Institutions* (London: Routledge & Kegan Paul, Ltd., 1950).

Morley, Sylvanus Griswold, *The Ancient Maya* (Stanford University, California: Stanford University Press, 1947).

Riemer, Svend, *The Modern City* (New York: Prentice-Hall, Inc., 1952).

Trever, Albert A., *History of Ancient Civilization*, 2 vols. (New York: Harcourt, Brace & Company, 1936).

Turner, Robert, *The Great Cultural Traditions* (New York: McGraw-Hill Book Co., 1941).

Walker, Robert Averill, *Urban Planning* (Chicago: University of Chicago Press, 1949).

CHAPTER 2

Urban Growth As World Phenomenon

By JERRY WALKER COMBS, JR.

At the close of the nineteeth century A. F. Weber wrote that "the tendency toward concentration or agglomeration is all but universal in the Western world," and called it "the most remarkable phenomenon" of the century.[1] Little more than half a century later it can now be said that although the urbanizing tendency is still marked in the Western world, it has become almost universal throughout the globe. Scarcely any area has not been affected by the trend, and, generally speaking, the most rapid rates of increase for cities are now in those areas with the smallest percentage of their population urban.[2]

Great urban concentrations are essentially the products of modern times. It is doubtful if Carthage, Rome, or Constantinople ever had as many as one million inhabitants at their peak, and, as indicated in Chapter 1, the worlds in which they existed were overwhelmingly rural. As recently as 1800 there was no city of more than one million, London, the world's largest city at that time, falling just short of that number. By 1890 there were eight such cities, and according to the most recent count shown in Table I there are sixty-three cities with over a million population if the suburban areas contingent to central cities are included. Weber could count only twenty-nine cities of 100,000 or more population in 1800,[3] but by 1951 or thereabout the number of cities of this size, including estimates for the cities of China, was at least 862.

Comparability of Urban Data. The tracing of urban development on a world-wide basis in anything like precise terms is limited by lack of essential and comparable data. In some countries censuses have either never been complete or are out of date. There are wide gaps in data covering Africa, very little accurate knowledge of China is available, and the most recent data for Soviet Russia is 1939. Lack of data is more serious concerning the historical development of cities. For only a small portion of the world can urban development over any prolonged

---

[1] A. F. Weber, *The Growth of Cities in the Nineteenth Century* (New York: The Macmillan Co., 1899), p. 1.
[2] United National *Demographic Yearbook 1952*, pp. 13-14.
[3] Weber, *op. cit.*, Table CLXIII, p. 450.

TABLE I

NUMBER OF CITIES BY POPULATION SIZE AND CONTINENTS, CIRCA 1950[1]

Continent	Size of City				
	1,000,000 and Above	500,000 to 1,000,000	100,000 to 500,000	50,000 to 100,000	20,000 to 50,000
Africa	1	5	34	25	71
North America[a]	15	15	108	145	346[b]
South America	4	5	38	38	125
Asia	20	21	221	333[c]	1,006[c]
Europe	19	26	231	345	1,189
Oceania and Pacific Islands	2	0	8	2	10
U. S. S. R.	2	9	78	92[a]	... [d]
Total	63	81	718	980	2,747

[a] Includes Central America and Caribbean Islands.
[b] Includes eleven cities in Cuba classified as 20,000 to 99,999.
[c] For cities below 100,000 population, no data is available for China.
[d] No information on cities of less than 50,000.
[1] Based on United Nations, *Demographic Yearbook 1952*, Tables 7 and 8.
[2] From Frank Lorimer, *The Population of the Soviet Union* (Geneva: League of Nations, 1946), Appendix Table A 24, pp. 250-253. The United Nations *Demographic Yearbook 1952* includes seven cities for Russia of over 100,000 population not included in Lorimer's tabulation.

period be delineated. Data prior to the beginning of the twentieth century is almost entirely restricted to Europe and the United States.

Comparisons between different countries are also difficult because countries differ widely in their definitions of what constitute urban populations and in their methods of classification. When cities were walled, their inhabitants isolated from the rural, and their separate character recognized by charters which gave them distinctive legal status, the problem of distinguishing rural from urban did not arise. But when cities began to overrun their traditional boundaries in the nineteenth century, and to extend their influence to all parts of a nation, it has been a continuing problem to decide where to draw the line between rural and urban categories.[4]

Some countries include in the urban category only places legally defined as urban either from an administrative standpoint or according to some characteristic other than numerical. The urban category of England and Wales, Ireland, and some European countries includes all places with urban status regardless of size. In Italy communities with less than 50 per cent of the economically active population engaged in agriculture are urban, and in many South American countries the administrative centers of departments or provinces are

[4] *Ibid.*, pp. 6-11.

classified as urban.[5] Others classify urban areas according to population, but differ with respect to the minimum size of community considered urban. In the United States and its possessions and territories, and in Mexico, the minimum is set at 2,500. The most generally used minimum in the rest of the world is 2,000. Among countries falling in these two categories no really material error in comparisons arises, but the minimum populations defined as urban are found to range from less than 500 in Iceland and Denmark to 20,000 in the case of the Netherlands and 30,000 in the case of Japan.[6] For the Netherlands the official urban percentage is 54.6, however, this would be 72.5 per cent if towns and cities 2,000 and above were included, whereas Iceland's official 71.7 per cent would be reduced to 46.7.[7]

When individual cities are compared, a further difficulty is encountered due to differences in degree to which town or city limits coincide with the limits of urban agglomerations. It is not always feasible politically or administratively to extend town limits with each expansion in population. Figures on the total urban agglomeration are available for some cities but not for others.

These several deficiencies and problems make comparison of the degree of urbanization or its rate for different parts of the world difficult and imprecise at best. But as long as the limitations are borne in mind and too fine distinctions are avoided, the data available do permit the delineation of major trends in world urbanization and meaningful comparisons between various countries and regions.

Urbanization in Europe. As indicated in Chapter 1, the most important developments to which the growth of modern cities is to be attributed are usually given as: (1) the expansion of commerce, (2) the increase in agricultural surplus, (3) the development of large-scale industry, (4) the development of rapid means of transportation and communication, (5) the improvement in sanitary and health conditions of cities, and (6) a phenomenal growth of population. Of these, commerce, industry and new forms of transportation form the immediately most important cluster. The others were essential conditions for their effectiveness, and all are closely related to changes in economic organization which accompanied them, fostered them, and in some cases were inspired by them.

The beginnings of the present trend in urban growth can be conveniently located in the same area where urbanism is most highly developed today—Europe. The increasing importance of commerce during the Middle Ages was marked by considerable urban growth and increase in the political importance of towns and cities. As these grew,

---

[5] United Nations *Demographic Yearbook 1952*, Table 6; T. Lynn Smith, "Population Analysis" (New York: McGraw-Hill Book Co., 1948), pp. 28-29.

[6] United Nations *Demographic Yearbook 1952*, pp. 9 and 177.

[7] *Ibid.*, p. 9.

an increase in agricultural products was gained by bringing new fields into production, more intense cultivation, specialization of products, and the adoption of crop rotation.[8] The improvement of tools, more scientific farm practices, and enclosures in England just prior to the advent of the Industrial Revolution effected not only a further increase in per capita product, but also led to the displacement of rural populations whose only recourse was to find their way into the cities or overseas.[9] Commercial activity also fostered the development of industry, especially textile manufacturing, and in England the metal trades, the manufacture of leather goods and paper-making also came into importance.[10]

Additionally, the more rational approach characterizing the Renaissance had culminated in the discovery of new continents, scientific inventions, advancement in the control of disease, and improvement in city sanitation, and, in the economic sphere, in rational capitalism.[11] As important as anything for the development which was to come was the emergence of the merchants, or the *bourgeoisie,* as the dominant class, and their creation of an economic and political structure capable of exploiting both events and resources to the fullest. The very mechanism of their endeavors generated capital needed to develop large-scale industry when it became technologically possible; and fortuitously, capital accumulation in England had been vastly increased by the profitableness of the Napoleonic wars and colonial exploitation.[12]

The phenomenal effect of the invention of steam power can therefore only be understood in terms of the circumstances in which it appeared, but it was nevertheless revolutionary. Before its appearance industry and commerce did not support large urban concentrations. At the height of textile manufacturing in Flanders, the largest town, Ghent, numbered probably less than 50,000 inhabitants.[13] By 1750 none of the towns of England were large except London. Cole reports that the population of Bristol was then 43,000, of Norwich 36,000, of Liverpool 22,000, and of Manchester and Salford and Birmingham as 20,000 "with their environs." [14] The great cities, London and Paris, were much larger and owed their importance as much to their political roles as to their commercial and manufacturing enterprises; and at

---

[8] Henri Pirenne, *Economic and Social History of Medieval Europe* (New York: Harcourt, Brace and Co., no date), pp. 69-85; Lewis Mumford, *The Culture of Cities* (New York: Harcourt, Brace and Co., 1938), pp. 22-23.

[9] G. D. H. Cole, *Introduction to Economic History, 1750-1950* (London: Macmillan and Co., Ltd., 1952), pp. 41-43, 150-151.

[10] *Ibid.,* pp. 22-26.

[11] Max Weber, *The Protestant Ethic and Spirit of Capitalism* (New York: Charles Scribner's Sons, 1948), p. 20 ff.

[12] Cole, *op. cit.,* pp. 40-48.

[13] Pirenne, *op. cit.,* p. 172.

[14] Cole, *op. cit.,* p. 21.

least London, with between 500 and 700 thousand population, was provisioned with difficulty.[15]

Steam provided the mechanism for the increase in factory size and freed the factory from the limitations upon location dictated by available water power sites. Thereafter the factory could be more efficiently organized in terms of available capital, labor resources, and markets, and greatly enlarged. Other inventions, such as the power-loom, followed, and when steam power was applied to land transportation, the industrial age came into full swing. Railroad building greatly expanded the metal trades and the iron and coal industry. It also served to open up the interior of continents for commerce, where before heavy trade had been limited to coastal points.

The combined effects of these two revolutionary events, industrialization and railroad building, were to speed urban growth phenomenally. England, where both industrial and rail development occurred earliest, showed its greatest urban development in the decades 1820-1830 and 1840-1850.[16] By 1850 London's population was approaching two and one-half million. Manchester-Salford, Glasgow, and Liverpool contained more than 300,000 inhabitants, Birmingham numbered 232,800, and Leeds, Edinburg-Leith, and Sheffield all contained more than 100,000. Virtually 40 per cent of the population of England and Wales lived in urban places of more than 10,000 inhabitants, and more than 30 per cent of the population of Scotland lived in such cities. By the end of the century, England and Wales were more than 60 per cent urban, and London's population was over seven million.

On the rest of the continent the greatest impact occurred after 1850. The only other country whose greatest period of urban increase occurred before that date was the United States. France's great growth came between 1850 and 1870, Belgium's between 1866 and 1890, and Denmark's and Prussia's not until after 1870, although after that date it was very rapid in the latter. Of the countries of northwestern Europe only the Netherlands showed little increase in per cent of the population living in cities of 10,000 or more, but it was singular in that at the beginning of the century its percentage urban was higher than in any other European country; at the end of the century only England and Wales, Scotland, Belgium and Saxony had surpassed it. The dates of maximum increase in percentage urban corresponds generally to the period of greatest increase in industrialization and railroad building.[17]

The twentieth century has seen the continuation of the process of urban growth in these countries and its expansion in other parts of Europe. As can be seen in Table II, by 1950 or thereabouts Germany,

---

[15] *Ibid.*

[16] A. F. Weber, *op. cit.*, pp. 150-152.

[17] *Ibid.*, pp. 151-152.

TABLE II

PERCENTAGE URBAN IN SELECTED COUNTRIES OF THE WORLD[1]

Rank	Country	Date	Per Cent Urban[2]	Rank	Country	Date	Per Cent Urban[2]
1	Scotland	1951	82.9*	34	Mexico	1940	35.1*
2	England and Wales	1951	80.7*	35	Hungary	1949	34.5*
3	Israel	1951	77.5*	36	Bolivia	1950	33.6*
4	Netherlands	1947	72.5	37	U.S.S.R.	1939	32.8*
5	Germany (Fed. Rep.)	1950	71.1	38	Finland	1950	32.3*
6	Hawaii	1950	69.0*	39	Tunisia	1946	32.0*
7	Australia	1947	68.9*	40	Guatemala	1950	31.6*
8	Germany (Dem. Rep.)	1946	65.4	41	Brazil	1950	31.2
9	United States	1950	63.7*	42	Portugal	1940	31.1
10	Belgium	1947	62.7*	43	Ecuador	1950	30.3*
11	Argentina	1947	62.5	44	Egypt	1947	30.1*
12	New Zealand	1951	61.3*	45	Columbia	1938	29.1*
13	Spain	1950	60.5	46	Costa Rica	1950	28.8
14	Denmark	1950	58.8	47	Nicaragua	1950	27.6
15	France	1946	52.9	48	El Salvador	1950	27.5
16	Sweden	1950	51.9	49	Federation of Malaya	1947	26.5*
17	Canada	1951	51.9	50	Turkey	1950	25.2*
18	Venezuela	1950	49.8*	51	Bulgaria	1946	24.6*
19	Cuba	1943	49.6*	52	Morocco (Fr.)	1947	24.2
20	Chile	1940	49.2	53	Philippines	1948	24.1*
21	Austria	1951	49.1	54	Dominican Republic	1950	23.8*
22	Czechoslovakia	1947	48.8	55	Algeria	1948	23.6*
23	Greece	1940	47.2	56	Romania	1948	23.4*
24	Italy	1936	44.6	57	Iran	1950	20.0*
25	Norway	1950	41.1	58	Korea (Rep. of)	1949	19.6*
26	Puerto Rico	1950	40.5*	59	Jamaica	1943	18.2*
27	Union of South Africa	1951	39.4	60	India	1951	17.3*
28	Japan	1950	37.5*	61	Yugoslavia	1948	16.2*
29	Switzerland	1950	36.5*	62	Belgian Congo	1950	15.8*
30	Ireland	1951	36.4	63	Ceylon	1947	15.4*
31	Paraguay	1950	35.9*	64	Haiti	1950	12.5*
32	Poland	1949	35.8*	65	Burma	1931	10.4*
33	Peru	1940	35.4*	66	Nigeria	1931	8.5*

[1] Based on United Nations *Demographic Yearbook 1952*, Table 6.

[2] Urban category includes residents of localities of 2,000 or more inhabitants unless designated by *. Definition of urban for other countries (*) numbered as in Table above, as follows:

(1, 18, 19, 29, 49) All cities, burghs and villages of 1,000 or more inhabitants;

(2, 12, 31, 32, 38, 51, 56, 57) places with urban status, regardless of size;

(3) predominantly non-agricultural centers: towns, urban settlements and urban villages;

(6, 26, 36) cities and towns of 2,500 or more inhabitants;

(7) capital cities of states and territories, other cities which are separately incorporated and other agglomerations within boundaries determined for census purposes and classified as urban;

(9) incorporated and unincorporated places of 2,500 or more inhabitants, including the urbanized zones around cities of 50,000 or more inhabitants;

(10, 59) communities of 5,000 or more inhabitants;

(24) communities with less than 50 per cent of the economically active population engaged in agriculture;

(28) municipalities, most of which contain an agglomeration of 30,000 or more inhabitants;

(29) communities of more than 10,000 inhabitants;

(31, 57) definition unknown;

(33) capitals of departments, provinces and districts and other populated centers the number of whose inhabitants exceeds the average for the capitals, provided such centers do not have typically rural characteristics;

(34) autonomous cities and county towns;

(35, 40, 43, 54, 64) administrative centers of departments, provinces and cantons (Bolivia and Ecuador); of municipios (Guatemala); of communes and municipal districts (Dominican Republic and Haiti);

(37) localities having an urban form of government;

(39) centers with the status of communes;

(44) governments and chief towns of provinces and districts;

(45) centers of more than 1,500 inhabitants which are seats of municipios or districts;

(50) places with a municipal organization, i. e., administrative centers of provinces and districts regardless of size, and other agglomerations of 2,000 or more inhabitants;

(53) chartered cities and administrative centers of municipalities;

(55) agglomerations of 2,000 or more inhabitants that are administrative centers of communes having local self-government;

(58) incorporated cities of 40,000 or more inhabitants;

(60) 1951 definition unknown; prior to 1951 the urban population included inhabitants of places of 5,000 or more inhabitants, possessing definite urban characteristics and included a few places of less than 5,000;

(61) administrative units that are governed by City People's Committees;

(62) agglomerations containing 100 or more non-indigenous inhabitants and all indigenous population living outside the regular districts;

(63) municipalities, urban council areas and Local Board areas;

(65) municipalities and towns—see India, No. 60;

(66) the forty (40) largest towns.

Belgium, the Netherlands, Denmark, France, and Sweden all exceeded 50 per cent urban, and England, where the process began earliest, was more than 80 per cent urban. As late as 1890 Ireland, Norway, Sweden, Switzerland, Austria, Hungary, Portugal and Russia contained less than 20 per cent of their populations in cities of 10,000 or more, the last named having less than 10 per cent. By 1950 all of these except Hungary and Portugal exceeded 35 per cent of their population urban. Russia, retarded in development and difficult to study, and still in 1939 with only 32.8 per cent urban, had shown remarkable growth since 1926—a growth undoubtedly continuing.[18] Lorimer lists forty-nine Russian cities of more than 50,000 inhabitants in 1939 which had increased more than three times since 1926. At least twenty-three million persons migrated to cities from rural areas during the period.[19] Moscow was a city of 4,137,000 in 1939 as compared with slightly more than two million in 1926 and 822,400 in 1890; and Leningrad had increased from about one million in 1890 to 1.7 millions in 1926 and more than three millions in 1939.

It was only in some southern and eastern European countries, like Yugoslavia, Romania and Bulgaria, where 75 per cent or more were still rural, that urbanization had not gained a firm foothold.

Urbanization outside Europe. Urbanization in Europe was accompanied by an expansion of European economy and population into almost every part of the world. In the Americas, New Zealand and Australia it was borne by European settlers and kept alive by trade between these and the continent. In Africa and Asia the penetration was only partially done by settlers, rather primarily by commercial agents. Only one country, Japan, successfully adopted it from Europeans. These areas provided the raw materials and agricultural products necessary to Europe's rapid urbanization; they provided markets for manufactured products; and to urbanize and make available these resources and markets was one of the functions of the extensive railroad building outside Europe. Financed and supplied with steel from Europe itself, this process contributed further to the industrial growth and prosperity of the continent.[20] But it also brought about the extension of urbanization into other parts of the world.

1. *North America.* Outside Europe urban development has been on a grander scale in the United States than anywhere else. Because it will be dealt with more fully in the following chapter, it will suffice to point out here that urbanization in the United States and Canada paralleled that in Europe during the nineteenth and twentieth centuries. North America was early an area of substantial European settlement and, because of rich resources and a population which turned

[18] Frank Lorimer, *The Population of the Soviet Union: History and Prospects* (Geneva: League of Nations, 1946), pp. 175-181.

[19] *Ibid.,* pp. 148-150.

[20] Cole, *op. cit.,* pp. 90-92.

itself readily to their development for home consumption, was able to combine an extensive agricultural development with a phenomenal urban growth. It played a crucial role in the redistribution of European populations during the nineteenth and twentieth centuries, absorbing millions of the surplus populations of Europe in its cities and expanding farm lands. Canada has been influenced by many of the same factors as has the United States; and the urban and industrial development in the latter and commerce with northwestern Europe has led to considerable urbanization in the southeastern portion. Less densely settled than its southern neighbor, Canada has relatively few large cities, but in 1950 more than 50 per cent of its total population lived in towns and cities of more than 2,000 inhabitants. Including suburbs, two of its cities numbered more than a million, ten more than 100,000.

2. *South America.* South America's early settlement was accomplished about the same time as North America's, and in 1800 Rio de Janeiro's population of about 125,000 made it the largest city in the western hemisphere with the possible exception of Mexico City. But climate, nature of the continent, dynamics of settlement and the culture of the settlers differed from that of North America, and the southern continent maintained both political and economic ties with Europe longer than did the United States. Exploitation of the continent has been characterized by a large estate economy, oriented commercially toward Europe, and the hinterland of the continent has been poorly developed. As a consequence, urbanization is not so far advanced as in North America, and the principal cities are almost all located on the coast or on navigable rivers and "face outward toward . . . other continents." [21] Urban growth in the past has had a predominantly commercial base, made possible in part by a territorial division of labor between the continent and the more industrialized countries of Europe and North America.

Considering the relative lack of industrialization, there has nevertheless been a remarkable urban development, particularly of large cities. Paralleling the industrial development of Europe and the construction of railroads, the growth of large cities has occurred principally since 1850. Although both Rio de Janeiro and Buenos Aires were larger than New York in 1800, they grew only moderately until 1850. Between 1850 and 1890, however, both grew more rapidly than New York, and Buenos Aires has continued to grow faster than any city of its size or larger in the western hemisphere. By 1950 there were eighty-five cities of over 50,000 population, nine of more than half a million, and four above one million.

Although the continent is predominantly rural, Argentina, Uruguay

---

[21] Kingsley Davis and Ana Casis, "Urbanization in Latin America," *Millbank Memorial Fund Quarterly*, Vol. XXIV (April, 1946), p. 192.

and Chile were more urbanized than Canada, Argentina almost as much as the United States.[22] The most rapid urbanization has occurred in the latter, Argentina's urban population having increased from 37.4 per cent in 1895 to 62.5 per cent in 1947. On the northern coast Venezuela is almost 50 per cent urban. The rest of the continent and of the Caribbean area to the north is predominantly rural. But two of the cities of more than one million, each with more than two million inhabitants, are in Brazil, which boasts only 31.2 per cent of its population urban; and among the Caribbean countries, Mexico, with only 33.5 per cent urban, contains one city of more than two million inhabitants. Cities are growing more rapidly than the total population in all areas.

3. *Australia and New Zealand.* European populations have also largely supplanted the indigenous populations of Australia and New Zealand. Settlement of these two areas, however, came later than did settlement of either North or South America, and when urbanization was already proceeding rapidly on the continent of Europe. Perhaps partly due to this factor, and also due to the nature of the areas, rural settlement has not achieved great density, and urban development has been part of the pattern of settlement. In 1881 the population in cities of 10,000 or more was already 41.4 per cent of the total.[23] Furthermore, the Australasian population has been singularly concentrated in its large cities, and smaller towns and villages have tended to cluster close to the larger ones, so that they could be considered suburbs of the latter even from the beginning. Both Australia and New Zealand are among the most highly urbanized countries today, as shown by Table II, and the rate of growth of their large cities since 1890 or 1900 has been slightly greater than that of the cities of northwestern Europe.

4. *Asia and Africa.* Diffusion of urban civilization from Europe has met in both Asia and Africa with somewhat different conditions than elsewhere. Europeans have settled on these two continents in relatively small numbers. The indigenous populations have remained and their predominantly rural cultures have only gradually been modified by contact with western influences. Such urbanization as has occurred resulted largely from commercial and transport activities incident to the exploitation of raw materials of the two continents for consumption in the more industrialized areas. Although an important consequence has been to establish the basis of an urban structure which may well develop more fully in the future, another has been to confirm reliance upon primarily extractive endeavors, making the transition to urban conditions more difficult.

Partly because western culture has been imposed upon native agriculturism, partly because Asia is both the largest continent and the most densely settled, that continent presents the anomaly of overwhelming

---

[22] *Ibid.*
[23] A. F. Weber, *op. cit.*, p. 140.

agriculturism co-existing with an urban development which in number and size of cities is second only to that of Europe (Table I).

Urbanization has proceeded more rapidly in Japan than anywhere else, and that country represents the sole example to date of a non-European people adopting western industrial civilization and carrying it to such a high state of development. The event is very recent. Japan was opened to western commerce only after 1850 and as late as 1920 only 18.1 per cent of its population resided in cities of 30,000 or more inhabitants. By 1950 approximately double the proportion in 1920, or 37.5 per cent, lived in cities of that size. Using a definition of urban as nearly comparable to that in other countries as possible, Japan was more than 60 per cent urban, ranking at least above the United States.[24] Data for 1946 indicate that in the last days of the war Japan's urban population was considerably reduced, but recovery since then has been rapid. Besides Tokyo there were sixty-three cities of more than 100,000 population in 1950, eighty-six others with 50,000.

Elsewhere commerce with Japan and the West and modest industrialization have maintained some urban development. Remarkable agricultural success in southern and eastern Asia has, however, made possible the support of dense agricultural populations which tend now to retard urban-industrial development, and the bulk of the population remains rural.[25]

The percentage of urban population in China is unknown, but it is certainly low. There are in China nine cities of more than one million inhabitants, according to estimates, and twenty-four cities of more than 100,000. The imbalance in these figures among themselves and in comparison with estimates of the total population of China suggests a high concentration of urban population in large cities and not a widespread urban structure.

Other predominantly agricultural and rural countries also boast large cities. Korea and Pakistan each contain eleven cities of more than 100,000 population, Thailand has ten, the Philippines and Iran have eight each, Indonesia seven, Indochina, Formosa and Turkey, five each. Available figures for these countries do not reflect very rapid increases in per cent of the population which is urban.

India, the other great Asiatic country, excluding Asiatic Russia, has less than 20 per cent of its population in cities, but that percentage is increasing. From 1881 to 1951 India's urban population increased from 9.3 per cent to 17.3 per cent, by far the greatest increase occurring after 1941.[26] Despite this still small percentage, how-

---

[24] *Infra.*, p. 17.

[25] Kingsley Davis, "Population and the Further Spread of Industrial Society," *Proceedings of the American Philosophical Society,* Vol. XCV, No. 1, (February 13, 1951), pp. 15–16.

[26] Part of the increase from 12.8 per cent (1941) to 17.3 per cent (1951) may be due to a change in definition of urban place in 1951, but that definition is not yet available. See United Nations *Demographic Yearbook 1952,* p. 177.

ever, India has four cities of more than one million, seventy-one others of more than 100,000, and in all 152 cities of more than 50,000. Its two largest cities are thirteenth and fifteenth in the list of the world's great cities (Table III) and have increased almost three and one-half times (346 and 342 per cent respectively) since 1891. The large cities have shown a more rapid increase than has the total population.[27]

Africa, less densely settled than Asia, has likewise experienced only moderate urbanization. As in South America, urban development in Africa is largely restricted to the coastal area, emphasizing the importance of commerce in such development as has occurred, as well as difficulties of developing the interior.

The Union of South Africa, the most Europeanized of African countries, shows the most rapid urban development and contains several important cities. Its European population is, in fact, almost as highly urbanized as are the English. Its mining region provides the only important interior urbanization in Africa. Urbanization there is fairly recent with the major increase having occurred since 1921.

Urbanization has likewise proceeded on the northern coast at both the western and eastern end of the Mediterranean. Egypt, though a country which is less than one-third urban, nevertheless contains one of the great metropolises of the world, Cairo, whose population has increased four-fold in the last half century.

Present Distribution of Urban Population. Altogether the process of urbanization over the past century and a half has given rise to sixty-three cities of more than one million inhabitants and 862 cities of more than 100,000. These figures are, of course, only approximate. Where known, the total urban agglomeration was included in determining the number of cities of over one million (Tables I and III). For a number of cities this figure is not known, and the most recent data for Soviet Russia are for 1939 and those for China are estimates. For cities below 100,000 population the number is probably even more inaccurate, for the enumeration includes no cities in China of less than 100,000, none for Soviet Russia of less than 50,000 as enumerated in 1939, and none for Japan of less than 30,000. There are unquestionably more than 4,589 cities of 20,000 or more inhabitants in the world today.

These cities are largely located in the northern hemisphere. Of the sixty-three cities of more than one million, almost two-thirds are on the great Eurasian land mass, which also contains most of the world's population, and almost another one-third are located on the continent of North America. Only one-ninth are found in South America, Africa and Oceania together.

Most of the important cities, moreover, are concentrated in three clusters, corresponding with a single exception to areas with the highest

---

[27] Kingsley Davis, *The Population of India and Pakistan* (Princeton: Princeton University Press, 1951), p. 129.

TABLE III

GROWTH OF MAJOR CITIES OF THE WORLD[1]

City	1950[2]	1900[2]	1850[2]	1800[2]
New York	12,296,117*	3,437,202	660,800	62,900
London	8,346,137*	6,581,372	2,362,100	958,800
Shanghai	5,406,644†	620,000	......	......
Tokyo	5,385,071	1,818,655	......	......
Chicago	4,920,816*	1,698,575	29,963	......
Paris	4,775,711*	2,714,068	1,053,300	546,900
Buenos Aires	4,603,035*	821,293	120,000‡	70,000‡
Moscow	4,137,018	1,092,360	360,000‡	300,000‡
Los Angeles	3,996,946*	102,479	1,610	......
Berlin	3,336,475	1,888,848	378,200	173,400
Leningrad	3,191,304	1,313,300	490,000	270,000
Philadelphia	2,922,470*	1,293,697	121,376	41,220
Bombay	2,839,270	776,006	560,000‡	150,000‡
Detroit	2,659,398*	285,704	21,019	......
Calcutta	2,548,677	1,026,987	400,000‡	800,000‡
Manchester	2,421,011*	543,872	388,500	90,400
Rio de Janeiro	2,377,451*	750,000	170,000‡	125,000‡
Birmingham	2,236,723*	522,204	232,800	70,700
Mexico, D.F.	2,233,709	541,516	150,000‡	137,000‡
Boston	2,233,448*	560,892	136,881	24,937
Cairo	2,090,654	570,062	250,000‡	250,000‡
Sao Paulo	2,041,716	64,934	......	......
San Francisco	2,022,078*	342,782	34,776	......
Osaka	1,956,136†	995,945	......	......
Peiping	1,940,290†	1,000,000	......	......
Tientsin	1,785,813†	750,000	......	......
Vienna	1,760,784	1,674,957	431,100	232,000
Glasgow	1,758,193*	735,906	329,100	77,100
Rome	1,695,477	462,783	175,900	153,000
Leeds	1,692,190*	428,968	172,300	53,200
Madrid	1,618,435	539,835	281,200	156,700
Hamburg	1,605,606	705,738	205,000	120,000
Pittsburgh	1,532,953*	321,616	46,601	1,565
Budapest	1,571,205*	732,322	156,500	61,000‡

* Population figure includes total urban agglomeration. This figure used whenever data were available. Otherwise the population figure is for city proper and may or may not include total urban agglomeration.

† Estimated population circa 1950.

‡ Denotes approximate population as cited in Weber, apparently based on estimate of population.

[1] Data for 1950 from United Nations *Demographic Yearbook, 1952;* for 1900 largely from *The Statesman's Yearbook, 1905;* for 1800 and 1850 from A. F. Weber, *The Growth of Cities in the Nineteenth Century* (New York: The Macmillan Co., 1899) Table CLXIII, p. 450, and U. S. Department of Commerce, Bureau of the Census, *1950 United States Census of Population,* "U. S. Summary, Number of Inhabitants," Series P-A1 (Washington: U. S. Government Printing Office, 1952).

[2] Understand in each case as circa 1950, 1900, 1850 or 1800; majority of data in 1950 column are for 1950 or 1951, but in a few cases for 1947, 1948 or 1949, and Russian data are for 1939.

proportion of the population urban. Of first rank in terms of number and size of cities and percentage of the population urban is north-western Europe. Five of the first ten countries listed in Table II are in that area, and ten of the first twenty are also located there. This is the seed-bed of modern urbanism. Second in importance is the north-eastern United States. The United States is only ninth (tenth, if Japan is properly placed) on the list of countries in terms of percentage urban. Many of its states, however, are as large and as highly urbanized as the countries of Europe. It boasts the world's largest city, New York, and five of the world's twenty-three cities of more than two million inhabit-ants are found in its northeastern portion. The third urban cluster of importance is in eastern Asia—Japan. In Table II, Japan is listed as twenty-eighth, but the percentage urban is based on a definition of urban which rarely includes population agglomerations of less than 30,000 persons. Actually Japan should rank at least ninth on the list, ahead of the United States. As early as 1935 the percentage of popula-tion residing in cities of 5,000 or more in that country was 64.5,[28] and although a comparable figure is not available for 1950, some increase has undoubtedly occurred since then. If the great cities of China are included in this configuration, then eastern Asia contains the third and fourth in rank among the world's large cities and fourteen of the cities in the world with more than one million inhabitants.

It is to be noted that all three of these areas are characterized by heavy industrial development and are on the edge of continents. Com-mercial access to sources of supply and markets of the world has been most important. At the same time, the development of interior cities in all these areas contrasts sharply with the predominantly coastal location of urban centers elsewhere in the world.[29] In part the latter indicates the locational importance of sources of raw materials like coal and iron; in part the ability of industrial societies to develop the material and market resources of interior areas through rail and highway networks.

In addition to those regions named above, Australia, New Zealand, Hawaii, and the three southernmost countries of South America are also among the most highly urbanized areas of the world from the standpoint of percentage of population in cities. But they have smaller populations and smaller urban concentration.

These four regions, however, contain only one-fourth of the world's population. Three-fourths live in countries which are more than half rural.[30] No country in Europe outside those rimming the North Sea and its sea arm into the Baltic and Spain, has as much as 50 per cent

[28] *Ibid.*, Table 45, p. 129.

[29] Paul K. Hatt and Albert J. Reiss, Jr., "World Urbanization," in Paul K. Hatt and Albert J. Reiss, Jr. (ed.) *Reader in Urban Sociology* (Glencoe, Ill.: The Free Press, 1951), p. 147.

[30] Kingsley Davis, "Population and the Further Spread of Industrial So ciety," *op. cit.*, p. 9.

of its population urban, although Austria, Czechoslovakia, Greece and Italy are close to it. The major portions of South and Central America, of Asia and of Africa are overwhelmingly rural. Despite the great growth of cities in the last 150 years, the world is far from urbanized; but, significantly, urban populations in virtually all areas are increasing more than rural.

Population Growth and Urban Development. The urbanization process is to be explained ultimately as the development of a way of organizating man's control of his physical environment so as to free large numbers from direct and primary dependence upon the soil; but as it has occurred historically it is not to be completely understood apart from the demographic changes which have accompanied it. Especially the phenomenal growth of large cities is inexplicable except in terms of the remarkable population growth which has also taken place during the last two centuries. Since 1750 the population of the world has increased almost three times, and since 1850 has approximately doubled. During the two centuries Europe's population has quadrupled and persons of European descent have increased 600 per cent.

Urban growth has both a cause and effect relationship to population increase. The civilization which created the commercial, industrial and urban development of the recent past has also channeled its technical skill into the control of disease and removal of the threat of famine. Mortality rates have fallen everywhere that European civilization has penetrated, but gains have been greatest in Europe, America, and Australasia. Whereas average life expectancy at the end of the eighteenth century was probably less than forty years,[31] by mid-twentieth century it was for whites in the United States approaching seventy years. Urban living has in turn been among the primary conditions fostering a reduction in the birth rate during the twentieth century. Urbanization has thus been instrumental in bringing about a demographic revolution as important in its way as the industrial revolution which set the urbanization process going.

The change in demographic balance has reciprocally affected the rate of urban growth. During the nineteenth century when birth rates were still high and death rates were falling, European populations grew very rapidly. Much but not all of the increased population found its way through migration into the cities of Europe and overseas into both the farms and cities of the New World. This was the century which witnessed such phenomenal growth of cities in Europe and in eastern North America. In the last half century, as the birth rate declined by virtue of increased proportions living in cities or coming under the influence of urban conditions, the rate of population growth has been less rapid. Urban growth has in consequence also slackened.

---

[31] Louis I. Dublin, Alfred J. Lotka, and Mortimer Spiegelman, *Length of Life* (New York: The Ronald Press, 1949), pp. 42-43.

In those countries where urbanization occurred earliest and the demographic transition has virtually run its course, both the rate of urban increase and the rate of population growth have recently been relatively low. Urban growth continues to be greater than population growth, however, and in some countries of Europe rural populations have actually declined in recent years.[32] Basically the result of diminishing growth in population, this fact of rural declines illustrates also the gradual urbanization of all parts of the highly developed countries. Not only do large centers continue to attract rural migrants, but rural communities also increase in size until they become themselves urban centers.

Both population growth and urban development have generally proceeded more rapidly where the demographic transition began later. High rates of urban increase were maintained in the United States and Canada for a longer period in the twentieth century than in England or Germany, and it is now going forward most rapidly in such countries as Argentina, Venezuela, Union of South Africa, Japan, U.S.S.R., and Egypt.[33]

Outside Europe it is only in Australia and, since 1940, in the United States, that rural populations even in countries of European settlement have not continued to increase. In Canada a four-fold increase of urban population since 1901 has been accompanied by a 50 per cent increase of rural residents, and Argentina's six-fold urban increase since 1895 has been accompanied by a doubling of its rural population. In these countries the rate of population growth has been more rapid than in Europe; but they have had agricultural areas which, because of low densities, could continue to be exploited more efficiently while at the same time aborbing increased rural populations. The rapid increase of urban populations in those countries has, in fact, been partly dependent upon the extension of the agricultural base, partly instrumental in bringing it about. By virtue of the growth of cities the economic basis for an efficient and profitable agriculture has been maintained, with a reciprocal effect upon urban enterprise and development. Increasing urbanization is also being followed here with diminishing rates of growth, so that near stabilization of population at a favorable man-land ratio can be anticipated.

The process of urbanization and the first phases of the demographic transition are also under way in the U.S.S.R., in portions of Africa, and in Asia. As we have seen, urban growth in the U.S.S.R. from 1926 to 1939 was very large, and the population increased from 147 million to 170 million. In Asia there is substantial urbanization already in Japan, especially, and in China and India, and population has been increasing throughout Asia.

---

[32] Belgium, Denmark, France, Germany, Sweden, and Scotland. In England and Wales and the Netherlands, rural populations have increased only slightly.
[33] United Nations Demographic Yearbook 1952, Table C, p. 14.

Just what will be the ultimate urban and population development in Asia, however, cannot be foreseen with confidence. If the demographic and urban processes were to follow the same course in these areas as in the West, then the greatest growth of cities and of populations lies in the future. Where room for expansion and resource base permit, as in Russia, rapid growth appears inevitable. But in some areas of Asia population has already expanded under the impact of western influence without a corresponding urban development taking place. The resulting high agricultural densities retard the transformation in agriculture required for the support of extensive urban populations and make for low levels of living which impede industrial and urban development. On the other hand, as urbanization proceeds, the depressing effect of heavy densities upon general levels of living, or the inability of the changing social structure to integrate large portions of the population, may prevent as striking population growth for the continent as a whole as has been observed in the West. Much of future Asiatic history will undoubtedly be written in terms of the efforts of various Asiatic countries to solve this basic dilemma.

Although three-fourths of the world's people live in countries which are still more than half rural, and the complex relationship between population, social organization and resources is such as to retard urban development in some areas, the last century and a half has seen a phenomental growth of cities in practically every part of the world. The dynamics of the new order which led to urban development emerged first in Europe, and urbanization has gone forward most rapidly in those countries settled by Europeans. Gradually, and as other peoples come under the influence and adopt certain portions of western European culture, urbanization is proceeding among non-European populations also.

The industrial base which has contributed to the greatest development of urbanization is heavy industry, close to coal and iron deposits. The great concentrations of urban population in the world are in northwestern Europe, northeastern United States, and in Japan, where the bases for heavy industry have been exploited. Industrial development has in turn been aided by an extension of commerce which has integrated endeavors of many peoples widely separated in space. Thus, while industrial countries show considerable urban development located close to raw materials, the largest of the inland cities are rail centers, and the world's greatest cities are still those with access to ocean transport.

Industry can, of course, exist in a country without heavy urban concentration resulting, as in the case of Switzerland, with only 36.5 per cent urban population. Conversely, the absence of extensive industrialization does not rule out substantial urbanization, as in Spain and several countries of South America. Variations in both industrial and agricultural organization affect the relationship between these and urban development.

Extension of urbanization to agricultural countries or regions, however, usually results from commerce with industrial areas which depend upon both food and raw materials from less industrialized ones. Northeastern United States, for example, has drawn upon continental North America as well as other regions. European urbanization was facilitated by access to products from widely scattered regions. Japan, lacking in many resources, has drawn upon those of less developed Asiatic regions. Where commercial relations are thus established, the urbanizing influence of trade then favors the growth of other cities at strategic points along transportation routes; and the new commercial centers become loci of more extensive urban development. Industries which find locations close to markets and labor supply equally or more advantageous than locations close to raw materials frequently locate in commercial and transportation centers, providing further diversification to the urban structure. If and as this process continues, the major portion of mankind may one day be urbanized.

The first phase of urbanization has been accompanied by remarkable population increase, the latter phases by a declining rate of growth. In Europe and areas of European settlement, however, the growth phase occurred under relatively favorable population-resource conditions. Population was able to expand into agricultural as well as urban areas. Future urbanization and population growth in countries where the two processes are just beginning also depend largely, at least, upon the extent to which favorable population-resource ratios, in terms of given social and economic structures, can be achieved.

WORKSHOP AND PROBLEMS

1. What are the chief difficulties in comparing urban data of different countries?

2. What forces led to the urbanization of Europe?

3. What five countries of the world are most urban? What five the least urban?

4. Why has urbanization in South America not advanced as rapidly as in North America?

5. What sections of Asia are most highly urbanized? Why?

6. What are the five greatest cities in size?

7. What is the relation between world population growth and urbanization?

8. Where are the places in the world where the outlook for urbanization is greatest?

BIBLIOGRAPHY

Cole, G. D. H., *Introduction to Economic History, 1750-1950* (London: Macmillan and Co., Ltd., 1952).

Davis, Kingsley, *The Population of India and Pakistan* (Princeton, N. J.:

Princeton University Press, 1951), Chapters 15-16.

————, "Population and the Further Spread of Industrial Society," *Proceedings of the American Philosophical Society*, Vol. XCV, No. 1 (February 13, 1951).

Davis, Kingsley, and Hertz, Hilda, *Pattern of World Urbanization* (New York: The Macmillan Company, 1954).

————, and Casis, Ana, "Urbanization in Latin America," *Millbank Memorial Fund Quarterly*, Vol. XXIV (April, 1946), pp. 186-207.

Gist, Noel P., and Halbert, L. A., *Urban Society* (New York: Thomas Y. Crowell Co., 1950).

Hatt, Paul K., and Reiss, Albert J., Jr., *Reader in Urban Sociology* (Glencoe, Ill.: The Free Press, 1951).

Hoover, Edgar M., *The Location of Economic Activity* (New York: McGraw-Hill Book Co., 1948).

Lorimer, Frank, *The Population of the Soviet Union: History and Prospects* (Geneva: League of Nations, 1946).

Mumford, Lewis, *The Culture of Cities* (New York: Harcourt, Brace & Co., 1938).

Pirenne, Henri, *Economic and Social History of Medieval Europe* (New York: Harcourt, Brace and Co., no date).

United Nations, *Demographic Yearbook, 1952* (New York: United Nations, 1952).

Weber, Adna Ferrin, *The Growth of Cities in the Nineteenth Century* (New York: The Macmillan Co., 1899).

CHAPTER 3

Urban Growth in the United States

By Jerry Walker Combs, Jr.

In few places of the world has urbanization gone forward as rapidly during the nineteenth and twentieth centuries as in the United States. Little more than a century and a half ago, the country was largely wilderness. The European settlements transplanted to America were restricted to the Atlantic seaboard, and among these only twenty-four towns, containing a mere 5.1 per cent of the total European population, had as many as 2500 inhabitants. In the 160 years since the area of settlement has been extended across the continent, the economy has been so transformed from its predominantly rural character that the United States ranks today among the three great urban-industrial areas of the world.

Despite its relatively large size among the countries of the world, it is high on the list from the standpoint of percentage in cities of 2500 or more, and its total urban population is greater than that of the United Kingdom, France and Belgium. Only England and Wales and Scotland have higher percentages in cities of 100,000 or more, and the more than 44 million inhabitants in cities of that size in the United States is larger than the combined populations in such cities in England and Wales, Scotland, Belgium, the Netherlands and Germany.[1] Not only does the country contain the world's largest metropolis, but also 7 of the 23 world cities of more than 2 million inhabitants (Table III, Chapter 2). There is no comparable urban population under the same politico-economic system in the world today.

According to the definition of urban population used in the 1950 census, 64.0 per cent of the population in that year, or 96,467,686 of the 150,697,361 persons in the continental United States, were urban. For certain areas the percentages were much higher. In the North East, where almost one-third of the urban population is located, the percentage urban was 79.5 per cent. By far the greater number lived in the more populous Middle Atlantic States (80.5 per cent urban), but more than three-fourths of the New England population was urban. Five states contained populations which were above 80 per cent urban—

---

[1] United Nations, *Demographic Yearbook 1952* (New York, United Nations, 1952), Table B, p. 11, and Table 7, pp. 188-201.

31

Massachusetts, Rhode Island, New York, New Jersey and California—and two others—Connecticut and Illinois—were more than three-fourths urban. In all, thirteen of the forty-eight states exceeded the national average of 64.0 per cent in the percent of their population which was urban.

The amazing growth of the urban population in the United States has been the result of rapid industrial development and population growth in a country abounding in natural resources. The industrial development on which urbanism rests, in turn, derives from the energy and initiative of a people who, drawn from diverse origins, shared a culture particularly favorable in its ideology and technology to the exploitation of the country's natural wealth. Although it has occurred under especially favorable circumstances, the growth of cities in America affords an excellent example of the urbanization process. That growth also helps to explain the cultural and social transformation in American society and many of the pressing problems to which it gives rise.

Increase of the Urban Population. Urban development in this country is singularly easy to trace, since the decennial censuses over the past 160 years cover virtually the whole period of significant urban growth. Equally important, although the definition of the term "urban" has varied, the Bureau of the Census has been able to adjust the earlier data to conform to the definition in 1940, thus providing for comparability as well as continuity.

1. *Definition of urban.* Essentially the population considered urban up to the present in the United States has been that residing in incorporated places of 2500 or more inhabitants. Because incorporation practices have varied among the states, certain additional categories of population which were clearly urban, though living outside of incorporated places, have also been included.[2] All other population was classified as rural, separated from 1920 onward into rural-farm and rural-non-farm. Although the minimum population of 2500 is entirely arbitrary, it can be consistently applied, and the 1940 definition has been adequate to reflect the growth of cities and the spread of urbanism throughout most of the period. Its chief inadequacy has been in reflecting the changing patterns of living among the urban population in the last several decades, and that was at least partially corrected in the 1950 census. In that year the definition of urban population was extended to include, besides the population in incorporated places of 2500 or more: (1) inhabitants of unincorporated places of 2500 or more where concentration of settlement gave these the same characteristics as incorporated places, and (2) inhabitants of the densely settled areas in the urban "fringe" around cities of 50,000 or more.[3] The diffi-

---

[2] U. S. Bureau of the Census, 1950 United States Census of Population, *U. S. Summary, Number of Inhabitants,* P-A1 Preprint of Vol. I, Chap. 1 (Washington: U. S. Government Printing Office, 1952), p. xiv.

[3] *Ibid.*

culty presented by the change is that the 1950 definition cannot be applied to earlier data; but only the interpretation of decade by decade growth since 1920 or 1930 is seriously affected, since it is doubtful if the additional population included under the latest definition was, prior to 1930, either large or essentially urban.

2. *Increase in Percentage Urban.* Tables IV and V present the pertinent statistics of increase in the total urban population from the first census in 1790 until the present. Comparison of the earliest figures with those for England at the same period shows that the United States was far behind in urban development at the end of the eighteenth century. Early settlement was almost entirely rural, the major portion of the localities which served for distributing and service centers being small villages or trading posts.[4] The largest of the cities, Philadelphia, contained less than 30,000, Boston contained 20,000, and all the towns later to be incorporated into the city of New York contained together less than 50,000. In fact, fifty years later, in 1840, the country was still predominantly rural, only 10.8 per cent of the entire population living by then in towns of 2500 or more.

The United States was, however, on the verge of expansion, and at least a partial basis for future urban growth already existed. Settlement of America itself had resulted from that burst of discovery, invention, commercial development and population growth which preceded large urban growth in Europe, and most of the United States' initial European population came from those countries where urbanization developed earliest. American culture was but an extension of the European. The similarity in culture made communication between the two continents easy; and a thriving commerce in the New World's abundant resources and the manufactured products of Europe had already been established, largely explaining the existence of such cities as there were. Here, as elsewhere, it was commerce which provided the first stimulus to urban growth.

The development of native manufactures soon followed. The first power loom was installed in 1814; steam engines were introduced in 1830; and iron production increased rapidly in the first four decades of the nineteenth century.[5] Railroad building, beginning after 1830, stimulated heavy industry and the growth of large cities as it did everywhere, and also made possible the development of the continent and the utilization of its vast resources with a speed which was not possible with earlier modes of transportation.

As a result of rapid expansion of industry, commerce and population,

---

[4] Non-inclusion of this village population in the urban reflects its essential rurality, but fails to give a true picture of growth of such places during the early period, since a very small gain in population which moved a town into the 2500 category counted as a gain of 2500 at the next census enumeration.

[5] Richard A. Lester, *Economics of Labor* (New York: The Macmillan Co., 1947), p. 78.

TABLE IV

GROWTH OF THE POPULATION, URBAN AND RURAL,
UNITED STATES, 1790-1950[a]

Census Date	Total	Urban	Rural	Per Cent Increase Over Preceding Census		
				Total	Urban	Rural
1950*	150,697,361	96,467,686	54,229,675	...	...	...
1950	150,697,361	88,927,464	61,769,897	14.5	19.5	7.9
1940	131,669,275	74,423,702	57,245,573	7.2	7.9	6.4
1930	122,775,046	68,954,823	53,820,223	16.1	27.3	4.4
1920	105,710,620	54,157,973	51,552,647	14.9	29.0	3.2
1910	91,972,266	41,998,932	49,973,334	21.0	39.3	9.0
1900	75,994,575	30,159,921	45,834,654	20.7	36.4	12.2
1890	62,947,714	22,106,265	40,841,449	25.5	56.5	13.4
1880	50,155,783	14,129,735	36,026,048	30.1	42.7	25.7
1870	38,558,371	9,902,361	28,656,010	22.6	59.3	13.6
1860	31,443,321	6,216,518	25,226,803	35.6	75.4	28.4
1850	23,191,876	3,543,716	19,648,160	35.9	92.1	29.1
1840	17,069,453	1,845,055	15,224,398	32.7	63.7	29.7
1830	12,866,020	1,127,247	11,738,773	33.5	62.6	31.2
1820	9,638,453	693,255	8,945,198	33.1	31.9	33.2
1810	7,239,881	525,459	6,714,422	36.4	63.0	34.7
1800	5,308,483	322,371	4,986,112	35.1	59.9	33.8
1790	3,929,214	201,655	3,727,559	...	...	...

* Rural and urban in accordance with new definition adopted in 1950. All other figures accord with the old (1940) definition.

[a] U. S. Bureau of the Census, 1950 United States Census of Population, U. S. Summary, Number of Inhabitants, Series P-A1 (Washington: U. S. Government Printing Office, 1952) Table 4, p. 5.

both the number and size of towns and cities grew rapidly, and the percentage of the population living in cities increased steadily. In only two decades during the century after 1790 did the number of persons living in urban places fail to increase by more than 50 per cent, and in only one, 1810-20, did the urban population fail to grow percentage-wise more than the rural population (Table V). After that single decade, the next two showed urban increase above 60 per cent and more than double the percentage increase in rural areas. The population of New York had by 1840 reached almost 400,000,[6] and two other cities, Baltimore and New Orleans, had passed 100,000 population. Philadelphia and Boston had reached more than 93,000 each and, along with Cincinnati, would pass the 100,000 mark before 1850.

The greatest percentage increase in the nation's history occurred from 1840 to 1850. The growth of industry in New England and the extension of rail lines led to the growth of cities in both the North

---

[6] Including all the boroughs incorporated in 1890.

TABLE V

PERCENTAGE OF POPULATION URBAN, UNITED STATES, 1790-1950[a]

| Year | United States | Regions | | | |
		North East	North Central	South	West
1950*	64.0	79.5	64.1	48.6	69.8
1950†	59.0	74.9	60.7	44.0	59.2
1940	56.5	76.6	58.4	36.7	58.5
1930	56.2	77.6	57.9	34.1	58.8
1920	51.2	75.5	52.3	28.1	52.5
1910	45.7	71.8	45.1	22.5	48.7
1900	39.7	66.1	38.6	18.0	40.6
1890	35.1	59.0	33.1	16.3	37.4
1880	28.2	50.8	24.2	12.2	30.8
1870	25.7	44.3	20.8	12.2	25.8
1860	19.8	35.7	13.9	9.6	16.0
1850	15.3	26.5	9.2	8.3	6.4
1840	10.8	18.5	3.9	6.7	...
1830	8.8	14.2	2.6	5.3	...
1820	7.2	11.0	1.1	4.6	...
1810	7.3	10.9	0.9	4.1	...
1800	6.1	9.3	...	3.0	...
1790	5.1	8.1	...	2.1	...

[a] U. S. Bureau of the Census, *1950 United States Census of Population, U. S. Summary, Number of Inhabitants*, Series P-A1 (Washington: Government Printing Office, 1952) Table 15, p. 17.

* Percentages based on new definition of urban adopted in 1950.

† Percentages based on old definition of urban for this and all other dates, 1790-1940.

Atlantic and the recently settled midwestern states. Such towns as Buffalo, Pittsburgh, Cincinnati and Louisville more than doubled in population, and Chicago jumped from a town of less than 5,000 to just less than 30,000. Total urban population increased 92.1 per cent, and the percentage of the country's population urban jumped from 10.8 per cent to 15.3 per cent.

Although after 1850 the slowing rate of population growth affected urban growth also, the urban population grew at an increasingly more rapid rate than did the rural. In the decade 1840-50 the urban percentage increase was triple that of the rural; in 1860-70, 1880-90, and 1900-10, it was 4 times as great. By the close of the Civil War decade, in 1870, one-fourth of the total population lived in cities, and by the end of the nineteenth century two persons in every five lived in towns and cities above 2500 in size. The North East was already more than half urban, two out of three persons there residing in cities.

The trend toward a society dominated by cities, already firmly established in the nineteenth century, was actually speeded during the early twentieth. The percentage increase to the urban population was nine times as great as the rural from 1910 to 1920, and the end of the

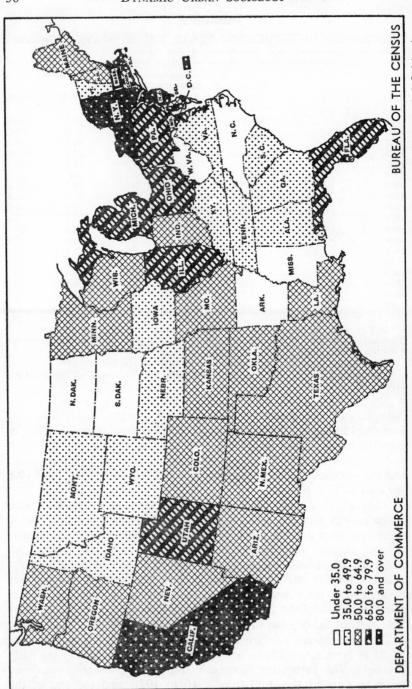

FIGURE 3. Percent of The Population Which Is Urban, By States, 1950. (Based on the new urban-rural definition.)

DEPARTMENT OF COMMERCE   BUREAU OF THE CENSUS

decade found the entire country more than 50 per cent urban. The increase in the following ten years was only slightly less. Urban growth was sharply curtailed by the economic depression of the 1930's, but it was stimulated again by the war-time activity of World War II, with the result that by 1950 virtually two-thirds of the population was urban.

3. *Growth in Number and Size of Cities.* The rapid expansion of the urban population manifested itself in the enormous increase in size of individual cities, on the one hand, and the emergence of more and more cities, on the other (Table VI). Urban places, numbering only 24 in 1790, were 61 in number by 1820, doubled in number from 1820 to 1840, tripled in number from 1840 to 1860, and more than quadrupled from 1860 to 1900. The rapid multiplication of urban places resulted from the establishment of more and more settlements as population and civilization moved westward and the growth in the older areas of small villages strategically located for trade, industry or extraction of raw materials as population expanded. Both processes have continued during the twentieth century. The number of urban places increased from 1,737 to 4,023 from 1900 to 1950,[7] but the number of places too small to be enumerated as urban also increased from 8,931 to 13,235.

As the number of cities increased, so did the size of the important ones. New York passed half a million people by 1850 and one million by 1880. By the latter date three other cities were larger than half million, and two of them joined New York in the one million category a decade later. By 1930 five cities in the country contained more than one million inhabitants, eight others were larger than half-million, and there were eighty additional ones of more than 100,000, for a total above the latter figure of ninety-three. According to the definition used in 1950, the number of cities larger than 100,000 was 106, and if the urban population contingent to each of the large cities is counted, there were in 1950 twelve cities of more than one million inhabitants.[8] New York contained more than twelve million, Chicago nearly five million, and Los Angeles virtually four million.

Regional Growth of the Urban Population.[9] Expansion of the urban population in the United States reflects not merely the transition from

---

[7] In this comparison, the 1940 definition has been used. The 1950 definition gives a total of 4,741 urban places and 13,807 rural places under 2500 inhabitants.

[8] See Chapter 2. There were actually only five central cities with one million inhabitants within their corporate limits.

[9] The U. S. Bureau of the Census divides the forty-eight states into four regions, and further subdivides these into Divisions. We will follow this classification in the present discussion. The four regions, with their divisions are: North East: New England and Middle Atlantic; North Central: East North Central and West North Central; South: South Atlantic, East South Central, and West South Central; West: Mountain and Pacific.

TABLE VI

NUMBER OF URBAN PLACES, BY SIZE, IN THE UNITED STATES SELECTED YEARS, 1790-1950[a]

Size of City	1950[b]	1950[c]	1940	1910	1880	1850	1820	1790
1,000,000 & over	5	5	5	3	1	.	.	.
500,000–1,000,000	13	13	9	5	3	1	.	.
250,000–500,000	23	23	23	11	4	.	.	.
100,000–250,000	65	66	55	31	12	5	1	.
50,000–100,000	126	128	107	59	15	4	2	2
25,000–50,000	252	271	213	119	42	16	2	3
10,000–25,000	778	814	665	369	146	36	8	7
5,000–10,000	1176	1133	965	605	249	85	22	12
2,500–5,000	1846	1570	1422	1060	467	89	26	.
Under 2,500	457	.	.	.	.	.	.	.
Total	4741	4023	3464	2262	939	236	61	24

[a] U. S. Bureau of the Census, 1950 United States Census of Population, U. S. Summary, Number of Inhabitants, Series P-A1 (Washington: Government Printing Office, 1952) Table 15, p. 17.
[b] New (1950) definition.
[c] Old (1950) definition.

a predominantly agricultural to a predominantly industrial society, but also the territorial and population expansion which has taken place. It has also reflected changing modes of transportation, which have opened up new possibilities for movement and land use.[10]

1. *North East.* Important urban development first occurred along the Atlantic seaboard where the earliest European settlements were established and where commerce with Europe promoted urban growth. In 1790 the five largest cities, Philadelphia, Boston, New York, Charleston and Baltimore were all seaport towns; and, except for Charleston which in subsequent censuses steadily dropped in rank, all were in the northeastern section of the country. In the first forty years of United States history these same northeastern cities maintained their pre-eminence, and the early lead established by the region when water transportation and ocean commerce were dominant factors in urban development has been maintained ever since. While the South retained its agrarian mold for a long time, industry grew rapidly in the North East. Its important industrial and commercial position made it the center of capital growth, the locus of many of the earliest railroads, and the focal point of the expanding network of rail lines which spread over the country throughout the latter half of the nineteenth century. By 1880 just over 50 per cent of its population was urban and 75 per cent was urban by 1920.

2. *North Central.* As long as the principal mode of long-distance transportation was via water routes, important urban growth was largely confined to the Atlantic Seaboard and the Mississippi Valley, and America's hinterland could be settled, but slowly and tediously. The Erie Canal led to some westward urban development in New York State, but it was actually the railroad which made possible the rapid development of the western portion of the country. Beginning just before 1840, the construction of railroads gave fresh impetus to urban growth in the North East through the expansion of its market area and of the coal and iron industry, and also stimulated a rapid urban growth in the west.

Population moved westward swiftly, and in the three decades following 1840 the urban population of the North Central States then in the union increased 286.0, 152.9 and 113.9 per cent. Over the same period the percentage of the population increased from less than 4.0 to 20.8. By 1870 Cincinnati contained 216,239, St. Louis had increased from just less than 5,000 in 1830 to 310,000, and Chicago from less than 5,000 as late as 1840 to 298,977.

After 1870 industry developed rapidly in the eastern portion of the region.[11] The growth of the country westward also expanded the com-

---

[10] See R. D. McKenzie, *The Metropolitan Community* (New York: McGraw-Hill Book Co., 1933) Chapter 10 for a treatment of the role of types and routes of transportation in the location and development of cities.

[11] The States of Ohio, Indiana, Illinois, Michigan and Wisconsin.

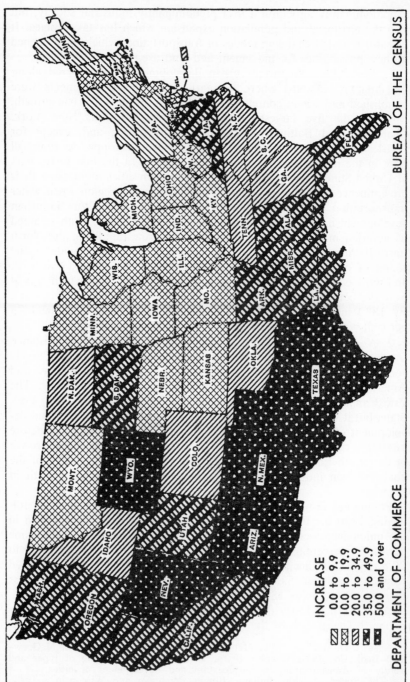

FIGURE 4. Percent Urban Population Increase, by States: 1940-1950. (Based on old urban-rural definition.)

DEPARTMENT OF COMMERCE

BUREAU OF THE CENSUS

INCREASE

0.0 to 9.9
10.0 to 19.9
20.0 to 34.9
35.0 to 49.9
50.0 and over

TABLE VII

PER CENT INCREASE IN URBAN POPULATION, BY
REGIONS, UNITED STATES, 1790-1950[a]

Census Period	North East	North Central	South	West
1940-1950	7.2	15.2	35.9	42.5
1930-1940	3.2	4.9	18.5	16.2
1920-1930	19.2	25.7	38.8	49.5
1910-1920	20.7	31.8	40.4	40.7
1900-1910	33.4	32.7	49.8	100.0
1890-1900	35.5	37.0	35.6	43.3
1880-1890	39.3	76.7	61.7	113.2
1870-1880	35.3	55.4	34.8	113.0
1860-1870	43.8	113.9	40.3	157.8
1850-1860	65.5	152.9	43.4	772.8
1840-1850	82.7	286.0	60.7	....
1830-1840	59.6	210.8	53.9	....
1820-1830	63.5	331.8	47.6	....
1810-1820	26.3	279.6	42.4	....
1800-1810	55.4	....	83.7	....
1790-1800	53.3	....	84.6	....

[a] U. S. Bureau of the Census, *1950 United States Census of Population,
U. S. Summary, Number of Inhabitants,* Series P-A1 (Washington: Government Printing Office, 1952) Table 15, p. 17.

mercial and transportational functions of cities there, just as commerce with the New World was one factor in the growth of cities in the Old World, and the first westward movement had helped foster urban expansion in the North East. In the decade 1880-90 urban growth was almost twice that in the North East, and Chicago became the second largest city in the country. Since about 1890 the percentage urban of the region has been close to the national average. Rapid population and urban growth continued through the third decade of the twentieth century, and although the West has a higher percentage of urban population, the number of those living in cities in the North Central States is second only to that in the North East.

3. *West.* Just as striking as the fact of impetus given urban development in older regions by the opening of new territory is the effect upon the urban pattern of settlement in the new area exerted by the urban growth already achieved in the old. Settlement of America was initially stamped with the rural orientation of its colonizers. When the North Central States were settled, urban growth had already gone forward in the North East and the rate of urban growth in the new territory was very rapid. The influence of urban development eastward is even more

clearly seen in the settlement of the far west, which has been the most recent and the most urban in its pattern of settlement.[12]

Less than one million persons inhabited the Mountain and Pacific States in 1870, the year after completion of the Union and Central Pacific Railroad. But one-fourth of these were residents of urban places,[13] and since then the pattern of development has been much more urban than it had been for any other region. The West has been, since 1870, the second most urban section of the country, and, more sparsely settled than the other regions, has enjoyed by far the most rapid population growth of any section. Greatest urban and total population growth has occurred since 1900 in the Pacific States. Between 1940 and 1950 the entire region increased in population 40.9 per cent, and the Pacific states increased 48.8 per cent. Although during the last two decades the rural population has grown more rapidly than the urban, this circumstance apparently reflects the sparseness of earlier settlement and the suburban pattern of growth of the urban population. The change in definition of urban adopted in 1950 makes a greater difference in the statistics for the West than for any other region.[14]

4. *The South.* By contrast, the states of the South have been outside the developmental trend of other regions. Despite the fact that its total population has been approximately as great as that in the North East and its rate of natural increase greater, the stamp of agrarianism and agriculturism upon the section during the period of settlement retarded urban growth. The industrial development which did occur, moreover, did not generate the same concentration of population as it did in New England.[15] As recently as 1920 less than one-third of its population was urban, as compared with three-fourths in the North East and more than one-half in both the North Central and Western states. Much less urbanized than the North East in 1790, its cities grew slower after 1820 than those of any other region. One of its cities, New Orleans, was able by virtue of its strategic position at the mouth of the Mississippi to maintain a position as fifth among the nation's cities until 1860; but thereafter, as a result of the devastating effect of the Civil War on the South's economy and the westward extension of the railroads, it grew more slowly and steadily dropped in rank.

The gradual alteration in traditional farming practices in the direction of increased production, and changes in the character of pro-

---

[12] Weber has noted the same phenomenon in comparing the difference in the patterns of settlement in America and Australia. See A. F. Weber, *Growth of Cities in the Nineteenth Century* (New York: The Macmillan Co., 1899) p. 1.

[13] The country as a whole became one-fourth urban in 1870.

[14] As noted above, the new (1950) definition includes the suburban population of cities of 50,000 or more. According to the 1950 urban definition, the Pacific States in 1950 were 75 per cent urban.

[15] Rupert B. Vance, *All These People* (Chapel Hill: The University of North Carolina Press, 1945), pp. 280-286.

duction, and the rapid increase of industry in the section has, in the twentieth century, wrought a rapid transformation in the region. Every decade since 1900 has registered a greater proportionate gain for cities there than anywhere else except in the West; and the increase to cities in that section has been a greater proportion of total population increase than in the West. Of the South's total gain in population since 1900, 82 per cent found its way into cities by 1950.[16] The South, like the West, was especially affected by the location of war industries and training camps after 1940. The most phenomenal growth has occurred in the West South Central States, their urban population increasing almost 50 per cent between 1940 and 1950.

Variations in the rate of urban development and industrial growth in different parts of the country underlie some of the important political and cultural differences within the United States. The recent great urban increases in the West and South, however, indicate that not only is the total population becoming more urban, but also that urbanization is extending to all parts of the country. It is proceeding most rapidly, in fact, in those areas which are least densely settled or have the lowest percentage of urban population. There is apparently some tendency toward equalization of both population density and urban concentration throughout the entire country.

Nevertheless, the impress of the course of development of our urban civilization still remains. As America's economic position in the world has risen, New York's location with reference to the continental interior, on the one hand, and world markets, on the other, has made it the world's largest city, and the region in close proximity to it one of the most heavily urbanized and industrial areas of the world. Here are the highest percentages urban in the country. The position of the North Central States relative to the North East and to the heart of the continent, as well as to abundant mineral resources, have given it an industrial and commercial importance second only to the North East, which it still retains. Although its percentage urban is less than that of the West, due to the fact that it also embraces rich agricultural lands, it has a far larger urban population. Despite the great gains in the West, its urban population is still relatively small compared with that in the North East and North Central Regions, or even in the South; and the South's rapid gains have brought it still just short of 50 per cent urban.

Population Growth and Urban Development. Underlying the territorial and economic expansion associated with the country's urban growth has been an amazing population growth. The original thirteen states contained just less than four million persons inhabiting 867,980 square miles. The United States of 1950 contained approximately one

---

[16] Using this basis of comparison, the North East's percentage of increase going to cities was 95, the North Central's was 101, and the West's was 77.5.

hundred fifty-one million inhabitants, which amounted to about thirty-eight times the original four million, in a territory about three and one-half times as large. The concurrent change from 5 per cent to 64 per cent urban means that in the process of growth the rural population has increased by some fifteen times its size in 1790, while the urban population has been multiplied by 480.

Growth of the United States population has been, of course, part of the general expansion of European population which, because of the unique historical role and favorable geographic situation of the country, is revealed here with particular clarity. The United States received millions of migrants from Europe when population expansion of that continent necessitated population readjustment, and frontier conditions were also especially favorable for an even more rapid natural increase than that which occurred in Europe. A doubling of the population through the excess of births over deaths in twenty or twenty-five years was apparently not uncommon under frontier conditions,[17] and the birth rate around 1800, as indicated by child-woman ratios, was very high indeed.[18] Together, migration and the high rate of natural increase contributed a very rapid population growth during the early period, especially marked in each new territory opened for settlement. For the entire country until 1860 the increase in population was more or less constantly around 35 per cent per decade, very much higher in some regions just opened for settlement.[19]

1. *Declining rate of growth.* Increasing urbanization, as it progressed, resulted, in the United States as elsewhere, in a diminution in the rate of growth. Immigrants continued to enter the country in large numbers until the first World War. But after 1860 the percentage increase each decade declined, due to the falling off in the rate of natural increase.

Throughout the nineteenth century the censuses reveal a steady rise in the average age of the population, and, especially after 1860, an increase in the proportion of the population over forty-five years of age. This increase among persons who were beyond the child-bearing period and at ages where death rates are high, although in part the result of changing mortality and fertility, tended to raise the death rate and lower fertility rates, since both these latter are based on total population. The tendency of the age structure to increase the death rate was probably offset to some extent by declining mortality throughout the century,[20]

---

[17] T. R. Malthus, *An Essay on the Principle of Population* (New York: E. P. Dutton and Co., Inc., 1952) Vol. I, p. 7.

[18] P. K. Whelpton, *Forecasts of the Population of the United States, 1945–1975* (Washington: U. S. Government Printing Office, 1947), p. 17.

[19] For the North Central States, for example, rates of growth were as follows: 1800–10: 472.7 per cent; 1810–20: 194.2 per cent; 1820–30: 87.4 per cent; and 1830–40: 108.1 per cent. U. S. Bureau of the Census, *1950 United States Census of Population, U. S. Summary, Number of Inhabitants,* Series P-A1, Table 7, p. 10.

[20] Louis I. Dublin, Alfred J. Lotka, and Mortimer Spiegelman, *Length of Life* (New York: The Ronald Press Co., 1949) Rev. ed. pp. 39–41.

but its tendency to lower the birth rate seems only to have accentuated a trend due also in part to a reduction in average number of children per woman.[21] Since the result of these changes was to decrease the difference between the crude birth and death rates, natural increase was consequently less.

Although beginning in the latter half of the nineteenth century, the change was greatest after 1900. The death rate dropped steadily, and the spread of family limitation caused the birth rate to decline more rapidly still. The latter, which in 1915 was still about 25 births per 1000 population, declined to 16.6 per thousand in 1933;[22] and with the almost complete cessation of immigration, the increase in the decade 1930-40 fell to 7.2 per cent, the lowest on record. A much higher birth rate during the 1940's led to a population growth of 14.5 per cent from 1940 to 1950, but this was still less than the percentage gain for any decade before 1930.

Both increasing longevity and declining fertility are characteristic of urban-industrial civilizations; and the decline in fertility is directly related to the growth of cities. Urban populations appear almost universally to have lower fertility than do rural ones.[23] Furthermore, as Table VIII shows, urban fertility has declined more rapidly in recent years than has the rural. The causes of this decline lie in the changing family relationships which occur in large cities, especially; and the rapidity of the decline in fertility is due to the concurrent reduction in urban fertility and the increased proportion of the population residing in cities. More about this in the chapters on rural-urban differentials.

2. *Internal Migration.* The slower growth of population resulting from the decline in fertility has inevitably led to smaller percentage gains for the urban population, but the ratio of urban to rural increase has grown steadily larger. In the first fifty years of the nation's history the ratio of urban to rural growth was about 2 to 1; in the last fifty years it has been close to 12 to 1. The rural population in 1950 was not quite twice the rural population in 1870; the urban was almost ten times the size of the 1870 urban population, and had more than doubled since 1910.

This circumstance of greater relative growth of the population having the lowest fertility is due to the radical change in population movements in this country, a fact which further underscores the progressive urbanization. Throughout most of the nineteenth century, it was immigration from Europe and the westward movement of peoples from the eastern seaboard which overshadowed all other migration, as the terri-

---

[21] P. K. Whelpton, *op. cit.,* p. 17.

[22] National Office of Vital Statistics, *Vital Statistics-Special Reports, National Summaries,* Vol. 36, No. 1, May 14, 1951, "Summary of Natality Statistics, United States, 1949," p. 4.

[23] A. J. Jaffe, "Urbanization and Fertility," *American Journal of Sociology,* Vol. XLVIII (July 1942), pp. 48-69.

TABLE VIII

FERTILITY OF NATIVE WHITE WOMEN, URBAN, RURAL NONFARM,
AND RURAL UNITED STATES, 1940 AND 1910[a]

Date and Residence	Children Ever Born		
	Per 1000 women 15-74	Per 1000 women 15-74 ever married	Per 1000 mothers 15-74
1940			
Cities:			
250,000 and over	1,103	1,745	2,424
25,000 to 250,000	1,351	2,020	2,665
2,500 to 25,000	1,486	2,176	2,770
Urban	1,292	1,961	2,610
Rural nonfarm	1,875	2,552	3,123
Rural farm	2,408	3,374	3,839
1910			
Cities:			
100,000 and over	1,414	2,527	3,189
25,000 to 100,000	1,616	2,659	3,290
2,500 to 25,000	1,849	2,925	3,484
Urban	1,609	2,704	3,325
Rural nonfarm	2,354	3,347	3,840
Rural farm	2,833	4,169	4,574

[a] U. S. Bureau of the Census, *Sixteenth Census of the United States, 1940, Population, Differential Fertility 1940 and 1910*, "Women by Number of Children Ever Born" (Washington: Government Printing Office, 1945) Tables 7 and 10, pp. 11-13.

torial expansion indicates.[24] The majority of those moving west sought lands to till, but the rapid growth of cities in the new territories shows that many of them also found their way into towns and cities.

As the century progressed, the urban-directed movement grew, and the Far West, as we have already noted, reflected in its percentage urban the increasingly urban character of the nation's population. A reverse movement, which seems almost altogether urban in its direction, also first appeared during the latter part of the nineteenth century. This movement, from west to east and from south to north, was evident in the states along the northeastern seaboard as early as 1860, and by 1900 was reflected in all the northeastern states and in Ohio in the North Central states.[25] It gained rapidly during the decades 1910-20 and 1920-30, when increased industrial activity in these regions corresponded also with the virtual stoppage of immigration.

Since 1930 the rural-urban migration has continued, but with two

[24] See Carter Goodrich, *et al.*, *Migration and Economic Opportunity* (Philadelphia: University of Pennsylvania Press, 1936), p. 676, especially the maps prepared by C. W. Thornthwaite from "state-of-birth" data in the censuses from 1850 onward.

[25] *Ibid.*, p. 677.

major changes. During the period of the depression, the net gain to cities dropped sharply from previous periods, and when it rose again during the period of World War II and after, its direction had somewhat altered. An increasing share of the migration has recently been going to cities in the South and West. In so far as they indicate migratory shifts, the greatest net losses between 1940 and 1950 show that movement has been out of Central United States, particularly the states of the West North Central Division and Mountain States and in the direction of the peripheral states.

3. *Consequences of Population Changes.* The population changes just discussed bear an important relationship to the character of urban-industrial civilization and some of the latter's great advantages and great problems. The problems frequently attract the greatest attention. Declining fertility is related to what is often referred to as the modern crisis of the family. From it derives also the prospect of eventual declining population which has created some fears for the ability of the economic order to maintain high levels of living in the future. From it derives in part also the continued increase in proportions of the aged in society, and a train of problems, personal and societal, which are related to this increase. From the fact of migration from rural to urban environments stem many of the problems of adjustment occurring in the city and much of *anomie* of city life.

The consequences of a problematical nature are, however, balanced by material advantages. The increase to the urban population has meant a more efficient utilization of manpower in industrial production and the provision of services, while it has helped to maintain a relatively efficient man-land ratio among the agricultural population in most areas. Much of America's high standard of living may be attributed to the favorable distribution of population which urban growth has made possible. It may in part also be attributed to a more efficient balance between births and deaths. Longer life expectancy and lower infant mortality rates have meant that society gains more productive-adult years for each child born and educated. They have also meant that relatively less effort need be expended in child-bearing and child-training to maintain the population, and that the same educational outlay, by being concentrated on proportionately fewer individuals, can provide for more intense training of the young, with consequent gains to the society. The recent decline in fertility occurring as it has during a period of declining mortality, has also created at least temporarily a society with a very favorable ratio of adults in the productive years of life to dependent young and old. As a result of migration, this characteristic is most marked among urban populations, since it is among young adults that most movement takes place. The increase in the aged population is in reality the result of the inevitable aging of the presently favorably structured population.

Recent Trends in Urban Growth. The relation between population growth and urban development has already been sufficiently emphasized, but we may return to it briefly by way of summary and evaluation of recent trends. Urban growth first occurred along the eastern seaboard, especially in the northeast, and from there spread westward as population moved across the continent. The causes of urban growth are, of course, to be found in the economic and social organization of a society, but the ultimate magnitude of urban growth is dependent upon population size, and the enormous growth of urban population in this country was made possible by the rapid increase in population. As the urban trend gained momentum, however, population growth after 1860 became slower, in large measure due to the effect of urban life upon fertility. Inevitably, although the urban population increased at an ever more rapid rate than did the rural, the slower growth of population led to declining rates of urban increase.

There are, however, some indications that there has been a relative decline in urban growth quite apart from the slower population increase, and that a point of equilibrium between the urban and rural populations is approaching. If our attention is directed solely to the decade 1930-40, such a decline in growth of cities is obvious. The urban increase of 7.9 per cent was only slightly higher than the rural increase of 6.4 per cent (Table IV), and some cities actually lost population. The decline is also manifest, though to a somewhat lesser degree, in the figures for the period 1940-50. The increase for the urban population was then 19.5 per cent compared with 7.9 per cent for the rural, but the contrast in these two figures is far less than in the decade 1920-30 when the urban population increased 27.3 per cent and the rural only 4.4 per cent. There is some reality in the claim that there has been a relative decline in the growth of the urban population when it is noted further that since 1920 the percentage increase for the urban population has been downward while that for the rural population has been up. The following data summarizes the trend, based on the definition of urban used in 1940, by showing the percentage of the total population increase which accrued to cities in each decade:

Period	Per Cent	Period	Per Cent
1940-50	76.2	1860-70	51.8
1930-40	61.5	1850-60	32.4
1920-30	86.7	1840-50	27.7
1910-20	88.5	1830-40	17.1
1900-10	74.1	1820-30	13.4
1890-00	61.7	1810-20	7.0
1880-90	62.4	1800-10	10.5
1870-80	36.5	1790-00	8.8

Re-evaluation of the trend since 1920 in terms of the 1950 definition of urban population, however, tends to refute the evidence of a decline in the urbanward movement. There is, of course, no doubt that cities grew more slowly during the 1930 to 1940 period, but this occurrence was an extreme manifestation of the effect of economic depressions upon the growth of cities. Cities draw population because of what they have to offer, the most important among which in modern industrial society is employment opportunities. Thus cities grow rapidly when economic activity rises, more slowly when it falls. But even for the period 1930-40 the degree of falling off in urban growth has probably been exaggerated. For behind the statistics available for analysis there lies an important change in the pattern of urban residence which the 1940 definition imperfectly reflected.

Just as the railroad and the factory promoted concentration of population in the nineteenth century, so the motor car, as it has become an almost universal means of private transportation, has contributed to the city's partial decentralization in the twentieth. The automobile made it possible for more and more people to work and trade in cities, but for more and more of them also to live on its outskirts. The decentralization resulting from increased suburban living, outside the corporate limits of cities, has been reflected in slower rates of urban increase as urban was previously defined. But far from meaning an actual decline in urbanization, the movement means rather an extension of it to the countryside.[26]

It was for the purpose of reflecting more accurately the totality of urban population that the definition of urban referred to earlier in the chapter was adopted in the census of 1950. As shown in Table V, the new definition increased the percentage urban for 1950 from 59.0 (given by the definition used in 1940) to 64.0. It increased the percentage urban in every region to some extent, and makes a drastic change of from 59.2 to 69.8 per cent for the West.

Unfortunately, data prior to 1950 cannot be interpreted in terms of the new definition, so that it cannot be used to assess changes for 1930-40 or 1940-50. It is probably reasonable to assume, however, that the suburban trend was not fully under way by 1920, and the new definition, if applied to the 1920 data, would not materially change the figure for that year. If that assumption is made, then it becomes possible to evaluate the change over the last thirty years, in the same way that the table above has done for decades, that is, by computing the percentage of the total population gain from 1920 to 1950 which accrued to cities in that period. The result is enlightening. Total population increased 44,986,741, while the urban population, according to the 1950 definition, increased 42,309,713, or very close to 94.5 per cent of the total. This rate of increase is higher than that even for the decade 1910-20, and indicates, rather than an abatement in the trend in urban growth, a continuing increase in it.

[26] Kingsley Davis, *Human Society* (New York: The Macmillan Co., 1949) pp. 325-326.

WORKSHOP AND PROBLEMS

1. To what do you attribute the rapid urbanization of population in the United States?

2. Contrast the definitions of "urban" in the 1940 and 1950 censuses.

3. Why the low percentage increase in urban population between 1930 and 1940? Why the large increase between 1940 and 1950?

4. What areas of the United States were most urban in 1950? Least urban?

5. What sections of the United States had the greatest percentage increase in urban population between 1940 and 1950?

6. Discuss the relative fertility rates of the urban, rural non-farm and rural farm populations.

7. Prepare a report on the urban population increase in your state and compare it with the national increase over the period 1900 to 1950.

8. Discuss the future trends in population growth in the United States.

BIBLIOGRAPHY

Davis, Kingsley, *Human Society* (New York: The Macmillan Company, 1949), Chapter 12.

Gist, Noel P., and Halbert, L. A., *Urban Society* (New York: Thomas Y. Crowell Company, 1950), 3rd Edition.

Hallenbeck, Wilbur C., *American Urban Communities* (New York: Harper and Brothers, 1951).

Hatt, Paul K., and Reiss, Albert J., Jr., *Reader in Urban Sociology* (Glencoe: The Free Press, 1951).

McKenzie, R. D., *The Metropolitan Community* (New York: McGraw-Hill Book Company, 1933).

National Resources Committee, *Our Cities: Their Role in the National Economy* (Washington: U. S. Government Printing Office, 1937).

Schlesinger, Arthur M., *The Rise of the City* (New York: The Macmillan Company, 1933).

Smith, T. Lynn, and McMahan, C. A., *The Sociology of Urban Life* (New York: The Dryden Press, 1951).

U. S. Bureau of the Census, *1950 United States Census of Population, U. S. Summary, Number of Inhabitants.* Series P-A1 (Washington: U. S. Government Printing Office, 1952).

Weber, Adna F., *The Growth of Cities in the Nineteenth Century* (New York: The Macmillan Company, 1899).

CHAPTER 4

The Metropolitan Area

By WILLIAM E. COLE

A New Phenomenon. The metropolis, under the variable terms that
have been used to describe it, represents a new phenomenon in American life and the life of many countries. The relatively isolated single
large city is old, as evidenced by Rome, Athens, Paris, and many cities
of prehistoric eastern world exerted wide ranges of influence over great
populations, but the metropolitan "community" or "area," as it now
is popularly referred to, is the result of improved means of communication—the inter-urban train and trolley, the bus, the automobile, the truck and now the aeroplane.[1] N. S. B. Gras conceives of
the metropolitan economy as the end result of a long series of economic
and historical stages scaled upward as follows:

    5. Metropolitan economy
    4. Town economy
    3. Settled village economy
    2. Agricultural nomadic economy
    1. Collectional economy[2]

He conceives the metropolitan economy as an economic organization—economically integrated areas—having large cities as nuclei. In
this organization producers and consumers are interdependent. Towns
remain in the metropolitan areas as they did in the town economy but
they are economically subordinated to the metropolis, their economic life
revolving around the larger places. In this metropolitan economy towns
serve different functions, some of them quite specialized, but they are
all subordinate to the large central cities of the metropolitan area.[3]

In the *Recent Social Trends* series, developed in the 1930's, Professor Roderick D. McKenzie prepared a volume, which has since
become classic, on the *Metropolitan Community,*[4] in which he went

---

[1] See Stuart A. Queen and David B. Carpenter, *The American City* (New
York: McGraw Hill Book Co., 1953).
[2] N. S. B. Gras, *An Introduction to Economic History* (New York: Harper
and Brothers, 1926).
[3] *Ibid.,* p. 184.
[4] Roderick D. McKenzie, *The Metropolitan Community* (New York:
McGraw-Hill Book Co., 1933).

51

52   DYNAMIC URBAN SOCIOLOGY

into great detail on the development of the metropolitan community.
He indicated, as we have, that it is a new social structure in social life
and indicated ways and means by which the boundaries of its influences could be established and its influences studied.[5] At a later
date, Don Bogue reviewed the theory of metropolitan dominance and
proceeded to test it with the data and procedures available prior to
1949.[6]

The Idea of Metropolitan Dominance. In discussing the nature of
metropolitan dominance Bogue says:

"The hypothesis of metropolitan dominance assumes that there is a
system of interdependency among cities, and that there are considerable
differences between the activities of individual cities. It maintains that
the organizing agent, and one of the forces making for intercity differentiation, is the metropolis.

"Sufficient evidence has been accumulated to make of this view a
very plausible hypothesis. Smaller cities and villages lying in the region
about great cities appear to have been drawn into a division of labor
with the larger urban centers. They exchange for the specialized goods
and services of the metropolis such other products as can most effectively be produced from the resources in their immediate locality. Farm
operators also appear to have become more dependent upon metropolitan markets, and consequently have regulated their activities to produce,
if possible, those products which will yield them the greatest return in
the metropolitan market. With these exchanges of material goods has
also gone the exchange of ideas and human values. The metropolis
appears to have become the focal point not only of our material activities, but of much of our moral and intellectual life as well. Repeatedly
it has been pointed out that not only in activities such as non-agricultural production, distribution, and finance, but also in matters of government, progress in the arts and sciences, news dissemination and the
formation of public opinion, changed philosophies of religion and the
emergence of human values, the great metropolis is now the domi-
nating center."[7]

Hubert indicates the nature of the dominance of the large metropolis
over the surrounding hinterland. He says:

The hinterland of the large metropolis may, and usually does, include many other cities and towns. But these cities and towns are
subsidiary centers which facilitate the functioning of the community
as a whole and are under the financial and commercial dominance
of the metropolis. Some of these are of specialized nature—industrial centers, political capitals, etc. But the major commercial and

[5] Ibid.
[6] Don J. Bogue, The Structure of the Metropolitan Community: A Study
of Dominance and Subdominance (Ann Arbor: University of Michigan
Press, 1949).
[7] Ibid., pp. 5-6.

industrial concerns in the subsidiary cities are controlled by the financial interests of the metropolis. The securities of the local corporations, for instance, are bought and sold on the metropolitan securities markets. The larger the metropolitan center is and the more important its economic institutions are, the larger is the hinterland over which it has dominance. Here also alternative costs of transportation determine the orientation of the points farthest removed in the trade area to one or the other metropolitan centers.[8]

Various attempts have been made to isolate and test some of the indices of urban dominance. Park used newspaper circulation as a measure of urbanization.[9] Wholesale trade area lines are frequently used, especially by chambers of commerce. Hubert, in his discussion of the "super metropolitan-orbit" indicates that "at several locations in the world there have developed large urban commercial and industrial agglomerations. The three largest of these are (1) that which has grown up around the North Sea in Western Europe, (2) that which has developed in the Laurentic basin (New York to Chicago) in North America and (3) that which has grown around the Japan and China seas in Eastern Asia."[10] Vance says:

"It is no answer to this problem of sectional interest in sheeps' clothing to state it in the familiar terms of the provinces against the metropolis. Ruralism against metropolitanism is not exactly the regional issue. We mediate our lives, our economy, and much of our cultural and artistic productivity today through cities. It is not a rural-urban issue, simply because each great region must finally develop its own regional centers and sub-centers. Such regional capitals may well be artistic, literary, and cultural centers, as well as major livestock markets, cotton markets, and grain markets for the areas' economic production. An example of the danger to be avoided can be found in France. The extent to which Paris dominates the nation's artistic and intellectual life has reduced French provincial cities to cultural monopoly. French travelers often remark on the economic and cultural rank of our regional cities as compared to those of France. Regional capitals need not be provincial. They should be regional, which to me means functional in relation both to the region and to the nation.

"The New York-Chicago Axis will, I suspect, continue for some time to dominate, with occasional help from Hollywood, the financial, artistic and cultural trends of our national life. As our great major areas pass from frontier to sections, to regions, as they fill out their complex structures, they too will develop metropolitan centers and sub-centers—centers which will realize their function and thus relieve

[8] Giles A. Hubert, "A Framework for Study of Peripheral Economic Areas," *Journal of Farm Economics*, Vol. 28 (August, 1946), p. 806.
[9] Robert E. Park, "Urbanization as Measured by Newspaper Circulation," *American Journal of Sociology*, Vol. 35 (July, 1929), pp. 61-79.
[10] Hubert, *op. cit.*, p. 807.

the megalopolis of its centralizing tendency, thereby preventing "apoplexy at the center and paralysis at the extremities."[11]

Status of Metropolitan Areas. On April 1, 1950, according to the Bureau of the Census, more than half of the population of the United States was living in a standard "metropolitan area" ranging in size from 56,141, in the case of Laredo, Texas, to 12,911,994 in the case of the New York-Northeastern New Jersey area.[12] Each metropolitan area comprises the county and counties containing a central city of 50,000 or more population and the contiguous counties economically integrated about the city. From 1940 to 1950 the population of these areas increased from 69,276,481 to 84,500,680.[13]

Some four-fifths of the national population increase between 1940 and 1950 took place in metropolitan areas. The urbanized areas containing more than 1,000,000 population in 1950 were as follows:[14]

New York-Northeastern New Jersey	12,911,994
Chicago	4,920,816
Los Angeles	3,996,946
Philadelphia	2,922,470
Detroit	2,659,398
Boston	2,333,448
San Francisco-Oakland	2,022,078
Pittsburgh	1,532,953
St. Louis	1,400,058
Cleveland	1,383,599
Washington, D. C.	1,287,333
Baltimore	1,161,822

The Bureau of the Census lists in all 168 standard metropolitan areas in 1950.

The rates of population growth of the various parts of metropolitan areas are, of course, not uniform, showing varying rates of growth between 1940 and 1950, as indicated in Table IX. These data show that while the population of the United States increased 14.5 per cent between 1940-50, the population of metropolitan areas increased 22.9 per cent. It is significant that the central cities of these areas grew

[11] Rupert B. Vance, "The Regional Concept as a Tool for Social Research," *Regionalism in America*, Merrill Jensen, ed. (Madison: University of Wisconsin Press, 1952), pp. 139-140.

[12] Bureau of the Census, *1950 Census of Population, Advance Reports*, "Population of Standard Metropolitan Areas: April 1, 1950," Series PC-9, No. 6 (November 24, 1952).

[13] *Ibid.*, p. 12.

[14] Bureau of the Census, *1950 Census of Population, Advance Reports*, "Population and Land of Metropolitan Areas: April 1, 1950," Series PC-9, No. 4, October 7, 1952. The figure for the New York-New Jersey area is from a similar release dated November 24, 1952, previously cited.

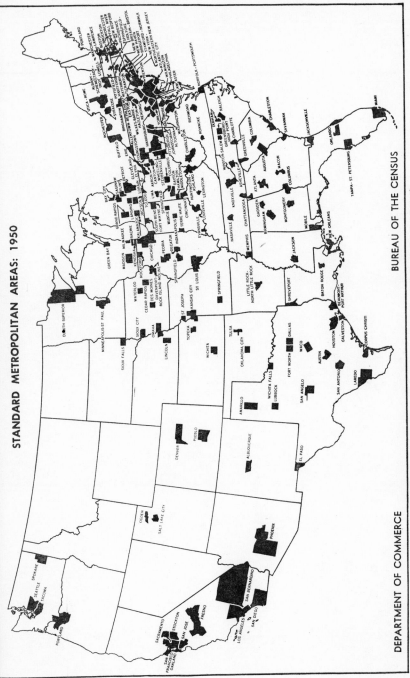

STANDARD METROPOLITAN AREAS: 1950

DEPARTMENT OF COMMERCE

BUREAU OF THE CENSUS

FIGURE 5. Metropolitan Areas In The United States, 1950.

only 13.9 per cent between 1940 and 1950, whereas, the outlying parts of the areas grew 35.6 per cent.[15]

TABLE IX

COMPARISON OF RATES OF POPULATION INCREASE 1940 TO 1950
IN METROPOLITAN COMMUNITIES AND UNITED STATES[a]

Area	Population Increase 1940 to 1950	
	Number	Per Cent
United States	19,028,086	14.5
Standard metropolitan areas	15,224,199	22.0
Central cities	6,021,074	13.9
Outlying parts	9,203,125	35.6
Outside standard metropolitan areas	3,803,887	6.1

[a] Source: Bureau of the Census, *1950 Census of Population* (Advance Reports), "Population of Standard Metropolitan Areas: April 1, 1950," Series PC-9, No. 6 (November 24, 1952), p. 1.

Some Problems Created by Metropolitan Expansion. Metropolitan areas have a series of complicated problems some of which individual large cities with less satellite growth have had in the past. Some of these more serious problems are:

1. *The variable and complicated layers of government in metropolitan areas.* Most metropolitan populations find themselves under complicated layers of government—state, county and local, and within the local level, various specialized districts of one type or another. Not only are there layers of government but forms are also variable. Taxable resources are highly variable in the various units and governmental leadership invariably shows varying degrees of progressiveness, conservatism and lethargy.

2. *Irresponsibility in fringe development.* Within the fringes of metropolitan areas, one notices much evidence of the lack of planned growth and development. The lack of land-use planning, adequate zoning and lack of building control is often due to the lack of legal responsibility on the part of satellite towns or county governments for planning. In passing one finds that frequently counties do not have the necessary planning powers, or, if they do, they lack adequate staff for carrying out a comprehensive program of planning. Jurisdiction for certain functions may also end with the boundary lines of each unit of government. As a result there is lack of planning and development which flows evenly across the boundary lines of political jurisdictions within standard metropolitan areas.

3. *Lack of regional development.* In planning for the future, as well

[15] For additional information on this point see Donald J. Bogue, *Metropolitan Decentralization: A Study of Differential Growth* (Miami, Ohio: Scripps Foundation for Research in Population, August, 1950).

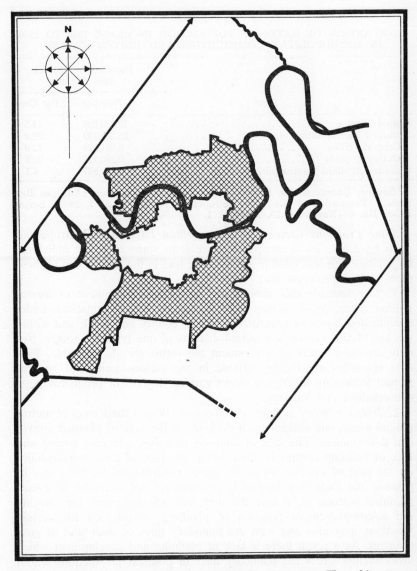

FIGURE 6. The Suburban Area around Nashville, Tennessee. The white space in the center indicates the present incorporated area.

Source: The Community Services Commission for Davidson County and the City of Nashville, *A Future for Nashville* (June 1952). p. 2.

as taking care of current needs, many cities find that it would be unwise simply to plan to meet the needs of the population of the central city without including the other areas of the metropolitan region. Highways, tunnels, parks, utilities—electricity, water, gas, sewage and garbage disposal—should be planned for the region and not just for the central city. The absence of responsibility for planning and development on such a scale is obviously a tremendous problem and one that is not easily met.

Some Attacks on the Problem of Metropolitan Expansion. Some attacks have been made upon the problems of metropolitan expansion with variable degrees of effectiveness. Some of the more important measures are:

1. *Annexation.* Historically, when the population of a city expanded beyond its legal boundaries, the thing to do was for the city to annex the "built up" territory to the city. With the expansion of suburbs, through the use of the automobile, annexation has become more and more difficult. Many arguments may be made for annexation:

  a. Most suburban residents work in or use the central city as a service area, therefore, they should help support it. They actually are a part of it.

  b. Annexation would enlarge the tax base and add to existing taxable resources of the central city.

  c. Suburban territory must be part of the official boundaries of the city in order that they may be properly controlled by the city.

  d. The costs of annexation, to the annexed home owner, are not greater than the direct and indirect costs he bears in higher utility rates, higher fire insurance costs and special assessments for fire or police protection, garbage removal and other services offered by the central city or by private companies under contract in the central city.

In a Nashville study:

  Approximately two-thirds of the persons interviewed would pay less for urban services as City taxpayers—after annexation and the proposed transfer of functions to the County—than they would pay if they remained residents in the unincorporated area. Savings range from $4.93 to as much as $115.24 each year, with the typical figure around $30.00. When costs are compared on the basis of existing City and County tax rates, over 60 per cent are now paying more for the inadequate services received than they would be paying if inside the City of Nashville. The typical excess expenditure is approximately $25.00 per year; the excess ranges from $1.18 to $112.44 per year.[16]

  e. Annexation may clear up certain hazards to the population of a

---

[16] The Community Services Commission for Davidson County and the City of Nashville, *A Future for Nashville,* June 1952, p. 20.

central city. Frequently suburban populations are unsewered and septic tanks serving a large population may constitute a health hazard to the people of the suburbs and the central city. Un-

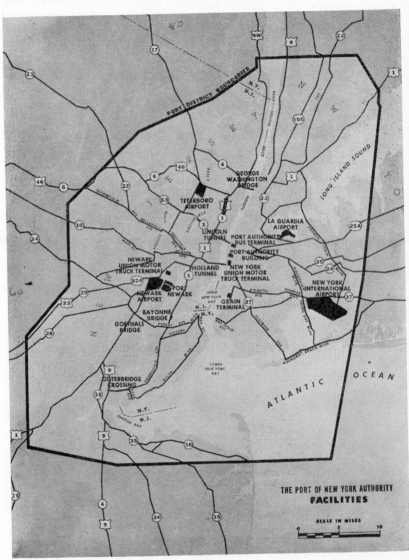

FIGURE 7. Facilities operated by The Port of New York Authority.
Source: Courtesy Port of New York Authority.

policed or inadequately policed territories may constitute a delinquency and crime hazard to an urban population.

In a way the foregoing arguments for annexation indicate the arguments against it. More specifically, opposition to annexation runs as follows:

    a. A city cannot possibly keep up with expanding suburbs through annexation in this day of expanding commuting areas.

    b. Annexation will increase the taxes of those whose properties are annexed.

    c. The cost of providing facilities, services and utilities to the newly annexed territory will be greater to the city than the new revenues derived from annexation and will, therefore, become a burden to the central city to which the territory is annexed.

    d. Annexation will cause suburbs to lose their identity. This loss of identification is looked upon as critical by long established suburban communities.

2. *Functional consolidation.* City-county consolidation of certain functions such as health and hospital care, especially for the medically indigent, education and planning offer some relief to problems created by metropolitan expansion, especially in the case of smaller metropolitan areas. It is not unusual to find suburban communities supporting certain services such as police protection, welfare services, streets and roads and recreational facilities and services which might well be provided at public expense by the county.

3. *Widened state responsibility for certain functions.* Some states have transferred some functions from local responsibility to state responsibility. Thus we find states assuming complete responsibility for the road system, for education, health and welfare. How much of this trend is due to expanding metropolitanism is difficult to say. The problems in this case are solved by moving it to a larger unit of government.

4. *The creation of metropolitan regional planning bodies.* Some city planning boards have the legal right to carry on planning activities beyond the boundary lines of the city. Others are combined boards covering a city and a county. One of the best examples of metropolitan planning agencies in this country is the New York Port of Authority. This regional agency, created by the States of New Jersey and New York, has responsibility for planning the harbors, the roads, the bridges, the airports, tunnels and terminal facilities for the metropolitan region of New York City. Its operations and its integrity as a planning agency speak well for this corporate type structure as a planning mechanism at the metropolitan level.[17] It offers one technique for handling the complicated problems of metropolitan planning through a corporation that is really regional in scope.

---

[17] See the various Annual Reports of the Port of New York Authority.

WORKSHOP AND PROBLEMS

1. What peculiar factors have led to the growth of the metropolitan area?
2. Do you agree with the hypothesis of urban dominance?
3. What are the more important indices of urban dominance which you consider reliable?
4. Why the higher rate of growth of the "outlying parts" of metropolitan areas between 1940 and 1950 as contrasted with the growth of central cities?
5. What major problems are created by metropolitan expansion and how may each be attacked?
6. What is being done in metropolitan planning in your city or state?
7. Study and evaluate the work of the New York Port Authority.

BIBLIOGRAPHY

Bureau of the Census reports on urbanization.

Bogue, Donald J., *The Structure of the Metropolitan Community: A Study of Dominance and Subdominance* (Ann Arbor: University of Michigan Press, 1949).

———, *Metropolitan Decentralization: A Study of Differential Growth* (Miami, Ohio: Scripps Foundation for Research in Population Problems, 1950).

Gras, N. S. B., *An Introduction to Economic History* (New York: Harper and Brothers, 1926).

Hubert, Giles A., "A Framework for Study of Peripheral Economic Areas," *Journal of Farm Economics*, Vol. 28 (August 1946) pp. 805-820.

Jensen, Merrill, Ed., *Regionalism In America*, Chapter 3, "The Regional Concept As A Tool For Social Research" by Rupert B. Vance (Madison, Wisconsin: The University of Wisconsin Press, 1952).

McKenzie, Roderick R., *The Metropolitan Community* (New York: McGraw-Hill Book Co., 1933).

Park, Robert E., "Urbanization as Measured by Newspaper Circulation," *American Journal of Sociology*, Vol. 35 (July 1929), pp. 61-79.

Queen, Stuart, and Carpenter, David B., *The American City* (New York: McGraw-Hill Book Co., 1953).

The Community Services Commission for Davidson County and The City of Nashville, *A Future for Nashville* (Nashville: The Commission, June 1952).

Wirth, Louis, "Urbanism as a Way of Life," *American Journal of Sociology*, Vol. 44 (1938-9), pp. 1-24.

CHAPTER 5

The Quantitative Differentials between
Rural and Urban Peoples

By PAUL M. and LEAH G. HOUSER

The purpose of this chapter is to focus attention upon a few care-fully chosen quantitative differentials between rural and urban people, and to suggest perspectives for interpreting the differentials meaning-fully. An attempt is made to avoid the use of undigested census facts, and, in simple nontechnical language, to point the student in directions recommended by Rupert B. Vance in a recent article, "Is Theory for Demographers?"[1] Thus far there are few, if any, adequate systematic explanations of our rural-urban differentials and the direction of their trends, although they are among the more popular census facts as judged by the number of times cited. This popular interest in these differentials and the absence of completely satisfactory explanations of trends are among the principal reasons for studying them. But there are other important reasons and a summary of them would be an ap-propriate place to begin.

Importance of Rural-Urban Differentials. It is important to be alert to the fact that we are studying urban people as a part of the whole American society; we accept the proposition that the fullest under-standing of urban life cannot be reached without considering its rela-tion to the "whole," and to the rural part of the dichotomy. The rural and urban societies are not independent of each other; rather they are inter-dependent. To omit one would be to eliminate many relationships upon which the urban society is partially dependent for its existence.

Although the present population of the United States is 64.0 per cent urban (new definition), a large proportion of that percentage was born and reared on farms. From a socio-psychological point of view, they are rural oriented, carrying many rural values with them into the urban situation where they persist, modifying the attitudes of urbanites toward their present environment. For example, Freedman's

---

[1] Rupert B. Vance, "Is Theory for Demographers?" *Social Forces,* Vol. 31, No. 1 (October, 1952) p. 10. (Presidential address read before the annual meeting of the Population Association of America, April 25, 1952.)

study of migration to Chicago showed that next to the large city migrants, rural farm migrants are most like Chicagoans.[2] Of course, a sociological study of the city is possible without making reference to rural hinterlands and rural-urban relations, but it also follows that the scope and range of understanding is limited accordingly.

It is desirable to keep a close check on the differences existing among the major parts of a society because there should be fewer differences and more similarities, this is, common interests, if the society is to hang together as a whole and perform its necessary functions effectively. To accept the assumption of the dominance of similarity over dissimilarity, which presumably is necessary for survival, is equivalent to placing organization over disorganization or anarchy; it also means certain "ways" are dominant over other "ways." In general, when differences are great, misunderstanding and intolerance are great, and instability and social disorder become real probabilities.

Differentials may be viewed as indices of cracks in the total society. Willard Waller often told his graduate students, "If you wish to learn how society works, study the cracks, or the places where it breaks down and troubles appear." When something goes wrong it attracts the eye because it is different, which implies that it is not the usual or the expected occurrence. The sex-ratio for the United States dropped below 100 in 1950 for the first time in its history. That was something different, and it made the newspapers. Fewer males than females is a condition viewed as undesirable and which some think ought to be corrected. The sex-ratio for urban people is traditionally below 100, while the rural figure has never dropped below 100. Many of the differentials, such as birth and death rates, are publicized because people interpret them as indicative of cracks or breakdowns in the social structure or living conditions which should be repaired.

It is probably true that we learn by noting differences. Whenever there are striking differences between groups, they seldom go unobserved and are sometimes used to perpetuate separation; similarities between groups of ten go unnoticed until challenged by other segments of the society, and may be indicative of integration. It is probably true, also, that individuals are more aware of differentials than of similarities because they identify themselves with certain groups and then become enmeshed with the competitive or conflicting relationships which stem from in- versus out-group differences.

Finally, the study of quantitative rural-urban differentials is a fruitful area for research for those interested in building and testing theories. Rupert B. Vance recently sounded a call for students to develop systematic theories and hypotheses in order to bind diverse demographic facts together in some meaningful fashion. He deplored the undigested

[2] Ronald Freedman, *Recent Migration to Chicago* (Chicago: University of Chicago Press, 1950).

use of census information as ". . . bad for the development of the theoretical muscles."[3] This is a worthy goal for it calls for a better demographic science. But the chief task of the census demographer in our government structure is to collect and present accurate information on the population, and his role not only does not include but is probably antagonistic to the construction of systematic theories of the "high level" type for the interpretation of reports. It is the scholars in the universities who have traditionally contributed the basic theories of knowledge and might try their hand at analyzing the extensive population data available. As in almost any area of related activity, there must be union of effort. Scholars cannot analyze if census takers do not collect key types of information. This is a very real problem in the analysis of migration data, for example, which has been carefully examined by Thomas.[4]

On the other hand, there is little need for collecting data someone does not analyze. Social scientists outside of government, including sociologists, and especially demographers, have been guilty of citing rural-urban differentials as interesting facts inviting further analysis but have then failed to utilize the data for purposes of theory building.[5] If we place the tendency of the theory specialists to neglect population differentials side by side with the tendency of demographers to neglect theory, we are forced to conclude that an unintended consequence is a one-sided development in certain scientific fields. Unsupported theories and undigested facts are equally bad for the development of scientific muscles in any of the scientific disciplines.

Rural-urban differentials give promise of contributing to a better understanding and appraisal of certain aspects of social structure and group integration in American society if approached with a proper balance of both theory and method. Theories of the "middle range" as Merton defines them seem more appropriate for the analysis of such differentials than more complex, universalistic theories of the so-called "higher range."[6]

Point of View. Some of the rural-urban differentials are large, some small; some of them are widening and some are decreasing or narrowing, One viewpoint holds that the facts should be permitted to speak for themselves without being twisted to fit a preconceived theory, while another view holds that it is more scientific to provide a theoretical basis for interpreting them for otherwise the facts have no scientific meaning. Both of these views have their strong points and proper roles

---

[3] *Op. cit.,* p. 10.

[4] Dorothy Swaine Thomas, *Research Memorandum on Migration Differentials,* Bulletin 43 (New York: Social Science Research Council, 1938).

[5] See any of the current books in social theory. An exception is Amos H. Hawley, *Human Ecology: A Theory of Community Structure* (New York: The Ronald Press Co., 1950).

[6] Robert K. Merton, *Social Theory and Social Structure* (Glencoe, Illinois: The Free Press, 1949).

in science and education; therefore, it is appropriate that we attempt to clarify them briefly. Both of them are employed in outline form in this endeavor. The first view is characterized below as "the factualists" and the second as "the schematists." The reader should find it interesting to locate himself in one of these extreme groups, partly in both, or somewhere in between them. It is believed that this will help develop a better understanding of changing rural-urban differentials and their implications to present-day America.

1. *The factualists: let the facts speak for themselves.* The "factualists" stand for the right and responsibility of each group to interpret and evaluate for itself how the facts are related to its own and other groups, and they demand that objective facts be presented distinctly separated from interpretations, points of view, and theories of the analysts. Members of this group contend that letting the facts speak for themselves really means letting each group interpret the facts according to its interest and viewpoint. Emphasis is placed upon the contention that facts do mean different things to different groups of people, and that these are the only meanings that count in social life irrespective of what they may mean for a particular theory. A rise in the consumer price index might mean a wage raise to a labor group and an increase in income taxes to an employer group. The loss of a college football or baseball game may mean something quite different to the professor teaching urban sociology than it does to the students taking the course. From his viewpoint, the right team won but from the viewpoint of the students the wrong team won.

The leaders and members of the urban society will not view the quantitative differentials presented in this chapter in the same light as do those of the rural society. Like the game referred to above, both of the residence groups cannot be completely satisfied with some of the population scores computed by the U. S. Bureau of the Census, the score keeper. For example, the rapid increase of the urban population and the corresponding decline of the rural segment may give the urbanite a secure feeling that he is in a strong position and on the winning side, while to the ruralite it may be the source of insecurity and displeasure.

But members of the urban society do not win all of the "population games." Many of them feel uncomfortable and even frustrated when reminded that until very recently their group had a poor birth rate record with very low scores for several decades (except for the war years to the present), and that it has a serious shortage of men and a surplus of women. On the other hand, the rural person may point to the record of his group in this respect with pride and feel his society is doing very well.

It is clear that factualism is, a strong, widely practiced point of view: it calls for the presentation of facts in an objective fashion and demands the right to interpret them as it sees fit. There is little doubt that whatever basis is used to interpret quantitative rural-urban differentials, those results which are inimical to a given group are likely to be rejected, ignored and discounted whenever possible, or accepted reluctantly. This is as it should be, for groups which accept defeat without being stirred are dead for all practical purposes.

2. *The schematists: make the interpretations factual.* The "schematists" seek to provide bases for interpreting facts which they claim can be equally useful to both ruralists and urbanists. They claim to be more scientific and free of subjectiveness than the group referred to as the factualists. Rather than interpret rural-urban differentials from the standpoint of either of the two groups, the schematist sets up a third viewpoint, a schema with complete definitions and explanations of how to use his approach. This is referred to as a systematic theory, or something short of one, which provides new explanations and insights to empirical data when used carefully. The use of such a procedure permits one to refer to the interpretations as factual because the point of reference of the theory is known, however hypothetical it may be. There are no vested interests in the interpretations aside from those involving the prestige and status of the scholar, and he expects them to be replaced by others sooner or later.

The schematists agree that facts mean different things to different groups of people, and for this reason they contend that interpretations obtained in this manner are subject to great error. There may be as many interpretations of a given fact as there are groups, when in reality there can be only one best for the total society. The schematists contend that interpreting facts from the viewpoint of each group is likely to be "fuzzy," and to that extent in error, because the frame of reference of the group is usually not stated precisely and often not known. The factualist view encourages the selection of only the facts which agree with a group's point of view, which may mean that one fails to see the significance of other facts. In other words, urban people may pay little heed to certain facts, while rural people overlook others, and the total society pays the penalty. All of the available facts must be examined by the same point of view, according to the schematists, irrespective of whether we like the interpretations that result.

Group Mergence Hypothesis for Interpreting Rural-Urban Population Differentials. Two groups which are socially adjacent to each other always influence one another and, through assimilation, take on similar characteristics. The tendency to join, to merge, is demonstrated repeatedly throughout the social and economic organizations of the society. Quantitative differences between them decrease according to the rate of change common to each characteristic and in relation to the degree that the group members mingle with one another, that is, their intragroup interaction rate. Certain societal characteristics come to be accepted by both groups as more needed and desired than others. In time the group which possesses the more important of these characteristics tends to become dominant, the other increasingly more subdominant. The latter may lose its identity entirely, or it may continue as a group entity. To maintain its identity, the subdominant group must meet two basic conditions: (1) it must develop sufficient awareness of the meanings of the interaction underway to offer resistance successfully to proposed changes in its technology, structure, and basic values; (2) it must be able and willing to maintain sufficient organization to pass on its essential cultural norms to succeeding generations. Unless these two key conditions prevail, the subdominant group is eventually absorbed into the dominant one by coalescence and by the general process of assimilation.

In the final stages of the mergence process the two groups develop essentially similar characteristics, and the subdominant group gradually becomes unaware of itself as a group. Nothing remains to prevent the completion of the process at this stage except when the dominant group recognizes a social need or function which may be fulfilled by the lesser group. The process may be then blocked by the dominant group. The blocking of a group mergence process in this sense is a kind of "caging" or containment of the lesser group, that is, it is revived and permitted to grow only enough to fulfill a need of the larger group.

Rural-urban quantitative differentials may be employed as rough measures of the rural-urban mergence process up to but not including the final stage.* Decreases in differentials may be regarded as proof that the process is underway. Similar characteristics will be interpreted as integration for that characteristic. This should aid us in interpreting the differentials more objectively from the standpoint of the whole, while giving due consideration to them from the standpoint of the rural and the urban people. Some questions to keep in mind include: Whose characteristics are becoming dominant in the total society? Are rural and urban people contributing to the emerging national norms equally? How close are we to the final stages of the mergence process? Can counter trends, or increasing differentials, be explained satisfactorily?

Change in Size of Rural and Urban Groups. As Simmel has pointed out, there is probably no more important characteristic of a group than its size for it is related to many other functional and structural charac-

---

* This requires, of course, that we assume the two groups began the process as two different social systems; secondly, that there is a connection between population characteristics and cultural norms, institutional values, and roles. There is considerable evidence to support the latter assumption, and the first one is important only for analytical purposes. It should be noted that the two groups are interdependent parts of a whole, but the data and discussions proceed as if they were two distinctly separate societies.

teristics.[7] The addition of even a small number of people to a group greatly increases the potential number of interactions which may

TABLE X

PERCENTAGE DISTRIBUTION OF THE POPULATION OF THE UNITED STATES BY RESIDENCE, 1790-1950 (FOR CONTINENTAL UNITED STATES)

Year	Total number	Percent Distribution			
		Urban	Rural	Rural-nonfarm	Rural-farm
*1950	150,697,361	64.0	36.0	20.7	15.3
**1950	150,697,361	59.0	41.0	25.7	15.3
1940	131,669,275	56.5	43.5	20.5	23.0
1930	122,775,046	56.2	43.8	19.3	24.5
1920	105,710,620	51.2	48.8	19.1	29.7
1910	91,972,266	45.7	54.3	19.7	34.6
1890	62,947,714	35.1	64.9	....	....
1790	3,929,214	5.1	94.9	....	....

* *New Residence Definition, 1950.* Urban now includes all persons living in places of 2,500 inhabitants incorporated as cities, boroughs, towns (except in New England, New York, and Wisconsin where "towns" are minor civil divisions) and unincorporated places of 2,500 outside any urban fringe: it refers to any concentration of population of 2,500 or more regardless of legally prescribed limits, powers, or functions. *Rural-nonfarm* includes all persons living outside urban areas who do not live on farms, including persons in villages and hamlets of fewer than 2,500 inhabitants and those who live on farms in open country, if they pay cash rent for their homes and yards only, in institutions, summer camps, "motels," and tourist camps. *Rural-farm* includes all persons living on farms without regard to occupation; it does not include persons in institutions located in open country, summer camps, "motels," and tourist camps, and those who rent a house and yard for cash only.

** *Old Residence Definition, 1940.* According to the old definition, *urban* population was limited to all persons living in incorporated places of 2,500 inhabitants or more and in areas (usually minor civil divisions) classified as urban under special rules relating to population size and density. *Rural-nonfarm* included all persons living outside of incorporated cities of 2,500 inhabitants but not on farms. *Rural-farm* included all persons living on farms without regard to occupation; this segment also included persons in institutions located in open country, summer camps, "motels," and tourist camps, and those who rented for cash a house and yard only.

Source: The total populations are given in the dicennial censuses. The total urban and rural per cents are adjusted to the 1940 (old) definition or residence. The Rural-nonfarm and rural-farm estimates are from Margaret Jarman Hagood, "Rural Population Characteristics," in *Rural Life in the United States* by Carl C. Taylor, et al., Table 29, p. 219. The old and new definitions of residence are summarized from *United States Census of Population:* 1950, Vol. 11, Part 1, U. S. Summary, Chapter B, pp. vi and vii. Data from 1950 from Table 34, p. 87.

---

[7] N. J. Spykman, *The Social Theory of Georg Simmel* (Chicago: University of Chicago Press, 1925), p. 129. See also Amos Hawley, *Human Ecology* (New York: The Ronald Press Company, 1950), p. 122, and Louis Wirth, "Urbanism as a Way of Life," *American Journal of Sociology*, Vol. 44 (July, 1938), pp. 1-24.

occur and the addition of large numbers invariably results in specialization of function and division of labor. The United States has shown
one of the most phenomenal increases of population known to man.
It increased from approximately four million in 1790 when the first
census was taken to 150.7 million in 1950 and to 162 million in 1954.
(See Table X.) During the period 1790 to 1950, as Combs points
out in Chapter 3, the urban population increased from two hundred
thousand to 96 million; the rural population from 3.7 million to
54.2 million. In absolute numbers, the urban segment always has increased from decade to decade, but the rural population began to
decline in the forties, dropping from 61.8 million in 1940 to 54.2
million in 1950. Relatively, or percentage-wise, the rural decline
started in 1800, falling below the 50 per cent mark between 1910
and 1920. The rural nonfarm population has been slowly increasing
but the farm population has been dropping rapidly, moving from 34.6
per cent of the total population in 1910 to only 15.3 per cent in 1950.

If present trends in agricultural technology continue, the farm population may stabilize eventually at approximately 5 per cent of the
total population. With improved machinery and scientific farm practices, fewer farmers will be needed to produce the required amounts
of food. If food production becomes the only reason for the farm
group's existence, it will be incorporated, without doubt, into the industrial system of the country. But there are those who believe that
rural people are adapting too readily to urban ways of life and that
the roles which they play in the larger society in the cultivation of
humanitarianism, in democratic ideology, the maintenance of cultural
continuity, and the development of personality are more important
than their agricultural roles. These people are apprehensive over
indications that the rural community is gradually failing in its efforts
to maintain its identity and to inculcate its way of life. To the ruralite
today, the prospects of his being able to continue his role in the
preservation of the national culture—even his survival culturally—
presents a gloomy picture.[8]

The new definition of "urban" employed in the census for 1950
(see Chapter 3 or the first note in Table X, for an explanation of the change) transferred about 5 per cent of the total rural
nonfarm population to the urban classification. It is partly the inclusion of this 5 per cent living in the suburban areas which accounts
for the accentuation of certain rural characteristics in the urban
population, for example, the increase in the number of children. They
are said to be similar to urban people because they work in the city
for a livelihood, are cosmopolitan in viewpoint, and aspire to an

---

[8] For an excellent discussion of this point see the section entitled "The
Role of the City and the Country in Innovation, Disruption, and Preservation
of the National Culture," in P. A. Sorokin and Carle C. Zimmerman, *Principles
of Rural-Urban Sociology* (New York: Henry Holt and Company, 1920).

urban standard of living. However, if we consider their emphasis upon family life and children and their interest in small group activity and community life, they are more like rural people. Neither the rural nor the urban society has tried to assimilate them as members, and that is one reason why the "urban fringe" has been defined as a social problem by some.[9]

Birth Differentials Decreasing. The birth rate for the United States as a whole has been the source of considerable worry for several decades until World War II. Even in 1940, we were not reproducing ourselves as a nation, and the urban people, thoroughly adjusted to depression behavior, were failing to reproduce themselves by 30 per cent. By 1950, apprehension diminished for the situation had reversed itself and we were producing children at a rate approximately 38 per cent more than enough to maintain our present population size. Many people wonder how long this trend will continue. Most population experts think that the birth rate will decline to where it was prior to the war "when things return to normal." But there is some evidence[10] based on analyses of differential fertility among population classes and income groups that the increase in the urban birth rate is more permanent and represents a continued acceptance of our more traditional attitudes toward parenthood.

So called normal conditions in the future may not correspond to normal conditions of our recent past. One can scarcely doubt that "cold war" prosperity and the continued operation of the maintenance provisions of the G. I. Bill for Korean soldiers has had much to do with the persistence of our birth rate at such high levels. But these programs are not based on norms of the past, and there is no certainty that the new norms will be continued in our future society. Although the G. I. Bill may be regarded as the most successful indirect population policy experienced by modern nations, it seems unlikely now that this program will be perpetuated in the United States either for educational purposes or to stimulate the birth rate further.

The most striking fact about the current picture of birth trends is

[9] See Stuart A. Queen and David B. Carpenter, *The American City* (New York: The McGraw-Hill Book Company, Inc., 1953), pp. 118-131, for a discussion of types of suburban communities, many of which started as fringe concentrations, and Solon T. Kimball, *The Fringe*, Spec. Bull. 360 (East Lansing: Michigan State College Agricultural Experiment Station, June, 1949), p. 19 ff., for a discussion of open country areas.
[10] For references to several studies see, Evelyn M. Kitagawa, "Differential Fertility in Chicago, 1920-40," *American Journal of Sociology*, Vol. 58, No. 5 (March, 1953), pp. 481-2. In a study by George Harris and Pat M. Panella, "Relationships of Level of Living Status and Selected Population Characteristics," Research Paper, Department of Sociology, Kent State University, Kent, Ohio, 1950 (Unpublished), p. 12, the authors found the level of living index computed for minor civil divisions in Portage County, Ohio, to be negatively correlated, with fertility ratios in the middle level of living class highest, 417.4. The fertility ratio for the high level of living group was 333.9, and for the low 366.2.

that the urban rate is higher now than it has been since 1900, and before, while the farm rate has decreased 10 per cent during the same period. Although the farm rate is still higher than the urban, considerable importance should be attached to the decreasing excess of rural over urban rates, which is caused by the converging effect of decreasing farm rates and increasing urban rates during and since the war. From 1900 up until 1940, farmers had a reproduction rate two times that of urbanites, while in 1950 their rate exceeded the urban only by about 50 per cent (See Table XI).

TABLE XI

NET REPRODUCTION RATES AND RURAL-URBAN DIFFERENTIALS
UNITED STATES, 1905-10 TO 1944-49

	NET REPRODUCTION RATES *				DIFFERENTIAL: PERCENTAGE	
Year	Total U.S.	Urban	Rural Nonfarm	Rural Farm	Rural Excess over Urban Rate Nonfarm	Farm
1944-49	1,385	1,186	1,628	1,806	37.3	52.3
1942-47	1,292	1,085	1,465	1,859	35.0	71.3
1935-40	978	726	1,150	1,661	58.4	122.6
1930-35	984	747	1,150	1,632	53.9	118.5
1905-10	1,336	937	1,499	2,022	60.0	115.8
Per cent change 1905-49	3.7	26.6	8.6	—10.7	—37.8	—54.8

* The net reproduction rate represents the number of daughters a cohort of 1,000 female infants beginning life together would have during the course of their lives if the cohort were subject to both the death rates at each age level that prevailed at the time specified. These rates have been adjusted to allow for under-enumeration of children under 5 years of age.
    Source: U. S. Bureau of the Census, *Statistical Abstract of the United States, 1952,* Washington, D. C., Table 41, p. 43.

What do these quantitative facts mean when interpreted from the standpoint of the group mergence hypothesis? Since the differential is decreasing, we conclude that behavioral patterns in the two societies are converging to produce similar birth rates. The society as a whole requires that somehow the population be maintained or increased. The rural people have conformed to this social imperative, though probably not consciously so, and it is therefore their birth patterns which prevail as dominant models for the whole society. The urban population, with birth rates previously below survival level, have increased their birth rates until they are now reproducing themselves by 18.6 per cent. This is a small margin and if they cannot maintain a net reproduction rate of over 1,000, we must expect to eventually have a decreasing population, since the total population is already more urban than rural. Moreover, within four decades, the urban population is likely to compose 70 to 80 per cent of the total population, and it will have a birth rate only slightly lower than the rural, if the birth differential continues at its present trend. Thus the urban segment must depend more and more upon itself for population replacements, if it is to survive. The ideal situation is a birth rate rationally and responsibly maintained by both residence groups in accordance with societal requirements.

Rural people place great emphasis upon children and family, but they have become increasingly aware of the great responsibility and cost of rearing and educating them. Their traditional pattern which produced four to six children is being replaced by that of the small family—one to three children. They are ceasing to be a "population pipe line" for the city. Let us emphasize again that the urban people, even though they continue the small family pattern, must manage to reproduce themselves, something they have now demonstrated they can do. The fact that they have been maintaining a positive population balance for the past decade is being used by many teachers, speakers, and writers to foster further community pride in family responsibility.

Rural-Urban Age Differentials Decreasing. The median age of our population was 23 years in 1900; it was 30 years in 1950, an increase of almost a third in 50 years. Almost half of this increase, 14 per cent, occurred during the last 20 years largely during the thirties when births were few. We added only slightly over one year (1.2) from 1940-50 (Table XII). This failure of the median age to advance much

TABLE XII

MEDIAN AGE, RURAL-URBAN DIFFERENTIAL, UNITED STATES, 1930 TO 1950 (NEW RESIDENCE DEFINITIONS)

	Median Age				DIFFERENTIAL: PER CENT Urban Excess Over:	
Year	U.S. Total	Urban	Rural Nonfarm	Rural Farm	Rural Nonfarm	Rural Farm
1950	30.2	31.6	27.9	26.3	13.3	20.2
1940	29.0	31.0	27.7	24.4	11.9	27.0
1930	26.5	28.4	25.8	21.6	10.1	31.5
Per cent increase 1930-50	14.0	11.3	8.1	21.8	—31.7	—35.9

Source: Statistical Abstract of the U. S., 1950, Table 14, p. 13. U. S. Census of Population: 1950. Vol. 11. U. S. Summary, Chapter B, Table 38, p. 90.

during the forties was due to the unusually large number of children added to the population. As long as the high birth rates continue the median age will not advance much, in fact, if they continue indefinitely the median age will decline. Suffering from "cultural depression" we had been easily convinced that aging of the population was under way at an alarming rate. The birth rate was depressed noticeably resulting in accentuated aging population trends. Perhaps there is some connection between our fear of eventually developing an old, stable population and the current birth rate hump. We are socially against having a very aged population, but we all want to live to a ripe old age.

Contrary to popular opinion, the rural society has the youngest population from almost every standpoint. The urban median age is 31.6 years, which is 20.2 per cent higher than the rural-farm median. If the point to this population game is to have the lower score, then the rural group wins hands down; however, it is having a difficult time holding its gains since its median age increased 21.8 per cent from 1930 to 1950, approximately twice the urban increase. In 1930 the farm population had almost the same percentage of its total population under five years of age, as in 1950, 11.0 compared with 11.4; in contrast the corresponding percentages for the urban population were 8.1 and 10.1, respectively, for these decades. Observe also in the left hand columns of Table XIII that both the farm and non-

TABLE XIII

PERCENTAGE DISTRIBUTION OF THE TOTAL POPULATION BY AGE AND RESIDENCE, 1950; AND RURAL-URBAN DIFFERENTIAL PERCENTAGES FOR 1950 AND 1930

	1950			PERCENTAGE DIFFERENTIAL			
	Percentage Distribution			Farm Excess Over Urban		Nonfarm Excess Over Urban	
			Rural				
Age Group	Urban	Nonfarm	Farm	1950	1930 *	1950	1930 *
0— 4	10.1	12.1	11.4	1.13	1.36	1.20	1.28
5—19	20.5	25.7	30.9	1.51	1.38	1.25	1.13
20—29	16.7	15.5	12.0	.72	.77	.93	.89
30—44	23.0	20.5	18.6	.81	.70	.89	.84
45—64	21.4	17.5	19.4	.91	.91	.82	.93
65—over ...	8.2	8.6	7.5	.91	1.00	1.05	1.29

* Computed from Warren Thompson, *Population Problems*, 1942, Table 15, p. 111.

Source: Computed from *U. S. Census of Population: 1950*. Vol. 11. U. S. Summary, Chapter B, Table 38, p. 91.

farm segments have lower percentages of their population in each age group above 19 years than the urban, except for the nonfarm segment at age 65.

The rural-urban age differential is decreasing; the urban median age was 31.5 per cent greater than the rural-farm in 1930 as compared with 20.2 per cent in 1950. This is also true for many age groups; a notable exception is age group 5 to 19 in which the percentage of the farm population in this age group in 1930 exceeded the urban by

38 per cent and increased to 51 per cent in 1950. Both median age trends slowed down from 1940 to 1950, the urban increasing only 2 per cent from 31.0 to 31.6 years while the rural-farm increased 8 per cent from 24.4 to 26.3 years. It would appear that the urban group is struggling toward a younger age norm.

Although median age differentials between the rural and urban segments of the population are thus converging, it does not follow that this pattern will characterize all of the respective age groups for the two populations. The age group differentials reflect the caprices of the birth and death rates for particular generations. For age group 0-4, the differential is converging, a reflection of the upward trend of the urban birth rate during post-World War II years. But for age group 5-19, the differential is diverging, a reflection of the depression.

Rural-Urban Sex Ratio Differentials Increasing. The facts given in Table XIV suggest that the United States is rapidly becoming a female

TABLE XIV

SEX-RATIO AND RURAL-URBAN DIFFERENTIAL, UNITED STATES, 1930 TO 1950

| Year | Number of Males Per 100 Females | | | | DIFFERENTIAL Percent Excess of Rural Over Urban Sex-Ratio: | |
	U.S.	Urban	Rural-Nonfarm	Rural-Farm	Rural-Nonfarm	Rural-Farm
1950	98.6	94.1	102.0	110.1	9.4	17.0
1940	100.7	95.5	103.7	111.7	8.6	17.0
1930	102.5	98.1	105.0	111.0	7.0	13.1
Per cent change 1930- 50	—3.8	—4.1	—2.0	—0.8	34.3	29.8

Source: Computed from 1950 Population Census Report P-B1 (Preprint of Vol. 11, Part 1, Chapter B), Table 34, p. 87; based on the old residence definition.

centered society.[11] Steadily increasing, the sex-ratio for the nation, now 98.6, fell below 100 for the first time in our history in 1950. It will probably continue to decline until it approximates that of the urban segment (94.1), since our society is growing steadily more urban. Since the rural ratio is also declining, the imbalance may be expected to continue. We seem to be following the course of western, industrialized nations, including England, France, Germany, and Sweden, whose sex-ratios dropped below 100 before 1900.[12] European nations lost

---

[11] For an excellent discussion of the sex ratio, its causes and effects, see Paul H. Landis and Paul K. Hatt, *Population Problems* (New York: The American Book Company, 1954), Chapter IV.

[12] Warren S. Thompson, *Population Problems* (New York: McGraw-Hill Book Company, 1942), p. 100.

some of their males through emigration to other countries, and many others through wars. Since our immigrants have been predominantly male, we stand to lose males through immigration restriction, and there seems little likelihood of any reversal of policy.

There are also other reasons for the declining sex-ratios in the United States. These causes lie in the following factors:

1. The high element of risk in male as compared with female social and economic roles.
2. The division of labor between the sexes.
3. The invasion by women of white collar jobs in both manufacturing and the distribution of goods as these areas increasingly become mechanized and freed of physical labor and personal risk.
4. The favorable female balance in extended life expectancy. Obviously, there are some biological differences but these are considered of minor importance in explanations of the sex-ratio declines.

The sex-ratio is 105.7 at birth. By age 51, it has been whittled down to 100.[13] Much of this decrease can be attributed to differential risks in the sex roles which favor female survival. As the proportion of the total population above 50 years of age increases, the sex-ratio decreases. We cherish highly the values and rights underlying all four of the causes of declining sex-ratios, mentioned above, and it remains to be seen how the dilemma will be solved.

The shortage of males in a society, especially ages 20 to 45, deters marriage and undermines the sex mores because it intensifies the competition among females for husbands. Ogburn estimates that cities deter marriage about 10 per cent;[14] the rate is probably much greater in large cities. At present, our rural-farm sex ratio is 110.1, which is 17 per cent greater than the urban ratio. The farm white population has 22 per cent more males than females at ages 20-24, and large excesses also at 55 years and over. In contrast, the urban white population has only 91 males for each 100 females in age group 20-24, and likewise shortages in age groups over 55. Smart girls should tarry in the country to get their man (Table XV).

The rural-urban sex-ratio differential is increasing only slightly. The farm-urban differential, however, did not increase from 1940-50; although it is now 30 per cent above its magnitude as of 1930, a condition due to the rapid urban decline. Rural-urban convergence is occurring from this characteristic, in part, because both residence groups are adopting "low sex-ratio patterns of behavior," that is, greater risk roles for males than for females in an environment where

[13] J. Yerushalmy, "The Age-Sex Composition of the Population Resulting from Natality and Mortality Conditions," *Milbank Memorial Fund Quarterly*, Vol. 21 (January, 1943), pp. 37-63.
[14] W. F. Ogburn, *Recent Social Trends in the United States* (New York: McGraw-Hill Book Co., Inc., 1933), p. 681.

high risk jobs and social situations involving hazards are gradually being eliminated.[15] This is a condition in which the customs permit the females to take advantage of improvements which extend the length of life, while the male tends to be limited to improvements which come from completely eliminating the hazardous factors. For example, women willingly consult physicians for minor ills whereas their mates are expected to be "he-men" and wear them out. The sex-ratio may be expected to remain low, that is under 100, or decrease, as long as the sex roles are unbalanced in respect to risk taking, or environment is not risk free.

TABLE XV

SEX-RATIOS OF THE WHITE POPULATION, UNITED STATES,
BY RESIDENCE (NEW DEFINITION), 1950

Age Group	U.S.	Urban	Rural Nonfarm	Rural Farm
Total All Ages	99.0	94.9	103.6	111.4
Under 5	104.4	104.0	104.7	105.2
5— 9	104.1	103.1	104.8	106.4
10—14	104.1	102.1	105.0	108.5
15—19	100.9	92.5	109.1	120.7
20—24	96.6	91.1	103.0	121.9
25—29	96.0	94.3	98.1	102.8
30—34	96.3	94.3	101.1	99.7
35—39	97.1	93.7	104.5	100.3
40—44	99.1	95.1	107.1	108.6
45—49	99.8	96.0	106.9	110.2
50—54	99.4	95.6	105.3	111.8
55—59	100.2	96.0	103.0	118.0
60—64	100.2	94.9	101.9	126.6
65—69	94.1	86.2	98.6	131.5
70—74	90.7	80.6	100.2	134.3
75—84	84.3	72.9	99.2	125.3
85 over	69.5	60.0	84.4	97.2

Source: U. S. Census of Population: 1950. Vol. 11. U. S. Summary, Chapter B, Table 38, p. 91.

Very high or very low sex-ratios may be considered indicative of undesirable conditions. With the exception of certain groups, Negroes, and the foreign-born, the ratios are not seriously out of balance but such a condition is not far ahead. Although urban people are becoming aware of this imbalance of the sexes and its implications, they see little opportunity to remedy the situation.

---

[15] For a discussion of the effects on mortality of differential risks inherent in sex roles see Paul M. Houser, "Mortality Differentials and Sex Roles: An Explanatory Hypothesis," pp. 376-393, in *Mortality Differentials in Michigan:* Microfilm No. 1151 (Ann Arbor: University Microfilm, 1948).

*Family Size Differential Increasing.** The gap between the average size of rural and urban households has been increasing gradually since 1910. Before that, from 1890 to 1910, when families were slightly larger, the rural-urban difference was slowly decreasing. A very natural question is "Why this reversal of trend? Why did convergent behavior trends become divergent ones? An examination of Table XVI will give us some clue.

The average size household has gradually decreased for all residence groups from 1890 to 1950, but the urban household has decreased at a much more rapid rate than the rural one since 1910. This can be seen from column 4 of Table XVI. In 1950, rural households were 13.3 per cent larger than urban units, a rural excess of members three times greater than that of 1890 and four times greater than that of

TABLE XVI

AVERAGE SIZE HOUSEHOLD AND RURAL-URBAN DIFFERENTIAL, UNITED STATES, BY RESIDENCE, 1890 TO 1950

| Year | Average Size Household | | | Differential |
	U.S.	Urban	Rural	Per Cent Rural Excess
1950	3.38	3.24	3.67	13.3
1940	3.78	3.61	4.01	11.1
1930	4.11	3.97	4.29	8.1
1920	4.34	4.23	4.46	5.4
1910	4.54	4.47	4.60	2.9
1900	4.76	4.61	4.75	3.0
1890	4.93	4.81	5.01	4.2
Per cent change 1890-1950	—31.5	—32.7	—26.8	216.7

Source: Average size households, 1890 to 1940, are from Paul C. Glick, "Family Trends in the United States, 1890 to 1940," *American Sociological Review*, Vol. VII, No. 4, August 1942. 1950 data from *United States Census of Population: 1950,* Vol. II, United States Summary, Chapter B, Table 47, p. 97.

1910. The explanation of this rural-urban reversal of trend in household size from convergence to divergence lies then in a differential rate of decrease between the two groups. Such differential rates of decrease in the average size household cannot continue indefinitely for eventually they must reach a minimum below which the unit cannot exist.

Some of the conditions which account for the decreasing family

---

* Two definitions of family are used—"Family" and "Household." In the 1950 Census, a family is defined as "a group or two or more persons related by blood, marriage, or adoption, and living together." A household includes all the persons who occupy a house, an apartment, or other group of rooms, or a room that constitutes a dwelling unit. Population per household is greater than average size family because it includes one person units. Historical data for the first definition are not available and hence the second definition is used in this chapter. In this discussion the two terms are used synonymously.

size are unavoidable. Children grow up and leave the parental home, which means that even families which had several children eventually become two-member units again. The number of such two-member families above 45 years of age is increasing. When one of the two members dies, the home becomes a one member family. The number of these is increasing. In the past, a single household might include two or even three generations of families. As we conquer the diseases of old age and extend the average expectation of life, we keep alive more one and two member families and this helps push down the average size of the household.

The low birth rates for the few decades prior to 1945 explain much of the decrease in family size. The fact that a counter mergence trend exists, that is, that the rural household has been decreasing in average size proportionately slower since 1910 than the urban, may result from two major influences: (a) from interruptions or accelerations in the mergence process which is directed toward a common norm, or (b) because one of the groups rejects the common norm substituting another in its place. Population specialists in the past, observing the behavior of the birth rate and sociologists specializing in family trends have tended to hypothesize that different family goals favoring individualistic rather than familistic and secular rather than sacred norms were emerging in the city. However, recent studies of increases in the birth rate and in fertility might cast some doubt upon this. These studies show an increase in upper class and in upper income group fertility, raising considerable question as to any change in basic attitudes toward parenthood.

Mortality Differentials Declining. Mortality has long been recognized as an important measure of the health of a population. As early as 1662, John Graunt, an English demographer, wrote that rural people had lower death rates than urban persons. During our history, death rates have been decreasing, and likewise, the mortality differentials between rural and urban populations have been declining. The drastic changes which have occurred among these differentials are shown in computations made by Harold Dorn (Table XVII). He compared crude and age-adjusted death rates in 1900-02 with those of 1940 for the two residence groups. The urban age-adjusted death rate, 20.8 per 1,000 population in 1900-02, dropped to 11.4 by 1940, a decline of 45 per cent. The rural rate decreased only 28.8 per cent, falling from 13.9 to 9.9 per 1,000 population during the same period. Thus the urban death rate was 50 per cent greater than the rural rate in 1900-02 but was only 15 per cent greater by 1940. Although both residence death rates fell noticeably during the forty year period, the converging trend was a reflection of the rapidly decreasing urban death rate as compared with the rural rate.

A more rigid analysis of mortality, making use of life tables, also

TABLE XVII

CRUDE AND ADJUSTED DEATH RATES AND RURAL-URBAN
DIFFERENTIALS, UNITED STATES, 1900-02 AND 1940 *

| | DEATH RATES | | | | DIFFERENTIAL | |
Year	Urban Crude	Adjusted	Rural Crude	Adjusted	Per Cent Crude	Urban Excess Adjusted
1940	11.5	11.4	9.8	9.9	17.3	15.2
1900-02	18.4	20.8	14.2	13.9	29.6	49.6
Per cent change	—37.5	—45.2	—31.0	—28.8	—41.6	—69.4

* The rates for 1900-02 are for the original registration states by place of occurrence of death. The 1940 rates are for the total United States by place of residence. Rural in 1900-02 included places under 8,000 population: in 1940, places under 2,500. The total population of the United States, 1940, was used as the standard population to adjust the rates.

Source: Harold F. Dorn, "Rural Health and Public Health Programs," *Rural Sociology*, Vol. 7, p. 25, March, 1942. Data for 1940 are from the Bureau of the Census, Special Reports, *Vital Statistics of the United States, 1940*.

demonstrates these declining rural-urban differentials. Using life tables prepared by Glover for 1900 and by the Metropolitan Life Insurance Company for 1930, Smith shows the life expectancy of the white population for both sexes, by age and residence.[16] In 1900, the expectation of life at birth was 23 per cent greater for rural than for urban males. By 1930, this differential had dropped to 9 per cent. Trends for females were similar.

Convergence patterns of the future between the rural and urban societies will depend upon the adequacy and equity of distribution of health facilities and health education in the areas, and upon differential health hazards which characterize them. The rural community now has the advantage of a more favorable natural environment—pure air, sunshine, and space; urbanites that of a more favorable social environment—scientific attitudes toward health care, better hospitals, and accessibility to facilities. Off hand, it would seem that the rural population has an advantage in that it might be easier to bring the social advantages of the city, which are man-made, to the country than to bring the natural advantages of the country to the city.

If mortality is examined in terms of differential rates such as those by age, sex, or race, the same trends indicated above prevail in most of the population segments.[17] For example, urban death rates for children under five years exceeded those of rural children by 10 per

[16] See T. Lynn Smith, *The Sociology of Rural Life* (New York: Harper and Brothers, 1953), p. 153. Data are based on the Death Registration States of 1900.

[17] See Paul M. Houser and J. Allan Beegle, *Mortality Differentials in Michigan*, Special Bulletin 367 (East Lansing: Michigan State College Agricultural Experiment Station, February, 1951).

cent in 1940 as compared with 73 per cent in 1900-02. This phenomenal decrease resulted largely from modern sanitation and improved
control of communicable diseases. Although the pattern of the trend
remains the same, it should be pointed out that the size of the differential varies among series of rates. Thus in contrast to that of the age-
group under five, urban death rates for rural persons over age seventy-
five only exceeded that of rural people by 16 per cent in 1902 and
fell to 4 per cent by 1940 (Table XVIII).

TABLE XVIII

NUMBER OF DEATHS PER 1,000 POPULATION UNDER FIVE YEARS
OF AGE AND 75 YEARS AND OVER IN EACH RESIDENCE
GROUP; AND RURAL-URBAN DIFFERENTIALS,
UNITED STATES, 1900-02 AND 1940

Year	RESIDENCE				DIFFERENTIAL	
	Urban		Rural		Per Cent	Urban Excess
	*Under 5 Years	Over 75 Years	*Under 5 Years	Over 75 Years	*Under 5 Years	Over 75 Years
1940	13.5	131.5	12.3	126.1	9.8	4.3
1900-02 ...	55.5	155.4	32.1	133.6	72.9	16.3
Per cent decrease .	—75.7	—15.4	—61.7	—5.6	—86.6	—73.6

*This is an age-specific death rate and should not be confused with the
infant death rate.
   Source: Harold F. Dorn, 'Rural Health and Public Health Programs,"
Rural Sociology, Vol. 7, p. 25, March, 1942. Data for 1940 are from the Bureau
of the Census, Special Reports, *Vital Statistics of the United States, 1940.*

Home Ownership Differential. The goal of home ownership and the
values which revolve around it are among the more powerful of our
social norms. The aggressive center of the drive is located in the social
roles of the family, which stem from the reproductive and child rearing
functions of the female. She has always been the impelling force which
makes the man settle down. Marriage, children, houses, and social
life in the home are her forte. It is no wonder that the symbol of
achievement for the agricultural social ladder consists essentially of
successfully attaining a home ownership status.

Home ownership is still a basic social norm of the total society,
but more so of the rural than of the urban segment. Some of what we
call the "housing problem" today is the struggle of the urban man to
carry out this rural norm.[18] In reality, home ownership does not fit too
well in the modern industrial social structure, except in those instances
where flexibility and mobility offer no economic opportunities to the
family. However, all efforts to modify it have failed as indicated by

[18] See the Chapter on housing.

the increasing proportion of homes occupied by owners. (See Table XIX). This fact is one challenge to the contention that the economic institution dominates and controls all others.[19]

In 1950, more homes (55 per cent) were occupied by owners than at any other time in our history; this is a 15 per cent increase over the 1930 figure. From 1930 to as far back as 1890, home ownership has fluctuated very little. In fact for those two years, it was identical, 48 per cent. The low point was reached during the thirties, a reflection of the increased foreclosures during the depression years. In 1940, only 44 per cent of American homes were owner occupied. During the next decade, home ownership increased 26 per cent, over half of the homes of the nation now being owner occupied.

TABLE XIX

PERCENTAGE OF HOMES OCCUPIED BY OWNERS, AND
RURAL-URBAN DIFFERENTIALS, UNITED STATES,
1930 TO 1950

	RESIDENCE				DIFFER-EN-TIAL	PER-CENT-AGE
Year	U.S.	Urban	Nonfarm	Farm	Rural Excess Nonfarm	Over Urban Farm
1950	55.0	50.5	62.6	65.4	24.0	29.5
1940	43.6	37.5	51.7	53.2	37.9	41.9
1930	47.8	43.4	53.7	53.9	23.7	24.2
Per cent change 1930-50	15.1	16.4	16.6	21.3	1.3	21.9

Source: Statistical Abstract of the United States, 1952, Table 910, p. 740. (The 1950 figures are based on preliminary samples, and they use the new definition of residence.)

Homes owned by farmers exceed those of all other residence groups. Approximately 65 per cent of all farm homes were occupied by owners in 1950 as compared with 55 per cent for urban dwellers. Moreover during the depression urbanites were most affected, home ownership decreasing 14 per cent from 1930 to 1940 for this group as compared with 4 per cent and one per cent respectively for nonfarm and farm families. The shock effect of the depression on home owners stimulated initiative to the extent that home ownership more than made up for its losses during the next decade in all residence groups. By 1950,

[19] Although home ownership is an economic act, it is a symbol of family status. Walter Firey demonstrates how certain houses and their locations are symbols of noneconomic values. See "Sentiment and Symbolism as Ecological Variables," American Sociological Review, Vol. 10. No. 2, (April, 1945) pp. 140-148.

half of the urban dwellings were owner occupied and two thirds of the farm homes, with nonfarm families falling between.

The farm-urban home ownership differential is temporarily increasing but it can be expected to move downward in the future. It is not anticipated that this differential decrease will result from any modification of the ownership norm but rather from further increases in the urban home ownership rate. Adaptations in types of housing now current include flexible housing units such as trailers, small, less expensive, prefabricated houses, and apartment units which can be bought and sold. The decrease in family size has also made these smaller family units more feasible. Since the number of families is increasing and the size of the family is decreasing, real estate men may well anticipate future shortages in small houses, or small dwelling units.

Level and Standard of Living Differentials Declining. Some of the more important measures of rural-urban differentials are the indices of level and standard of living. The level of living refers to the actual possession of goods and services and to the opportunities to consume these while standard of living refers to the values attached to things possessed or things desired. *What we have* is level of living; *what we strive for* is standard of living. The latter is attitudinal and hence is more difficult to measure, particularly for large populations.

Items in a level-of-living index include possession of your own home, an automobile, a telephone, a bath, income, education, and similar items. Individuals who rank lowest in level-of-living tend to rank lowest in standard of living.[20] Highly refined mathematically validated indexes of level-of-living based on census data have been worked out for the rural segments of all counties of the United States by Margaret Jarmon Hagood but the work is not complete for urban segments of the population.

We shall examine the rural-urban differentials of two of these items of level of living, median income and median grade in school attained. Median income as used by the Bureau of Census refers to cash income and the term is used here in this sense.

The differential between the income of farmers and urban workers is narrowing, having declined 56 per cent from 1939 to 1950 (Table XX). Irrespective of this, the income of farmers on the average, is still only about half as high as that of urban people, $1,729 as compared with $3,431.

This does not mean that urban people are twice as well off as farmers, for the latter have income in kind which is not easily measured, such as eggs and housing. However, income in kind is not transferable and cannot be used ordinarily as a medium of exchange to buy such things as television sets and automobiles, unless converted into cash.

---

[20] Paul M. Houser and Robert E. Galloway, *Rural Reading Habits,* Bulletin A 69 (College Park, Maryland: University of Maryland Agricultural Experiment Station, June, 1952), p. 16.

TABLE XX

MEDIAN INCOME OF URBAN AND RURAL FAMILIES, UNITED
STATES, AND RESIDENCE DIFFERENTIALS, 1939 TO 1950

	MEDIAN INCOME			DIFFERENTIAL: PER CENT	
				Urban Excess Over	
			Rural		
Year	U. S.	Urban	Nonfarm	Farm	Nonfarm	Farm
1950	3,073	3,431	2,560	1,729	34.0	98.4
1949	3,107	3,486	2,763	1,587	26.2	119.7
1939	1,231	1,463	976	453	49.9	223.0
Per cent increase 1939-50	149.6	134.5	162.3	281.7	—32.0	—55.9

Source: U. S. Census of Population: 1950. Vol. II. U. S. Summary, Chapter
B, Table 57, p. 104. (New urban definition used for 1950.) *Statistical Abstract
of the United States: 1952,* Table 318, p. 264; 1947, Table 314, p. 280.

Money income is what gives flexibility of action in purchasing the
things considered important in achieving one's standard of living. To
achieve equality in this sense, the rural person must be guaranteed a
certain cash income over and above his subsistence level of living.
This is in part one of the factors operating in the rationalizations over
farm subsidy and the parity index. It is a controversial way of providing purchasing power to the rural group for commodities on sale in
the urban market. It is a kind of a guarantee of a "decent wage."

The differential between the income of nonfarm and urban people,
in lesser degree than that of the farm population, has been decreasing,
the income of urbanites exceeding that of the nonfarm group by 50
per cent in 1939, decreasing to 34 per cent in 1950. Corresponding
figures for the farm population are 223 per cent and 98 per cent
respectively.

TABLE XXI

MEDIAN GRADE OF SCHOOL COMPLETED BY THE URBAN AND
RURAL POPULATION 25 YEARS AND OVER, 1940 TO 1950*

	MEDIAN GRADE OF SCHOOL COMPLETED			DIFFERENTIAL: PER CENT	
				Urban Excess Over:	
			Rural		
Year	Urban	Nonfarm	Farm	Nonfarm	Farm
1950	10.2	8.8	8.4	15.9	21.4
1940	8.7	8.4	7.7	3.6	13.0
Per cent increase	17.2	4.8	9.1	341.7	64.6

*1950 data based on New Bureau of Census definition of urban.
Source: United States Census of Population: Vol. II, Part I, U. S. Summary, Chapter B, Table 44, p. 96.

Urban people are raising their educational level considerably faster than farm people. They added a full grade and a half from 1940 to 1950, an improvement of 17 per cent (Table XXI). In contrast, the farm population increased its educational base seven-tenths of a grade and the non-farm only four-tenths, during the same decade, increases of 9 per cent and 5 per cent, respectively. This relatively low educational gain for the nonfarm population may reflect ineffective social motivation arising out of inadequate participation in either the urban or the rural social institutions. Hence nonfarm persons may occupy fewer status positions and have fewer drives toward educational achievement.

Increasing rural-urban educational differentials are examples of the trends of other noneconomic level of living measures as well. In contrast, economic level of living differentials such as median income are decreasing. These trends reflect the relationship between the level and the standard of living and suggest that economic level of living characteristics start converging first and then the noneconomic ones follow. Economic life for the farmer is rapidly becoming as complex as that of the urban man. Since his financial solvency remains insecure and outside of his control, resting on government subsidies and the like, he is often averse to voting increasing funds for schools, irrespective of his felt need for higher education.

Summary. An attempt has been made in the foregoing pages to focus attention upon several carefully chosen rural-urban differentials and to interpret their meanings and implications for contemporary America. The use of undigested census facts is discouraged because it contributes little to one's understanding. The question of why concern ourselves with differentials was discussed briefly. Among the more important reasons are:

1. The fact that each individual is interested in the residence segment of which he is a member and has vested interests in its survival.

2. People in general are quick to note differences because they are easier to observe than similarities. Many of these differences are large and their implications are subjects of conversation, rationalization and planning both at scientific and personal levels.

Rural-urban differentials, however, have probably been neglected by students who have tried to appraise the integration process in American society.

Quantitative factual information is difficult to interpret, whether it pertains to rural and urban peoples or other classes of the population. We pointed to two viewpoints, "factualists" and "schematists," and contended that both were useful and proper in their place. The factualist view infers that the meaning of facts are what the strongest groups say they are, but it is also true that the viewpoint emphasizes democratic interpretation and that all groups have inherent rights to present their position. In contrast, the schematist claims to be more scientific, relating his findings to specific theoretical frames of reference.

Examination of several differentials indicates that the direction of their trends is fairly well established, irrespective of the point of view by which we interpret them. These may be summarized as follows:

1. The difference between the sizes of the rural and urban societies is increasing. The rural farm population is decreasing; the rural non-farm shows slight increases; the urban is increasing rapidly.

2. The former wide gap between the urban and rural birth rate is narrowing, the urban having moved upward and the rural having started a slow decline.

3. The trend toward similar median ages of rural and urban people is slow but steady. Age in both groups is increasing, but the farm median is still considerably under the urban.

4. Sex-ratios are declining in all residence segments but the rural-urban difference is increasing due to greater drops in the urban sex-ratio.

5. Rural-urban differentials for average size family have increased since 1910; family size is decreasing in both groups.

6. The urban death rates, formerly much higher than the rural, have decreased more rapidly than the rural, until now they are quite close together.

7. Home ownership differentials between rural and urban peoples are decreasing; both groups own their homes at increasing rates although relatively more farm than urban people own homes.

8. Economic level-of-living items such as median income show decreasing residence differentials but noneconomic level-of-living items such as education are apparently increasing faster in urban than in rural areas, resulting in an increasing differential between the two residence groups.

Current differential trends suggest that the total society is temporarily, at least, adopting the following norms which have characterized rural society: high birth rates, home ownership, low mortality and long life, and young age. From the urban society come such characteristics as high level-of-living (income and education), families of small size, low sex ratios, and the advantages of large population size.

Our conclusion is that convergence patterns are not completely dominated by either of the two groups. Rural norms are not being destroyed, as some claim, but are gradually being adapted and reincorporated into the total society. On the other hand, the urban society, ever becoming more powerful, is contributing greatly to the nation as a whole by developing economic standards and a level-of-living base which permits the further development of personal and small group values.

WORKSHOP AND PROBLEMS

1. Why are rural-urban differentials important?

2. What is the position of the factualists and the schematists with respect to rural-urban differentials? What is the "group mergence" approach?

3. Discuss the trends in birth differentials between rural and urban populations.

4. What are the more important age differentials between the two populations?

5. What are the more important sex ratio differentials? Why the declining sex ratio differences in the United States?

6. Why the gap in family size differentials and what is the trend?

7. What are the death rate differentials between the two populations?

8. What is the trend in home ownership differentials?

9. To what extent do educational differentials exist?

10. Taking all of the trends collectively, what differentials do you expect to widen in the future and which ones do you expect to narrow? Why?

BIBLIOGRAPHY

Bogue, Don J., *The Structure of the Metropolitan Community, A Study of Dominance and Subdominance* (Ann Arbor: University of Michigan School of Graduate Studies, 1949).

Dorn, Harold F., "Rural Health and Public Health Programs," *Rural Sociology*, Vol. 7 (March 1942), pp. 22-32.

Dublin, Louis I., Lotka, Alfred J., and Spiegelman, Mortimer, *Length of Life* (New York: The Ronald Press Co., 1951).

Edin, K. A., and Hutchinson, E. P., *Studies of Differential Fertility in Sweden* (London: P. S. King and Son, 1935).

Ericksen, E. Gordon, *Urban Behavior* (New York: The Macmillan Co., 1954).

Firey, Walter, "Sentiment and Symbolism as Ecological Variables," *American Sociological Review*, Vol. 10 (April, 1945) pp. 140-148.

Freedman, Ronald, *Recent Migration to Chicago* (Chicago: University of Chicago Press, 1950).

Gist, Noel P., and Halbert, L. A., *Urban Society* (New York: Thomas Y. Crowell Co., 1945).

Glick, Paul C., "The Family Cycle," *American Sociological Review*, Vol. 12 (1947), pp. 164-174.

—————————————, "Family Trends in the U. S. 1890-1940," *American Sociological Review*, Vol. 7 (August, 1942).

Goode, William J., and Hatt, Paul K., *Methods in Social Research* (New York: McGraw-Hill Book Co., Inc., 1952) Chapter 18.

Graunt, John, *Natural and Political Observations Made on the Bills of Mortality* (Baltimore: The Johns Hopkins Press, 1939).

Hagood, John Jarman, "Development of a 1940 Rural-Farm Level of Living Index for Counties," *Rural Sociology*, Vol. 8, No. 2 (June, 1943), pp. 171-180.

Hatt, Paul K., and Reiss, Albert J. Jr., *Reader in Urban Sociology* (Glencoe: The Free Press, 1951).

Hawley, Amos, *Human Ecology: A Theory of Community Structure* (New York: The Ronald Press Co., 1950).

Houser, Paul M., *Mortality Differentials in Michigan* (Ann Arbor: University Microfilm, Publication 1151, 1948) Appendix IV.

————————————————— and Beegle, J. Allan, *Mortality Differentials in Michigan* (East Lansing: Michigan State College Agricultural Experiment Station, Special Bulletin 367, 1951).

—————————————————, Galloway, Robert E., and Hoffsommer, Harold, *Rural Reading Habits* (College Park: University of Maryland Agricultural Experiment Station, Bulletin A69, June 1952).

Jaffe, A. J., *Handbook of Statistical Methods for Demographers* (Washington, D. C.: Government Printing Press, 1951).

Kiser, C. V., "Fertility Trends and Differentials in the U. S.," *Journal of the American Statistical Association*, Vol. 47 (March, 1952).

Kitagawa, Evelyn M., "Differential Fertility in Chicago, 1920-40," *American Journal of Sociology*, Vol. 58, No. 5 (March, 1953).

Koos, Earl L., and De S. Brunner, Edmund, *Suburbanization in Webster, New York* (Rochester: University of Rochester, 1945).

Landis, Paul H., and Hatt, Paul K., *Population Problems* (New York: The American Book Co., 1954).

Loomis, Charles and Beegle, J. Allan, *Rural Social Systems* (New York: Prentice-Hall, Inc., 1950).

Martin, Walter T., "Associational Activities of Rural-Urban Fringe Residence," *American Sociological Review*, Vol. 17, No. 6 (December, 1952), pp. 687-694.

Merton, Robert K., *Social Theory and Social Structure* (Glencoe, Illinois: The Free Press, 1949).

Mott, Frederick D., and Roemer, Milton I., *Rural Health and Medical Care* (New York: McGraw-Hill Book Co., Inc., 1948).

Ogburn, W. F., *Recent Social Trends in the United States* (New York: McGraw-Hill Book Co., Inc., 1933).

Queen, Stuart A., and Carpenter, David B., *The American City* (New York: McGraw-Hill Book Co., Inc., 1953).

Schmid, Calvin F., *Social Trends in Seattle* (Seattle, Washington: University of Washington Press, 1944).

Smith, T. Lynn, *Population Analysis* (New York: McGraw-Hill Book Co., Inc., 1948).

—————————————————, *The Sociology of Rural Life* (New York: Harper and Bros., 1953).

Sorokin, P. A., and Zimmerman, Carle C., *Principles of Rural-Urban Sociology* (New York: Henry Holt and Co., 1929).

Spykman, N. J., *The Social Theory of Georg Simmel* (Chicago: University of Chicago Press, 1925).

Taylor, Carl C., et. al., *Rural Life in the United States* (New York: Alfred A. Knopf, 1949).

Thomas, Dorothy Swaine, *Research Memorandum on Migration Differentials* (New York: Social Science Research Council, Bulletin 43, 1938).

Thompson, Warren S., *The Growth of Metropolitan Districts in the United States: 1900-1940* (Washington, D. C.: U. S. Bureau of the Census, 1948).

—————————————————, *Population Problems* (New York: McGraw-Hill Book Co., Inc., 1942).

U. S. Bureau of the Census, *Population: Differential Fertility 1940 and 1910: Women by Number of Children Ever Born and Fertility by Duration of Marriage* (Washington: U. S. Government Printing Office, 1945 and 1947).

U. S. Bureau of the Census, *Statistical Abstract of the United States* (Washington: U. S. Government Printing Office, 1952).

U. S. Bureau of the Census, *U. S. Census of Population: 1950* (Washington: U. S. Government Printing Office, 1952).

U. S. Bureau of the Census, *Vital Statistics of the United States, 1940,* Part II, Residence (Washington: U. S. Government Printing Office, 1943).

Vance, Rupert B., "Is Theory for Demographers?" *Social Forces,* Vol. 31, No. 1 (October, 1952), pp. 9-13.

Whelpton, P. K., and Kiser, C. V., "Social and Psychological Factors Affecting Fertility. I. Differential Fertility Among 41,498 Native-White Couples in Indianapolis," *Milbank Memorial Fund Quarterly,* Vol. 21 (July, 1943).

Willcox, Walter F., *Studies in American Demography* (Ithaca, New York: Cornell University Press, 1940).

Wirth, Louis, "Urbanism as a Way of Life," *American Journal of Sociology,* Vol. 44 (July, 1938), pp. 1-24.

Yerushalmy, J., "The Age-Sex Composition of the Population Resulting from Natality and Mortality Conditions," *Milbank Memorial Fund Quarterly,* Vol. 21 (January, 1943), pp. 37-63.

CHAPTER 6

Rural-Urban Contrasts in Socialization

By EDWIN L. LIVELY

A major consideration for any society is the preservation of its way of life over the years. The life span of individual members is very short compared to the length of time many societies and many social systems exist. In order for the continuance of the society, the membership must devise means by which the knowledges and beliefs of the past and the present may be extended into the future. Modern industrial societies have developed mechanical means of reproducing writings and pictures so they may be kept more or less indefinitely. Some records of the present are being buried in "time capsules" to be opened in the future. It should be remembered, however, that all societies have not had and do not have these modern tools, and some do not even have a system of writing, and yet these simple and preliterate groups have managed to survive and maintain cultures through many generations with a high degree of continuity. In both simple and complex societies, one technique for survival is always present. This technique is called *socialization*.

Socialization encompasses those processes involved in fitting the coming generations into the existing society with a minimum of tension and maladjustment. The broad area called education is a part of socialization, and some aspects of government, religion, and family life, indeed every phase of life, may have value for the adjustment of someone to the society and its culture. In the following pages the term socialization will be examined more fully with special emphasis on the broad differences in the growing up processes of rural and urban environments. Most of the chapter is devoted to an emphasis of these contrasts, however the last section attempts to show some of the recent changes that have taken place, particularly in the United States, in rural and urban areas, which affect the socialization process. A note of caution should be added, namely that this is a general discussion of rural and urban contrasts, consequently the reader will not be likely to find a perfect description of his own community, whether he lives on a farm in Kansas, or in an apartment on a busy street in New York City. Keeping this in mind, we turn to an examination of those processes by which societies extend their existence through the years.

The Nature of Socialization. The adult in any society develops his personality through the interaction of three factors, culture, heredity, and personal experiences.* The human organism begins life with a great number of unchannelled biological potentialities out of which emerge specific behaviors performed in specific situations. These behaviors include role patterns accompanying social statuses, motor habits, language, and skills of various sorts, plus their covert aspects such as attitudes, values, and superstitions. Also involved is the learning of the situation in which each behavior is not only useful but socially acceptable. The acquisition of these behaviors, both overt and covert, and the learning of the contexts in which they are to be used, is known as socialization, and it operates from birth until death. Thus, as the individual matures in a biological way, he also matures socially. Similarly, just as there is a wide variety of sizes, shapes, and colors among the members of a society (although there are tendencies for certain types to be more common than others) so there are numerous varieties of social behaviors within a given society with the same tendencies toward certain more or less repetitive patterns.

All societies have a number of agencies and techniques through which the socializing of the youth is initiated and maintained. The agencies include the formalized institutional areas such as the family, the school, the church, the media of communication, and the government, using such methods as teaching and law, plus the more informal techniques of gossip, ridicule, reward and punishment. There are also imitative learnings which are not structured within the institutions, plus the neighborhood and peer group interactions which are mostly informal. Through these devices the child is taught the role behaviors associated with the many statuses or social positions he occupies and will occupy during his life in that society. He also is aided in developing a concept of "self" including the inhibitions necessary for acceptable participation in the society; he learns the language, the customs and traditions, fashions, skills, and trades. All of these and many other behavioral requirements for becoming a useful and desirable member of society are achieved through the processes of socialization.

It should be pointed out that, in addition to differences in degree of proficiency in the aforementioned behaviors, there are various actions and attitudes which are defined as undesirable or threatening to the welfare of the group. It follows that as societies contribute to the socially acceptable behaviors acquired by its youth, they may also contribute in some way to these deviations which impair the efficiency of that society. The ineffectiveness of the socialization processes is likely to be a major factor if the number of these deviants, including delinquents, transients, idlers, or whatever form the unacceptability may take, becomes large. As we examine the types of socializing agencies

---

* The usual conditioning factors of natural environment are noted and taken for granted.

and techniques, and draw some contrasts between rural and urban societies in these areas, we also should watch for any deficiencies or failures in these processes which might account for some of the contrasts between these two segments of our society. Clues to these differences might be found in such divergent areas as educational levels of attainment, physical rejections for military service, church attendance, crime rates, and voting behavior.

Culture in Socialization. The direction of the socializing processes will be limited by the values or ideology of the social grouping in which they are operating. This direction and the content within the processes, along with the values that underlie them, will vary from society to society. Within a given society, however, the adults are likely to attempt, as nearly as possible, to prepare their offspring for the society in which they believe those children are going to be living, namely, one very much like that of the parents themselves. This cultural preparation is usually concerned with the mores, taboos, avoidances, and other such values in the area of human interaction, rather than specific behaviors related to material cultural objects, such as the family's possessions, items in the stores, and the furnishings in the school.

Culture, including values, behaviors, and material items, is primarily concerned with man's adjusting to his environments by making use of his multipotential original nature. Due to geographical differences, differences in inventions, both planned and accidental, man's fertile imagination, and the many transportation and communication channels through which diffusion takes place, a tremendous variety of cultures have been found on the earth's surface. Studies such as those of Herskovits,[1] Kluckhohn,[2] Mead,[3] Redfield,[4] and Thompson,[5] which describe aspects of preliterate societies, and those of civilized people's societies, e.g., Young,[6] Hollingshead,[7] Arensberg,[8] and the Lynds,[9] illustrate variations, not only in the culture patterns and complexes in any almost indefinite number of divergent ways, but also of the many socializing techniques used in those societies and designed to insure their survival with a high degree of stability and continuity. In the rural, isolated, preliterate so-

---

[1] Melville Herskovits, *Dahomey: An Ancient West African Kingdom* (New York: J. J. Augustin, 1938).

[2] Clyde Kluckhohn and Dorothea Leighton, *The Navaho* (Cambridge: Harvard University Press, 1946).

[3] Margaret Mead, *From The South Seas* (New York: William Morrow, 1939).

[4] Robert Redfield, *The Folk Culture of Yucatan* (Chicago: University of Chicago Press, 1941).

[5] Laura Thompson, *Culture in Crisis* (New York: Harper & Bros., 1950).

[6] Pauline V. Young, *Pilgrims of Russian-Town* (Chicago: University of Chicago Press, 1932).

[7] August B. Hollingshead, *Elmtown's Youth* (New York: John Wiley and Sons, 1949).

[8] Conrad M. Arensberg and Solon T. Kimball, *Family and Community in Ireland* (Cambridge: Harvard University Press, 1940).

[9] Robert S. Lynd and Helen M. Lynd, *Middletown* (New York: Harcourt, Brace & Company, 1929). Also *Middletown in Transition*, 1937.

cieties, specific techniques of child rearing and training do not seem as important as in the modern, complex areas, because the high degree of homogeneity in the former limit the acceptable directions and possible alternatives to those already in use by the adult population. Consequently, socialization as a formalized process or series of processes occupies comparatively less time in these societies, whereas in the United States, as an example of a society with a high degree of heterogeneity of population in concentrated areas, much of the socialization is highly structured to assure at least a minimum of continuity and stability in the society as a whole.

In spite of the difficulties in classifying the major values underlying the culture of the United States, due primarily to this heterogeneity, some consensus[10] has been reached on such things as democracy, monogamous marriage, monotheistic religion, freedom, education, and a few others. This means that in a vast majority of families, schools, churches, and other institutional areas which function in the socialization processes, there are unifying bonds or themes of consistency and continuity. There would probably be more agreement, however, among sociologists and other students of society regarding the cultural differences existing between regions, and communities within them, in this country.

Since it has been demonstrated [11] that there is a reciprocal relationship between the existing social structure and the personalities of persons behaving within that structure, it follows that to the extent that social systems differ from one another, the personality types of the members of different systems, including those performing in socializing capacities, would differ. Many writers have tended to construct rural and urban as either ideal community types, or as polar types on a social order continuum, and some suggest that there are specific or distinctive personality types associated with those communities toward the continuum extremes, especially when contrasted with one another in a given society.[12] One caution should be noted, that these differences are attributed to the cultural traits which reflect the ideological system and have been disseminated through the processes of socialization and not to innate differences. Since change is inherent in the concept of culture, these traits are not to be treated as constants but rather as changing with the culture in which they exist. It will be suggested later

---

[10] See John F. Cuber and Robert A. Harper, *Problems of American Society: Values in Conflict* (New York: Henry Holt and Company, 1951), pp. 474-477. Other problem texts seem to make the same assumptions of a nucleus of common values in American culture.

[11] See Abram Kardiner, *The Psychological Frontiers of Society* (New York: Columbia University Press, 1945). Others using projective techniques, and some of the followers of Kurt Lewin, have demonstrated this relationship.

[12] This point is suggested in the writings of Kardiner, *Ibid.*, and also in those of Ruth Benedict, *Patterns of Culture* (New York: Houghton Mifflin, 1934).

in this chapter that this dichotomous treatment of rural-urban differ-ences has two problematical aspects. First, it emphasizes greater con-trasts than really exist, and secondly, any applicational value it may have had seems to be rapidly disappearing through the operation of such trends as urbanization, mobility, and secularization.

Contrasts in Rural and Urban Cultures. In the course of the develop-ment of sociology, there have been many attempts to classify cultures or sub-cultures into types or categories. One area with a profusion of such attempts has been that of rural-urban differences, usually de-veloped on a continuum with rural and urban defined as ideal types using certain criteria and representing the two extremes on the various continuua. Many of these earlier classificatory attempts have become familiar, such as Tonnies' Gemeinschaft and Gesellschaft,[13] Becker's sacred-secular,[14] Durkheim's mechanical and organic,[15] Cooley's pri-mary group with the implied secondariness,[16] the folk-urban con-tinuum constructed by Redfield,[17] each of these having been used to differentiate some aspects of rural and urban societies. A more recent breakdown which helps to clarify some of the contrasting culture traits and patterns is that of Loomis and Beegle[18] which combines some aspects of the earlier conceptualizations into the familistic Gemeinschaft, representing the rural, and the contractual Gesellschaft, representing the urban. These authors utilize a number of specific communities in applying to their continuum such criteria as rationality of behavior, the diffuseness of activities, community responsibility, and role integra-tion, both within and outside the system, in order to more effectively contrast rural and urban cultures. Both this scheme and the others are useful in illustrating that there are definite rural-urban differences in behavior patterns, roles, and the accompanying expectations, and gen-erally in the whole sphere of cultural activities.

On the basis of these differences, the education and training of chil-dren will differ in the degree to which the communities fall toward one

---

[13] Ferdinand Tonnies, *Gemeinschaft Und Gesellschaft* (Leipzig, 1887).

[14] Howard Becker and R. C. Myers, "Sacred and Secular Aspects of Human Sociation," *Sociometry,* Vol. V, No. 3 (August, 1942), pp. 207 ff. See also Howard Becker, "The Process of Secularization," *Sociological Review* (Eng-lish), Vol. 24, pp. 138-154, 226-286 (1932).

[15] Emile Durkheim, *The Division of Labor in Society,* translated by George Simpson (Glencoe: The Free Press, 1947), Book I.

[16] C. H. Cooley, *Social Organization* (New York: Charles Scribner's Sons, 1909). The primary group concept has been widely used.

[17] Robert Redfield, "The Folk Society," *American Journal of Sociology,* Vol. LII, No. 4 (January, 1947), pp. 293-308. For an application, see Redfield, *op. cit.,* and for a recent evaluation, see Horace Miner, "The Folk-Urban Continuum," *American Sociological Review,* Vol. 17, No. 5 (October, 1952), pp. 529-537.

[18] Charles P. Loomis and J. Allan Beegle, *Rural Social Systems* (New York: Prentice-Hall, Inc., 1950). A very interesting discussion of social systems and the use of continua in analyzing concepts. The emphasis on value orienta-tion is especially useful here.

or the other end of the continuum. Many studies[19] have suggested that rural people are more provincial, isolationist, traditional, conservative, religious or sacred, immobile, and primary in their broad outlook on the community, the world, and life itself, when compared with urban populations. In an intensive analysis of the Miami Valley area of Ohio, Mangus[20] found that the rural children in this area are more self-reliant, have a greater sense of personal worth, of belonging, show fewer neurotic symptoms, and greater social skills than a corresponding group of urban children. If we can accept these findings as having general applicability, then two alternative hypotheses are suggested; either the rural and urban areas are unique with reference to their socializing techniques, or the techniques are the same but the results are different due to a different cultural setting within which these techniques are being applied. It is probable that the correct answer lies somewhere between these two alternatives because these differences have been developed through the use of ideal types and few societies really approximate them very closely. We now turn to an examination of socialization in rural and urban environments, with the major question being the degree of difference between them, and the significance of any differences that might be found.

Primary Forces in Socialization in the Rural Setting. The family is usually defined as the most primary contact a child may have, and probably the most influential force in the socialization of the child. The rural family has been found to be larger in size, has a higher birth rate, and tends to be more of an extended family or kinship group than the urban family.* It is, therefore, less likely that the rural child will be reared as an only child, so his peer groups and the older and younger siblings will play an important part in the training and disciplining program. It also means that the individual child may get proportionately less attention from his parents and other adults. On the other hand, there exists a larger number of adults, other than his parents, with whom there exists a primary relationship, and he is likely to be supervised and guided in any situation in which he finds himself. Bossard[21] and Bales[22] have developed indices showing that interaction becomes more

---

[19] See Howard M. Bell, *Youth Tell Their Story* (Washington, D. C.: American Council on Education, 1938); Noel P. Gist and L. A. Halbert, *Urban Society* (New York: Thomas Y. Crowell Company, 1948), esp. Ch. 15; J. H. Kolb and E. deS. Brunner, *A Study of Rural Society* (Boston: Houghton Mifflin, 1940), Ch. 11.

[20] A. R. Mangus, "Personality Adjustment of Rural and Urban Children," *American Sociological Review*, Vol. 13 (1948), pp. 566-575.

* See Chapter 8 on "The Urban Family System."

[21] James H. S. Bossard, "The Law of Family Interaction," *American Journal of Sociology*, Vol. 50 (January, 1945), p. 293.

[22] Robert F. Bales, "A Set of Categories for the Analysis of Small Group Interactions," *American Sociological Review*, Vol. 15 (April, 1950), pp. 257-263. Also O. J. Harvey, "Status Relations in Informal Groups," *American Sociological Review*, Vol. 18 (August, 1953), pp. 357-367.

complex when more people are involved, but further research is needed to indicate the effect of complexity on socialization.

A prime consideration in the rural-farm family is the common interest of all the members in the farm as a family occupation and means of livelihood. Each member of the family has a definite role in the daily functioning of the farm, and as the children grow up these tasks gradually change without interfering in the unity of the group. All the associates of the farm child will have similar tasks with the corresponding free time and recreational activities, thus facilitating the integration of play group and peer group behavior patterns. It is also likely that the same children participate in the school and church programs together and a high degree of intimacy develops and functions as an internalized social control through mutual understanding and empathy. The Gestalt psychologists have helped to indicate the importance of role relationships, and the rural child is in a position where his roles are unlikely to be incompatible with each other. He also is reinforced in his playing of these roles and his transition from one to another through his ability to imitate his peers and elders and identify with them. The homogeneity of the rural families in their interests and activities provides a support and also a widespread supervision of personality development through indirect kinship ties covering much of the surrounding area as well as the immediate environment.

The rural environment, which seems to be a more traditional, custombound influence, provides not only more definite patterns for the child to acquire, and constant supervision, but emphasizes these patterns consistently from infancy so that they are likely to be well learned, with little need for formal enforcement in order to be effective. Due to the homogeneity of agricultural areas as a whole, there is little opportunity for setting up comparisons or developing alternative behaviors without leaving the rural setting. It should be pointed out that as the isolation and lack of outside contacts break down through diffusion of urban characteristics, the rural areas lose this homogeneity in time and acquire the more varying urban values, thus rendering less effective these informal and unconscious types of social controls. During this transitional period the family gradually loses its effectiveness as it becomes more difficult to impose its value system and role concepts on the child. Accompanying this reduction of family influence has been a decrease in the amount of time spent in the home, and a corresponding increase in the influence of the school and church as socializing agencies in the development of rural youth.

Secondary Forces in Socialization. The schools in rural areas have frequently been deficient in space, equipment, and in both quality and quantity of instruction. Curricula, likewise, have been limited. These limitations have not been too important from the standpoint of socialization because of the tremendous importance of the family, but with the acquisition of urban characteristics the schools will tend to increase in importance. The Amish and other strongly farm-oriented groups have recognized this fact by minimizing the school in their socialization programs. The primary function of the school has been to provide the child with the mechanical functions as exemplified by the three "R's," as generalized cultural equipment. Personality development and social adaptation, however, were not usually emphasized in the educational sphere. Whether this is a cause or effect of the inadequacies of the rural schools is not important here, as we are concerned with the broader aspects of social growth. Whether he attends a one-room school, or the more recent type of consolidated one, the rural child ordinarily spends as little time as possible at the school due to the demands of his farm home. The distance between home and school which frequently involves considerable time in transit further reduces the role of the school in providing extra-curricular activities as sources of social interaction. Probably the most significant function of the school in socialization is as a community center for the family. It is here that the members of the community gather for graduation ceremonies, community meetings, and social gatherings. The emphasis is not on the school as such, but on the social aspects of the gatherings of entire families, with the school buildings as the physical setting.

The rural church is in a similar position to the rural school with regard to its socializing aspects, church membership and participation being primarily on a family basis. The church provides the setting and a certain amount of religious information but the family as a unit, even in ritualistic observances, is always in the background as the functional group. In addition, a religious theme is often present in the home, with the whole family participating in such activities as Bible and prayer reading sessions, overt acknowledgements of supernatural forces influencing their successes or failures in agriculture, and admonitions of proper behavior to the youth. Landis[23] discusses the predominance of the sacred influences in the rural environment, as contrasted with secularism in the cities. It is suggested that the person engaged in farming is more aware of the past and the future, while the city person thinks more about the present and changes in his man-made world.

Empirical evidence is largely lacking to support the above thesis although many authors agree with Landis in their writings on the same topic. If it is assumed that religion exerts a considerable, although indirect, influence upon the rural child,[24] then the church as a socializing agency ranks second only to the family. Rural areas have been largely Protestant, and contain many small sects as well as segments of larger

---

[23] Paul H. Landis, *Social Policies in the Making* (New York: D. C. Heath and Company, 1952), Part I.

[24] Dwight Sanderson, *Rural Sociology and Rural Social Organization* (New York: John Wiley & Sons, 1942). See Chapter 15 for a discussion of several of the points suggested in this paragraph.

denominations, so that any generalizations as to religious influence need qualifications in specific community and open-country studies. Religious census data for 1936 show that a larger proportion of rural people belong to churches, but a larger proportion of urban people attend church when rural and urban attendance figures are compared. It was also found that open-country churches are closing or decreasing in membership, with their members transferring to churches in the small towns and villages. The higher rural membership may be explained by the less voluntary nature of joining the church due to family influence in the country. Sanderson[25] points out that most people grow up in the church of their parents, and are likely to adopt the attitudes and beliefs of the adults in their primary group contacts. The proportionally smaller attendance figures are more difficult to explain but might be due to a minimal operation of the prestige factor that often is attached to church attendance in the city. The smaller number of church activities, and the greater distance from home to church could also be operative in rural areas to hold down attendance.

Summing up, the family is *the* primary force in the socialization of the rural child. Its influence extends into the other institutions such as the church and the school, and creates a highly homogeneous, primary group environment in which socialization takes place. In one small community known to the author, twenty-eight of thirty pupils in the graduating class, the class advisor, and the principal all had the same surname and were related to one another. The rural government and the institutions of health and economics also tend to function primarily through the family and kinship ties.

Primary Forces in Socialization in Urban Areas. Socialization in the city takes place under quite different circumstances than in the rural areas, and much of this is reflected in the differences in rural and urban families. The smaller urban family is enabled to devote more time to each individual child, but it is an open question as to whether this is actually the case. The secondary agencies will be shown to play a much larger part in the socialization processes concerned with training the urban child, and consequently the boy or girl in the city is away from home a great deal of the time. The opportunities available and demands made upon the urban youth are likely to be much more specialized, and distributed over a much wider range, and the parents are less well equipped to provide the necessary orientations. The urban child, for example, is likely to come into contact each week with a heterogeneous group of schoolmates, and meet children at church who come from many different areas of the city. In addition, he may visit the movies, take music or dancing lessons, see and hear a variety of conversations of his parents with neighbors and strangers, and some children might visit a museum, a library, a baseball game, or go for

[25] *Ibid.,* p. 309.

an automobile ride with the family covering a considerable amount of territory. Even lower class children see more variety in their daily routine than would be possible on the farm. Within the school itself, demands of many types are likely to be a regular occurrence, e.g., plays, parties, clubs, and athletics, and school work of a more or less "progressive" type, involving trips outside the school. The introduction to and orientation in these activities is performed for the child by a number of persons, with the parental contacts constituting a relatively small part of the whole.

The numerous associations of the child outside the home are indicative of some of the changes in functions of the family as a society becomes urbanized. The urban family is relatively less important as a unit in educational, recreational, economic, and protective functions in modern society.[26] The functional emphasis of the family has shifted toward affectional roles, providing a source of security for the child in the midst of the rapidity of movement and constantly shifting focii of interests in the city. In addition, the family provides a base of operations from which the child emerges to participate in a dynamic society, and to which he may return for a moment of stability before moving in a quite divergent direction for his next activity. While the adults in an urban family are unlikely to be qualified to offer specific guidance for the child, they do provide a set of values with which the child interprets these activities outside the home. The advantages from the standpoint of socialization are the integration of the values obtained from many varied sources which may provide a source of objectivity, or cognizance of differences existing in the overall urban society. Nevertheless, if parents are unable to recognize or interpret these cultural differences emanating from the varied value systems, due to heterogeneity in occupations, neighborhoods, age and sex groupings, and the many racial, religious, and nationality backgrounds, then the socialization of the child falls even more heavily on the secondary contacts. This seems to be a frequent occurrence if our present criteria of family disorganization are adequate, as they consistently show higher rates for the urban family. Regardless of the aspects of the family that are being disrupted, it seems probable that the socializing processes would be interfered with.

Secondary Forces in Socialization. In contrast with the school and the church in the rural community, the population of the urban schools and churches is not likely to include the same children in both institutions. The child must thus make adjustments to a greater number and

---

[26] Although the changes in functions of the family have been a source of much argument among students of the family, much of the disagreement has been centered around the amount of change rather than the direction. For analyses of this point, see Ernest W. Burgess and Harvey J. Locke, *The Family* (New York: American Book Company, 1945), pp. 501-517; also Harold T. Christensen, *Marriage Analysis* (New York: Ronald Press, 1950), pp. 34-40; Francis E. Merrill, *Social Problems* (New York: Alfred A. Knopf, 1950), pp. 290-296; Chapter 9 of this volume.

variety of children in the urban setting. In the degree that the family has developed in the child a flexibility for meeting change and confidence in himself and his family, his adjustment will likely be quite satisfactory for his adult roles. If, however, the family is unaware of the many sociological and psychological principles underlying the structure and growth of urban areas,[27] then the task of orienting the child in his complex, heterogeneous social milieus rests upon the institutions within which he must function.

A slightly different approach to urban difficulties in socialization of the child is indicated by Tomars;[28] namely, that the transitional problems inherent in a society moving in a more or less unplanned manner from a rural to an urban orientation create socializing problems, among others, as a "normal" part of social change. The emphasis in these writings is that the values and behavior patterns of rural America are inadequate as bases for present day urban areas, and will likely become so if present urbanization trends continue. Here we still have a problem of role development. The difficulty lies in the lack of clear definitions of statuses and roles as a result of change, rather than the failure of socializing agencies to provide proper training for established roles. It has been pointed out that a rural society is more likely to be integrated than an urban one, even though it is undergoing changes in the direction of urban characteristics. These changes are taking place more slowly, giving the adults greater opportunity to adjust their behavior to the new conditions, and to develop techniques for rearing their children in the fluctuating scene with less instability in role-playing. Combining the difficulties suggested above, the conclusion seems to be that the rural societies are better equipped for the training of the rural child for the rural environment than urban societies are for the urban child in his environment, but that both are generally inadequate for the child who will live in the city, regardless of birth place.

Contrasts in Role Development. By role we mean a pattern of required, expected, and tabooed behaviors associated with specific group or social statuses, determined by the relation of the person to other members of the group. In terms of the previously delineated contrasts between the rural and urban societies, the statuses and associated roles to be achieved by the young people in the society will be differentiated

---

[27] This unawareness on the part of the great majority of citizens would seem to be a valid assumption when we consider the fact that the average schooling completed by the adult population is slightly above the ninth grade, plus the probability that most who completed high school or college did not have a lot of social and behavior science.

[28] See Adolph S. Tomars, "Rural Survivals in American Life," *Rural Sociology,* (December, 1943), pp. 378-386; reprinted in Logan Wilson and William L. Kolb, *Sociological Analysis* (New York: Harcourt, Brace and Company, 1949), pp. 371-378. Another article illustrating the problems of a rural background in the urban community is Arnold W. Green, "The Middle-Class Male Child and Neurosis," *American Sociological Review,* Vol. 11 (February, 1946), pp. 31-41.

in part by the environment in which the children are being reared. Though a role consists of both overt and covert behavior, the ideology of the society underlies the manifestations of roles. This means that the broad values held by the adult members will help determine the attitudes and actions which they exhibit to the child and which they attempt to inculcate in him. It is essential for survival purposes that these values be integrated into an ideological pattern with some degree of consistency. It is this factor that tends to make it difficult for the rural or urban child to make any rapid transition to the other culture, and gives us a basis for elaborating upon rural and urban contrasts in behavior, attitudes, and personalities.

A significant part of socialization consists in creating in the child a knowledge of the statuses he now occupies and those he will occupy in his society with the passing of time. This is accomplished through the primary and secondary agencies discussed above, and will be effective in the degree that these agencies are coordinated and complementary in their definitions of these statuses and the accompanying roles. A common example of a failure of coordination in defining statuses and accompanying behavior is when the family defines a son as a servant to his parents' wishes, while his teachers emphasize that he is a young man and should think for himself. Whichever one prevails, the other will likely display dissatisfaction with the young man; if he tries to please both, achieving any degree of psychological stability in his own mind is almost impossible. Frustration, and possibly rebellion, are the likely result.

It is in the rural society that this consistency is most likely to occur due to the common interests centering around agriculture and prevailing among the entire adult population, and to a lesser degree among the peers. The same personnel is likely to be operating in all areas of activity, or at least to have considerable contact with each other. In other words, the parents, or relatives, or neighbors, the members of the primary group associates for the child, are likely to be his associates and leaders in the school, church, recreation, and other secondary situations. This fact enables the adults in the rural environment to continually reinforce their values in the mind of the child but it minimizes the chances for comparisons or the awareness of alternate patterns. It is also true that the totality of role possibilities is lessened as the cultural homogeneity increases, and the rural society is characterized by much greater homogeneity than the urban. In essence, this means the rural child is reared in an environment with well defined goals based on highly integrated values, and it is only in recent years that he has been exposed to cultural differences which might distract him in his social indoctrinations toward those goals.[29]

---

[29] Recent innovations which tend to reduce rural isolation would also include such factors as television, drive-in movies, and especially the rural electrification program.

The urban society requires a somewhat different configuration in its personality types, consequently the statuses and role behaviors are distinct from those desired in the villages and on the farms. The variety and range of personality types is also greater in the city as the population is' more diversified and the needs are also much more varied. While the urban community has more alternatives in the socialization of its youth, there is more difficulty in devising the techniques by which these youth can be successfully oriented to its system. As Linton[30] suggests, statuses whose roles are fundamentally incompatible with each other may become fairly frequent under modern urban conditions. Thus the difficulties in making choices, in feeling secure in those choices, and in assurances in the reciprocal behavior of others is likely to lead to frustrations and personality disorganization. Most college students have experienced the difficulties in remaining true to parental teachings, and yet conforming to the suggestions and desires of classmates or fraternity brothers. As suggested, our present data indicate that this situation probably prevails in a comparatively higher degree in the cities than in rural areas.

One of the most effective ways of defining and maintaining roles over the years is through the various techniques of social control such as the pressure of mores, tradition, gossip, public opinion, and law. If the adult population consistently adheres to the role patterns which are being taught to the child, it provides that child with a model for imitation and someone with whom he can identify himself. Sanderson[31] believes that the rural community is likely to have a relatively strong social control structure due to such factors as a common interest in agriculture, a strong primary group organization including the extended kinship system, permanency of residence, and the supervision of members through an inability to escape recognition throughout a wide area. This last factor, the lack of anonymity over a large sphere, may defeat the parental conception of the socializing process because of the youth's desire for independence and recognition as an individual rather than just a member of an extended family. Television and greater mobility would stimulate the adolescents along these lines, possibly leading to rebellion and perhaps migration from the community of orientation. All in all, the rural society has the means for enforcing its patterns upon the youthful members through an intensive emphasis upon the prevalent values, and maintaining them through a continued supervision. The urban situation tends to be just the opposite, inasmuch as anonymity, mobility, a lack of primariness, and the small conjugal family are characteristic patterns.

---

[30] Ralph Linton, *The Cultural Background of Personality* (New York: D. Appleton-Century Company, 1945), pp. 81-82; however, the entire book is useful for this general area. Also Ralph Linton, *The Study of Man* (New York: D. Appleton-Century Company, 1936), Ch. 8.

[31] Sanderson, *op. cit.*, p. 639.

Summing up, the person who is *aware* of the expected behavioral interactions moves through his social situations with confidence while the one who lacks that awareness or faces questions or problems for which his society has been unable to develop satisfactory procedures, must rely on his own ingenuity and initiative and the concomitant uncertainty in his actions. The urban youth is more likely to be in the latter position because he lives in a more dynamic environment with more problems arising, and because his parents and other adults are less likely to provide satisfactory means for teaching him the qualities needed as they themselves have not faced them nor been prepared for them during their own socialization.

Deviation from Rural-Urban Norms. One useful approach to the effectiveness of socialization as a process for a given society is in terms of the amount of deviation from the socially approved norms of that society. These norms are the behavioral standards which manifest themselves through the mores, laws and customs which the members of that society expect, demand and require of its members inasmuch as they are believed to be not only desirable but necessary to insure survival. If the coming generations are properly inculcated with these norms, then the behavior of these young people should cluster closely about these norms. If, for any reason, the techniques of socialization are inadequate, or are improperly used, we might expect a much wider range of behavior from those undergoing that type of socialization. It is important to keep in mind that each society will develop its own norms and that deviation must be measured within a society on the basis of its own standards. It has been shown above that some differences exist between the generalized rural and urban societies in the United States, so we can draw generalizations from a study of these norms and the deviations thereof.

It has been customary in the past to attempt to apply the same criteria to both rural and urban communities. It has consistently been demonstrated that according to these "standardized" measures of personality disorganization (immorality, vice, crime, and other such indices), the urban community shows much greater frequencies of such deviant behaviors. Recently, however, several authors[32] have tended to question the validity of such findings. It has been pointed out that possibly our previous data have been distorted by the use of "urban" indices and definitions, inasmuch as most researchers have been affiliated with schools and governments in an urban location. The recent Miami Valley study,[33] for example, suggests that rural children may

[32] Edwin M. Lemert, *Social Pathology* (New York: McGraw-Hill, 1951), pp. 293-95, 397; S. Kirson Weinberg, *Society and Personality Disorders* (New York: Prentince-Hall, Inc., 1952), pp. 98-106; Herbert A. Bloch, *Disorganization, Personal and Social* (New York: Alfred A. Knopf, 1952), pp. 167-68, 304-10.

[33] Mangus, *op. cit.*

not be quite as stable mentally and socially as has previously been believed. Draft records from World War II show that a considerable percentage of draftees with rural backgrounds were rejected for mental reasons. Other reasons suggested by these authors for urban rates, compared to rural, are more accurate records in the cities, greater awareness of deviations, and the inability of psychological deviants to make some types of useful adjustment. Thus future findings may reveal that the previously accepted differences are the result of faulty methodology because of weaknesses in measuring techniques and a lack of information about our rural populace.

Our existing criteria of personal disorganization tend to indicate that those factors conducive to deviation are more likely to appear in the urban rather than the rural areas. By the same token, the techniques for socialization of the youth in a rural community are more likely to be effective in preventing deviation if it is true that tensions, frustrations, rapid change, and societal instability are major contributors to poorly-adjusted personalities. These factors seem to be more frequently found in cities and the youth are faced with more problems in the growing up process due to the presence of these elements. As Landis[34] points out, no person is adjusted for life in the city merely because he has mastered the patterns of his particular group. The urban youth has a variety of contacts during his growing up period, and in late adolescence will likely leave his family group to make his way in a secondary world. In this secondary environment, law is the major provision for maintaining the direction the socialization processes have taken, and laws are based on the assumption that their existence is sufficient to provide order.

There seems to be no limit to the theories of deviation. The writers[35] in this field have included physical, mental, social, and cultural explanations in their attempts to define the field more clearly. All of these

---

[34] Paul H. Landis, *Social Control* (New York: J. B. Lippincott Company, 1939), see all of Chapters 11, 20, 21.

[35] The following are a few of the many books and articles devoted to this tremendously complex topic. Abraham A. Brill, *Freud's Contribution to Psychiatry* (New York: W. W. Norton & Company, 1944); Ruth Benedict, *Patterns of Culture* (Boston: Houghton Mifflin, 1934); L. Guy Brown, *Social Pathology* (New York: McGraw-Hill Book Company, Inc., 1942); Abram Kardiner, *The Individual and His Society* (New York: Columbia University Press, 1939); Paul H. Landis, *Social Control* (New York: J. B. Lippincott Company, 1939); Edwin Lemert, *op. cit.;* Alfred R. Lindesmith and Anselm L. Strauss, *Social Psychology* (New York: The Dryden Press, Inc., 1949); S. Karson Weinberg, *op. cit.;* Kimball Young, *Personality and Problems of Adjustment* (F. S. Crofts & Company, 1945). Articles include Ruth Benedict, "Continuities and Discontinuities in Cultural Conditioning," *Psychiatry* (May, 1939), pp. 161-167; Karen Horney, "Culture and Neurosis," *American Sociological Review*, Vol. 1, No. 2 (April, 1936), pp. 221-230; Mirra Komarovsky, "Cultural Contradictions and Sex Roles," *American Journal of Sociology*, Vol. 51 (November, 1946), pp. 184-189; Robert K. Merton, "Social Structure and Anomie," *American Sociological Review*, Vol. 3 (October, 1938), pp. 672-682.

theories seem to have some utility and yet they all have their limitations. In a discussion of socialization, these limitations prevent the reaching of conclusions as to how important efficient socializing techniques are in the prevention of deviation in either rural or urban communities. In general, however, many of the pathological conditions seem to thrive where social controls are weakest, and social organization is relatively poor. On the basis of present knowledge, this seems most likely to exist in urban areas, or in rural areas which are in the process of acquiring urban characteristics. Some of the explanation then may be found in the rural origins of the United States and its rapid transition toward urbanity, without sufficient time to alter the systems of control and methods of socialization to prepare our youth for the changes that have resulted. These problems of deviation should be kept in mind while reading the next section devoted to some of the recent trends in rural and urban socialization patterns.

Trends in rural-urban socialization patterns. Throughout the foregoing discussion, there has been an assumption of definite differences between rural and urban culture, personalities, and socialization patterns. This assumption has plenty of support from other writers in the field, using either a dichotomous distinction, or graduated differences as demonstrated on a continuum. Although there seems little doubt that in the past rural and urban communities could be clearly differentiated, many recent articles intimate that these differences are diminishing, and in some cases have disminished almost to the point of non-existence. For example, a recent article,[36] discussing the South which is usually considered the most rural region in the United States, suggests that it is almost impossible to distinguish significant differences between the rural and urban families there. Other writers have concentrated on the rural-urban fringe,[37] the activities of non-agricultural rural families,[38] the relocation of urban-employed families in rural areas,[39] the lack of a true "rural behavior,"[40] and the accuracy of the rural-urban distinction.[41] While we cannot settle the question here, some trends can be pointed out and their importance for socialization indicated.

---

[36] D. Dickins, "The Southern Farm Family," *Rural Sociology*, Vol. 15, pp. 232-238.

[37] Walter T. Martin, "A Consideration of Differences in the Extent and Location of the Formal Associational Activities of Rural-Urban Fringe Residents." *American Sociological Review*, Vol. 17, pp. 685-694; "Some Socio-Psychological Aspects of Adjustment to Residence Location in the Rural-Urban Fringe." *American Sociological Review*, Vol. 18, pp. 248-253.

[38] Rudolf Heberle, "A Sociological Interpretation of Social Change in the South," *Social Forces*, Vol. 25 (October, 1946), pp. 9-15.

[39] Noel P. Gist, "Ecological Decentralization and Rural-Urban Relationships," *Rural Sociology*, Vol. 17, pp. 328-335.

[40] Howard W. Beers, "Rural-Urban Differences: Some Evidence From Public Opinion Polls," *Rural Sociology*, Vol. 18, pp. 1-11.

[41] I. A. Spaulding, "Serendipity and the Rural-Urban Continuum," *Rural Sociology*, Vol. 16, pp. 29-36; John L. Haer, "Conservatism-Radicalism and the Rural-Urban Continuum," *Rural Sociology*, Vol. 17, pp. 343-347.

There seems to be a reasonable consensus that many urban characteristics are now prevalent in traditionally rural areas. Such phenomena as specialization, mechanization, electrification, increased recreational and educational facilities, paved roads, radios and television sets, and many others are coming to be the rule rather than the exception in many farming areas. What impact will this have upon the farm youth? Will these factors result in increasing rural-urban similarities in personality traits, role-taking and role-playing[42] and deviant behaviors? Will the differences in social controls, degrees of conservatism,[43] primariness, secularization, and disorganization disappear, and be replaced by a society quite homogeneous insofar as its social characteristics are concerned? These questions seem pertinent to the whole future of the United States, and to the students of that society; the discussion to follow raises some possibilities as to the answers.

A number of years ago, William F. Ogburn, in a discussion of social change, developed the concept of "culture lag."[44] He stated that material culture tends to change first with a lag or delay in non-material aspects of culture leading to a more or less continuous maladjustment in the society so affected. It seems that this is the case in rural communities today with a considerable resistance to many of the values and attitudes that have accompanied similar material changes in the cities. It seems doubtful if television, automatic washers, and the many other inventions now in rural homes have the same meaning to the rural people that they do to the city dweller. Consequently, rural youth is likely to show increasing symptoms of maladjustment in coming years as they are exposed to the wide variety of urban devices without being taught the concomitant behaviors for their most functional utilization.[45]

Two trends that seem especially important for socialization are the increasing number of rural youth seeking further education, and the consolidation of rural schools into larger units containing a broader curriculum and many extracurricular activities.[46] The latter factor has brought several characteristics of urban areas to the rural educational scene. These include an increased amount of time spent in school (both in hours per day and in total years spent in schooling), an increase in activities as sports, clubs, and plays. There may also develop more

---

[42] For a discussion of these concepts in detail, see Walter Coutu, "Role-Playing Vs. Role-Taking: An Appeal For Clarification," *American Sociological Review,* Vol. 16, No. 2 (April, 1951), pp. 180-87.

[43] Beers, *op. cit.*

[44] William F. Ogburn, *Social Change* (New York: Viking Press, 1922).

[45] Kingsley Davis, "The Sociology of Parent-Youth Conflict'" *American Sociological Review,* Vol. 5, No. 4 (August, 1940), pp. 523-535; reprinted in J. E. Nordskog, E. C. McDonagh, and M. J. Vincent, *Analyzing Social Problems* (New York: The Dryden Press, 1950), pp. 288-296.

[46] See Douglas Ensminger, "The Rural School and Education," in Carl C. Taylor, et al., *Rural Life in the United States* (New York: Alfred A. Knopf, 1949), pp. 92-115; also Stuart A. Queen and David B. Carpenter, *The American City* (New York: McGraw-Hill, 1953), Ch. 17.

emphasis on grades and honors, as well as a greater detachment between school and home. The rural youth is undoubtedly becoming more sophisticated, more conscious of social distinctions,[47] and less well-adjusted to his rural home. As Nye[48] points out, the adolescent-parent adjustment is poorer in rural families than in city families according to his scale, and his explanation is partly the same one we have been discussing—secondariness and urbanization. These same factors contribute to the increased desire and attainment of an academic career beyond grade and high school. Even if the youth return to the farm, they desire a higher plane of living, are more conscious of the "human" factor in social relationships, and are more machine-minded and perhaps specialized in their agricultural endeavors. Thus the rural youth is acquiring many of the social attributes previously associated with urban societies. It should be remembered, however, that the noise, smoke and dirt, crowding, and rapid pace of urban life are not present and unlikely to appear in the rural community due to the nature of the farming occupation which prevails there. A number of years ago, Stuart Chase, in his book *Men and Machines*,[49] described behavior in the urbanized culture of American cities. Most readers would agree that similar scenes are unlikely to be duplicated in rural communities. The rural parents are less likely to emphasize health factors, to keep warning of dangers of the street, request silence for the benefit of the neighbors, or be so concerned about protecting their property from youthful hands. While none of these behaviors are significant in themselves, together they symbolize a value system which is unlikely to exist as a part of the socializing processes of the rural sections of the United States.

One area still under investigation which may have tremendous importance for socialization trends in rural-urban populations is the migratory pattern in the United States. The particular factor of interest is the relationship between migration and intelligence.[50] It has been assumed that migration from the farms drains off the most capable persons, leaving an inferior quality to man the farms. If true, the effects

---

[47] See Harold W. Pfautz, "The Current Literature on Social Stratification," *American Journal of Sociology*, Vol. LVIII (January, 1953), pp. 391-418, for articles on stratification including rural studies. Also Arthur F. Raper, "Rural Social Differentials," in Carl C. Taylor, *op. cit.*, Ch. 18.

[48] Ivan Nye, "Adolescent-Parent-Adjustment—Rurality As A Variable," *Rural Sociology*, Vol. 15, pp. 334-339.

[49] Stuart Chase, *Men and Machines* (New York: Macmillan Company, 1929). See also W. Lloyd Warner and Paul S. Lunt, *The Social Life of a Modern Community* (New Haven: Yale University Press, 1941).

[50] See Noel P. Gist and Carroll D. Clarks, "Intelligence As A Selective Factor in Rural-Urban Migrations," *American Journal of Sociology*, Vol. XLIV (July, 1938), pp. 36-58; W. Parker Mauldin, "Selective Migration from Small Towns," *American Sociological Review*, Vol. 5, No. 5, pp. 748-758. A classic book touching on this problem is Otto Klineberg, *Negro Intelligence and Selective Migration* (New York: Columbia University Press, 1935); and a follow-up study, Everett S. Lee, "Negro Intelligence and Selective Migration," *American Sociological Review*, Vol. 16, No. 2, pp. 227-233.

would be multiple; a reduction of rural population, less capable parents among the remaining rural persons, and perhaps a deterioration in the quality of all rural institutions, and even the national economy. Recent studies[51] have tended to refute the above assumption by using improved measuring tools which allow for cultural differences and show insignificant differences between rural and urban populations. Inasmuch as the family has been shown to be of major importance in socialization, the quality of parents and schools is going to be directly affected by any mass shifts in intellectual quality which might affect present day families and their ability to train their offspring.

Finally, and significantly, an aspect of urbanization unlikely to have a major impact in rural socialization trends is the improbability of rural people ever being able to achieve the anonymity possible in heavily populated areas. Consequently, the strength of the informal, internalized controls so effective in the country is likely to remain. Primariness is still present in the group interactions, and the adolescents seeking emancipation from the home are still under relatively greater supervision than are their city cousins. In many escapades, the family remains the primary disciplining agency. All in all, it would still seem to be true that the rural youth is reared in a different social and psychological atmosphere from that of the urban youth despite increasing similarities in the material surroundings. These differences do not seem likely to disappear as a result of any of the trends taking place in American society today.

The major technique by which all types of societies insure their survival is known as socialization. This includes all those processes directed toward the preparation of youth for a place in the sun of the adult society in which they are being reared. It includes not only the educational system but aspects of other institutions such as the family, government, the economic system, and the church. No two societies tend to train their young people in precisely the same way, because no two societies have the same material cultures, behavior patterns, and value systems. Due to the reciprocal nature of culture and personality, this means that each society is likely to have unique personality types.

Rural and urban are usually defined as distinct cultural types. As such, they have different programs of socialization because they have different goals to strive for and toward which to prepare their children.

---

[51] The influence of culture upon personality and intelligence has been the subject of much discussion and debate in recent years. In a recent study, William H. Sewell and Bertram L. Ellenbogen, "Social Status and the Measured Intelligence of Small City and Rural Children," *American Sociological Review*, Vol. 17, No. 5, pp. 612-616, found no significant differences between urban, rural non-farm, and farm children with respect to intelligence, when their parents are equated for occupational and intellectual levels. Articles by Rupert B. Vance, Ronald Freedman, Natalie Rogoff, and Ronald Freedman and Amos Hawley, in Paul K. Hatt and Albert J. Reiss, Jr., *Reader in Urban Sociology* (Glencoe: The Free Press, 1951), also discuss migration problems.

It is generally accepted as true that rural and urban people do differ in personality traits, social values, and philosophies of life, but that these differences are decreasing.

The family is the primary socializing agency in the rural environment. Such secondary forces as the school and the church are much less influential than the family unit in influencing the social growth patterns of the youth, not only infants and children but throughout the period of adolescence. The immediate family is reinforced by the extended family system and the neighborhood, all of which comprise a primary organization under whose supervision the children, and also the community services for socialization, must continually function. The rural church is frequently strong but from the standpoint of socialization tends to reinforce the values of the primary group because of the overlapping of membership.

The school and the church play a much larger role in the city youth's growing up, as the urban culture is so heterogeneous that the family is unlikely to be qualified to help prepare the young people for more than a small part of their daily experiences. The primary function of the urban family is to provide a broad value framework with which the youth can interpret their experiences and into which the totality of experiences can be integrated. If this familial value system is obsolete, unreal, or idealistic, then the city boy or girl must rely upon himself, his peers, and the adults in the secondary situations for integrating those experiences. Some writers believe that the problems of the city are so complex and varied that any urban socialization program cannot guide but must train young persons to think for themselves and to meet the problems of the day as individuals rather than as members of a highly integrated social order.

A major task in socialization is to create a knowledge of the statuses, or positions in society, the child will likely assume, and an understanding of the roles that accompany each status. A rural society is likely to maintain a more consistent relationship between its statuses and roles. The urban community may develop varying degrees of incompatability in status and role relationships due to the rapidity of change and the general randomness of its growth. The informal controls used in the rural areas to prepare children for their adult roles are more likely to be effective because they are internalized, whereas in the city, law, as the major control, is highly impersonal both in theory and enforcement.

Deviation is often the result of poor socialization techniques. Due to the cultural differences between rural and urban communities, it is difficult to compare their respective rates of deviancy but recent studies suggest that the rate differentials may not be very great. Uncorrected rates using our present criteria indicate that urban areas contain considerably more personal disorganization than rural areas, and urban areas contain more social disorganization as well. Major contributors to this difference are the dynamic nature of the city, and the relatively stable and homogeneous rural culture.

The foremost trend in rural-urban socialization patterns seems to be the gradual acquisition of urban characteristics by many farm families and communities, with the concomitant problems of adjustment for the youth as their society becomes less stable and the traditional guides become less useful. The educational system, especially, seems likely to play an increasing role in the preparation of tomorrow's farm youth. As rural areas become more urbanized, the rural family acquires those traits previously associated only with the urban family, namely, greater mobility, increased secondariness, and emphasis on education and climbing the class ladder. Certain traits of the city seem unlikely to ever invade the rural realm, however, due to the nature of agriculture, so the two areas are unlikely to ever become completely homogeneous. While the material aspects of the city are extending into the rural sections of the country, the values surrounding them remain quite distinct between the two.

Summary. The whole area of socialization is one of the most pertinent for the understanding of human behavior, and yet it is perhaps one of the least understood. Here sociology, psychology, and anthropology come together, and as these disciplines advance, singly and collectively on a framework basis, so will our knowledge of the processes of human interaction. Much of culture is devoted to the effective functioning of the social order, but as long as socialization is ineffective to some degree, then the functioning of society will be impaired in the same degree. Thus many of the problems of the United States at the present time have their origin in a rural socialization being utilized in an urban society.

WORKSHOP AND PROBLEMS

1. What is meant by socialization?

2. What is the role of culture in socialization?

3. What are the chief differences between rural and urban cultures?

4. What are the major primary forces in socialization in a rural setting? The major secondary forces?

5. What are the major primary forces in socialization in urban areas? The major secondary forces?

6. What are the outstanding contrasts in role development in rural and urban areas?

7. Contrast deviation from rural-urban farms as between the two cultures.

8. What are some important trends in rural-urban socialization patterns? What trends do you predict for the future?

BIBLIOGRAPHY

Angell, Robert C., *The Integration of American Society* (New York: McGraw-Hill Book Company, Inc., 1941).

Arensberg, Conrad M., and Kimball, Solon T., *Family and Community In Ireland* (Cambridge: Harvard University Press, 1940).

Beers, Howard W., "Rural-Urban Differences: Some Evidence From Public Opinion Polls," *Rural Sociology*, Vol. 18 (March, 1953), pp. 1-11.

Bell, Howard M., *Youth Tell Their Story* (Washington, D. C.: American Council on Education, 1938).

Benedict, Ruth, *Patterns of Culture* (Boston: Houghton Mifflin, 1934).

Bloch, Herbert A., *Disorganization, Personal and Social* (New York: Alfred A. Knopf, 1952).

Bossard, James H. S., *The Sociology of Child Development* (New York: Harper & Brothers, 1948).

Brill, Abraham A., *Freud's Contribution to Psychiatry* (New York: W. W. Norton and Company, 1944).

Brown, L. Guy, *Social Pathology* (New York: McGraw-Hill Book Company, Inc., 1942).

Burgess, Ernest W., and Locke, Harvey J., *The Family* (New York: American Book Company, 1945).

Chase, Stuart, *Men and Machines* (New York: Macmillan Company, 1929).

Christensen, Harold T., *Marriage Analysis* (New York: Ronald Press, 1950).

Cooley, Charles H., *Social Organization* (New York: Charles Scribner's Sons, 1909).

Cuber, John F., and Harper, Robert A., *Problems of American Society: Values In Conflict* (New York: Henry Holt and Company, 1951).

Durkheim, Emile, *The Division of Labor in Society*, translated by George Simpson (Glencoe: The Free Press, 1947), Book One.

Ericksen, E. Gordon, *Urban Behavior* (New York: The Macmillan Co., 1954. Crowell Company, 1948).

Gist, Noel P., and Halbert, L. A., *Urban Society* (New York: Thomas Y.

Harvey, O. J., "Status Relationships in Informal Groups," *American Sociological Review*, Vol. 18 (August, 1953), pp. 357-367.

Hatt, Paul K., and Reiss, Albert J., Jr., *Reader In Urban Sociology* (Glencoe: The Free Press, 1951).

Herskovits, Melville J., *Dahomey: An Ancient West African Kingdom* (New York: J. J. Augustin, 1938).

Hollingshead, August B., *Elmtown's Youth* (New York: John Wiley and Sons, 1949).

Kardiner, Abram, *The Individual and His Society* (New York: Columbia University Press, 1939).

——————, *The Psychological Frontiers of Society* (New York: Columbia University Press, 1945).

Klineberg, Otto, *Negro Intelligence and Selective Migration* (New York: Columbia University Press, 1935.

Kluckhohn, Clyde, and Leighton, Dorothea, *The Navaho* (Cambridge: Harvard University Press, 1946).

Kolb, J. H., and Brunner, E. deS., *A Study of Rural Society* (Boston: Houghton Mifflin, 1940).

Landis, Paul H., *Social Control* (New York: J. B. Lippincott Company, 1939).

——————, *Social Policies in the Making* (New York: D. C. Heath and Company, 1952), Part I.

Lemert, Edwin M., *Social Pathology* (New York: McGraw-Hill Book Company, Inc., 1951).

Lindesmith, Alfred R., and Strauss, Anselm L., *Social Psychology* (New York: The Dryden Press, Inc., 1949).

Linton, Ralph, *The Cultural Background of Personality* (New York: D. Appleton-Century Company, 1945).

——————, *The Study of Man* (New York: D. Appleton-Century Company, 1936).

Loomis, Charles P., and Beegle, Allan, *Rural Social Systems* (New York: Prentice-Hall, Inc., 1950).

Lynd, Robert S., and Lynd, Helen M., *Middletown* (New York: Harcourt Brace and Company, 1929).

—————————————————, *Middletown in Transition* (New York: Harcourt Brace and Company, 1937).

Mead, Margaret, *From The South Seas* (New York: William Morrow, 1939).

Merrill, Francis E., *Social Problems* (New York: Alfred A. Knopf, 1950).

Nordskog, J. E., McDonagh, E. C., and Vincent, M. J., *Analyzing Social Problems* (New York: The Dryden Press, Inc., 1950).

Ogburn, William F., *Social Change* (New York: Viking Press, 1922).

Queen, Stuart A., and Carpenter, David B., *The American City* (New York: McGraw-Hill Book Company, Inc., 1953).

Redfield, Robert, *The Folk Culture of Yucatan* (Chicago: University of Chicago Press, 1941).

Riemer, Svend, *The Modern City* (New York: Prentice-Hall, Inc., 1952).

Sanderson, Dwight, *Rural Sociology and Rural Social Organization* (New York: John Wiley and Sons, 1942).

Taylor, Carl C., et al., *Rural Life in the United States* (New York: Alfred A. Knopf, 1949).

Thompson, Laura, *Culture in Crisis* (New York: Harper and Brothers, 1950).

Tonnies, Ferdinand, *Gemeinschaft Und Gesellschaft* (Leipzig, 1887).

Warner, W. Lloyd, and Lunt, Paul S., *The Social Life of A Modern Community* (New Haven: Yale University Press, 1941).

Wilson, Logan, and Kolb, W. L., *Sociological Analysis* (New York: Harcourt, Brace and Company, 1949).

Weinberg, S. Kirson, *Society and Personality Disorders* (New York: Prentice-Hall, Inc., 1952).

Young, Kimball, *Personality and Problems of Adjustment* (New York: F. S. Crofts and Company, 1945).

Young, Pauline V., *Pilgrims of Russian-Town* (Chicago: University of Chicago Press, 1932).

CHAPTER 7

The Urban Class System

By RUSSELL R. DYNES

The city is a study in contrasts. It is a kaleidoscope of different social types and areas. There the Bowery bum lives a few actual miles but many social miles from Park Avenue. Nob Hill and Beacon Hill stand higher socially than they do geographically. The Gold Coast has little in common with the slums except that they exist side by side in Chicago. Other areas of most cities provide a glimpse of transplanted Europe. The Black Belts support a density of population that no other area of the city could endure. Rows of identical homes show the effects of mass production not only upon housing but also upon their occupants. Any Main Street will provide a vantage point to see, at least superficially, a great range of urban types. Here the mink coat may brush the tattered sleeve on the crowded sidewalks of the city. The driver of the Cadillac may honk impatiently at the owner of the push cart who is more concerned with his search for junk than he is with his traffic obstruction. All of these contrasts are associated with urban living and urban life.

Most of these contrasts reflect social class differences. The everyday language of the urbanite betrays the class position of both the speaker and the topic of his conversation. "He is one of the Four Hundred." "He comes from a shiftless family and he shows it." "They are in the Country Club set." "They are our kind of people." "You can't expect more than that from those kind of people. The things they do!" These statements refer to class membership and class behavior.

What, then, does social class mean? What are the criteria for class membership? How many classes are there in the urban community? If social class is so important, how does it affect a person's behavior and attitudes? What are the complicating factors which tend to blur the urban class system? How are social class differences manifest in urban life? This chapter will be concerned with these questions.[1]

Criteria of Social Class. The inhabitants of any city can be ranked in many ways. Any difference that is expressed in terms of more or less

---

[1] For an extensive source on social class see Reinhard Bendix and Seymour Martin Lipset, *Class, Status and Power* (Glencoe, Illinois: The Free Press, 1953).

115

can be placed in some kind of hierarchy and the city is full of these potentialities for ranking. For example, since individuals differ in economic and political power, they could be ranked from least to most power. Individuals could be ranked from the least to the most educated, the least to the most wealthy, or the least to the most occupational skill. One such ranking system, which is summary of many of these differences, is that of *prestige* in which individuals are judged by comparison with other members of the community. The individual may gain his prestige by his own efforts or he may receive it by the fortuitous accident of parents. In fact, it is more realistic to speak of the family as the unit of prestige as the male head of the family is usually the focus of prestige and his wife and children derive their prestige from him.

How does an individual get prestige? The most common way is to have possessions and characteristics which are important in the terms of the value systems of their community. The logical reasons for prestige may not be apparent as each value system has its own peculiar logic. Each city may have a distinct and unique value system, but the following factors will have some generality in all urban areas in the United States. These factors are some of the ingredients that make up the final products—prestige.

1. *Family background.* For some urbanites, it is important to trace their ancestry back to the Mayflower, the Revolution, or some other illustrious or momentous point in history. Inheritance involves more than biology as an individual also gets a heritage of family prestige. In judging a person's merit, family membership is often taken as a sufficient criterion because family names and connections provide easy referents in assigning prestige.

2. *Money.* Any monetary or exchange system depends upon a standard of common value and nothing is more comprehensible to most urbanites than dollars and cents. It provides a standard basis for evaluation. For example, something is frequently taken to be beautiful because it is expensive and it is not expensive because it is beautiful. Other illustrations about the importance of money would be as useless as they would be familiar. One should note, however, that distinctions are often made between "good" and "bad" money, inherited wealth and the new rich, and wages and salary. These subtle distinctions may be the reason for the exclusion or inclusion of certain individuals in different degrees of prestige.

3. *Occupation.* One of the key questions asked about everyone is his occupation. An answer will provide an indication of the person's skill, training, income, power, and style of life. Since many of the male's working hours are spent in occupational pursuits, his prestige from this course carries over into other activities. In fact, occupation largely includes many of the other factors which give prestige. It pro-

vides income which is spent on status goods—clothing, cars, and housing, and it requires education and sometimes involves kinship. If any one factor could be known about the person, occupation would be the best single predictor of prestige.

4. *Residence type and area.* Residential areas in the city are farther apart socially than they are geographically. Some of these areas are restricted against the invasion of "social impurities" and to gain admittance the impure have to cleanse themselves with the correct prestige traits. Socially desirable real estate is priced far beyond the intrinsic values of the soil, the frontage or location. The desire to move out of the smoke is more often a desire to move into a socially cleaner atmosphere. In some areas, the function of housing is not to provide shelter for a house is not to live in but to live for. Where and how a person lives is then another important prestige source.

5. *Education.* For prestige purposes, education is useful as long as you don't have too much. Learning is secondary to "serving" time in an educational institution as the mere attendance at the "right" schools can provide an entré into certain social circles without any further question. While too much education might be a deterent in a prestige sense, a minimum "sentence" is a prerequisite for acceptance and participation. Education may, however, be used as a path for mobility, and individuals, through the educational channels, may achieve some of the other ingredients of prestige.

6. *Other factors.* Every city will have its own unique set of prestige sources. Drinking may be a social expectation in one group and a reason for expulsion in another. Church attendance or church avoidance may be important. Certain political attitudes may be imperative to acceptance; and membership in certain groups and interest in certain activities may be compulsive if the individual expects to maintain his standing. Preference for types of literature, art, furniture, and entertainment may be tickets for companionship, and ways of thinking and ways of behaving may be the conditions for association.

All of the preceding factors are generally used as the basis for judgment of the individual's worth. Individuals are evaluated by others and these evaluations are expressed in terms of more or less prestige. *All communities, rural and urban, can be seen as layers of prestige called social classes. These classes are strata of individuals who have approximately equal prestige. The individuals who occupy these strata have somewhat similar attitudes and behavior which differentiate them from individuals in other strata.*

Since small communities have a more consistent and uniform value system as the factors which give prestige tend to be agreed upon, there the class system will be less ambiguous. In rural areas, for example, since a person's life activity is under the scrutiny of the whole community, it is easier to know what he is "really" like and worth. The city, however, presents a more complicated class picture. Within the city, competing value systems exist and there is not complete agreement on the "important" things. Since only segmentalized facets of the "total" person are exposed in urban life, evaluation is most often made by judging a few easily perceived factors. What does a person do? Where does he live? What kind of a car does he drive? These are used as indicators of where a person fits into the total prestige structure of the city. Even in the complexity and the heterogeneity of urban areas, social class still is a useful category to understand behavior.

In summary, an important part of every community and every city is the prestige hierarchy. Individuals are evaluated in terms of the prevailing value systems and are rewarded by differing amounts of prestige by the community. A stratum of similarly prestiged individuals may be said to constitute a social class and membership in one or another stratum is shown by the behavior and attitudes of the class members.

Methods of Determining Social Class. Although there has been an avalanche of research in recent years, with the focus on social class, few researchers have attempted to utilize the large city for field work. This is perhaps a justifiable omission since the techniques utilized in the smaller community are still unperfected. Some researchers have implied that their specific methods used in the small community can be applied everywhere, but it is doubtful that any one technique can be used in every type of community since many of these approaches currently used are based on somewhat different conceptions of social class. In recent class studies, at least the three following approaches to the prestige structure have been used.

First, in many studies, one or more objective indices are used to delineate the class structure. Usually occupation and/or income are used as the major determinants. In some cases other factors are added as the amount of education, type of house, and the area of residence. Individuals who differ in some degree with respect to one or a combination of these factors are said to constitute a social class. For example, in this approach families who earned between three and five thousand dollars a year might be considered a social class. Many different types of research have used this approach, and the research by Kinsey on sexual behavior would be one example.[2] This technique might be called the *objective approach* to social class.

The second approach has been characterized by the research of Warner and Hollingshead.[3] They treat social class as stratum of individ-

[2] Alfred C. Kinsey, W. B. Pomeroy, and C. E. Martin, *Sexual Behavior in the Human Male* (Philadelphia: W. B. Saunders Co., 1948).

[3] W. Lloyd Warner, Marchia Meeker, Kenneth Eells, *Social Class in America* (Chicago: Science Research Associates, Inc., 1949); and A. B. Hollingshead, *Elmtown's Youth* (New York: John Wiley and Sons, Inc., 1949).

uals who interact and participate on the same prestige level. Although economic factors are still considered central, they must be translated into socially approved behavior and possessions. With these status goods and actions, the individual participates and is accepted by others on the same prestige level. The social class configuration of a specific community is determined by observation and interviewing, so individuals are judged by the sources of prestige which are unique to the specific community. Community members are placed in strata by the status accorded to them by the community. This technique might be called the *accorded status approach* to social class.

The third approach has concentrated on the subjective aspects of class—the communalities of attitudes and ideologies of groups within the community. Since individuals within the city have different life experiences, they develop different concepts and attitudes toward life. These interest groups, which are characterized by a sense of "belongingness," feel a part and identity with a particular class. Their attitudes differentiate them from the strata above and below. Research utilizing this conception of social class has been conducted by Centers and Jones.[4] Classes, in this approach, imply a similarity of attitudes and involve a consciousness of their loyalty to the interests of their class. Since this technique depends on factors "inside" the individual rather than "outside" this may be called the *subjective approach* to social class.

These three approaches are not as separate as they might appear. Warner used such objective factors as occupation, source of income, type of residence, and neighborhood area to closely predict the status accorded an individual by other community members. Centers has found a close relationship between occupations, the objective approach, and class affiliation or identification, the subjective approach. It is safe to assume that individuals who have the same accorded status in the community, and who associate with each other, have or will develop a similarity of attitudes and a feeling of belongingness to the class. In other words, although there is no perfect relationship between these three approaches, knowing one will aid in the prediction of a second or a third. Starting at any one conception of class, one can construct with great accuracy, but with some discrepancy, the other two conceptions.

How Many Classes? Asking the question of how many classes are there in a specific city is similar to asking how many pieces in a pie. Since most of the differences among the occupants of any city shade into one another, obviously no distinct breaks will appear. The pie and the community can then be cut in half, thirds, quarters, or any other fraction depending on one's appetite and the methods used in cutting. This

---

[4] Richard Centers, *The Psychology of Social Classes* (Princeton: Princeton University Press, 1949); and Alfred W. Jones, *Life, Liberty and Property* (Philadelphia: J. P. Lippincott Co., 1941).

division will depend on the conception of class utilized and the instruments used to draw the class lines. There is currently some controversy and confusion in stratification research about the number and the nature of class lines. Some of this difficulty would be avoided if the researcher made explicit his conception of the nature of class, and the three approaches to class mentioned previously would make a difference in the focus of attention and the division. Still more clarity could be achieved if it were made explicit how the number of classes were decided and how the lines between classes were drawn. These decisions can be made either by the researcher or simply recorded from the conceptions of the community members. Each source is equally valid.

1. *The researcher's decision.* When the researcher has to make some analysis of the community structure, usually his particular data are capable of more than one type of interpretation. In *Middletown* it made sense in the analysis of the class structure to divide the city into two major classes—business and labor.[5] To others, it seemed more profitable to classify a community into five classes with perhaps a sixth added in older cities where family tradition is considered important. For many problems, the traditional upper, middle, and lower classes will be sufficient. From the viewpoint of the researcher, then, the particular problem under analysis will largely determine the type of the division. The fact that he divides the data in one way does not preclude the same data being divided in other ways. Figure 8 shows some of the ways communities have been divided.

2. *The community's conception.* Community members, of course, make their own division of the class structure. No researcher will ignore their conceptions and, in many cases, he simply tries to record these. The differences in prestige ultimately stem from the evaluation of the individual by other community members. In small communities, there is more consensus on the sources of prestige, and the characteristics of the community members are sufficiently well known to make a somewhat consistent evaluation, but in the city an unambiguous class structure is impossible. Because of these conflicting community conceptions, some individuals have come to the conclusion that no classes exist. Even if community members disagree on or disclaim class differences, this is not sufficient reason to deny their existence. Individuals may have different reasons for their ideas about the class structure. For example, a socially mobile person may be very conscious of the traits of the class into which he is trying to move, and he may be purposively unclear about those below and around him. In addition, community members may be using different criteria in placing an individual or group in the total class system. Some of these complicating factors will be taken up in another section. There does seem to be, however,

---

[5] R. S. Lynd and Helen M. Lynd, *Middletown* (New York: Harcourt, Brace Co., 1937).

some common agreement that certain objective factors as occupation and perhaps housing type and residential area confer prestige. These do provide some common denominator for the evaluation of the urban-

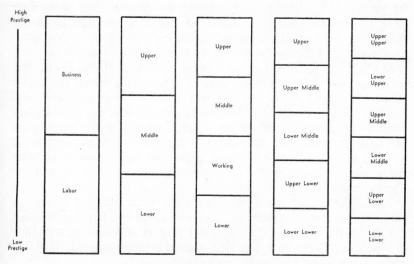

FIGURE 8. Urban Class Pictures.

ite. In any case, community conceptions, regardless of their consistency, can be used to determine the number of the classes and the position of the class lines.

The classes of any city, then, can be divided in a number of ways. Since the differences between community members are not absolute but only a matter of degree, a division can be effected by the researcher or by the community members. Depending on the focus of research, the investigator will utilize any definition or division necessary for the analysis of his problem. While the urbanite will present conflicting divisions of the class structure, these differences should not obscure and do not deny the fact that the class structure, however divided, is still crucial to the understanding of the city.

The Class Structure—An Example. The various factors which act as sources of prestige can be shown in a specific example. The criteria mentioned earlier—family background, income, occupation, residential area, education, and others—will be shown in their relationship to prestige in a small city in the mid-west.[6] In this community, the structure was divided into five classes and the accorded status approach was used to determine the class structure.

---

[6] See A. B. Hollingshead, *op. cit.*, Chap. 5, and also his "Selected Characteristics of Classes in A Middle Western Community," *American Sociological Review*, Vol. 12 (August, 1947), pp. 385-395.

1. *Class I*. Position in this class tends to be passed on by inheritance but a few attain it by their own efforts. There is consequently some subdivision in Class I between the old families and the newly rich. Although wealth is a prime prerequisite for achieving position, once the position is acquired there is no need to reinforce their status with more money. The members emphasize that their position is due to their superior traits which are an expression of their hereditary qualities, and they believe that the lower classes show "bad blood."

Most of the families had an income over $5,000 (in 1941), and some had over five times that much. In addition, the banks, the largest industries, almost all of the business buildings and extensive farm lands are owned by Class I families. Occupationally, the men are engaged in large business or farming enterprises, plus a few independent professionals. Generally little effort is expended at work since many of the families have supervisors or agents for their investments. With the minimum supervision that is necessary, there is much time to dignify leisure.

All of the homes are owned and many were inherited. They are concentrated in one residential area, with some overlap into another, the next best area. Education does not play an important part in their life pattern. Those who attended college seldom finished, but they managed to attend the "right" colleges.

2. *Class II*. Almost one half of the families have achieved their position in this class by their own effort. Their rather humble origins, however, are too well known to permit them to climb to Class I. They try to identify with Class I but realize that the difference between the two classes is greater than their wishful thinking permits them to hope. About four out of five families trace their ancestry directly to pioneer "American" stock.

Annual incomes range from $3,000 to $10,000, with a mode around $4,500. This income is earned largely by the male head, who is a professional, operates a family owned business, or is a salaried executive. Income may be supplemented by a farm or two, some securities, and perhaps rental property.

One half of Class II families live in the best residential area, and 90 per cent live in their own homes. The house is generally run with help which allows the wife to participate in community activities. Civic leadership is a very important function, as both the husband and wife are expected to devote a large portion of time to community affairs.

Class II comprises the most highly educated group in town. Those who lack a college education indicate that they could have gone farther with a better education, and parents emphasize the need of a college education to their children.

3. *Class III*. Family lineage does not play a large role in Class III.

They believe that those below them lack the hereditary traits to move up, but insist that the individuals above them keep them down regardless of their own efforts. Family incomes ranging from $2,000 to $4,000 are largely earned by the male head, but it is no disgrace for the wife to work. Less than half of the group own small businesses, farms, or are independent professionals; the rest are employees of the mines, mills, offices, banks, or are in public service.

This class has enough income for the convenience and comforts of life but has little left to invest in wealth producing activities. About two-thirds of the homes are owned. About a quarter of these houses are in the best residential area but not on the best streets. Another half live in the second best residential area. Class III is not as highly educated as the classes above them. In addition, there is a differential in education between husband and wife. While half of the fathers have not gone beyond the eighth grade, almost all of the mothers have had some high school training.

4. *Class IV*. This group is aware of their inferior position and resent the attitudes of those above them concerning their status. They conceive of themselves as the "backbone" of the community. The annual family income ranges from $800 to $2,700 with the mode at about $1,500. Family incomes are spent as they are earned, and about a third of the wives supplement this income.

The members of this class work for wages on the farms, in the mines, mills, and shops of the city, and a few are owners of very small businesses. While about one-third of the members own their homes, Class IV farmers and laborers are almost exclusively tenants. They are largely excluded from the best residential areas; on the other hand, they avoid the lowest rated area.

Formal education is limited to elementary and high school. Although the children are receiving more education than their parents received, the parents do not object if their children leave school and start to work.

5. *Class V*. Class V is at the bottom of the prestige structure, and they are the object of contempt by those above it. The members of this class realize that they are on the bottom and believe that they can do nothing to improve their position. When they do attempt to improve their position they are accused of "putting on airs." In length of residence, these families have as long a history as the best families, but, unfortunately, their notorious ancestors are remembered more than their illustrious ones.

Family support comes from many sources, and income ranges from $500 to $1,500, with a mode around $800. In addition to the father as the main breadwinner, over half of the wives are employed. Occasionally the income may be supplemented by welfare grants and, at times, the families receive an indirect form of wages through gifts of clothing and food from their employers.

Occupationally, they are almost exclusively unskilled and semi-skilled laborers and machine operators. They are excluded from the best residential areas and live in the sections of town that are labeled for their undesirability. Four out of five houses are rented. The houses are crowded and lack privacy since one room has to serve many functions. Educational experience is generally limited to elementary school. Only a few have been to high school and fewer have graduated.

Other factors could be emphasized, in addition to these, which are important in this particular class structure. Leisure and social ritual are as important to Class I families as civic leadership is to Class II families. Class III families are the active members of the churches of the community and keep the religious organizations functioning. Differences in recreational activities and political participation are other differentiating factors.

Looking at this example in terms of the conception and method of arriving at the class structure, a social class in this particular study was defined as families with equivalent degrees of prestige. This prestige was derived from the status accorded the families by other community members. The specific method used to determine the class structure involved interviewing community members about the prestige structure, and from these interviews thirty families were selected for their distribution and representativeness in the community structure. Nineteen of the twenty-five initial community raters divided these thirty families into five strata, and there was consistent agreement on the relative positions of twenty families. Taking these agreed-upon families as a standard list, thirty-five raters then ranked all of the families of the community into these five strata. The greatest agreement among the raters was found at the top of the prestige hierarchy, and the greatest disagreement over the placement of families was found in Classes III, IV, and V—particularly in Class IV, the largest group. This would seem to indicate that the "middle" class divisions were rather confused in the minds of the community, and it would also point to the fact that with an increase in the size of the classes (and the community) placement becomes more difficult. If there is this much confusion in a small city (6,000) one cannot anticipate too much consistency in a city of 600,000.

What Class Membership Means. Class membership is more than a simple difference in prestige as one's position in one class or another has an influence on all aspects of life. At birth the individual is faced with a set of expectations coming from the class system, which have little to do with the biological structure that he brings into the world. The child is surrounded by a set of social relationships which are unique to his class position. Since class position does involve such a pervasive influence, only a small segment can be considered here—its influence in certain aspects of the urban family system. Chapter 11 has a similar analysis of organized religion and stratification. The findings to be presented are from a number of studies using somewhat different conceptions of class, so the distinctions to be utilized here will be the traditional upper, middle, and lower. In the previous community example, Class I would be equivalent to the upper, Classes II and III to the middle, and Classes IV and V to the lower.

There are many contrasts that could be made between family life on the various class levels in the city. One way, which makes a number of these other differences intelligible, would be to stress the values which these families seek—the goals which are the focus of their activity. To somewhat over-simplify, the upper class family can be considered as tradition oriented; the middle class family as ambition oriented; the lower class family as survival oriented. These orientations provide a basis upon which their actions and behavior become understandable. The following class pictures of urban family life will summarize a number of class differences.[7]

1. *The urban upper class family—tradition oriented.*[8] The upper class child has all the specialized help needed to officiate at his antiseptic entrance into the world. His parents, who are older than average since they postponed marriage, are looking for someone to carry on the important family name. Since the child has fewer brothers and sisters, he becomes an important link in the larger kinship unit. At least a few children, however, are wanted to assure family continuity, and the Roman numerals which follow his name are an indication of this. With birth a place opens in the family business, plans are made for education, and perhaps informal arrangements are made for marriage. The birth is more a class event than a family event.

The cost of the birth is neither financially nor psychologically heavy. The responsibility for rearing can be delegated to nurses, governesses, boarding schools and summer camps, and the child's progress can be scrutinized during vacations with his parents. Financially, the child has no actual insecurity, and psychologically he is protected by specialized help and a net-work of kinship. This cushion against in-

---

[7] More complete descriptions of the class variations in family structure can be found in Ruth S. Cavan, *The American Family* (New York: Thomas Y. Crowell Co., 1953), and Robert F. Winch, *The Modern Family* (New York: Henry Holt and Co., 1952). This description also draws from Allison Davis and Robert J. Havinghurst, "Social Class and Color Differences in Child-Rearing," *American Sociological Review*, Vol. 11 (1946), pp. 698-710, and Kinsey, Pomeroy and Martin, *op. cit.*

[8] Unfortunately, the upper class family has not been studied scientifically to the extent that the middle and lower class families have; therefore, most of this material depends heavily on novels. If these literary sources are descriptions, then the authors have mirrored reality, but if they are fiction, the authors are perpetuating a stereotype. In any case, if this class picture is accurate it only applies to a very small portion of the urban class system.

security exists for a long period since there is little emphasis on striving or moving out of the family to prove one's self. The striving, which is characteristic of the middle class, is scrupulously avoided since the upper class position is secure. If he avoids bringing disgrace on the family name, he can wait for the rewards that are due him. Adolescence is not a period of great stress or strain since the transition to adulthood is clearly marked out through the channels of appropriate parties and debuts, and these announce to the class the maturity of the individual.

Courtship and mate selection is dictated less by the Hollywood variety of romance than it is for considerations for family tradition. Since the person has learned to hold a reverence for the sanctity of his family, love is somewhat a by-product of fulfilling family obligations. The family has to be satisfied with the prospective in-laws' status and property, so the arrangements proceed at a leisurely rate while the prospective partnership is evaluated. While some upper class men marry down, the upper class female who does this has to drop to the prestige level of her new husband. Many would rather keep their dignity and position in a single state than compromise it for such a prosaic reward as marriage. When marriage does come, and early marriage is not encouraged, it is more a class affair than a personal or a family affair. Then the cycle of the upper class family starts again as an endless chain providing for the continuity of the family tradition.

2. *The urban middle class family—ambition oriented.* The middle class child hardly has such an auspicious beginning as his upper class counterpart, perhaps not less sterile but less specialized. He will come into a family with more brothers and sisters and younger parents. Although his parents have plans for him, they would scarcely be as articulate or formalized. He belongs to his immediate family and not to his kinship unit. Since he scarcely knows his relatives, this serves to focus all his emotional attachments on his small family group.

The middle class child is a costly investment to his parents, not only for support in helping him attain his life goals, but, also, he may take the mother out of the labor market and he may also take his parents out of activities which are an aid to their own social and economic striving. To compensate for this parental investment, the child is expected to repay in kind—he must be a success. He does not have to worry about the necessities as the lower class child does, nor can he wait for the rewards assured the upper class child. He is expected to start striving during his early years to fulfill the goals and expectations.

Child rearing practices make these expectations explicit. He is required to wean himself and is started on the road to toilet training earlier than the lower class child. Generally, toilet training is started before the child has adequate muscular control, so he must suffer the consequences of his parents' lack of anatomical knowledge. The middle class child is expected to take responsibility earlier in the home, even when economic necessity does not require it. The girl must work, sew, and care for children at a younger age as a part of learning the sex role. Responsibilities are presented as "musts" even when the child is not emotionally or physiologically ready to assume them. With these high expectations and a lack of resources for meeting them, anxiety is produced and this anxiety may be intensified since the parents often use the threat of the withdrawal of their love as a means of punishment.

Realizing these success goals necessitates a great deal of self-discipline and postponement of immediate gratification. Money is to be saved and thrift is to be encouraged. Fighting is frowned upon and aggression is channeled into competitive activities. Premarital sex experience is denounced, but petting allows some of the same satisfactions without the same risks. These factors, along with the willingness to undergo long years of frustration in the process of education, are seen as necessary to attain their goals.

While the middle class teen-ager is economically dependent on his parents, psychologically he feels that he is ready for adulthood. Adolescence, then, is a period when he is caught between these conflicting demands. His dating experience often is used as another means of attaining status. Since marriage has to be deferred until the completion of occupational goals, the dating time may be used for ego satisfaction rather than dedicated to mate selection. While mate choice still tends to occur within class lines, the middle class person has more flexibility than the upper class person, since he is expected to start an independent family. While there are informal parental pressures, the parents cannot refuse to accept the new couple in the non-existent kin group and the child himself represents their inheritance. With marriage, the middle class family focuses again on ambition—this time perhaps on goals that the parents themselves did not quite reach.

3. *The urban lower class family—survival oriented.* The lower class child makes his entrance into the world without too much concern for new theories of obstetrics. Consequently, he not only has more brothers and sisters, but the members of his family have had a higher mortality rate. Chances are that his mother has taken the total responsibility for the child, since the death, divorce, separation and desertion rates are much higher in this class. The child cannot depend too much on his family for support so he often has to work himself to contribute to the meager family income.

The cost of the child can be viewed in two ways. Financially, the birth will take the mother out of the labor market for a period, and she may be the sole means of support. Psychologically, he will be no great threat to parental ambitions and may become an economic asset very early. The insecurities that he will face do not concern success but the necessities of life. Irregularity of his parents' employment leads to an unpredictable income. Relief often has to be utilized and, since one has to establish a "need" for relief, there is little incentive to save. If the family has money it is spent, not tucked away for a rainy day that they may not survive to see. According to middle class values the money is spent foolishly, and "those kind of people" don't know the value of the dollar, but for the lower class family survival is a day to day affair.

In growing up the lower class child follows a leisurely pace. There is no great urgency to wean him, and toilet training is not started as early, nor is it as compulsive as in the middle class. In one sense the lower class child rears himself, or, at least, does not have to contend with parental expectations which surpass his infant abilities. When he does not conform to his parents' expectations, they spank him and don't threaten him with the loss of their love. Even though adult responsibilities are not forced on him, these tasks are assumed in a real and not an artificial sense. Caring for other brothers and sisters, earning money, and helping his parents are necessities and not busy work. The child works, not for long term goals but because it is necessary. Since he is not college oriented, many school subjects have little relation to lower class reality. A course in French makes little sense when there are more direct ways for expression. Fighting is one much more effective means of expression and it is utilized much to the horror of his middle class school teachers. The "better students"—those from a higher class—get most of the individualized attention from teachers, and the lower class family does not insist that the child stay in a school that holds little interest and occupation value for him. Higher education becomes not imperative but an impossibility.

The crowded conditions of the lower class homes are conducive to learning about sex. Petting, so characteristic of middle class, is considered perverted, and intercourse, premarital or otherwise, is a more natural mode of expression. Moral ideals about chastity are usually contradicted by their parents' example and the behavior of those around them. School does not provide the locale of courtship, but the tavern, the street corner, and the factory are the logical places. Since they can't go lower, mate selection occurs in the class, but an occasional person will move up, especially the more attractive girls. Courtship is short and often the marriage is announced to the family after a quick ceremony. The new couple may move in with the parents, whose only concern is whether he got a "good" woman or she got a "good" man. The kinship group, which is more important than in the middle class, is not concerned with family tradition but only with family existence. The energy spent on striving for ambition in the middle class is channeled into a struggle for survival in the lower class.

If class differences create such contrasts in this one area of urban life, think of class differences in the many other areas. Think of an upper and a lower class male standing before a judge. The lower class offender has stolen a ten dollar pair of pants and he gets six months for every dollar of merchandise. The upper class offender has embezzled $100,000, and he gets two years, but the sentence will probably be reduced by his "good behavior." Or think of two first graders confronted by an I. Q. test on their first day at school. The one from the middle class family can answer the questions about a library since he goes there with his family. The boy from the lower class knows about many other things but not about libraries, and the things that he knows well are not asked in the test. By the test scores the lower class child may not be rated as intelligent, at least about the questions asked. The quest for class differences can be endless. Class membership affects voting behavior and party affiliation. Class affects recreational and leisure time activities. Class affects who goes to school and how well they get along. Class affects who gets caught for being a delinquent or committing a crime. Class affects religious affiliation and religious belief. In fact, one might pose the question, "What areas of urban life are *not* affected by class membership?"

The Urban Class System and Sources of Confusion. It is doubtful that one can speak of *the* urban class system, or a uniform system which is common to every city. Discussing a particular class system in a specific city is a complex task, but generalizing about *the* urban class system, at least, has these two disadvantages—first, the dangers involved in any generalization, and second, the lack of relevant research on which to base these generalizations. Since the conferring of prestige depends upon the consensus by the community members on the factors, possessions, and traits which are used in the evaluation, urban life presents certain problems which complicate and confuse the class system.

A clearly consistent urban class system would have the following characteristics. First, there should be a parallel relationship among all of the sources of prestige, and there should be agreement by the community members on the relative values of these sources. Second, individuals should identify with and label themselves as members of a particular class. They should exhibit the same set of unique attitudes and behavior patterns as the other members of their class. Third, an individual's associations with others should be within class lines. In other words, friendships would be with others of equivalent prestige. In this way the objective sources of prestige, the subjective aspects of class consciousness, and the person's friendship patterns would come into agreement.

The city, however, complicates this ideal type in many ways. Not only can each of the ingredients of prestige be treated as a separate ranking system, but also there are many class systems in the city, not just one. Urbanites perceive the total class system in different ways and they will disagree on what they see. One urbanite, also, may use a different set of prestige factors than others use when he places a person in a particular class. The class system is also confused since some individuals do not have the "appropriate" class attitudes for their class position. The class system is blurred because the system itself is changing and individuals within the system are moving. While one's friends in the city tend to be chosen from the new class, other bases of friendship may give false clues to a person's objective class position. Since each of these factors confuses the urban class system, more attention will be given to them in the following sections.

1. *Confusion from the multiplicity of ranking systems.* A city can be seen as a number of somewhat separate ranking systems. Individuals differ on all of the various factors—income, occupation, education, etc. —which go into the final product of prestige. Each one of these component factors, however, can be seen as a separate ranking system, and there may be discrepancies between them. While discrepancies also exist in small communities, they tend to be average and a composite prestige evaluation of the person is given. Also, in the small community the differences between the various ranking systems tend to be less discrepant. In the city these different systems will give somewhat different views of the same person. For example, a college professor and a bartender may be next door neighbors. The professor is evaluated more highly in occupational and educational rank, the bartender has a higher income, yet they share the same ecological area and housing type. The gambler may hide his somewhat disapproved occupation behind the walls of a suburban mansion, and the eccentric rooming house tenant may have a large bank account. This lack of equilibrium among the many facets of life patterns presents a confused picture, and since some of these discrepancies are hidden from other community members by the complexity of the city, they cannot easily be averaged into a single prestige score.

Other systems divide the city. The Negro community is always somewhat distinct. In fact, in one way it may be seen as an isolated island, not as separate spatially as it is socially. With the Negro community a comparable but socially distinct set of prestige levels exists, and certain occupations, as the mail carrier, may have a higher prestige there than in the white system. To a lesser degree ethnic origin provides another differentiating factor. Little Italy, Germantown, Spanish Harlem, and other names describe not only an area but a self contained community. In some cases groups with similar regional origins, as Southerners, become somewhat equivalent to ethnic groups in the city. The major religious divisions, Protestant, Catholic, and Jewish, also are social divisions as religious affiliation encompasses behavior which extends past the church door into other community activities. These many divisions in the social structure are shown in New Haven, where eight different Junior Leagues were "needed" to serve young upper class women.[9] There was one Negro organization, one Jewish organization, three Catholic groups, each composed of a different ethnic group, Irish, Polish, and Italian, and, finally, three Protestant Junior Leagues, differentiated again along the ethnic lines of "Old Yankee," Danish, and Swedish. While all of these organizations ostensibly served the same function, the racial, ethnic, and religious divisions were sufficiently intense to prohibit joint activity and membership.

In addition, there are groups within the city which are, in a sense, "declassed." These declassed groups, to some extent, do not accept and often depreciate the factors which other community members use to judge prestige. Particularly some individuals who are engaged in artistic and intellectual pursuits—the artist, the musician, the writer, and the entertainer—may substitute creativity for easy-judged objective factors, and this makes it difficult for the outsider to evaluate. These groups may also withdraw and feel that they are not a part of the total social system. Because of this their mode of life in Little Bohemia, Greenwich Village, or whatever label is applied, often becomes the subject of scorn and contempt by those who accept the usual prestige sources.

Summarily, in the city the various factors which give an individual prestige may lack uniformity or consistency, and the segmental knowledge that urbanites have of each other prevents any kind of a composite evaluation. In addition, racial, ethnic, religious, and "sophisticated" communities exist within the larger urban community, and they may utilize somewhat different criteria for prestige.

2. *Confusion from differential perception.* Many attitudes which are associated with a particular class are the result of differential perception. In other words, "reality" is not as much what actually exists as how the individuals define this existence. A doctor, a lawyer, an auto mechanic, and a policeman will not see an automobile accident in the same way, because they are looking for different things. Since this is a general principle, there is no reason to expect any exception in perceiving the class system. Part of the confused picture of the class system stems from the fact that one's own position will determine in part how others are seen. For example, in judging the prestige of certain occupations, both rural and metropolitan residents gave higher than average rating to jobs that were more closely related to their residential experience. Also, when a person rated his own job or one closely related to it, his evaluation was higher than the evaluation by others. Wealthy and highly educated people gave higher evaluation to scientific and profes-

<hr>

[9] A. B. Hollingshead, "Trends in Social Stratification: A Case Study," *American Sociological Review,* Vol. 17 (December, 1952), pp. 679-686.

sional occupations, while the less educated and lower economic groups rated skilled and semi-skilled jobs higher than average. Many other factors will enter into the particular decision to evaluate a job one way or another.[10] If these complications enter into this one dimension of prestige, the difficulties increase when one includes the total class system and not just occupation.

It has also been suggested that the greater the distance from an individual's own class position to other classes, the greater the difficulty a person has in knowing the characteristics of these distant classes.[11] The person more clearly recognizes those groups above and below him. He sees the class below more clearly, perhaps to refrain from identifying with it, and he tends to underestimate his distance from the class above him. Figure 9 shows the social perspectives of the classes, and it indicates very clearly that every class sees the total system somewhat differently. Centers has also suggested that a member of a particular class tends to include more individuals in his own class than individuals outside the class would include.[12] The person not only includes some of those with higher occupational prestige as being in his class but also some individuals of the lower prestiged occupations. This would enhance his own class position by both prestige and size. This confusion which stems from differential perception, then, not only affects how other classes are seen, but also how one's own class is conceived.

3. *Confusion from differential criteria.* Another confusing element in the class structure stems from the fact that on different class levels individuals may use different criteria for placing others in the class system. While there may be some agreement as to *where* people are in the class system, there is less agreement *why* they are there. It has been suggested that upper class individuals think of the class system in terms of time and family background; the middle class is concerned more with moral behavior; and the lower class thinks almost solely in terms of wealth. Research by Centers seems to indicate that the upper class and the lower class do consider family position and lack of wealth as more important characteristics of their class than do others outside these classes.[13] The middle range of the class structure, however, in this research seemed to place more importance on money, income, and working for a living as the more important characteristics for membership in their class. From other attitude and opinion studies, this middle range does tend to see the world and the class system in somewhat

---

[10] Cecil C. North and Paul Hatt, "Jobs and Occupations: A Popular Evaluation," *Opinion News* (September, 1947), pp. 3-13.

[11] A. Davis, B. B. Gardner, and M. R. Gardner, *Deep South: A Social Anthropological Study of Caste and Class* (Chicago: University of Chicago Press, 1941), pp. 63-83.

[12] Richard Centers, "Social Class, Occupation, and Imputed Belief," *The American Journal of Sociology*, Vol. 58 (May, 1953), pp. 543-555.

[13] Centers, *The Psychology of Social Classes, op. cit.,* pp. 89-106.

FIGURE 9. The Differential Perception of Social Classes.

moralistic terms, being particularly critical of the marital, sexual, and drinking behavior which they assume to be prevalent in both the upper and lower classes. So some confusion about the urban class system is due not only to the actual differences in the ways in which individuals perceive it but also from the fact that they tend to judge it by different criteria.

4. *Confusion from "false" class consciousness.* A person is "falsely" class conscious if his attitudes and behavior are inconsistent with his objective class position. If a person is class conscious, he has consistent attitudes with the interests of his class, and he labels himself as a member of that class. The urban class system, however, presents

many contradictions between a person's objective class position and his class-consciousness.

If classes are to be conceived as groups with unique interests, every urbanite might have to be considered as a separate class. It seems doubtful, also, that most people utilize a self-conscious label for their class, even though they recognize the different levels of prestige. If the urbanite is asked to choose a name for his position in the prestige hierarchy he is reluctant to violate the stereotype of the "common man" and he will claim he is middle class. A *Fortune* poll showed in their nation-wide sample that while 70 per cent claimed they were middle class, only 7 per cent claimed they were upper class, and 22 per cent claimed they were lower class. Centers, in his study, added a fourth choice, working class, and found only 4 per cent who would place themselves at the extreme ends.[14] If class-consciousness involves a self-label, then, by the choice of most urbanites, cities are almost totally middle- and working-class communities.

If classes are to be seen as groups that hold distinguishable attitudes and beliefs, there is still a great deal of contradiction. One can find lower class individuals who have "upper class attitudes," and upper class individuals who have "lower class attitudes." Many individuals not only believe but also implement their beliefs by voting in contradiction to their own "class" interest. These conflicts should not obscure the fact that there do seem to be somewhat distinct attitudes and beliefs at the top and the bottom of the prestige hierarchy, but the middle class seems to oscillate between these two poles.[15]

In short, if a class is conceived as being a self-conscious interest group with distinct attitudes and beliefs, then the city cannot present a precise class system. Most urbanites identify with the middle and working class and, although they do not always act contrary to their objective position in the prestige structure, they more often see their actions as motivated by self-interest rather than a particular class interest.

5. *Confusion from change and mobility.* Another reason why the urban class system appears blurred is that it is not a static system but it is constantly changing. It is changing in two directions; first, the system itself is undergoing change, and second, individuals within the system move up and down.

Industrialization is associated with urbanization and both are characterized by rapid social change. New and novel occupations are created which provide difficulties in assigning prestige since they are unique to the communities' past experiences. Many previously casual and unskilled laborers have now been assimilated into skilled jobs, and with an increase of occupations have moved up. Also, in recent years some

---

[14] Centers, *The Psychology of Social Classes, op. cit.*

[15] See, for example, *Ibid.,* and A. W. Kornhauser, "Attitudes of Economic Groups," *Public Opinion Quarterly,* Vol. 2 (1938), pp. 260-268.

occupations have changed their relative positions in the prestige hierarchy—the minister perhaps being one example. Today the income of the blue collar worker may be a more important inducement for occupational recruitment than the "dignity" of the white collar. Unionization has created new shifts in the power structure and has produced new men of power. The city also provides an impersonal environment in which skills are emphasized at the expense of family background. Since occupation provides such an important source of prestige, rapid technological changes are felt throughout the entire class system.

Within this changing class system vertical mobility or movement within the system occurs. There is currently some controversy as to whether the class system in the United States is becoming more or less rigid and whether vertical mobility is becoming easier or more difficult.[16] While a verdict on this controversy is not required here, it is sufficient to state that vertical mobility does occur, disregarding possible historical differences. While in America a great deal of mythology has centered around Horatio Alger and the "rags to riches" stories, most actual mobility has been hardly this dramatic. A great deal of so-called mobility is simply the result of the reasonable expectation that years of effort and experience are rewarded with increasing responsibility, income, and prestige. Also, the emphasis on education in America not only creates a need for more middle class school teachers, but

TABLE XXII

NET OCCUPATIONAL MOBILITY OF SONS OF PERSONS IN VARIOUS OCCUPATIONAL STRATA (N-637)

Occupational Stratum of Father	Percentages Having Sons Whose Occupational Status is:			Net Mobility of Sons in Per Cent and Direction
	Better Than Their Own	The Same as Their Own	Not as Good as Their Own	
All strata	35	36	29	6 upward
Large business	..	50	50	50 downward
Professional	15	32	53	38 downward
Small business	21	32	47	26 downward
White collar	27	45	28	1 downward
Skilled manual	41	31	28	13 upward
Semi-skilled	46	43	11	35 upward
Unskilled	63	37	..	63 upward

Source: Table 3 in Richard Centers "Occupational Mobility of Urban Occupational Strata," *American Sociological Review*, Vol. 13 (April, 1948), p. 201.

[16] See, for example, J. O. Hertzler, "Some Tendencies Toward A Closed Class System in the United States," *Social Forces*, Vol. 30 (March, 1952). pp. 313-323, and Gideon Sjoberg, "Are Social Classes in America Becoming More Rigid?" *American Sociological Review*, Vol. 16 (December, 1951), pp. 775-783.

leaves open a channel aiding mobility which is accessible to many. Technological changes, with a corresponding decrease in agricultural personnel, have created many generational shifts in occupations which appear on the surface as mobility. Table XXII gives some indication of the amount of occupational mobility by comparing a son's occupation with that of his father. While occupational "inheritance" is still common, the data can be viewed in two opposing ways. Optimistically, mobility in this one sphere is great because somewhat over one third of the sample had achieved higher occupational status than their fathers. The less optimistic way is also appropriate since nearly two thirds of the sample had occupations which were either the same or not as good as their father's. In addition, as those individuals who have higher prestige also have fewer children, members of the lower range of the class structure have to make up the net loss. It has been estimated that the net mobility will be somewhat over 20 per cent each generation, considering only the present differential birth rate and not other changes in the class system.[17]

Regardless of the actual objective chances of mobility in urban society, the common attitude that mobility is easy will hinder the development of any type of class-consciousness. The mere fact that individuals think that their children's chances of moving up will be much better than their own chances were will shift the focus of attention upon the individual and not the class. These expectations are rather common and the barriers to actual mobility apparently do not seem insurmountable to most people.

Since the prestige structure, in general, and the occupational structure, in particular, is changing, this will present a confused picture of the urban class system to the participants. Mobility does occur and a person may move up in one ranking system without moving in all of the ranking systems. Since individuals have attitudes which assume the ease of mobility, particularly for their children, stability and the actual difficulties in movement within the class system are minimized.

6. *Confusion from friendship patterns.* Although many studies have shown a close relationship between a person's associations and his class membership, there are enough exceptions to be somewhat confusing.[18] Some friendship patterns may have a basis which is not strictly aligned with class membership. Many of the origins of clique behavior may be found in childhood, adolescent, and college acquaintants, and these individuals may be somewhat disparate now in prestige. Others may be drawn together by their interest in art, music, hobbies, and politics.

[17] Carson McGuire, "Social Stratification and Mobility Patterns," *American Sociological Review,* Vol. 15 (April, 1950), pp. 195-204. See also Gregory P. Stone and William H. Form, "Instabilities in Status: The Problem of Hierarchy in the Community Study of Status Arrangements," *American Sociological Review,* Vol. 18 (April, 1953), pp. 149-162.

[18] Hollingshead, *Elmtown's Youth, op. cit.,* Chap. 9

Age and length of residence may provide communalities which even similar prestige could not. Standards of morality may be a basis for the formation of groups emphasizing, for example, drinking or non-drinking. Many urban working class families who do not participate in class-aligned voluntary organizations, may find their associational satisfactions still within their family and kinship structure.[19] The members of the family and kin group may have had the opportunity to move up or down in the class system and with time these initially homogeneous groups would not consist of similarly prestiged individuals. Again, while friendship and clique associations do tend to follow class lines, there is enough variation in the city to be concerned with these contradictions as well as the confirmations.

7. *Common elements.* To an undetermined degree, the inhabitants of cities do agree on the relative value of some possessions and personal traits. In one study there was somewhat general agreement that certain occupations have more prestige than others. This evaluation seems to be fairly consistent irrespective of the region of the country, size of the community, or the characteristics of the evaluator. For example, professional and executive governmental jobs were evaluated consistently high. This consistency would imply that the evaluators were using some common basis for their judgments. The most common criteria they used were income, length of training, the occupation's necessity, and its service to humanity.[20]

In addition, urbanites are exposed to common stimuli through the media of mass communication. Movies, radio, television, and newspapers provide a common source and comparison for the relative worth of certain status goods. By emphasizing the heterogeneity of the city, one can overlook these common factors in urban life.

The previous difficulties mentioned in conceiving a clear cut and consistent class system in urban areas do not mean that a class system does not exist. In terms of our ideal type of class system, there are some aspects that would have some generality from city to city. *First,* there are a number of separate class systems within the urban community. The Negro system is most distinct, while some ethnic divisions will approximate it. To a lesser degree, the major religious divisions can be treated as somewhat self-contained. Although it is impossible to ignore completely the generally accepted sources of prestige, some urbanites tend to emphasize unique prestige sources in their small groups. In terms of the overall urban class system, these groups are "declassed" and add to the number of separate systems. *Second,* the urban class system can be divided in a number of different ways and each way can point to actual differences in the characteristics and be-

---

[19] Floyd Dotson, "Patterns of Voluntary Association Among Urban Working Class Families," *American Sociological Review,* Vol. 16 (October, 1951), pp. 687-693.
[20] North and Hatt, *op. cit*

havior of the individuals occupying these class levels. For some purposes, the traditional upper, middle and lower will suffice. If finer distinctions are needed, each of these three can be sub-divided. The upper class can be divided between the old and new families, both in terms of time and wealth. The middle class can be sub-divided into an upper middle and lower middle, using degrees of occupational prestige and income as the divisors. The lower class can be divided in the same way, and all of these subdivisions have a foundation in the reality of differences in behavior. Regardless of the number of divisions, some individuals will be difficult to place because they are mobile or, in some other way, present a disparate set of factors for the community to evaluate. *Third,* most urbanites do not see themselves behaving explicitly in class terms and prefer to label themselves as middle or working class. While this aspect of class consciousness is lacking in urban society, the various class levels may be characterized by somewhat distinctive attitudes and interests. For example, those toward the top of the class system, in general, are opposed to change or governmental intervention in any aspect which would affect the status quo. While exceptions to this generalization do occur and are remembered, the overall conformity in urban areas outweighs these occasional non-conformists. *Fourth,* although urbanites may associate and participate in friendship groups which transcend class lines, most friendship is based on a person's compatibility with another's values and interests, and these tend to follow class lines. The banker has little in common with a bricklayer but much in common with another banker. Occupation, education, and place of residence are not only prestige sources but are also sources of friendship and association. Again, some discrepancy should not obscure the general consistency.

Summary. A city has a number of class systems, some markedly distinct, while others merge into the major one which encompasses the "Old American," white Protestant population. The total prestige system can be divided horizontally in a number of ways. In most cases, six classes will be sufficient for most analyses, although even this will not encompass all possible distinctions, and this division will represent distinctions which urbanites themselves make. While members of the urban class systems do not often think explicitly of their behavior in terms of class labels or interests, differences in attitudes, behavior, and patterns of association indicate the divisions between classes within the system. In terms of the "ideal," clearly consistent class structure mentioned previously, no urban community would measure up completely, nor would any community, large or small, in any society.

Urban life is synonymous with complexity and heterogeneity, but much of this complexity can be simplified by analyzing the city in terms of the class system. Every city can be seen as strata of individuals with differing amounts of prestige. Groups of individuals who have similar amounts of prestige constitute a social class. This prestige is derived from the possession of certain traits valued by other members of the community. In every city, family background, income, occupation, education, type of house, and the area of residence are more or less standardized prestige sources. In addition, each urban community may have other unique prestige sources.

There are currently three different research approaches to the class system. The first concentrates on certain objective criteria as income or occupational status; the second uses the prestige accorded an individual by other community members; the third is concerned with the subjective aspects of class consciousness. Each of these approaches, although distinct, can be translated into any of the others with some interpolation.

The lines between and the number of the classes can be determined either for the purposes of the particular problem or by recording the divisions made by community members. The way in which the various sources of prestige interact and produce the class structure was shown in an example from an actual community. The impact of class was shown in certain aspects of urban family life, and this was only one of a number of possibilities. The analysis of class differences could extend into every aspect of urban life.

Urban areas do not, however, present a clearly divided or clearly seen class system. There are actually many class systems which contain distinctive populations and distinctive prestige sources. Community members see the class system in different ways and they may judge it by different criteria. A person's class attitudes may not coincide with his actual objective position. Not only do individuals move up and down within the class system, but also the system itself changes. While these factors complicate the class system, one should not overlook the realities of the class system in urban life at any given time.

The class system is a source of real differences. Each class in the city provides a unique setting for the development of personality, both in the nature of the social relationships and in the content of what must be learned. These class patterns are internalized by the learning child and become a part of his total personality structure. Actually the values within these urban classes are so unique that they may be considered subcultures within the culture of the city. While some values are shared throughout the whole class system, each class usually judges other classes by its own unique values, and all classes assume that their own way is the "natural" way to do things.

The urban class structure might be compared to the steel girders of the rising skyscraper. Each floor and each class differs not only in its distance from the foundation but also in its composition. Each level is characterized by a unique set of surroundings and occupants. These occupants behave differently, think differently, and have different values than those on the other levels. The total skyscraper, called the city, can be seen as one structure from the outside, but it can only be understood in terms of the various levels inside.

WORKSHOP AND PROBLEMS

1. What is the meaning of social class?

2. What are the more important criteria of class in urban communities?

3. What are the more important methods of delineating social classes?

4. How may the community's concept of class differ from the researcher's concept?

5. Select a community with which you are acquainted and determine the criteria of class which are current.

6. What is meant by the fact that the urban middle class family is ambition oriented?

7. Why does one say that the lower class family is survival oriented?

8. What are some sources of confusion with respect to urban social classes?

9. What is meant by confusion from "false" class-consciousness?

10. What aspects of class have some generality or common elements from city to city?

11. What do you predict may be the trend in urban classes—toward more open or toward more closed classes?

BIBLIOGRAPHY

Bendix, Reinhard, and Lipset, Seymour Martin, *Class, Status and Power* (Glencoe, Illinois: The Free Press, 1953).

Centers, Richard, *The Psychology of Social Classes* (Princeton: Princeton University Press, 1949).

Davis, A., Gardner, B. B., and Gardner, M. R., *Deep South* (Chicago: University of Chicago Press, 1941).

Dollard, John, *Caste and Class in A Southern Town* (New Haven: Yale University Press, 1937).

Drake, St. Clair, and Cayton, Horace R., *Black Metropolis* (New York: Harcourt, Brace and Co., 1945).

Goffman, Erving, "Symbols of Class Status," *The British Journal of Sociology*, Vol. 11 (December, 1951), pp. 294-304.

Gross, Neal, "Social Class Identification in the Urban Community," *American Sociological Review*, Vol. 18 (August, 1953), pp. 398-404.

Hatt, Paul, "Stratification in the Mass Society," *American Sociological Review*, Vol. 15 (April, 1950), pp. 216-222.

Hollingshead, A. B., *Elmtown's Youth* (New York: John Wiley and Sons, Inc., 1949).

Jones, Alfred W., *Life, Liberty and Property* (Philadelphia: J. B. Lippincott Co., 1941).

Kaufman, Harold F., "An Approach to the Study of Urban Stratification," *American Sociological Review*, Vol. 17 (August, 1952), pp. 430-437.

Lynd, R. S., and Lynd, Helen M., *Middletown* (New York: Harcourt, Brace and Co., 1937).

—————————, *Middletown in Transition* (New York: Harcourt, Brace and Co., 1937).

Mills, C. Wright, *White Collar, The American Middle Classes* (New York: Oxford University Press, 1951).

Speier, Hans, "Social Stratification in the Urban Community," *American Sociological Review*, Vol. 1, pp. 193-202.

Warner, W. Lloyd, and Lunt, Paul S., *The Status System of A Modern Community*, Vol. II "Yankee City Series," (New Haven: Yale University Press, 1942).

Warner, W., Lloyd, Meeker, Marcia, and Eells, Kenneth, *Social Class in America* (Chicago: Science Research Associates, 1949).

West, James, *Plainville, U. S. A.* (New York: Columbia University Press, 1945).

CHAPTER 8

The Urban Family System

By VIRGIL E. LONG

The family constitutes a basic social unit in all contemporary cultures. Its form and functions have varied and continue to do so, not only interculturally but subculturally as well. Through all cultures, ancient, preliterate, or modern, it has retained some fundamental features. It remains a genetic group of two or more persons related by kinship, marriage, or adoption, usually residing together. As a social institution, it has retained sufficient adaptability to survive under social crises and the strenuous conditions of a rapidly changing social order. The family has not only been subjected to the influences of social change, but has, in and of itself, been a causal factor of change.

This treatment of the urban family focuses attention upon only its most salient features in a dynamic social order. It is so interrelated and interdependent with the matrix of society that it cannot be understood as an entity in isolation from other social groups and family classifications.

The Contemporary American Family. Any adequate understanding of contemporary family life must take into account its remote historical background, as well as the more immediate past through which it has undergone such radical change. Despite the impact of industrialization and urbanization upon the family, and the many changes which have been accredited to them, contemporary families possess some outstanding traits which are clearly rooted in the past. Vestiges of ancient Hebrew and Roman cultures appear in patterns of male dominance and semipatriarchal families, transmitted through our European background. Medieval chivalry put women on a pedestal and introduced the pattern of romantic love, although it was then disassociated from marriage. Religious influences both exalted woman to worshipful heights and warned against her as the temptress of men. From this background of mixed values, the American families emerged with predominantly semipatriarchal family types in which both women and children occupied subordinate status and roles to the dominant male. Although the orginal influences were predominantly British, the social, religious, economic, and political values of various European nationalities helped furnish

143

the initial elements out of which contemporary American families developed.

Whatever customs, traditions, and values entered into the family life of early American settlers, these have been modified in varying ways and degrees to adjust to the social and economic conditions of the new and changing environment. The major sources of influence for significant change in family patterns and functions are associated historically with an expanding frontier, agricultural economy, and, finally, with industrialization and urbanization. This does not tell the complete story, nor can it be told in toto. When such broad generalizations must be used, much of the detailed, factual background is often subordinated or altogether hidden. We know that through the interaction of a multiplicity of social forces, a new type of family is emerging.

The writers of fiction, philosophy, and theory present controversial characterizations of the "modern family" to a reading public which reacts with mixed emotions to deny or accept, according to its different points of view or value systems. Representatives of various academic disciplines, such as sociology, psychology, biology, and home economics, seek to apply the scientific approach for a better understanding of the nature and problems of contemporary families. Social workers, psychiatrists, ministers, doctors, lawyers, teachers, and counselors increasingly enter the family field in some phase of preventive or ameliorative practice. Although this multiple or "team" approach appears to be moving in the right direction with considerable impetus, the major tasks in this respect are still ahead. This is true for the family researcher as well as the practitioner.

1. *Families increasingly more urban.* The number of families continues to increase at a more rapid rate than the population growth of our country. For the period of 1790 to 1940, the population increased thirty fold, and in the meantime, the number of families increased sixty fold.[1] Even more phenomenal than the increase in number of families has been the increasing proportion of urban to rural families. In 1890, 64 per cent of the families in the United States were farm families. In 1950, only 14.5 per cent remained on the farm, and of the 85.5 per cent nonfarm families, 19.8 per cent were rural nonfarm and the remaining 65.7 per cent were classified as urban families (Fig. 8).

On a regional basis, the highest percentages of urban families are found in the Northeast, with 80.8 per cent, and in the West, with 70.2 per cent. Each of these is above the national average of 65.7 per cent.[2] It is especially significant that the most densely populated area of the Northeast has only 4.5 per cent farm families. The South and North Central regions fall below the national percentage, with the South being

---

[1] National Conference on Family Life, *The American Family: A Factual Background* (Report of Inter-Agency Committee on Background Materials, May 1948), p. 5.
[2] See Fig. 8.

14.4 per cent below the national level of urban families, and 29.5 per cent below the Northeast. In other words, the South (48.6 per cent rural) is the only region that approximates a 50-50 division between rural and urban families.

Urbanization and the Institutional Family. Conditions in the city are not conducive to the traditional type of family. The large institutional families of the past were favored by the socio-economic conditions which made the home a center of social, economic, religious, and educational activities. High birth rates and mass immigration gave impetus to the ever expanding agricultural economy. Emphasis was placed upon the

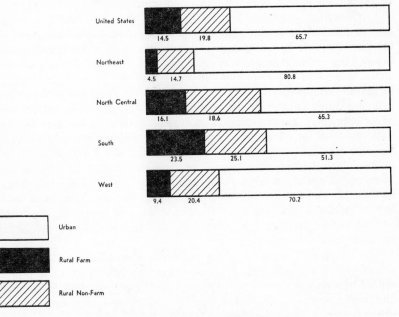

FIGURE 10. Families by Residence.

family as a unit of economic production. It was through the cooperative efforts of parents and their children that food, shelter, clothing, and other means of subsistence were produced. Thus children were assets and large families could be profitable economically, as well as desirable socially.

In the wake of the industrialization came the transfer of economic activities outside the home. Families, migrating to cities to be near their work, settled in densely populated urban areas where conditions were unfavorable to the rearing of children, and hence to large families. The factory system brought employment of men, women, and children, but often in different occupations and locations. Soon there were limitations upon the earning capacities of children. Child labor was restricted, and compulsory attendance laws made it imperative that the early years of the child's life be spent in preparation for later life as an adult. The child in the home became a dependent during the formative years of his life, and an economic liability rather than an asset. When mothers work to supplement the earnings of the family, children may be left without adequate supervision. The disorganizing effects of this arrangement may appear in pre-delinquency and problems of parent-child relations. As yet, the major responsibility for support of the family rests with the father. Since little or no provision is made for increased income, as the number of children increases the standard of living may be threatened by the increasing size of a family.

1. *Changing urban and rural differential.* The increased concentration of families in urban centers is one aspect of the urbanization of families. Another is recognized in urban influences which have spread beyond the political boundaries of cities and transmitted many of the characteristics of urban families to rural families. The automobile has increased the mobility of both the urban and the rural population, thus bringing direct contact in the economic, as well as the social spheres of activity. Newspapers, magazines, radio, and television provide the same medium for educational, recreational, religious, and aesthetic life for both rural and urban life. As rural electrification is extended, equipment of farm homes more nearly approximates that of the city. In the more prosperous farm areas, city families are rivaled in modern home equipment; and farm equipment also reflects the influence of urbanization and modern technology. The crude ways of preserving fruit and vegetables by salt water, in cellars, by drying and canning are being replaced by the freezer.

The one-room school is being replaced by modern, well-equipped schools, to which children are transported in private cars or public school buses from distant points. The school's organization, personnel, and program may approximate the education and standards of the urban centers.

The automobile has made it possible for youth and adults to go to the city for most of their recreational, social, and religious interests, if they so desire.

The effect of these influences upon rural family life is graphically described by two rural farm mothers who give the old in contrast with the new. A farm mother writes:

"My husband and I started out farming with his father in 1916, on a small farm. It was really work then to farm. We were up at four, while I got breakfast of meat and gravy, eggs, hot biscuits and coffee, on a wood stove, my husband went to the barn to feed and curry the horses preparatory to the day's work. When breakfast was over the day's work really began. In the spring, it was plowing, planting, etc., all done with machinery that was drawn by the faithful mule. At the house it was milking by hand, setting hens, feeding them, and doing thousands of things in the slow old-fashioned way, yet it was all interesting.

"Our son was born in 1919. By the time he was out of school, the depression had come. There was no money to buy modern machinery, so he became disgusted with farming and said he would never farm, but after serving in the army for four years he changed his mind and bought a dairy farm with modern equipment. Instead of the cellar to keep the milk cool for the meals, there is the electric refrigerator, instead of coal oil lamp there is electric light. The home is completely new and modern, with bath and hot and cold water, electric stove and washing machine, taking the place of the wood stove and wash board. These changes scare us who made ours the hard way.

"We go now to the farm, the herd of thorough-bred Holstein and Jersey cows have replaced the cross-breed milch cow of a few years ago. The modern milk house and barn is equipped with milkers and a cooler, everything government inspected.

"The tractor and its appliances has taken the place of the mule, and one man can do with it in three days what it took three men to do in a month. The rolling hills are covered with permanent pasture, where one time they had to be cultivated but also washed away. The incubator and brooder has taken the place of the old hen, yet we must have her to lay the eggs. The new foods for chickens have greatly reduced the death rate of chickens. The length of time it takes to raise fryers is the wonder of the poultry business.

"The only way to make money out of milk was churning butter, but now this son has the trucks collect his milk each day and the profits are larger. Our church going has been an interesting change too. We at one time walked two miles to the little country church every Sunday. We would not take worlds for the influence of that church on the life of this son. Later we got the buggy, then in 1929 we got the T-model. We felt fine then. The first six years of our son's school life were spent in a one-room school building to which he and his brother walked two miles. They rode a bus six miles the rest of the time until they were through school, then the War. When the boys went to war there was a shortage of teachers so I took up my old job as teacher."[3]

The technological factors, the social processes involved and their effects upon these rural families serve as forceful illustrations of cause and effect in the changing institutional family. It is important to note a number of factors involved, which give insight into what happens to the structure, functions, and traits of families undergoing change. Through case studies we are given a "ring-side seat" to view the *changing* institutional family, not just the *changed* family. Rural fam-

---

[3] A case study from the files of the author.

ilies usually write of changes in the *present tense,* which they are consciously observing, such as: (1) the higher level and standard of living; (2) the changing roles of family members, especially parents and children; (3) the shift of social, recreational, and religious activities to other institutions; (4) the increasing loss of personal-social relations within the family circles; and (5) the declining size of the family.

The Changing Functions of the Family. It is clear that the commonly recognized functions of the institutional family have changed, and are changing under the impact of urbanization which carries with it the force of modern technological development. But the extent and nature of these must be more clearly delineated. It is often asserted that the family has lost its major functions to other social institutions, and that its place in the social structure as a fundamental social group is threatened. In the light of present knowledge, this appears as a gross exaggeration. We may more accurately speak of *changing* and *modified functions,* than of lost functions. Outstanding among these changing functions are the biological, economic, protective, educational, recreational, religious, social, and affectional functions.

1. *Biological function.* Marriage is still the most popular institution for the biological union and amalgamation of male and female. Statistical evidence, presented on the following pages, shows that the proportions married in our population have reached an all time high. It now appears that the long term trends toward smaller families may be in process of reversing itself—at least to the extent of popularizing the moderate-sized family of from three to five children.[4]

2. *Economic.* The economically self-subsistent family, so characteristic of the agrarian economy of the past, is a rarity in American life. This does not mean that the economic function of the family has been lost. The importance of the economic function of the family and its members is a self-evident fact to all experienced breadwinners, homemakers, and/or budget keepers in families. Although urban families are not in the business of producing economic goods, they are in the business of receiving and dispensing income as well as the consumption of economic goods. Furthermore, income adequate for the maintenance of an acceptable level of living is one of the prerequisites to family integrity in modern economy. Researchers have credited economic or financial factors as being among the chief sources of marital conflict. According to Mowrer, "financial tension" is the "greatest apparent cause of divorce."[5] Terman's study of grievances of husbands and wives placed insufficient income as highest on the list.[6] Burgess and Cottrell found occupations, income, regular work, and savings to be the eco-

---

[4] See data in this Chapter and Chapter 5 for support.

[5] Ernest R. Mowrer, *Family Disorganization* (Chicago: University of Chicago Press, 1927), pp. 68-69.

[6] Lewis M. Terman, *Psychological Factors in Marital Happiness* (New York: McGraw Hill, 1938), pp. 96-97.

nomic factors significantly associated with adjustment in marriage. They concluded, however, that in so far as economic behavior affected marital adjustment, it was an expression of other non-economic factors associated with it.[7]

Some evidence of the rapidity and extent of the shifting economic function of the family is revealed by comparison of agricultural employment with urban employment. In 1850, agricultural employment accounted for 65 per cent of the nation's workers as against 35 per cent urban. Agricultural workers had declined to 31 per cent by 1910, and to 14 per cent by 1949, with urban employment accounting for 86 per cent of the workers.[8]

Urban family income is primarily from the employment of family members in occupations outside the home. Regular or full employment, with adequate income to maintain the various elements in a normal standard, is the goal. Full employment does not, however, guarantee economic security. Some safeguards are provided through various measures of the Federal Social Security Act, minimum wage laws, as well as by numerous other federal, state, and local government aids to families.

3. *Protective function.* The protective services provided for contemporary society by federal, state, and local governments touch many aspects of family life. Policemen, firemen, civil defense and public health workers combine to protect life and property. Private insurance companies will, for a price, furnish safeguards against almost all hazards to life and property.

The Federal Social Security Act of 1935 was designed primarily for the purpose of providing safeguards against economic insecurity of families. Among its provisions are: (1) public assistance to old people, dependent children and the blind and disabled; (2) old age and survivors insurance; and (3) unemployment insurance. Numerous other safeguards such as Railroad Retirement, Workmen's Compensation, state-federal unemployment insurance, and state and local government retirement, have been provided. Over six billion dollars was dispensed to slightly less than nine million beneficiaries from these various sources in 1950.[9]

Life would be hazardous indeed without the protective services of agencies. However, they do not and are not intended to usurp the protective functions of the family. They merely supplement and/or provide special safeguards to take care of family failure, or to provide beyond what is within the power of the family alone to do. Despite continued

---

[7] Ernest W. Burgess and Harvey J. Locke, *The Family,* Second Edition (New York: American Book Company, 1950), p. 435.

[8] Warren Thompson, *Plenty of People* (New York: Ronald Press Company, 1948), pp. 136-138.

[9] Source: U. S. Census Bureau, *Statistical Abstract of the United States, 1952,* No. 268, p. 22.

assertion to the contrary, the family remains the chief protective agency against the major mental, physical, moral, social, economic, and health hazards of its members, and more especially of its children.

4. *Educational function.* Before the coming of public schools, private tutors and itinerant teachers were available to those families who could afford to board them in their homes and pay the fees. Otherwise, the responsibility for education rested upon the family. The public schools took responsibility for the formal education of the child; but the educational function was not taken away from the home. The educational task, performed at its best, is a shared task and requires the contribution of both the parents and the school. A major portion of the essentially informal aspects of education remains with the home. The adequacy of performance of parents in the informal aspects of education and socialization has important bearing upon the success of the school. With the school taking responsibility for the formal aspects of education, parents may devote more time and attention to the informal aspects of training in the pre-school years, as well as the later phases of the child's development.

5. *Recreational function.* Commercialized recreation serves as a centrifugal force to pull the members of the family away from the home. Opportunities for family participation in these outside activities are limited, and individual interests separate them from each other. Technological development has placed facilities at the disposal of the home, that may serve as a centripetal force, making the home the center. Among these are the radio and television. The automobile may be used to promote recreation or destroy it. Family travel on vacation; a ride in the evening after the day's work is done; the trip to the park, mountain, or lake, all may serve to keep family members together and provide memorable occasions.

In the well planned and equipped home, family recreation is still a lively function, especially for the growing child.

6. *Religious function.* Without doubt religious teachings, ritual, and activities have diminished in the modern home. As in the case of education, religious training was an important phase of family life. The fundamental religious needs of the individual can best be met in the home environment. Parental responsibility for religion in the early years of the child's life cannot be delegated to others.

7. *Social function.* There is no adequate substitute for the family's role in the socialization of the child. This is peculiarly true with urban families. Other social agencies, such as the schools, the churches and the varied interest groups, may supplement the family, or make some provisions for family failures, but not supplant the family in this area. It is in the family that the attitudes and patterns of conduct so essential to effective citizenship in adult life are formed. More than any other agency, it is the responsibility of the family to meet the individual

needs for security, intimate response, recognition, and new experiences. Its status-giving function is still of major importance, despite modifications in this respect.

8. *Affectional function.* It is in the home during the formative years of the child's life that the foundation is laid for the later affectional life of the child. Special studies have shown a positive relationship between satisfactory affectional life of children with parents and their subsequent adjustment in marriage. Burgess and Cottrell found that husbands closely attached to their fathers had a positive correlation with successful marriage; and a similar correlation held for the adjustment of the wife who had close attachments to the mother.[10] Terman's study of 792 married couples supported this same conclusion. In addition, both of the above studies placed emphasis upon the importance of happiness in the parental family for successful marriage of the children.[11]

Changing Patterns of Authority. The patterns of family authority in the western world have been in process of transition from the patriarchal authority to equalitarian and democratic control. In the patriarchal family, authority was vested in autocratic control of the father.

With the ascendancy of woman and the accompanying changes in the habits and roles of other family members, there was a shift of authority in the direction of the equalitarian pattern, in which authority is shared by the father and the mother. The austerity and firmness of equalitarian authority varies greatly in the different families, but it is still essentially adult control.

During this period of transition from the old authoritarian patterns of adult control, a new basis of authority was emerging in the form of the democratic family. In this is implied: (1) that each member of the family, parent or child, may have a voice in decisions made which concern him and other members of the family; (2) that such controls as are established result from group action; and (3) that individual conduct is subjected to group control rather than to arbitrary decisions of dominant individuals. The extent to which this transition is achieved has important bearing upon the problems of adjustment of the individual in a changing and complex society.

In some segments of cities there are vestiges of the ancient forms, now more properly designated as semipatriarchal. Burgess and Locke cite the fact that the immigrant family transplanted from the Old World to the American city is typically a peasant family. Such families are described as semipatriarchal, "because by custom the father is head of the family and both the wife and children are subordinate to him.[12] In the large cities, such as Chicago, they tend to settle in congested

---

[10] Ernest W. Burgess and L. S. Cottrell, *"Predicting Success or Failure in Marriage* (New York: Prentice Hall, 1939), pp. 354-359.
[11] Lewis M. Terman, *op. cit,* pp. 145-146.
[12] Ernest W. Burgess and Harvey J. Locke, *The Family* (New York: American Book Company, 1953), pp. 165-175.

areas around the central business district and in the industrial areas. The theoretical scheme (Figure 11) shows the relative position of the immigrant zone (III) to the central business district of the city. Each of the other zones in this theoretical scheme has its characteristic form of family organization, based upon some degree of parental authority. Families of the workingmen's area (Zone IV) populated by rural-minded American families and descendants of the old immigration, have preserved the rural type of family in the city. Although there is apparent evidence of democracy in this type of family, "The husband and father is admittedly its head." These are classified as patricentric. The equalitarian family is associated with the apartment house area and hotel district (Zone V). This district has a high density of population, few open spaces for children to play, and the more impersonal relationship so characteristic of big cities.

In the suburban area, sometimes designated as the commuters' zone, there is a high ratio of women to men, of children to adults. Husbands commuting to the city for work are away from early morning until late evening. The dominant position of the mother is increased by the father's absence from the home. These have been designated as matricentric families.[13]

The trends toward individualism, so pronounced in cities, tend to break down the pattern of familism so characteristic of rural farm families.[14] The assumption is sometimes made that the same individualization also runs counter to adult dominance of the family in the city. Although some evidence lends support to this theory, Landis and Stone found little to confirm it in their study of 4,310 high school seniors in the state of Washington. Of the 1900 boys reacting to the questionnaire, 40.4 per cent placed their families in the democratic, 38.7 per cent in the intermediate, and 20.8 per cent in the authoritarian classifications, indicating a high degree of moderation in parental control of boys. Slightly more than 22 per cent of 2,410 girls thought their families were democratic, and 22 per cent fell in the authoritarian class. The majority, 55.6 per cent, scaled their families as intermediate in control. This would support the conclusion that parents are more inclined to shelter and protect the girl, and in doing so they deny her much of the freedom they grant the boy. With respect to residential groups, classified as farm, town, and city, 45.7 per cent of the town boys thought their families were democratic, compared to 39.4 per cent in the city, and 38.1 per cent in the farm group. Only slight differentials appeared for the girls on residential classifications and the family administrative pattern.

When the cities were reclassified according to size, no significant

---

[13] Based upon Burgess and Locke, op. cit. Those interested in more complete characterization of the designated areas and in other family traits, should read pp. 100-124.
[14] Ibid, pp. 60-61.

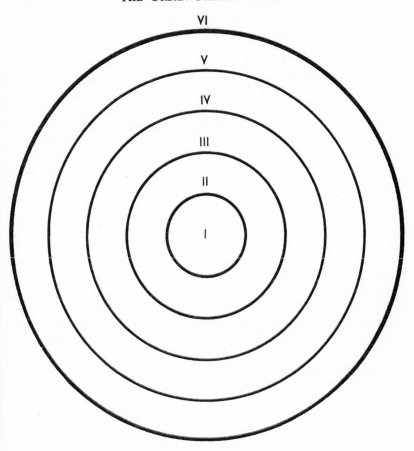

I. Business Zone, Non-Family
II. Rooming-house Zone, Emancipated Family
III. Immigrant Zone, Semi-Patriarchal Family
IV. Workingmen's Zone, Patricentric Family
V. Apartment-house Zone, Equalitarian Family
VI. Suburban Zone, Matricentric Family

FIGURE 11. The Theoretical Pattern of Urban Zones and of Family Types.

difference appeared between boys from the cities of 150,000 population and over, and farm boys, on the percentage of democratic families. But the cities of 10,000 to 50,000 had the largest percentage of boys living in authoritarian families. Interpreting the lack of farm-city differences in family administrative patterns, Landis gives two possible explanations. (1) Only one tenth of the farm population and 14 per cent of the urban population of the state were foreign-born. Foreign-born families are usually patriarchal in character, and therefore authoritarian in administrative pattern. (2) It is probable that farm young people from democratic families more often complete high school than those from authoritarian families.[15]

The Declining Size of Families Urban and Rural. The long term trends toward smaller families have affected both urban and rural families. Urban families were the first to make the transition from the traditionally large family pattern, with high fertility rates to relatively small families with low fertility rates. This is shown by the average size of urban, rural farm, and rural nonfarm families for the last three decades (Table XXIII).

Families in urban areas were smaller than in either rural nonfarm, or rural farm areas, for each census report since 1930. The urban family declined in size more rapidly than did the rural farm family. The farm family was 15.1 per cent larger than the urban family in 1930; 17.7 per cent larger in 1940, and by 1950 the margin of difference had declined to 13.6 per cent.

Other comparisons reflect differences in size of families according to the extent of urbanization. Of U. S. families having four or more children under eighteen years of age, in 1947, a 4.1 per cent were urban, 8.4 per cent rural nonfarm, and 12.7 per cent rural farm families.[16]

Differences appear on the basis of geographical areas. In 1947, there were about 164,000 births in families with six or more children—

TABLE XXIII

AVERAGE SIZE OF THE FAMILY IN THE U. S. BY URBAN
AND RURAL AREAS 1930-1950

Year	Urban ı	Rural Farm	Rural Nonfarm
1950	3.24	4.0	3.40
1940	3.61	4.25	3.78
1930	3.97	4.57	3.99

Sources: *U. S. Census, 1940, Housing, General Characteristics,* Part 1, p. 7; 1950 Census of Housing, U. S. Summary, General Characteristics, H-A1, Tables 3 and 4 (computed from).

[15] Paul H. Landis and Carol L. Stone, "The Relationship of Parental Authority Patterns to Teen-age Adjustments," Washington Agricultural Experiment Stations Institute of Agricultural Sciences, State College of Washington, Bulletin No. 538, September 1952.

[16] Bureau of the Census, Current Population Reports, *Population Characteristics,* Series P-20, No. 21 (Dec. 19, 1948), p. 12.

these were of the seventh order of births or over. This constituted 5 per cent of all births for that year. But 7.4 per cent of all births to white women in the East South Central states, predominantly an agricultural region, were of the seventh order or over, and 2.1 per cent were of the tenth order. Two other predominantly rural areas, the South Atlantic and Mountain regions, were next highest in the seventh order of births. In the highly urbanized Middle Atlantic and Pacific regions, the seventh order of births constituted only 2.2 per cent of all births.[17]

The Prospect of Larger Families. If former trends toward smaller families had continued, the nation's families would not now be replacing themselves. It is estimated that an average of three children for all fertile marriages would be needed to accomplish this. Landis estimates that 1940 reproduction rates were four points short for population replacement for the nation.[18] World War II accelerated the upswing in the birth rate which began in the pre-war period as the national economy recovered from the depression. It was natural to expect a downward trend in the birth rate when the influences of the war were dissipated, and that long term trends would be resumed. The predictions of population analysts were to this effect.[19]

Despite these predictions, present birth trends do not support this conclusion. Now that more detailed analysis of the post-war period is possible, there is substantial support for the conclusion that we are experiencing a reversal of the trend toward smaller families, in favor of moderate sized families. In the postwar upswing, the birth rate reached its highest peak in over twenty-five years in 1947, declined slightly in succeeding years, but remained at a high level in 1950. First births declined by nearly 30 per cent by 1950, thus following the declining marriage rate which reached its peak in 1946. Despite this downward trend, first births remained 20 per cent above those of 1940. Only first birth rates declined. The trend for higher orders of births, second through fifth, has been upward since 1940. The rate rose as much as 77 per cent for third births, 50 per cent for fourth, and 27 per cent for fifth births. It remained about the same for sixth and higher orders of births.[20] This evidence indicates some trend toward moderate-sized families of four or five children. The larger families of six or more children have not gained significantly, nor have they declined in popularity as shown by the birth trends. This may reflect an increasing popularity of children which may establish long term trends

---

[17] Metropolitan Life Insurance Company, *Statistical Bulletin*, Vol. III, No. 5 (May 1950), pp. 3-5.

[18] Paul H. Landis, *Social Policies in the Making* (New York: D. C. Heath and Company, 1952), p. 491.

[19] *Ibid.*, p. 495. Also P. K. Whelpton, "Cohort Analysis of Fertility," *American Sociological Review*, 14: 735-749, December 1949.

[20] Metropolitan Life Insurance Company, *Statistical Bulletin*, Vol. XXXIV, No. 1, January 1953, p. 6.

at a different level. On the other hand, it may be of short duration because of its relationship to the years of economic prosperity, when incomes will afford larger families, along with an acceptable standard of living.

Factors Related to Family Size. There are multiple factors which influence family size, of a biological, psychosocial, or socio-cultural nature. These have operated together in various complexes to produce long-term trends toward smaller families. The more significant factors may be summarized under (1) the standard of living, (2) increased knowledge of birth control, and (3) changing social values.

1. *Standard of living.* There is a constant pull between the *standard of living*—what families want and/or need; and the *level of living*—what the income will afford and/or what they get. Rarely do the two get together, especially in lower and middle class families. The relationship between level and standard of living is dynamic, ever changing. When increased income permits a higher level of living, the elements in the standard tend to rise to a higher level, and the struggle is resumed to achieve the new goal.

Some insight concerning the complexity of standards of living reveals a vital relationship to the birth rate and hence to the size of families. The standard of living is composed of many elements, such as food, shelter, clothing, and health, as well as the educational, recreational, religious, and aesthetic life of members of the family. Intermingled and inseparable from these elements in the standard are many cultural, as well as personal-social values, which determine the wishes and needs of different families and family members. These constitute what to them means desirable family life.

Perhaps the most important of these influences is related to social status as represented in family backgrounds, personal-social, and in-group-outgroup relations. In family planning, or family decisions in the absence of specific planning, these values influence choices between houses, automobile, refrigerators, radios, television, or other devices for the home and children. Value decisions also influence activities and membership in non-family groups of either social, religious, civic, or political nature. In the planned family, the decision to have or not to have children is inevitably linked with other decisions. The questions of how many children and when are related to "quantity and quality," according to the values of those in position to decide.

The above considerations do not affect all families to the same extent. The middle and upper class families are more subject to the influence of the rising standard of living, than lower class families. Some evidence for this is found in the relation of fertility rates to family income, occupational status, and educational achievement. Kiser's study showed that native white urban wives with incomes under $1000, had a fertility rate 50 per cent higher than those with incomes of $5000 and over.[21] Unskilled laborers had a fertility rate 15 per cent in excess of skilled labor, 22 per cent above professionals, and 34 per cent above the business class. Thus, we have a negative correlation with occupational classification.[22]

Levels of educational achievement show a negative correlation with fertility. Kiser found that those who had not reached the seventh grade in school had a fertility rate 30 per cent above those with high school training, and 38 per cent above those with college education.[23] Other supporting evidence for this negative relationship is found in the proportions of childless women, among those who have ever been married and have passed the child bearing period. According to the data of Table XXIV, a higher percentage of childless women is associated with each higher grade level in school for both rural and urban areas. Urban influence is reflected in the fact that the prevalence of childless women is greater for urban than for rural farm, on all equivalent educational levels.

2. *Increased knowledge of birth control.* Increased knowledge of birth control by contraceptive methods has been a factor in planned parenthood for both urban and rural families. Both federal and state

TABLE XXIV

THE PERCENTAGE OF CHILDLESS WOMEN AMONG NATIVE WHITE WOMEN WHO EVER MARRIED, AGE 50-54, ACCORDING TO EDUCATIONAL ATTAINMENT, UNITED STATES 1940*

	Maximum Years of School Completed					
	Grade School			High School		College
	Under 5	5-6	7-8	1-3	4	1 or more
Total U. S.	11.5	12.4	15.2	16.3	18.3	17.4
Urban	14.4	15.9	17.7	18.9	19.4	18.6
Rural Nonfarm	11.3	10.8	14.7	16.2	18.0	17.0
Rural Farm	8.5	8.3	10.7	9.9	13.0	14.2

*Source: United States Bureau of the Census, *Population, Differential Fertility*, 1940 and 1910, *Fertility by Duration of Marriage* (Washington, D. C.: 1947), Tables 9 and 24.

laws have relaxed restrictions, permitting a wider dissemination of prevenceptive information to the people. Clinics have been established in

---

[21] Source: Percentages computed from data given by Clyde V. Kiser, *Group Differences in Urban Fertility* (Baltimore: Williams and Wilkins, 1942), p. 124.

[22] *Ibid*, p. 56.

[23] *Ibid*, p. 91.

strategic areas, especially in the South, under both public and private auspices, to give instruction to prospective parents about birth control and other facts related to planned parenthood. Although the full effects of this increased knowledge cannot be fully evaluated, it doubtless has played a major role in controlling family size.

3. *Changing social values.* The strength of primary group controls has declined as families have become more urbanized and more mobile. In the urban community, standards of behavior become more personalized and self-directed; due in part to greater anonymity in urban than in rural communities. Social pressure has declined concerning the imperative "to multiply and replenish the earth." Wide latitude is given to the personal desires of married couples to have or not to have children. Increasingly, family size is becoming a function of personal desires and expediency.

Significant Marriage Trends: National, Urban and Rural.

1. *Increasingly more married.* Marriage is becoming increasingly more popular in the United States. A greater proportion of the population is married, than at any time in history. The long term trend in this direction has been accelerated by the increased marriage rates which came in the wake of World War II. So marked has been the upswing that the supply of single persons in the population has been significantly decreased.

The proportion of the male population, fourteen years old and over who were married, increased from 52.1 per cent in 1890, to 69.9 per cent in 1951. Similar increases were registered for the female population. The proportion of females married was higher than that of the males in 1890. By 1940, the proportion of married males had taken a slight lead over the married females. This lead was proportionately greater by 1951. (See Table XXV.)

The proportion of persons married increased for all age groups, male and female, during the last decade. From one point of view, this means that marriage prospects improved between 1940 and 1951. (See Table XXVI). On the other hand, the consequent reduction of single persons in the population may make marriage more difficult in the immediate future. Especially notable are the increases for the younger ages. For the girls, in 1951, the age groups 15-19, 20-24, and 25-29 showed an average per cent difference of 11 points over the 1940 proportions.[24] Excluding the lower age group (15-19), the average difference for the girls is approximately 14. For the men, the age groups 20-24, 25-29, and 30-34 had an average increase of 13.4. This increase in the married population may be attributed to two major factors: (1) the improvement in mortality and the consequent reduction

---

[24] A unit difference in proportions, and not a computed percentage.

in widowhood,[25] and (2) the high marriage rate of the war and immediate postwar period.

2. *Urban and rural marriage trends*. For several decades the urban

TABLE XXV

MARITAL STATUS OF THE POPULATION 14 YEARS OLD AND
OVER, BY SEX, 1890, 1940, AND 1951*

Year	Per Cent Married	
	Male	Female
1951	69.9	66.5
1940	59.7	59.5
1890	52.1	54.8

Statistical Abstract of the United States, 1952, p. 44.

TABLE XXVI

PER CENT OF POPULATION WHO HAD EVER MARRIED, BY SEX AND
AGE PERIODS IN THE UNITED STATES, 1940 AND 1951*

Age (Years)	Males		Females	
	1951	1940	1951	1940
15-19	2.7	1.7	16.7	11.9
20-24	48.3	27.8	66.8	52.8
25-29	79.5	64.0	89.0	77.2
30-34	87.5	79.3	90.6	85.3
35-39	88.6	84.7	92.2	88.8
40-44	90.8	87.4	93.2	90.5
45-49	91.6	88.8	93.0	91.4
50-54	91.4	89.0	92.8	91.3
55-59	92.8	89.2	92.5	91.3
60-64	92.8	89.5	92.3	90.7

*Source of basic data: Metropolitan Life Insurance Company, *Statistical Bulletin*, Vol. 34, No. 5, (May 1953), p. 8.

environment has been more favorable for the marriage of men than for women. Table XXVII shows a greater proportion of men married than of women for each decennial census from 1910 through 1950 and the

[25] Metropolitan Life Insurance Company, *Statistical Bulletin*, Col. 31, No. 7, July 1950, p. 6.

year 1951. In rural areas, the reverse is true. The proportion of women married exceeds that of the men. The proportion of men married was greater in the country than in the city before 1930; from that time on, the married proportion has been greater in the city.

3. *Fewer men in urban areas.* A factor conducive to the higher proportion of married males than females in the urban environment, is the imbalanced sex ratio. The 1920 urban ratio of 100.4 declined to 98.1 in 1930, and has declined to 94.1 by 1950. It is of interest to note that the national sex ratio of 98.6 in 1950, is near the level which the urban sex ratio was twenty years earlier.* The continued excess of males in rural areas creates better prospects for marriage of women, than is found in the urban areas.[26]

On a regional basis, significant sex differentials exist (Table XXVIII). On farms of the North Central and Western regions, the excess of men is above the national farm ratio; with men greatly exceeding women in the West. Other male excesses appear in the rural nonfarm category

TABLE XXVII

MARITAL STATUS OF PERSONS 15 YEARS OLD AND OVER, BY SEX AND RESIDENCE 1910-1951, PER CENT—DISTRIBUTION*

Year	Male		Female	
	Urban	Rural	Urban	Rural
1951**	70.5	68.4	64.9	69.8
1950**	68.6	65.8	63.8	69.8
1940	61.8	60.4	58.1	65.4
1930	60.5	59.3	58.5	65.0
1920	58.9	59.5	57.6	64.3
1910	54.7	56.8	54.6	63.3

*Computed from United States Censuses: *Statistical Abstract of United States,* 1952, p. 44, No. 43.
**1950 definition of urban, rural farm and nonfarm used. Age fourteen and over.

in the Northeast and the nonfarm Negro population of the South. Urban ratios for all regions show a deficiency of males. The Northeast, with 90.5, is nearer the national ratio for urban population than in the South with a ratio of 85.3.

The pull of the city is greater for young women than for young men. This is in part due to the fact that girls find more suitable employ-

---

*See Chapter 5 for more details on sex ratios.
[26] *1950 Census of the Population, Preliminary Reports, General Characteristics of the Population of the United States,* Series PC-7, No. 1, Bureau of the Census (April 1, 1951), pp. 6-7.

TABLE XXVIII

SEX RATIO FOR REGIONS, URBAN AND RURAL,
FOR AGES 15-29, 1950*

Region	Urban	Rural Nonfarm	Rural Farm
North East	90.5	116.2	108.6
North Central	93.5	93.4	117.6
South	85.3	99.5	106.4
West	93.3	105.2	124.7

*Source of basic data: *1950 Census of Population, Preliminary Reports, General Characteristics of the Population, by Regions,* Series PC-7, No. 3 (Bureau of the Census, April 1, 1951), pp. 12-13.

ment in cities than in rural areas. Men who migrate, tend to do so at a later age. Some cities, such as Detroit and Gary, Indiana, which have heavy industries, attract an excess of males. In each case, the selectivity seems to be predominantly upon a basis of seeking suitable employment.[27]

In many communities, migration which influences the sex ratio is a two-way process. The sex ratio which is unfavorable to women in the large cities, particularly the South, may be the result of the in-migration of women or the out-migration of men or both.[28] In a similar manner, an imbalance unfavorable to the marriage of men, results when men remain on the farm or migrate to rural areas for work, while the women are at the same time and for similar reasons, migrating to the city.

Unmarried males fourteen years old and over, constituted 34.8 per cent of all males in the 1940 population; this proportion had declined to 26.2 by 1950. Similarly, the proportion of unmarried women changed from 27.6 in 1940, to 19.6 in 1950.[29]

Marital Success and Family Unity. The measure of marital success is not found in mere numbers of people who marry, nor is failure to be gauged by the number of divorces, separations, and desertions. Under contemporary patterns of mate selection, couples may marry without minimum prerequisites for successful marriage. Many of these marriages are failures from the beginning. Divorce represents dissolution of marriage and can be tagged with a number, but not all marital failures reach the divorce court. Marriages may fail, although vows are kept "until death do us part."

[27] Ruth Shonle Cavan, *The American Family* (New York: Thomas Y. Crowell, 1953), pp. 72-77.
[28] *Ibid.*
[29] Source: *Statistical Abstracts of the United States,* 1952, p. 44.

Marriage has been defined as "unity out of diversity,"[30] and the family as "a unity of interacting personalities."[31] The major effort of successful marriage is related to achieving this unity. Couples who enter marriage with diverse interests, values, and backgrounds, may, in spite of this diversity, achieve unity and happiness. Yet some of these differences may persist as areas of tension, frustration and conflict, and hence marriage failure. "Successful marriage," according to Burgess and Locke, is one in which differences are so organized that they contribute to the equilibrium, stability, and harmony of the marital relationship. The unsuccessful marriage is one in which differences upset the equilibrium and make for instability and discord.[32]

Definitions of success or failure in marriage and family life cover a wide range of interactional patterns. Marriage and family life research seeks to identify those factors most clearly associated with marital success or failure. These items tend to fall into two general classifications: (1) premarital items, and (2) postmarital items.

Premarital items are background characteristics which have been found to be associated with marital adjustment. These characteristics may be known to prospective mates prior to their marriage. As many as seventy-five items have been reported by different studies, but some have been verified by several studios. Of these, the following are associated with success in marriage: a high degree of happiness of parents marriage; happiness of childhood; regular attendance at Sunday school a number of years of education.[33]

Postmarital items are conditions present after marriage which are associated with marital adjustment, such as the presence or absence of children, owning or not owning a home, or employment or unemployment. Also included are items which could have existed before the marriage, but are effective after marriage, such as personality traits and desire for children.

The different individual items entering into marital adjustment, have been classified under six basic factors: personality characteristics, cultural backgrounds, social participation, economic status, response patterns, and sex desires.[34]

Locke studied difficulties which placed the greatest strain upon the marital relationship, among happily married and among divorced persons. The items, ranked in order of importance, for the men are: (1) affectional relationships, (2) sex, (3) constant bickering, (4) interference of in-laws, (5) money matters, (6) drunkenness, and (7) no

---

[30] E. W. Burgess and Harvey W. Locke, *The Family* (New York: American Book Company, 1945), pp. 333-335.

[31] *Ibid*, p. 432.

[32] *Ibid*, p. 435.

[33] E. W. Burgess and Harvey J. Locke, *The Family* (New York: American Book Company, 1950), p. 296.

[34] *Ibid*, pp. 406 and 431.

having mutual friends. For the women, the order is (1) affectional relationships, (2) sex, (3) forms of socially disapproved behavior, (4) constant bickering, (5) economic difficulty, and (6) not having mutual friends.[35]

Landis ranked six areas of marital adjustments according to "the time required for adjustment." More time was required for adjustment in sex relations and in spending the family income, than in any other area. About half (52.7 per cent) of the husbands and wives agreed that sex adjustment was satisfactory from the beginning. There was some disagreement between mates (12.3 per cent) concerning the degrees of adjustment, other (22.5 per cent) agreed along a continuum of one month to twenty years of time required for adjustment, and some (12.5) agreed that they never had achieved adjustment. Other areas with the per cent of satisfactory adjustment from the beginning are: spending family income (56.2 per cent), social activities (67.1 per cent), in-law relationships (68.6 per cent), religious activities (74.0 per cent), mutual friends (76.4 per cent).[36]

These studies indicate the trend among family researchers to apply scientific methods for a better understanding of interactional patterns within families. This augurs well for a better understanding of *what makes families strong*, as well as *what makes families weak*.

Disorganization, Disintegration and Disruption of Family Life. Disorganization, disintegration, and disruption imply a prior state of organization and integration. Broadly interpreted, the terms include both the internal and external aspects of marriage and family living. Internal factors involve the interactional unity of family members, and external factors the relations which the family has with the society of which it is a part. Family members sustain membership in, and communication with other social groups, and families function within the framework of the greater society. These are not therefore discrete areas of social conduct. Those factors which significantly disturb the family internally tend to be reflected in both external and internal relationships. The disorganizing effects of tensions, frustrations, and conflict may bring failure in either marital or parental roles, regardless of the origin of causal factors.

Divorce, Desertion, and Death. The three D's, divorce, desertion, and death are the most commonly recognized forms of family disintegration and disruption. To many quarters, divorce and desertion serve as the chief criteria of marriage failure. The thesis here presented is that divorce is merely symbolic of internal conflict, tension, and frustration, which lead to disintegration of the relationship. Widowhood is a form

---

[35] Harvey J. Locke, *Predicting Adjustment in Marriage: A Comparison of A Divorced and A Happily Married Group* (New York: Henry Holt and Company, 1951), pp. 75-76.

[36] Judson T. Landis and Mary G. Landis, *Building A Successful Marriage*, Second Edition, (New York: Prentice Hall, Inc., 1953), p. 259.

of marital disruption which carries no necessary implication of conflict. Desertion is a disruption of family unity that usually implies the presence of conflict similar to that of divorce, although it may be temporary.

1. *Extent and trends in marital dissolution.* Evidence of need for more aggressive and constructive social measures to deal with marriage in trouble, is found in the extent to which divorce, desertion, and death affect marital dissolution. Death, not divorce, ranks highest as a cause of marital dissolution. However, between the early 1890's and 1948, the rate of marital dissolution because of death declined from 30 to about 19 per 1000 married couples.[37] In the meantime, divorce increased from three per 1000 married females to a peak of 17.8 in 1946, and declined to about 11 in 1948.[38] The combined rate of dissolution from death and divorce is somewhat lower than it was about sixty years ago. This, of course, is due to the declining death rate.

Social crises such as war and economic depressions influence divorce trends. During the prosperous 1920's, the divorces reached a peak of 1.7 divorces per 1000 population, and declined to a low of 1.3 for 1932-33. In 1934, the divorce rate began a rise which continued annually through the prewar years of increasing economic prosperity; was accelerated by World War II, and reached a peak in 1946 with a rate of 4.3. A rapid decline from this peak brought the divorce rate back to 2.5 in 1950, slightly above the prewar level.[39]

2. *Causes of divorce.* In seeking the causes of conflict leading to the dissolution of marriage, it is important to remember that a configuration of factors is usually involved; rarely does a causal factor stand alone. The same influences which make for unhappiness and conflict in the marriage *per se,* become basic causes of divorce. Illustrative of these are temperamental incompatability, difference in system of value and conduct, often involving financial, religious, social and sexual matters.

Certain factors of the socio-cultural order are associated with the incidence of divorce, such as the following: (1) it varies with occupations; (2) it is more prevalent among Protestants than among Catholics; (3) the mass of divorces take place in the middle class; (4) it is more frequent in homes where there are no childen; (5) it is more prevalent in urban than in rural areas; (6) divorce rates are high where social change is rapid; (7) it tends to rise with economic prosperity, and to decline during depressions; (8) it tends to rise during war and postwar periods.

---

[37] Metropolitan Life Insurance Company, *Statistical Bulletin,* Postwar Divorce Rates Here and Abroad, Vol. XXX, No. 11, November 1949, p. 2.
[38] Source: *Vital Statistics—Special Reports—National Summaries,* XXXV. No. 2, June 5, 1951, Federal Security Agency, Washington, D. C.
[39] Sources: *Metropolitan Life Insurance Company Bulletin,* Vol. XXXII. No. 6, June 1952.
United States Vital Statistics, Special Reports, Summary of Marriage and Divorce Statistics, 1949, Vol. 36, No. 2 (Federal Security Agency, June 1951), pp. 14, 25, 25.

3. *Effects of divorce.* Evaluation of the effects of divorce must begin with the premise that it is neither *good* nor *bad* in and of itself. Divorce is a social device, designed to achieve equity and expediency by legal dissolution of a marriage that has failed. Like the surgeon's knife, it may kill or cure. When divorce is not judiciously administered, it may serve the opposite ends for which it was designed. In any case, divorce is likely to have mixed values for the different persons involved. If it is used to serve the purposes of equity and expediency, the results should at least be better than the calculated effect of holding a poor marriage together.

It may be more difficult to decide when children are involved. They are often the pawns, and suffer most when the family is dissolved by divorce. But if the marriage is not dissolved, children may be forced to remain helpless victims of parental abuse and conflict. The divorced are faced with the problems of readjustment in terms of changed marital status.

4. *The problem of the widowed increasing.* Despite the declining rate of marriage dissolution by death, widowhood remains a major national problem, especially in urban areas. It is estimated that the actual number of widowed men and women in our country reached an all time high of 9,296,000 in 1951; an increase of 1,500,000 since 1940.[40] Of those who have ever been married, one out of every nine is widowed.

Almost all the increase in widowhood between 1940 and 1951 occurred among women, as may be observed from Fig. 12. There were three times as many widows as widowers in 1951. Widows increased by 24.3 per cent between 1940 and 1951. In the meantime, widowers increased by only 3.4 per cent.

5. *The widowed primarily a problem of urban areas.* The city has a higher proportion of widowed men and women than both rural nonfarm and rural farm areas combined. In 1951, there were an estimated 7,080,000 widows in the United States, 71 per cent of whom resided in urban areas. The total number of widowers was 2,216,000, 64 per cent of whom lived in cities.[41] The widowers constituted only 4.2 per cent of the total male population fifteen years old and over, of cities and rural nonfarm areas and 3.8 per cent of the rural farm areas. The proportion of widows to the total number of women fifteen years old and over reached the high of 13.3 in urban areas, and 8.7 for rural farm areas. This is due largely to the higher death rates of men than of women. The wife's chances of outliving her husband have been increased by the more rapid improvement in mortality among women than men.

[40] Source: *Department of Commerce, Bureau of the Census; Current Population Reports,* Series P-20, Nos. 35 and 38, as revised; *Statistical Abstracts of the United States,* 1952, p. 44.
[41] Source: *Statistical Abstracts of the United States, op. cit.*

Widowhood, at whatever age, may bring problems of social and economic adjustment for both men and women. The problems of adjustment are more difficult for women than for men. Women tend to become widowed earlier in life than men, and they live longer on the average. Furthermore, the chances that a widower will remarry are

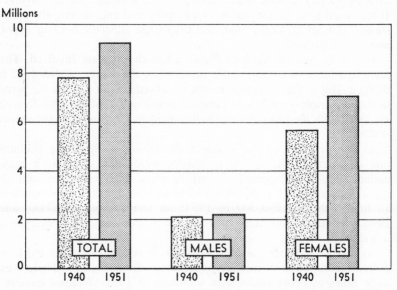

FIGURE 12. Number of Widowed in the United States; by Sex. 1940 and 1951. Source: Metropolitan Life Insurance Company, *Statistical Bulletin*, Vol. 33, No. 2 (August 1952), p. 9.

greater than for a widow. Besides, the opportunities for gainful employment of older women are more limited than for older men.

If there are dependent children associated with widowhood, the social and economic problems are augmented. It is estimated that nearly 400,000 children under eighteen years of age lose either their father or mother. Two-thirds of these children lose their fathers and one-third their mothers.[42] Fortunately, Federal Social Security provides economic assistance to the aged as well as aid to dependent children.

6. *Annulment.* Marriages which do not fulfill certain basic legal requirements, may be *voided* through court action, or annulment. The most common grounds for annulments are nonage, force, fraud, bigamy, impotence, and insanity. Divorce is more important than annulment as a legal means for dissolution of marriages. However, in some states, such

---

[42] Metropolitan Life Insurance Company, *Statistical Bulletin*, Vol. 33, No. 8, August 1952, pp. 9-10.

as New York and California, annulment is extensively used. In 1946, at their peak, the 22,000 annulments constituted 3.5 per cent of the total legal dissolutions of marriage.[43] In California, they constituted one-ninth of all legal dissolution in 1948; almost one-quarter in New York in 1940, and since 1946 almost one-third of the dissolution.[44] Jacobson says that "in at least five counties in New York the number of annulments now exceeds the number of absolute divorces."[45]

7. *Separation and desertion.* The extent of separation and desertion cannot be determined. The majority of those who separate or desert, do so informally and no records are made. The laws of twenty-four states provide for legal separations, but these are recorded with divorces. A legal separation is a partial divorce. Neither party may remarry, nor demand the privilege of living with each other as husband and wife. This is sometimes called, "divorce from bed and board." Desertion has been called "the poor man's divorce," because of its prevalence as a substitute for divorce on the lower economic levels. Such information as is available indicates that separation is a major factor in the disruption of families. A U. S. government survey on a sample basis in 1951, gave an estimated total of 450,000 separated, and 516,000 as "other married, spouse absent;" a total of 966,000. The same survey gave an estimated total of only 542,000 divorced.[46] Of course not all separations are permanent, but we do not know the extent of permanency.

Desertions and separations often involve children, and are more associated with lower economic levels than is divorce. These facts suggest that, as compared to divorce, separations constitute the greater social problem.

8. *Remarriage of the divorced and widowed.* The number of widowed and divorced in the population is reduced by a second or subsequent marriage. Remarriages constituted one-fifth of all marriages in 1950. The proportions were greater for the higher age levels, twenty-five years and over. In 1950, one-fourth of all brides for the ages 25-29, were divorcees. This proportion rose to nearly one-half in the age range of 35-44 years; but dropped to about one-third in the early 50's. The proportion of the grooms previously divorced increased from one-eighth for ages 25-29, to one-half, for those marrying at 40-49 years of age.[47]

[34] Kingsley Davis, "*Statistical Perspective of Marriage and Divorce,*" The Annals of the American Academy of Political and Social Science, Nov. 1950, p. 20.
[44] Paul H. Jacobson, "Marital Dissolution in New York State in Relation to Their Trend in the United States," Millbank Memorial Fund *Quarterly,* Vol. 28 (January 1950), pp. 35-37.
[45] *Ibid.*
[46] *Statistical Abstract of the United States, 1952,* p. 46, No. 47.
[47] Metropolitan Life Insurance Company, *Statistical Bulletin,* Vol. 34, No. 6, June 1953, p. 6.

Remarriage of the widowed increased in relative importance with advancing age levels. This accounted for one-fourth of the brides, ages 40 to 44, one-half at 50 to 54, and more than four-fifths at ages 65 and over.[48] Certain geographic variations are significant in the remarriage proportions. For instance, the proportions of divorcees among women getting married ranged from 8.6 in New York State, to 28.3 in Wyoming.[49] Such wide variations reflect differences in age groups, in attitudes toward divorce by religious groups, as well as the diversity of marriage and divorce laws. Since adultery is the major legal ground for divorce in the State of New York, many New Yorkers resort to the divorce meccas of Nevada and other states, and remarry outside the state. Others find it easier to dissolve their marriages through annulments, which meet with more ready approval of strong religious groups of the area. These factors taken together could account for the lower proportion of divorced among those who married in 1950.

Social Forces and the Family System. The socio-economic conditions associated with urbanization and industrialization were not favorable to the persistence of large self-sufficient families, so characteristic of the early agricultural economy. In the course of time, family structure and functions, customs and traditions changed to meet the demands of the urban environment and the dynamic industrial economy. In general, changes were so rapid and drastic that the term "industrial revolution," so often applied to the phenomenon, seems justified. But the material aspects of culture changed more rapidly than the nonmaterial. The family may not, and at times does not, have the inner resources to enable it to hold itself together, or to restore normal functions when they are weakened or destroyed. Individualistic theories to the contrary, families must, and do, draw upon *social forces* in the time of crisis, or fail. Some fail.

The last two decades have been notably characterized by (1) increasing recognition of the important needs and problems of families, and (2) the development of organized efforts to mobilize social forces for meeting the common family problems. These facts are amply substantiated by the multiplicity of agencies and institutions of both technical and non-technical nature, organized, and functioning to promote family welfare. All the major social institutions, such as the church, schools, and government, have either incorporated special programs in the marriage and family area, or are in process of doing so.

Many of the more recently established agencies have been organized and staffed to deal with special phases of family life problems. Still others deal with the general problems. The following general classifications are indicative of the various approaches to general and special-

[48] *Ibid,* p. 7.
[49] *Ibid,* p. 8.

ized areas of family welfare: (1) general family service, (2) social security for family members, (3) health aids for families, (4) mental hygiene clinics and programs, (5) marriage and family counseling, (6) organized religion, (7) home making skills, (8) better housing, (9) parent education, and (10) youth education.[50]

1. *General family service.* The agencies and institutions which furnish less specialized services for the family, are both public and private. Public welfare departments of city, county, and state governments administer services which touch various phases of family life. Other tax supported services, primarily federal, are aid to dependent children, maternity benefits, G. I. loans, veterans' services, aid to the handicapped, and hospitalization services. The most notable of the private agencies in this field is *The Family Service Agency,* a national organization founded in 1911, which has developed high standards for the rehabilitation of families in need.

2. *Security programs.* Security programs safeguarding the family are numerous. Insurance companies provide annuity plans, family plans, unemployment insurance, group hospitalization, and accident insurance. Some major companies now offer to give guarantees against loss of the regular income. Cooperatives, now touching many phases of the problem of economic security for families, are increasing in membership and volume of business. Many of these are farm cooperatives, but non-farm cooperatives are expanding as well. Some of the services included in the cooperative movement in both urban and rural areas are: cooperative wholesale associations, manufacturing cooperatives, retail cooperatives, cooperative housing, medical and hospital cooperatives, credit unions.[51]

The Federal Social Security Administration has responsibility for three major programs in this area: (1) *Federal Old Age and Survivors Insurance,* (2) *Public Assistance,* and (3) *Maternal and Child Health and Child Welfare.* Under the liberalized eligibility program, 60,000,000 persons were insured by Old Age and Survivors Insurance by the end of 1952. The Public Assistance Program for the aid of the permanently and totally disabled, initiated by the 1950 act, was aiding 633,000 families by the end of the fiscal year 1951. Old Age Assistance payments were going to 2,745,000 needy aged persons. Aid to the Blind payments went to 97,000 persons. General Assistance, which was financed by states and localities without federal funds, was given to 333,000 cases.[52]

---

[50] Modification of general categories used by Evelyn Millis Duvall, "Organization of Social Forces to Promote Family Stability," (New York: *The Annals of the American Academy of Political and Social Science,* Nov., 1950), p. 77.

[51] Florence E. Parker, Bureau of Labor Statistics, "Cooperatives," (New York: *The Americana Annual, 1952),* p. 176.

[52] Arthur J. Allmeyer, Commissioner, Social Security Administration, (New York: *The Americana Annual, 1952),* p. 636.

The Maternal and Child Health and Welfare grants, extended to improve the health and welfare services for mothers and children, totaled $13,200,000 for the year ending June, 1951. The service under this program includes prenatal clinics, child health conferences, school medical examinations, and nutrition, dental, and mental health programs. The number of dependent children in 563,275 families receiving aid to dependent children numbered 1,492,640 in 1953.

The United States Department of Labor administers the federal aspects of the *Unemployment Insurance System* and the *Employment Service*. Under this program, 3,700,000 unemployed workers were paid benefits amounting to $873,000,000. The *Federal Credit Unions* had increased to 5000 in 1950, with assets of $405,835,000.[53]

3. *Health aids.* The long list of health aids for families includes both preventive and curative services, such as: nutrition research, nutrition education, dental care, preventive medicine, therapeutics, prenatal clinics, fertility services, and laboratory services. Public health departments in the past, and generally at present, have confined their services to preventive medicine, but rapid strides have been made in some states in the control of special diseases, such as venereal disease control, and tuberculosis. Extensive case findings and treatment of venereal disease under local, state, and federal sponsorship, may be credited with the phenomenal reduction of the incidence of syphilis and gonorrhea.

In addition, nursery services have been elaborated in various ways such as emergency home nursing, and programs for training homemakers in home care of the sick and convalescent. Various group hospitalization programs, such as Blue Cross, provide protection to family members for hospitalization and surgical services. Included in this area are private associations for promotion of health and treatment of specialized afflictions, such as heart, tuberculosis, cancer, infantile paralysis and cerebral palsy.

Mental hygiene services extended to aid members of the family are: mental hygiene, psychiatric services, child guidance clinics, guidance programs in schools, personnel programs in industry, and personal guidance in schools.

Marriage and family counseling services, of both public and private types, are increasing. The two groups with which marriage counselors are most identified are: the National Committee on Marriage and Family Counseling of the National Council on Family Relations, and the American Association of Marriage Counselors. In addition to professional family life counselors, many other professionals are doing counseling. Among these are teachers of sociology, psychology, home economics, health, and biology and, in the medical profession, gynecologists, obstetricians, psychiatrists and general medical practitioners.

---

[53] *Ibid.*

Counselors are increasing among ministers, lawyers, psychologists, ond social workers.

Organized religion did much in family counseling long before the more professional spread of interest developed. The visiting pastor was often a family counselor upon whom his patrons relied. Of more recent date is the movement for better trained ministers who are prepared to make use of more modern techniques in counseling.

All three major religious faiths, Protestant, Catholic, and Jewish, have specific programs for strengthening marriage and family life. The Federal Council of Christ in America has an active program under the Commission on Marriage and the Home. The Catholic Church has the Cana Conference, which is effective in education and counseling. Jewish leaders have been active in the marriage and family life movement from the beginning. This increased religious interest in marriage and family life is shown by the introduction of training courses for ministers in theological schools, educational programs for youth and adults in local churches, and the dissemination of information on family life through the literature of the church school.

Homemaking departments in high schools and colleges have courses in the arts and skills of homemaking and the interactional phases of marriage and family life.

4. *Housing.* Our country has faced a condition of almost perpetual housing shortage, especially in urban centers. The factors creating this condition are: (1) the increasing population, (2) the increasing marriage rate, (3) the smaller sized families, and (4) the migration of families to urban areas. The ways and means of meeting the housing problem are discussed in another chapter.[54]

5. *Parent education.* The education of parents may serve four chief ends: (1) better understanding of the dynamics of marriage and family in (a) husband and wife roles and in (b) parental roles; (2) to better understand their children and their developmental needs; (3) increase parental resourcefulness for personal growth and satisfaction in marital relations; (4) to increase parental resourcefulness in providing for the growth needs of their children, physical as well as psycho-social.

Adult educational programs for parents are increasingly oriented to marriage and family life content, similar to the content of the college and high school courses which are designed to better prepare youth to assume the responsibilities of husband and wife, father, and mother roles.

A complete list of educational agencies engaged in some kind of work in the field of family life would be prohibitive at this point. A few of these are: American Association of Adult Education, American Home Economic Association, American Social Hygiene Association, Child Study Association of America, Children's Bureau, Family Service

---

[54] See Chapter 15.

Association of America, National Committee on Parent Education, National Congress of Parents and Teachers, National Council on Family Relations, and the Planned Parenthood Association.

Each year, more colleges and universities increase their course offerings to parents through on-campus and off-campus courses. Clinics, workshops, institutes, and special lectures extend family life education from the "ivory towers" of state universities to distant areas of their states. Especially notable among university programs are: (1) Florida State University, with institutes extended to various communities of the state upon invitation; (2) University of California, with six weeks' summer sessions on family life extended to the campuses of other state colleges in the system; (3) Vassar College, pioneering with seminars, institutes, and workshops for parents, teachers, and other professional workers.[55] Pilot projects in parent education were scheduled to start in the evening colleges of five universities, in 1953. Universities scheduled to participate were the University of Washington, (Seattle), Rutgers University, Dallas College of Southern Methodist University, University of Chattanooga, and Ohio State University. This experimental program is under the joint sponsorship of the National Congress of Parents and Teachers, and the Center for Study of Liberal Education for Adults. The Center is a research agency of the Committee on Liberal Education of the Association of University Evening Colleges, an independent agency of the Ford Foundation.[56] Successful parent education for marriage and family life is education at its best for the next generation of parents and their children.

6. *Childhood and youth education.* Education for marriage and family life was first introduced into the educational system at the college level. The early courses dealt with the institutional, historical, and sociological aspects of the family. At a later date, courses of a functional nature were introduced. Ernest R. Groves gave the first course of this type for college credit at Boston University in 1924. More extensive development came after he transferred to the University of North Carolina. The following years brought rapid development of courses designed to prepare young people for marriage. In his study of the nature and content of marriage courses, of colleges and universities for the year 1948-49, Bowman found that 632 colleges and universities of the 1,270 answering his questionnaire, were offering one or more courses dealing principally with education for marriage.[57] According to this study, such courses are popular, but they reach only

---

[55] Ray E. Baber, *Marriage and the Family* (New York: McGraw-Hill, 1953), pp. 660-661.

[56] Marion L. Faegre, "Parent Education," *Marriage and Family Living,* Vol. XV, No. 1; February 1953, p. 8.

[57] Henry A. Bowman, "Marriage Education in Colleges," *Journal of Social Hygiene,* 35: 407-417, December 1949.

an estimated 50,000 students per year, or about one in fifty college students.

In recent years, the demand has increased for marriage and family life education in the elementary grades and in high school. Some of the reasons for this are obvious: (1) only a small percentage of the population goes to college; (2) only a small percentage of college students takes marriage courses; (3) high school is a crucial development period for youth in relation to the opposite sex in general, and to marriage specifically; (4) much of the pertinent information could be given in the years prior to high school, in terms of the needs of the growing child.

If these assertions are valid, any adequate program for marriage and the family life education should begin in the grades and continue through high school and college. Some progress has been made in this direction with an increasing number of high schools throughout the country offering courses in selected phases of the subject. Much more progress has been made on the secondary level of education than on the elementary. However, significant progress is being made, primarily in an experimental way, on the elementary school level.

Summary. The family constitutes a basic social unit in all contemporary cultures. It varies as to its form and functions on an intercultural and subcultural basis. Our European backgrounds furnished the initial elements for American family life. The early pattern of large, self-subsistent institutional families, favorable for the agrarian life, has been drastically changed under the impact of industrialization and urbanization. This change has affected both its form and functions.

As families have become increasingly more urban, they have become less self-sufficient. The urban family is no longer a unit of economic production; rather it is a unit of economic consumption. By comparison, rural farm families remain largely units of economic production, but not of the totally self-subsistent type. The urban families are more dependent, since their source of income is from employment outside the home.

The urban way of life has brought other important modifications in family functions. The size of families has declined, which means that the reproductive function of the family has been subjected to greater control than it was in the agrarian past. Among factors influencing family size are the conditions of urban living, the rising standard of living, increased knowledge of birth control, and changing social values. The protective, educational, recreational, and religious functions have been modified by the more formal aspects shifting to institutions and agencies outside the home. These help families to accomplish the task of training and social conditioning, but do not of necessity relieve the family of responsibility for the less formal, but no less vital responsibilities for these in personal-social relationships of the home. The conditions of modern society make it important that the social and affectional functions of the family be strengthened.

The roles of family members have changed as well as the patterns of authority in the home. Children are no longer economic assets, but they occupy a position second to none in family relationships. This, with the improved status of women, has had important bearing upon the changing patterns of authority in the home. The trend has been from male dominated or patriarchal to equalitarian and democratic control.

Significant marriage trends are indicated in (1) a higher proportion of the population married in all age groups, (2) marriage prospects are better for women in rural than in urban areas, due to the scarcity of men in the city and the excessive number in rural areas, (3) important marriage differentials appear on a regional basis, with the urban South furnishing the poorest prospects for the marriage of women.

New approaches through scientific research give a better understanding of crucial areas of marital adjustment, as well as the factors which make for strength or weakness in families. Continuation of this trend should give a more scientific basis for reconstruction of the family than has existed in the past.

The most commonly recognized forms of family disintegration and disruption are: divorce, desertion, and death. Death, not divorce, ranks highest as a cause of marital dissolution. The combined rate of marital dissolution from divorce and death has declined, due, primarily, to the declining death rate. Divorce rates have increased on the long term basis, while the death rate has declined. On a short term basis, the divorce rate fluctuates. It has taken a downward trend since the peak of 1948.

The problem of the widowed in the population is increasing. Almost all the increase in widowhood for the last decade occurred among women. There were three times as many widows as widowers in 1951. The city has a higher proportion of the widowed than rural nonfarm and rural farm combined. Wives tend to live longer than their husbands, and are less likely to remarry. The economic problems are greater on the average for widows than for widowers. This is especially true if dependent children are involved.

Annulments constitute a significant factor in the dissolution of marriage in some states, especially New York State; but for the country as a whole, it is much less important than divorce.

The extent of separation and desertion cannot be properly evaluated, but available information indicates that they rank close to divorce as a cause of marital dissolution, and are perhaps more important.

The last two decades have been notably characterized by (1) increasing recognition of the important needs and problems of families, (2) the development of organized efforts to mobilize social forces for meeting common family problems. These facts are substantiated by the multiplicity of agencies and institutions, functioning to promote famly welfare. These measures are of both the preventive and correctional or curative types.

WORKSHOP AND PROBLEMS

1. How has urbanization affected the institutional family?
2. In what functions would you say the urban family rates superior and in what function is it weak?
3. Critically evaluate the relationships between theoretical zones and family types.
4. What would you say are the prospects of larger families in urban areas? Give reasons for your answer.
5. What are the more important urban factors related to family size?
6. What are the more significant marriage trends? Indicate those that are distinctly urban.
7. What is the relationship between marital success and family unity?
8. What is being done in urban communities to strengthen family life? Which of these apply in your community?

BIBLIOGRAPHY

Altmeyer, Arthur J., "Social Security" (New York: The Americana Annual, 1952).

Baber, Ray E., Marriage and the Family (New York: McGraw-Hill, 1953).

Bowman, Henry A., "Marriage Education in Colleges," Journal of Social Hygiene, Vol. 35 (December 1949), pp. 407-417.

Bryan, Jack H., "United States Housing and Home Finance Agency," (New York: The Americana Annual, 1952).

Burgess, Ernest W., and Cottrell, L. S., Predicting Success or Failure in Marriage (New York: Prentice Hall, 1939).

——————————————, and Locke, Harvey J., The Family (New York: American Book Company, 1953).

Cavan, Ruth Shonle, The American Family (New York: Thomas Y. Crowell, 1953).

Davis, Kingsley, "Statistical Perspective of Marriage and Divorce," (New York: The Annals of the American Academy of Political and Social Science, November 1950).

Duvall, Evelyn Millis, "Organization of Social Forces to Promote Family Stability" (New York: The Annals of the American Academy of Political and Social Science, November 1950).

Faegre, Marion L., "Parent Education" (Chicago: Marriage and Family Living, February 1953).

Jacobson, Paul H., "Marital Dissolutions in New York State in Relation to Their Trend in the United States," Millbank Memorial Fund Quarterly, January 1950.

Kiser, Clyde V., Group Differences in Urban Fertility (Baltimore: William and Wilkins, 1942).

Landis, Judson T., and Landis, Mary G., Building a Successful Marriage (New York: Prentice Hall, Inc., 1953).

Landis, Paul H., Social Policies in the Making (New York: D. C. Heath and Company, 1952).

——————————————, and Stone, Carol L., "The Relationship of Parental Authority Patterns to Teen-Age Adjustments," Washington Agricultural Experiment Stations Institute of Agricultural Sciences, State College of Washington, Bulletin No. 538, September 1952.

CHAPTER 9

Urban Education

By Lloyd H. Elliott

As early as the eighteenth century the schools in American towns and cities were offering instruction in evening classes for apprentices, employed youth, and other special groups. The private schools of secondary level apparently took the lead in adapting educational offerings to reach more and more people. As the public school was gradually fitted to urban life, it was quite natural that new and untried areas of educational service should be assessed in terms of the greater whole of urban living. Such experimentation, followed by a gradual broadening of the entire base of education, has characterized American efforts in both private and public education since the first meager beginning.

While many of the educational activities continue to be centered about the schools and colleges of a city, efforts to augment regular offerings have reached into practically all areas of living. The school remains the most formidable institution of society for the transmission of culture, but the necessity for coordinating its activities with other private and public groups or agencies is becoming more acute year by year. In fact, there is considerable evidence to suggest that one of the most complex tasks facing school authorities in every city of the country' is that of sorting out the services and responsibilities of an educational nature which other agencies may effectively assume. The coordination of all the various efforts has thus become a mammoth undertaking in large population centers.

Organization for Education. The organizational framework by which the people expected to provide appropriate education in this country was formally started, in 1647, by the issuance of "the old deluder act" by the General Court of Massachusetts. It is worth noting that this early ordinance directed the larger towns (one hundred families or more) to set up a grammar school as well as the "reading and writing" school required of townships with half as many people. This may well have been an omen of things to come in the three centuries which fol-

Note—See the Chapter on rural-urban differentials for educational differentials between rural-urban populations.

lowed since the cities were the scene for many more developments in education.

1. *The city—a school district.* Responsibility for education has, historically, been left to the states. State legislatures have consistently seen fit to delegate this accountability further to local school districts. Even in such a metropolis as New York City, where the annual budget for schools reaches toward 300 million dollars, a city district constitutes the legal framework for education. On the other extreme, districts exist, carrying full responsibility for all the education of young people below college level, which are not large enough to operate even a one-teacher school.

Since state responsibility has more and more been concerned with establishing minimum standards for the entire area while cities have consistently led the advance of educational progress, the relationship of state to city has gradually changed from one of meeting legal technicalities to the more important area of cooperation. In fact much of the worthwhile experimentation has been possible only because of the favorable position enjoyed by some of the city school districts. This observation should not be construed to imply that schools located in larger population centers are all the best quality and that rural schools are all second rate. There has been found, though, a positive relationship between quality and size of school and a fairly definite minimum as to size of student enrollment with regard to economical operation of an adequate program. While there is seldom any difficulty in meeting such minimums among city schools, great obstacles sometimes stand in the way in rural areas. At the same time that greater opportunities have existed in city districts so, too, have greater problems. An example is the great difficulty of keeping the schools close to the people when the size of the operation is alone enough to make enormous machinery necessary.

2. *Boards of education.* Policies regarding schools are now quite generally established by school boards. This represents the gradual change from the "town-meeting" type of policy-making which was characteristic of early education in this country. Perhaps, more importantly, it shows a concentration of educational authority in the hands of a small group of laymen who serve as instruments of the popular will in matters pertaining to schools. The fact that approximately 86 per cent of all board members are elected or appointed on a non-partisan basis is evidence that the people have taken considerable precaution to insure that education does not fall under the control of a political group.[1]

In the past half century school boards have changed considerably in make-up and in manner of action. The trend has been toward boards

---

[1] National Education Association, Research Division "Status and Practices of Boards of Education," *Research Bulletin,* Vol. 24 (April, 1946), pp. 47-83.

with fewer members, elected to represent the city at large, and serving longer terms. As a result of such developments it has been possible for the boards to give more continuity to the educational program and to devote less time to administrative details. As specialized services became more readily available to the schools, administrative and supervisory staffs were given many of the responsibilities previously performed by members and committees of the board.

Since the educational institution is one of the biggest management enterprises in each community, both urban and rural, and especially vast and complex in the large cities, school boards are becoming increasingly convinced that their greatest single task is that of selecting a competent administrator. This officer, now called the superintendent of schools, is the chief executive to whom the board hands the responsibility for carrying out its policies. In stating the solution desired by the superintendents themselves, the most important professional organization of that group recently used the analysis made by the President's Committee on Administrative Management:[2]

> Fortunately, the foundations of effective management in public affairs, no less than in private, are well known. They have emerged universally wherever men have worked together for some common purpose, whether through the state, the church, the private association, or the commercial enterprise. They have been written into constitutions, charters, and articles of incorporation, and exist as habits of work in the daily life of all organized peoples. Stated in simple terms these canons of efficiency require the establishment of a responsible and effective chief executive as the center of energy, direction, and administrative management; the systematic organization of all activities in the hands of a qualified personnel under the direction of the chief executive; and to aid him in this, the establishment of appropriate managerial and staff agencies. There must also be provision for planning, a complete fiscal system, and means for holding the executive accountable for his program.

3. *Superintendent of schools.* The professional head of a city school system is now one of the most important officials in the whole community. Subject to pressures from every individual and all kinds of groups, this office is located in the path of nearly all major developments in the city. The person who serves as superintendent is, by virtue of the office, in a position of community leadership as well as educational guidance. The school board which has appointed him must look immediately to his expertness for interpretation, advice, and direction. As an individual leader, he is expected to give guidance to broad

---

[2] American Association of School Administrators, *The American School Superintendency, Thirtieth Yearbook* (Washington, D. C.; National Education Association, 1952), p. 112.

community problems, as well as to be sensitive to the various needs for educational service.

After a century of experimentation with "clerk," "manager," "visitor," "acting visitor," "agent," inspector," and other related titles, the city superintendent of schools has now been charged with creative and socially intelligent leadership. While this official has been earning such high status through the years, the problems imposed have likewise grown. One group brought his difficulties into focus, and incidentally the plight of education, as follows:[3]

> The opening of the turbulent second half of the twentieth century finds the superintendent of schools . . . spotlighted from all directions. He and his board of education are sometimes caught squarely between the lessened buying power of the school dollar on the one hand and organized taxpayer resistance to higher budgets on the other. High current birth rates mean more children to be served by more teachers in more school rooms.

Like many other offices and positions in our society, that of superintendent of schools in a large city has grown beyond the scope of one person. Even with liberal staff allowances it has become a job with such responsibility and opportunity that no one person can hope to carry it. In such circumstances the one man who fills the office in each city can only work toward fulfilling his responsibility within his own human limitations.

4. *Teaching staff.* City schools have consistently attracted the better qualified teachers of the country, and, even in the days of a serious shortage of teachers, urban centers have been the last to feel this pinch. The normal path of advancement for public school teachers has been from training institution to rural area, from rural school to village, and from town or village to city. Most urban centers draw steadily on the schools in surrounding towns and villages for replacements and new appointments. Such a policy has tended to bring experienced teachers to the cities and to increase the rate of turnover of staff in other schools.

A number of factors have quite naturally contributed to this situation. Better salaries and more advanced personnel policies are basic attractions of most city school systems. Teachers are interested in the additional cultural attractions of the cities in contrast to the limited activities of many small places, as well as the opportunities for further education which are available in most urban areas. Another very real inducement which many city schools hold out to other teachers is the opportunity for more highly specialized service to pupils. For the most serious, conscientious teacher, it is important that he have help from various experts in problems of child or parent behavior which he has

---

[3] *Ibid.*, pp. 60–62.

neither time nor training to handle. Such additional specialized help is often lacking in rural areas.

Some of the advantages now enjoyed by city schools are in some danger of slipping away because of the problems confronting the whole of education. People in rural areas have recognized that they must provide salaries and working conditions for teachers comparable to those of the cities if they are to have schools open at all. Improvements in transportation now make it possible for teachers, as well as many others, to enjoy the advantages of living in the open country, working in an attractive consolidated or village school, and still have the city within reach as desired. The surburban movement is another development, the long-range effect of which is not yet fully known.

The increased birth rate since World War II, plus the teacher shortage, holds out the danger of larger classes for all schools. It may be a pressure harder to resist in the cities, though, than in other areas. After all, the children are already on the doorsteps in immense numbers, space for new buildings is available only at great expense, and local tax burdens continue to increase. Whether city schools can continue to attract the best teachers during this trying period, and retain classes at a desirable size, remains to be seen.

A certain degree of stability is desirable among teaching personnel but, under normal circumstances, staffs in large cities are apt to lack the balance of well-distributed age groups. Another potential difficulty that must be guarded against is the inbreeding of the total staff since most large cities will probably have local citizens who are technically qualified to fill every specialized position in the school system. By exercising care in avoiding these and related dangers, city schools can probably be managed so as to maintain their advantages as far as teaching staff is concerned.

5. *Pupil personnel.* As social scientists have long pointed out, an important factor in a person's life is where he is born. As far as education influences his life, it might be appropriate to ask, what are the opportunities for schooling which are within reach because of where one lives? The chance for greater variety of educational offerings is not the only influence between heavily and sparsely populated areas, but the number of years of basic schooling completed is also influenced by place of residence. Reports of the Bureau of the Census have consistently shown illiteracy to be less in urban areas than in rural, and the median years of schooling completed by the adult residents have likewise favored the city. Of more significance, especially in recent years, has been the research on holding power. One such study[4] is typical of the many because it reveals clearly that the larger high

---

[4] Federal Security Agency, Office of Education, *Holding Power and Size of High Schools* (Washington: U. S. Government Printing Office, 1950), Circular No. 322.

schools hold pupils longer than the small ones. Among other things, economic status and pupil-interest are important factors in relation to a youngster's achievement and advancement. Better enforcement of compulsory attendance laws, and more attention to the needy by various welfare agencies seem to contribute more significantly to school attendance in the city than in the rural areas.

Numerous investigations of recent decades have also contributed significantly to the knowledge of individual differences among boys and girls. Variations in mental and physical capacity, rate of growth in both areas, dominant and driving interest, aptitude, achievement, social development, and emotional stability have all been identified as fundamental factors in the overall educational guidance of a pupil. It is the providing for such differences in the most desirable way that has come to be recognized as the basic problem of effective teaching in today's schools.

It is correct to expect that all schools will have pupils from among the full range of variation insofar as the enrollment of each compares to an adequate sample of the entire pupil population. Provision for the extreme deviates is the difficulty which city schools have made far more progress toward solving than have rural schools. Since these deviates, whether they be emotionally disturbed or mentally superior, are to be found in the city in sufficient numbers to arouse the interest and attention of several persons, they are cared for more adequately. Such children may still be hidden or just ignored more easily when they live in less populated areas. An example which should suffice to point up the differences in opportunity is that of the crippled child. It is estimated that about one in 400 is badly enough crippled to need a special program of education. Such programs are practically non-existent in rural schools, yet outstanding work is being done in several city systems. It does matter, educationally, where a child lives.

6. *Curriculum.* The complete sweep of school-directed experiences which a youngster undergoes is now accepted as a workable definition of curriculum. A look at the total program of many city schools will show great differences from that of a similar view of a rural school.

In bringing the experiences of formal education to the pupil, it has long been accepted that the demands and needs of people form the basic criteria of selection. Keeping abreast of such needs, both individual and group, is a task of great challenge and one that requires much energy and attention from all educational workers. In our changing society this phase of planning is particularly important. Effective specialization by the staff of a school system is necessary. City school districts have been the most effective in meeting this problem. Curriculum specialists, research workers, and pupil personnel experts, working on closely coordinated projects, have been able to make the most significant contributions. With few exceptions such highly trained persons are available only to city schools.

Having recognized the great variations which are to be found among learners, it is easy to accept the principle that a broad, rich, yet flexible curriculum is the only answer to such educational needs. The example of good art and good music is often mentioned as one of the areas of significant difference between the city and rural community; but the real differences, as far as learning is concerned, reach even deeper. The first-grade child who can visit a fire station or listen to the local policeman talk about safety will be greatly motivated in his reading of stories which are centered on similar activities. The airport, railway station, and bus terminal are common observations of city children, and such knowledge adds significantly to the experimental background of pupils—so essential to success in the tasks of the formal school.

In many other areas where the rural setting might actually hold some natural advantage, a shortage of trained personnel often prevents the pupils from realizing the benefits. A field trip to study natural phenomena is an example. While rich experiences in the natural sciences are within reach of every rural school, such basic knowledge that may be gained and such incentives to further learning as may be realized are often missed entirely because the teacher lacks the time, training or imagination. On the other hand, a study of the health facilities of the community may have to be quite unreal in the rural area since medical personnel may be sparsely distributed and hospitals or public health offices completely beyond the first-hand knowledge of children. In contrast the city contains these resources and facilities in such readiness that a little planning can bring reality to such study. The advantages for community projects in such situations may be easily recognized.

While it may be said that the earlier years of formal schooling present a more common pattern from one community to another than the upper years, some of the possible advantages for enriching the curriculum in city schools over those in rural areas, even in the early grades, have been suggested. Even more noticeable are the differences which have grown up between city and rural schools at the junior and senior high school level.

Plans, dreams and aspirations for the pattern of one's life are important to the adolescent. Plans for a vocation, problems of growth and development, and challenges of adult life are all converging to make the teen-ager's educational needs more varied and more complex. Cities have been able to provide special vocational and technical schools and courses of study to answer the needs of some; work experience in conjunction with regular classwork has helped to fit others more adequately for adult activities, and specialized curriculums have been adapted in many other areas. While the small schools may be able to present an equally strong basic program at the secondary level of the common education for general citizenship in our society, they fall short in providing specialized training in the fields where such offerings often serve as the stimulation for further study in the general fields as well. The disagreement between educators over "general" and "specialized" courses and programs at the high school level has not been settled yet, but enough evidence has been accumulated to show that one strengthens the other. To the pupil the vocational course often serves as the vehicle to point up the need for further study in the general areas. City schools have thus been able to capitalize on pupil interests and abilities to a greater degree.

Another development of significance in city schools has been the establishment of libraries and depositories for teaching aids. Many cities now provide a large selection of films, slides, maps, and models for use by teachers on a circulating plan which is difficult to duplicate in less populated areas. Such central exchanges serve also as laboratories where teachers and supervisors, as individuals and committees, prepare units of work, courses of study and various guides to learning which other teachers in the system may adapt for their own use. All such resources contribute to the depth and breadth of the pupil's experiences when used appropriately in the classroom.

7. *Community participation.* Laymen have long participated in the educational affairs of the city through the ballot box. In selecting board members, approving operational expenditures, and voting on bond issues the lay public continues to control education in a very real sense. Groups and individuals use the newspapers, radio and telephone to make their wishes known to teachers and other school authorities as well as the personal visit. Some cities have conducted more systematic studies of public feeling regarding schools through opinion surveys, polls, and checklists.

While the parent-teacher association has been recognized for many years as the official organ of broad school-community cooperation, its effectiveness varies considerably from one community to another. With more than two million members this is a potentially powerful force for educational progress in every community. The national by-laws contain the aims of the organization, expressed as follows:

> First, to promote child welfare in home, school, church, and community; to raise the standards of home life; to secure more adequate laws for the care and protection of children.
> Second, to bring into relation the home and the school, that parents and teachers may cooperate intelligently in the training of the child; and to develop between educators and the general public such united efforts as will secure for every child the highest advantages in physical, mental, moral, and spiritual education.

Other semi-official bodies have been growing in recent years to supplement the work of others in securing greater public participation in school affairs. Known by different labels, they are developing as

"Committees of Citizens" with the work being coordinated at the national level by the National Citizens Commission for the Public Schools. Most of the activity of these groups has been centered in the cities and suburban areas, and the national organization has been very effective in bringing the problems of a growing pupil population and a shortage of teachers to the country's attention. These committees have sponsored broadcasts, telecasts, community surveys, forums, and other activities to stimulate interest in public school problems. Six regional offices of the National Commission are now located in Boston, Sacramento, Dallas, Louisville, Minneapolis, and Denver, with the headquarters in New York City.

One of the unique aspects of the work being carried on by this national group is the defense which it gives the schools against irresponsible attacks. While perhaps difficult to establish, it is probably safe to say that this is one of the first lay groups to take responsibility for informing the people of the country about their schools, and, at the same time, assuming defense of the schools against the efforts of selfish and bigoted groups who would destroy them.

The principles of action outlined by the New York State Citizens Committee are suggestive of the framework of these groups:[5]

(1) Be representative of the whole community.

(2) Keep well informed—the process of gathering, digesting and passing on information is all important.

(3) Earn the confidence of the community through tangible achievement and services.

(4) Strengthen the work of the parent-teacher and other school-minded groups through teamwork, close liaison, and not by duplicating efforts.

(5) Work cooperatively with school boards and school superintendents, but maintain independence of thought and action.

Perhaps one key to the success which these groups have thus far achieved is to be found in the stated desire to avoid duplication of the work of other groups, and, instead, to coordinate all the efforts of various individuals and organizations.

Problem Areas in Urban Education. In spite of the problems implicitly referred to already, it seems appropriate to examine a few of the basic ones at more length.

1. *Jurisdiction.* While the state has been accepted as the unit of government basically responsible for public education, there still exists a large area of undefined relationship between some states and some cities. The board of education, historically established as an extension of the state, is subject to a number of additional restrictions in some urban localities. Most frequently such difficulties are centered in

---

[5] As reported by Benjamin Fine, *New York Times,* July 12, 1953, p. E9.

the authority of local units of government over the financial transactions of the schools.

Since city school systems are operated by fiscally dependent boards, and by fiscally independent ones as well, a long-standing debate has emerged regarding the relative merits of one over the other. Educators and laymen have generally argued for the separation of school budgets from municipal authority, while authorities in public administration and political science have usually held the opposite view. Court decisions have favored the fiscally independent belief, but the research studies have failed to show conclusive evidence on one side or the other.

Obviously, this is neither the place to present evidence on one side nor to review the dispute. It should suffice here to point out the necessity for clarifying the problems of jurisdiction in each city in order that such difficulties may be brought within manageable bounds. Some of the present wrangling among mayors, city councils, and boards of education might be averted if the variations and degrees of financial authority were more clearly understood.

2. *Finances.* In addition to the problems resulting from certain municipal controls over educational funds, schools in some cities have been further restricted by state laws regulating tax rates, limiting bonded indebtedness, and prescribing the ways in which money may be spent. While the whole structure is but the system of checks and balances of a democratic government as applied to schools, in recent years of high costs they have often operated to obstruct educational advancement. Such controls, usually provided in terms of ceilings on tax rates or percentage of assessed evaluation for borrowing purposes, are either in the statutes of the various states or written into the constitutions in such fashion as to be cumbersome for meeting emergencies.

As the whole system of financing public education in the country has undergone changes in recent years, at least one trend remains a question for some cities. This aspect concerns the shift toward state and an increase in state funds for education, with local funds decreasing proportionately in payment of the total cost. The change became apparent when economists and other taxation experts began pointing to the excessive burden which real estate was carrying in the total tax structure. As taxes of the income, sales, inheritance, license, payroll, and other varieties mounted in volume, local school boards turned to the state level of authority for more aid. This trend may well return all questions of jurisdiction back to the state level in due time, but questions of source, distribution and control relative to school finance are still quite jumbled in many cities.

3. *Private schools.* The freedom of the parent to choose the kind of educational program he desires for his children has given rise to a non-

public school system in the United States which enrolls more than 10 per cent of the total elementary and secondary population. Without a doubt the recent Supreme Court decision on segregation in public education is likely to increase the demand for private schools in many communities.

Since most groups large enough to support private schools are found only in urban areas, these institutions are found in greatest numbers within easy reach of the large cities. As rather large numbers of various groups have built their own schools, some cities are found in which dual systems of education are competing for the interest and support of the total public. The situation is further complicated in those cities where the public schools are provided separately for Negroes and whites. In this latter case there are actually three school programs, with some duplication of facilities or overlapping of services, bidding for support from the same sources.

Obviously, the private school must remain a vehicle for individual freedom of choice, but its place must not jeopardize the public school on which the country has long depended for an informed citizenry. In the face of unusual costs in recent years the public schools in some cities have been endangered by the divided loyalties created through the appeals of dual systems of education.

4. *Home-school relations.* Considerable organizational machinery is required in order that adequate home contacts may be maintained in the large school. Quite often parents feel that the large school is impersonal, that teachers are strangers, and that day to day coordination between home and class is completely out of reach. While such feelings may often be unfounded, since they do exist to a greater degree than in the small neighborhood school, such impressions must be recognized.

The city schools have serious competition for the attention of the parents. More compelling pressures are present than in rural areas— pressures that interfere with pupil study as well as parent interest. Perhaps the key to this problem in urban education is to be found in the difficulty of getting "functional" learning into the setting. Pupil experiences at home and in the community, which might be used to inspire further school work, are often lost in the irritation and quickened pace of city life. The teacher, himself, is often lost in the bigness which surrounds pupils and parents. In all of this complexity teacher-parent co-operation becomes more difficult.

5. *Free public education.* At least two problems of pupil costs still remain for urban schools. One is the perplexing riddle of trying to bring under control the social position which money buys for even young pupils, and the other is the undefined boundaries of schooling which our society will provide at public expense.

Social and even academic status which economic level brings to the elementary or secondary pupil has been clearly established by many researches. Pressure for acceptable clothes, spending money and attendance at admission-type functions are very important factors in the degree to which a school is actually "free" to its pupils. Findings have shown that children change courses, lose interest and sometimes quit school because of such economic pressures. The city school, often located so as to serve a great cross-section of the public, is particularly vulnerable to the ill effects of social tensions thus aroused.

In extending the boundaries of public education the city has historically set the pace. Kindergarten and collegiate levels developed as parts of the public school system in the great population centers, and now the nursery school is gaining momentum mainly as a result of the experience gained in the cities. It will probably be a commonly accepted part of the free public school in another decade. Technical institutes, community colleges, and other provisions for post-high-school education are being accepted also as parts of the tax-supported system of cities.

Such extensions of public education are the natural outgrowth of the efforts of a free people to retain and strengthen that freedom. The problems attached to such developments have not yet been resolved satisfactorily. They present additional challenges to the ordering and enriching of urban life in the years ahead.

Education, as centered in the urban areas of America, is a vital part of human behavior in that environment. At this particular time in history there is no world-shaking decision pending within the framework of the city's schools. Its strength and progress are so bound up with the total welfare of the urban community that such cannot be separated. The important problems that do exist and that pertain significantly to schools will have to be resolved by the broader society within which the education takes place. This does not ignore the difficulties that are now upon the city schools but, instead, places them in their proper setting. Neither does this minimize the problems but, rather, it is hoped, places responsibility for their solution where it must be borne.

Viewed in retrospect, city schools have pointed the way for educational advance; looking ahead, the prospect is for continued leadership. As such schools change in scope and service, they reflect the changing nature of the basic values and resources of the people. Schools serve as gauges of societal beliefs and attitudes as faithfully as barometers reveal air pressure, and city schools further serve as pilots for the country's total educational efforts. To observe and to study society through the avenue of education is to use one of the most rewarding vantage points.

WORKSHOP AND PROBLEMS

1. In what phases of education did the early towns and cities take initiative?

2. What was the "old deluder act"?

3. In what respect is the city unit a school district?

4. What are the major functions of city boards of education?

5. What are the major functions of the city superintendent of schools?

6. What advantages does the city offer teaching staffs? What possible disadvantages do you visualize?

7. What has been done to bring about better adaptation of urban schools to student needs?

8. What is being done to bridge the gap between urban schools and the communities they serve?

9. What are some of the current major problems in urban education?

10. Bring a city superintendent of schools into the classroom to discuss his problems.

11. What responses are likely to be made by city schools in segregated systems to the recent U. S. Supreme Court decision on segregation?

BIBLIOGRAPHY

American Association of School Administrators, *American School Curriculum, Thirty-first Yearbook* (Washington: National Education Association, 1953).

————————, *The American School Superintendency, Thirtieth Yearbook* (Washington: National Education Association, 1952).

Bedford, Scott E. W., *Readings in Urban Sociology* (New York: D. Appleton Century and Company, 1927).

Bogue, Jesse Parker, *The Community College* (New York: McGraw-Hill, 1950).

Douglass, Harl R., and Grieder, Calvin, *American Public Education* (New York: Ronald Press, 1948).

Eby, Frederick and Arrowood, Charles Flinn, *The Development of Modern Education* (New York: Prentice-Hall, Inc., 1937).

Federal Security Agency, Office of Education, *100 Evening Schools*, Bulletin No. 4, 1949.

————————, *Education for A Long and Useful Life*, Bulletin No. 6, 1950.

————————, *Extra-class Activities for All Pupils*, Bulletin No. 4, 1950.

————————, *Holding Power and Size of High Schools*, Circular No. 322, 1950.

————————, *Identifying Educational Needs of Adults*, Circular No. 330, 1951.

————————, *Where Children Live Affects Curriculum*, Bulletin No. 7, 1950.

Johns, R. L., and Morphet, E. L., *Problems and Issues in Public School Finance* (New York: National Conference of Professors of Educational Administration, 1952).

National Education Association, Research Division, "Status and Practices of Boards of Education," *Research Bulletin*, Vol. 24 (April, 1946), pp. 47-83.

Otto, Henry J., *Principles of Elementary Education* (New York: Rinehart and Company, 1949).

Pfeiffner, John M., *Public Administration* (New York: Ronald Press, 1946).

CHAPTER 10

The Urban Religions

By RUSSELL R. DYNES

Poets have written of the city as the corrupter of man and the de-
moralizer of women. Popular writers have described our "cities of sin"
and the "shame of our cities." Journalists have written about the ab-
normality of the city, and theologians have pleaded the case of moral
man in an immoral society. Social scientists have constructed neat
formulas which state that any increase in urbanization is accompanied
by a corresponding upswing in disorganization and secularization. As
the insect that goes crashing to its death against the lighted window,
the bright lights of the city are pictured as the lure which leads man
to his ultimate destruction. Many reformers have envisaged Utopias,
most of which have a rural setting as a major ingredient. Here in
rural, idyllic simplicity, man could realize the fullest of his capabilities.
From this conception of the modern city, the religious man is a deserted
soul in a secular wilderness. Religion is a lost art for the city dweller,
lost in the forest of machines and skyscrapers. In this view, religion
is to be relegated only to a place in history; its loss today is to be re-
gretted, but its influence not to be regained.

The student may agree that while this is the prevailing conception of
the role of religion in urban life, this picture is not entirely accurate.
Does man change so much in his urban existence? Are urbanism and
religiosity opposites, as many imply? One might pause and think of the
central place that Mecca, Rome, Geneva, Wittenberg and Jerusalem
have played in religious history. In its inception, Christianity appealed
to the little man in the urban communities, while the ruralite was the
pagan. Today, prominent religious leaders and actionists find their
initial and largest audiences in urban centers. Architecturally impressive
churches are as much a part of the city landscape as machines and traffic.
Urban congregations are larger and urban ministers better trained and
better paid than their rural counterparts. More church members are
found in urban areas in proportion to the population than in rural
areas. The city is certainly not without religious expression.

Why, then, this paradox. The city is pictured as a "den of iniquity"
—the antithesis of religion—and yet, historically and currently, it has

played an important part in the religious life of man. What historical factors aid in the understanding of urban religion? What religious groups are found in the city? What are the functions of religion in the complexity of urban society? What is the influence of religion in the city? How does religious organization affect the rest of the social structure of the city? Since both urban living and religious expression seem to be indispensable ingredients of man's future, some understanding of their interrelationship is necessary. This is our task.

Historical Factors in Urban Religion. Understanding the urban adaptation of religion in America requires some knowledge of its historical antecedents. One can view religion as a part of the historical tradition, and an integral part of Western culture is the Judeo-Christian tradition. The motivation of many of the early colonists coming from this tradition to America was religious freedom, and they sought refuge across the ocean because of their unfortunate relationships with the state and the accepted or established church. Since there were these previous difficulties, religion in America was to rest on its own merits and there would be a separation of church and state. This provided fertile ground for the development of congregationalism which meant that local groups would direct their own religious fortunes and would not be subjected to a higher ecclesiastical or secular authority. This feature has given rise to the multiplicity of religious groups which Protestantism experiences today. Any minor disagreement in doctrine, dogma and practice may become a valid reason for separation from the main religious body and the establishment of a new sect to express the only "true" way.

Most of the initial colonizers in the United States were Protestants. Their doctrines of freedom, of grace, and of individual salvation fitted well with the values of individualism and frontier democracy. Protestantism followed the expanding frontier, not as an established church but as a manifestation of religious experience. Revivalism provided satisfactions for emotional starvations and recurrent frustrations of the frontier. The frontier minister shared the same set of experiences as his religious adherents. He felt the same religious feelings in the same way and he was not set apart by ecclesiastical garb or theological education. Converts were made and congregations were formed, bound by locality. In some cases, local groups were loosely bound to the larger denomination by circuit riders, which gave them continuity without authority. Protestantism made its greatest triumphs in rural areas and, because of its priority and flexibility, it provided a channel for religious expression to many groups who faced common problems along the expanding frontier of the new country.

America did not stay in the wilderness. Cities were growing and rural Protestants gave it nourishment. These migrants came to new experiences and to find many who did not share their religious heritage. Other immigrants were piling into the city who came from over the world and brought with them their different faiths as a part of their cultural tradition. Even today, Catholicism manifests many characteristics of the various national origins of its parishioners and it has provided a tie with the old for those who were bridging the chasm of two cultures. The Catholic Church gave organizational efficiency to its urban parishioners without exhausting its energies on sparsely populated rural parishes. Even more often to the cities came the Jews. Suffering in nations without the ethic of religious toleration, many Jews sought refuge here in anticipation of a truly democratic society. Without the ecclesiastical organization of the Catholic Church, Judaism still made an excellent urban adaptation. Depending more on a similarity of practice rather than a uniformity of ideas, they accomplished this orthopraxy

TABLE XXIX

PERCENTAGE DISTRIBUTION OF SELECTED RELIGIOUS GROUPS BY AREAS (N-12,421)

Religious Group	Farm	Under 2,500	2,500 to 10,000	10,000 to 100,000	100,000 to 500,000	500,000 and Over
Entire sample	16	9	20	21	14	20
Roman Catholic	9	6	14	25	18	28
Jewish	1	0	4	9	9	77
Methodist	23	13	25	19	10	10
Baptist	22	10	23	19	15	11
Presbyterian	16	8	26	21	13	16
Lutheran	25	9	20	20	11	15
Episcopal	8	10	20	23	19	20
Congregational	19	10	23	32	7	9
Christian Science	12	5	17	18	22	26

Source: *Information Service*, National Council of Churches of Christ in the United States of America, Vol. XXVII, No. 20, Part 2, Table V.

through the internalization of religious norms channeled by the family group. For the Jew, religion was life and life was religion—not a ritualistic activity accomplished in a short period of time on one day a week.

Urban Religious Groups. As might be inferred from the previous discussion of historical factors, the non-Protestant groups have their greatest strength in the city. For example, Table XXIX shows that 99 per cent of Jews live in the areas over 2,500 which the Census designates as urban. In addition, 77 per cent of Jews live in the large cities of the country, those over 500,000. Catholicism also has its stronghold in the cities as 75 per cent of the membership live in urban areas. There is considerable variation within Protestantism, but most of the older established denominations have large rural memberships. New groups, as the Christian Scientist Church, are overly represented in the city. Many new denominations which have developed within the tradition of

Protestantism, have had their origin and have found their support in the city. The Salvation Army churches are almost entirely urban and the Church of the Nazarene, some of the Assemblies of God, and other Pentecostal churches have arisen and flourished in the city. The broad contrasts show that the older established Protestant denominations either have more membership in rural areas or tend to approximate the distribution of population of the country as to residence. The non-Protestant and the new Protestant groups tend to be concentrated in the city. Generally, as the size of the community increases, the proportion of Protestants to non-Protestant groups decreases.

Some interesting contrasts between rural and urban religion were shown by the 1936 *Census of Religious Bodies.* Urban churches tend to have larger memberships than rural churches, and the size of the church tends to rise with the size of the city. In New York, Chicago, etc., the average size of the church was over 1,000 members, while in Kansas City, Louisville, etc., the average size was over 600 members. Larger churches, of course, require larger budgets. Urban ministers are better trained and better paid than rural ministers. Proportionately, more urban adults are church members than rural adults; however, many farm families may hold membership in the city. Since today the differences between rural and urban are merging, these contrasts between religious groups would certainly not be as great as they were in 1936.

The Function of Religion in Urban Society. Religion in urban society has many functions. It satisfies certain needs for both the individual and the society. Its groups may provide a network of social relationships to sustain the individual. It can provide common ties for groups in the city who have little else in common, and it may promote solidarity despite the mobility of the metropolis. It often encourages the internalization of social norms which are effective even in the impersonality of the city, and it has provided ethical norms which are aften essential to the survival of the community. Obviously, none of these can be adequately analyzed in a few paragraphs. One specialized aspect of the many functions of religion in the city can be considered here. For our specific purposes, religion may be defined as the *beliefs, practices and organizations which arise in response to uncertainties and frustrations which exist in any society.* It provides meaning, purpose and explanation to the complexities of social life.

A comparison of the function of religion in rural and urban areas shows both similarities and differences. The actual differences in these two polar types—rural and urban—are not as great as the following illustrative contrasts imply. The discrepancy between expectations and realizations in any society is an inherent source of strain. In rural areas there was, and perhaps still is, a closer relationship between what one did and what one was rewarded for. "Early to bed and early to rise" made sense in a rural economy, because one could see the value of this activity reflected in results. Of course, there were strains. Months of activity could be cruelly destroyed by the caprice of the weather, but your neighbors shared the same fate. Any stroke of ill fortune—as a barn burning—could be rectified by collective action, and the recipient of such aid would repay by helping others. The farmer could follow his work with satisfaction as he could see the relationship between planting and harvesting, growing and consuming—the total cycle of the farm economy. The farm family was the process, not an atomistic part, of a gigantic scheme of mass production.

These factors are reflected in differences in personal satisfaction between urban and rural areas. A recent study related certain factors with an index of urbanism.[1] It was found, interestingly enough, that satisfaction with job and residence was not related to urban but to rural living. In other words, the ruralite felt satisfied with his occupational fate; he sees, and we are going past the evidence here, a closer relationship with what he does and the results and rewards. Satisfaction, however, is always relative and it may be doubtful that rural living is any more inherently satisfying than life in the city. The ruralite is comparing himself to those around him and they, too, share his fate. While the ruralite is satisfied with his "poverty" of alternates, the urban dweller can make constant unfavorable comparisons. His life-chances might be objectively better than his rural equivalent but he has a more differentiated community in which to be dissatisfied. Achievements are fleeting and no matter how well the urbanite does in the race of life, there are others ahead of him. Others he can see and hear about. Others who have no more ability and who still pace him. These factors present sources of tension. In any case, the urbanite is subject to, or at least conscious of, more points of stress and strain.

What has all this to do with religion? Many have noted the relation between a dependence on religion and crisis and stress situations. The assumed turn to religion during wartime and the cliché that "There are no atheists in foxholes," point to this assumption. While these clichés are no doubt oversimplifications, there is some empirical verification of this relationship. In studying the motivations of ground troops in World War II, it was found that infantrymen said that they were helped by prayer.[2] While these answers were obtained by a checklist and prayer is a socially approved answer, the only other factor that approximated prayer as a motivation was "fear of letting their buddies down." Those individuals who said that they had been helped by prayer appeared on the average to have experienced greater strain—infantrymen as opposed to men in other branches, men who had seen their close buddies

[1] Stuart Queen and David Carpenter, *The American City* (New York: McGraw-Hill Book Co., 1953), pp. 28-38.
[2] Samuel Stouffer, et. al., *The American Soldier: Combat and Its Aftermath* (Princeton: Princeton University Press, 1949, Chap. 3.

killed, men who had taken air or artillery attacks from their own side. Other factors are involved, of course, in stress situations in addition to a reliance on prayer, as humor, magic, and pure fatalism, which all play a part. While the individual soldier might reject many of these alternatives in less stressful situations, the attitude seemed to be to use any and all pathways. While these complicating factors need systematic study, the fact remains that combat maximizes frustration and uncertainty, and a frequent adjustment technique in facing this situation was a reliance on prayer. We are not likening life experiences in the city to that of combat, although some rural idealizers would like this analogy. But if the urbanite is subjected to, or conscious of, points of stress and strain, and a usual response to this stress is a reliance on forms of religious adjustment, then the city should be a haven for religion. The city should teem with religious activity—the center of the search for meaning amidst the perplexities of modern life.

Why, then, is this searching not expressed in fervent religious activity? Simply, *organized religion in the city has many competitors.* In the early American rural communities, most people were very much alike as they had very similar occupation and economic interests, similar tastes, similar racial, nationality and religious backgrounds. In the urban community this similarity is lost and diversity is the theme. Any difference can become the basis for some new group. Organized religion, of course, has implicitly and explicitly taken cognizance of this differentiation. Protestantism, with its heritage of self determination, is divided into denominations, and more specifically churches within denominations, that serve specific socio-economic interests. Judaism also follows this pattern of elaboration. In Catholicism, parish lines follow the social differences of the parishioners. Within the program of the urban churches men's groups, women's groups, youth groups, young married groups, hobby groups, interest groups, and other groups try to service the diversity of their congregations. Judaism has provided a common tie for individuals with diverse national origins confronting new situations. Catholicism has cushioned the shock of assimilation for the Irish, Polish, Mexican, Puerto Rican, and a myriad other nationalities who came late to the American scene. Within the stream of Protestantism, the Negro has found some channel of protest and some consolation for his minority group status. Newer Protestant sects have provided meaningful association for rural migrants caught in the web of the impersonality of the city.

Spilling over from the churches, these diversities of interests have sought expression elsewhere. Specialized groups compete for some of these allegiances and provide expression for many needs which churches do not attempt to fulfill. While these voluntary organizations—fraternal, social, political, economic, etc.—are numerically impressive in urban areas, their importance in fulfilling group needs can be over estimated

It was found, in New York City, that the occupational classes that make up the bulk of the city's population were largely unaffiliated with these specialized groups.[3] In general, studies show that the higher the socio-economic status, the higher the social participation in these groups. One cannot conclude that the non-participant in these types of groups is a social isolate, attached to no meaningful group. Among many urban people, the family, kinship and clique groups still provide meaningful interaction.[4] These many groups, formal or informal, provide meaning, support, and reinforcement for the urban dweller, channeling off individuals who might seek these same things within organized religion.

There are other sources of values and points of identification in the urbanites' search for meaning. The gods and godesses of the movies and television provide a visual and glamorous morality. "Successful people" preach capsule sermons *via* radio.[5] These are the source of such pungent theology as "I believe in my God, my country, my family, and baseball," and these beliefs are possibly not in the order of importance. Nationalism has provided an absolute for many to use as an anchor in the turmoil of social change. Other ideologies, as conservatism, liberalism, aestheticism, humanism, scientism, and perhaps one could add alcoholism, have provided substitutes, alternatives, and escapes.

This, then, is the picture. Urban man today is confronted by a style of life new in the world, newer in America, and he faces a host of new problems, and complex ones, at least by their newness. Organized religion, which has provided meaning and guidance in the past for such situations, is caught by the new flexibility and fluidity of urban life. Religious experience, as universally expressed, is seeking other outlets. Other worldly rewards and punishments have lost their significance in producing conformity of belief. New groups promise their own brand of messianic salvation, and new ideologies explain away man's frustrations with simplicity and finality. The character of the gods today has shifted from justice and mercy to success and wealth. The task of urban religion is to interpret a universal experience in man's new surroundings. The verdict must wait the test of time, the validation of survival.

The Influence of Religion in Urban Life. Essaying the importance of religion in any context is a difficult task. The complexity of the city does not make the analysis easier. Some observers assign religion no influence and others see its influence present everywhere. One person can point to the educational, recreational, and welfare agencies spon-

---

[3] Mirra Komorovsky, "The Voluntary Associations of Urban Dwellers," *American Sociological Review,* Vol. 11 (December, 1946), pp. 686-98.

[4] Floyd Dotson, "Patterns of Voluntary Association among Urban Working-Class Families," *American Sociological Review,* Vol. 16 (October, 1951), pp. 687-693.

[5] Edward R. Murrow (Ed.), *This I Believe* (New York: Simon and Schuster, 1952), p. 137.

sored and supported by organized religion. He could point with pride that the ideal definition of the "successful man" in America often includes some religious affiliation. He could point to the role of religion in the integration of personality, the changes in life organization, and the disciplined lives which often ensue. Another might ignore this evidence and would highlight the opposite characteristics. He could point to the "hypocrisy" of church leaders and attenders. He could decry and deny the role of religion in any sphere of current affairs. Both of these approaches, like any half-truths, are half-false. To escape this dilemma of assertion without facts, one has the security of certain objective indices—the reader can interpret their significance.

1. *Church membership.* One way of looking at the influence of religion in urban life is by the criteria of church membership. The 1936 *Census of Religious Bodies* reported the total church membership of 256 denominations to be 55,807,366, or about 49 per cent of the total population. Of this total, 38,519,170 were urban and 17,084,410 were rural, while the general population was 12.4 per cent more urban than rural. Unfortunately, no census of religious bodies was completed in 1946 and there is agreement that the 1936 census was incomplete. Currently the *Yearbook of American Churches* gives estimates on church membership. The 1951 totals are 88,673,005, about 58 per cent of the total population. No rural-urban breakdown is made. Since migration has continued toward urban areas and the proportion of church members in relation to the total population has increased, there is no reason to believe that the city has declined in its importance as far as membership is concerned.

2. *Church attendance.* Membership may be one measure of influence but church rolls often do not keep pace with the changing population. In fact, much of the assumed increase in the proportion of church members in this country may be a statistical myth supported by rapid mobility and lethargic records. Church attendance should be a better index of influence as it requires some interest and effort to attend but not necessarily to belong. One study, conducted in Madison, Wisconsin, showed a great difference between Catholic and Protestant church attendance and a considerable variation within Protestantism.[6] The average church attendance per month was 3.52 for Catholics, 1.85 for Protestants, and 1.75 for Jews. Within the main bodies of Protestantism, the Lutheran was the highest (1.97) and the Episcopalian the lowest (1.52). The best attendance record within the Protestant family is among the small sectarian groups. On the average, the study seemed to indicate that on any one Sunday 10 per cent of the non-church affiliated people, 43 per cent of the Protestants, and 80 per cent of the Catholics attend church. About one-half of the seating

----

[6] Louis Bultena, "Church Membership and Church Attendance in Madison, Wisconsin," *American Sociological Review*, Vol. 14 (June, 1949), pp .384-389.

capacity of the Protestant churches is used every Sunday, while the Catholics fill their seating capacities twice each Sunday. This study seems to be corroborated recently for Catholic attendance.[7] It was found that about 79 per cent of the Catholics in a southern city attend mass every Sunday.

3. *Marginal church participants.* While attendance is probably a better index of influence than church membership, the non-attender and the non-member are not wholly outside the influence of the church. There are an unknown number of what Cuber calls "marginal church participants."[8] Actual participation within the influence of organized religion is not easily measured. The reach of the church extends far beyond the bounds of its formal indicators. For example, a person may not be an attender or member but he could not escape the influence of the role of religion in the socialization process of his past. A person might have no visible religious ties but, ideologically, he might be identical with the avid participant. These "marginal" individuals, without membership or attendance, might be a part of those who claim a church preference. In Madison, about 30 per cent of the sample indicated that they had no church membership, but about 60 per cent of these non-members stated that they had a church preference.[9] In a southern city, a canvass within the parish area found almost 11,000 who listed themselves as Catholic. Then a more intensive census was made and about 40 per cent of this group had to be considered marginal. They were a part of the geographical parish but not a part of the religious parish. They did, however, identify themselves as Catholics in the initial canvass.[10] It seems plausible that although they could not, in one sense, be considered a part of the parish, they shared more than the religious label with the active parishioners. Since many of our religious values have been secularized, and many of our secular values incorporated into religion, the separation of the religious from the non-religious is a difficult process. Many ideas and actions stem from religious orientations and the actor often is without knowledge of the source.

4. *Church related groups.* Since the city is often characterized by the multiplicity of interest groups, it is well to remember that some of these interests are religious, or, at least, church sponsored. In a study in New York,[11] women were shown to have more affiliations with church-related groups than men, irrespective of economic level. Church

---

[7] Joseph H. Fichter, S.J. "The Profile of Catholic Life," *American Journal of Sociology,* Vol. 58 (September, 1952), pp. 145-149.

[8] John Cuber, "Marginal Church Participants," *Sociology and Social Research,* Vol. 25 (September-October, 1940), pp. 57-62.

[9] Bultena, *op. cit.,* p. 384.

[10] Joseph H. Fichter, *Southern Parish Dynamics of A City Church* (Chicago: The University of Chicago Press, 1951), p. 20.

[11] Komorowsky, *op. cit.*

sponsored groups were especially important for white-collar women and men. Both Catholic men and women had a greater proportion of affiliations in religious groups than Jews or Protestants. In addition, many fraternal groups, as the Knights of Columbus and the Masons, have religious ties and they constitute an important outlet for participation.

A great deal of participation is emphatic rather than active, but another study showed that among urban working-class families membership in church affiliated groups tends to be active as contrasted to only nominal membership in unions, military, and fraternal groups.[12] Although church affiliated and church sponsored groups were important for men, they were a more important outlet for women and children.

5. *Beliefs and attitudes.* Most urbanites verbalize certain ideal religious patterns. Several Gallup-type polls have shown that about all Americans believe in God and believe that they are good Christians, without bothering to specify either their conception of the nature of the God or the nature of the Christian. This uniformity of answer would doubtlessly be destroyed by more specific questions. A study of pre-school Catholic children tested their knowledge of certain prayers and religious stories.[13] On these items, one-third or less of the children displayed the knowledge expected by the teachings of the Church. Rural children generally showed a greater knowledge on these items than did urban children, as is usually expected. Urban children, however, made a better showing in the Northeast and the Southwest regions of the country. Although the study does not explain this contradiction, these regions have the highest incidence of urban Catholics. This would seem to indicate that religious isolation is conducive to conformity of belief. Rural areas generally provide this isolation, but it can be found in certain cities. Contact with different beliefs and ideas may bring on question and doubt. While residential segregation along certain ethnic lines can produce ideological inbreeding, the city usually maximizes conflicting ideas.

Another study in a southern city seemed to indicate that among Catholics the greatest conformity of belief was on abstract ideas or items which were not too pertinent to every-day living.[14] On questions involving mixed marriages and fasting, i.e., those items having somewhat immediate application upon behavior, there was little conformity. Also, the official statement of the church regarding racial integration gave way to the community sentiment on segregation. Some comparisons can be made with reference to Protestantism. The usual assumption

---

[12] Dotson, *op. cit.*

[13] John L. Thomas, "Religious Training in the Roman Catholic Family," *American Journal of Sociology,* Vol. 57 (September, 1951), pp. 178-183.

[14] Fichter, *Southern Parish, op. cit.,* Chap. 20.

has been that there is a closer conformity between the teaching of the Catholic Church and the attitudes of its adherents. A similar study was conducted among the members of the Church of the Brethren in Cincinnati.[15] The members were surveyed on their attitudes in six areas ranging from church-state relationships and church ordinances to recreational patterns and personal attire. The traditional stand of the church was contrasted with the actual answers of the members. More questions were answered contrary to the church's traditional stand in the areas of personal attire and recreation. In other words, religious beliefs which are contrary to general cultural practices around them are most pliable on the behavioral rather than the ideological level.

6. *Integration and social well-being.* There is another way to try to indicate the influence of religion—this time "on the city" instead of "in the city." All cities are not characterized by complete anomie or disorganization, as their worst critics imply. Cities have varying degrees of integration, cohesion and morale. Angell has suggested that one way that this might be measured is by the differences between cities as shown by a crime index, and another index measuring welfare effort by the city.[16] The well-integrated cities would have presumably a low crime rate and a high welfare rate, and cities over the country vary considerably on these factors. In seeking the causal factors in these differences in integration, two hypotheses were tested. One was that the larger the proportion of church members in a city, the better the integration, and the second was that the larger ratio of Catholics to all church members, the better the integration. The last hypothesis was based on the idea that Protestants were more individualistic and the Catholics were more cohesive in their outlook. Neither of these hypotheses was substantiated. Church membership did not seem to be a factor in integration. Perhaps if other measures of influence, as church attendance, were utilized, they might prove to be related.

A similar venture was the construction of a composite statistical index called "Social Well-Being," by Porterfield.[17] The index was composed of scores on economic welfare, education and culture, housing, voting, medical facilities, and certain measures of health. These were constructed for states, using the average for the United States as a norm. Then a Church Index was constructed in a similar way, using the number of ministers, per cent of church members, and the number of churches. The relation between these two factors for the states was

---

[15] T. Quentin Evans, "A Study of the Opinions of Members of the Church of the Brethren in Cincinnati, Ohio," (unpublished M.A. thesis, University of Cincinnati, 1950).

[16] Robert C. Angell, "The Moral Integration of Cities," *American Journal of Sociology*, Vol. 47 (July, 1951), pp. 18-19.

[17] Austin Porterfield, "The Church and Social Well-Being," *Sociology and Social Research*, Vol. 31 (January-February, 1947), pp. 213-219.

negative. In other words, the higher the Church Index (number of ministers and churches, etc.,) the lower the social well-being of the states. States were then broken down by degrees of urbanization, and the relationship between church and social well-being seemed, at best, to be unrelated and, in most cases, negatively related. This does not imply that the church makes things "worse," since it is only one of many influences in the "goodness" and "badness" of certain areas. It does, however, make one pause and think of why the church was not a more potent factor in making things "better."

7. *Social action.* A growing conception in America has been that man is, in part, able to change some of his social conditions and is not the pawn of uncontrollable forces. If this is true, the church could play an important role. An interesting indication in the possible role of the church is provided by Porterfield in an unpublished study.[18] He showed that in those cities with a low crime index the ministers were "this worldly" and "present" oriented. In cities with a high crime index, the questionnaire responses of ministers were "other worldly" and "future" oriented. If this is cause rather than coincidence, then the church might play an important role in social change. The Roman Catholic Church has long had a well-organized social action program. Within Protestantism, the larger the membership in a denomination, the more likely it will look with favor upon social action by the church.[19] The smaller denominations tend to frown upon efforts of the church to change social conditions, even though they might think the conditions should be modified. Today, most Protestant denominations have some full-time staff member concerned with social action, but the attention paid is minute compared to the immensity of the problems. Most emphasis in social action by the large denominations is given to labor relations, interracial and urban social problems. The actual effectiveness of these programs is difficult to measure and, for most purposes, unknown.

Religion as a Part of the Social Structure. The indicators, mentioned above, give only part of the picture. The difficulty with any and all of these measures is that the influence of organized religion and religiously motivated behavior is filtered through and is bound up with a number of other factors. The net result is produced by a combination of these and religion is only one of them. There is sociological truism that social institutions are interrelated. This simply is a disciplinary way of saying that parts of society fit together and interweave instead of being insulated and compartmentalized. For example, economic

---

[18] Austin L. Porterfield, "Aspects of Organized Religion, Suicide, and Crime as Variables Codependent upon the Societal Contexts of States and Selected Cities." Unpublished paper read at the American Sociological Society, Chicago, September, 1951.

[19] Judson T. Landis, "Social Action in American Protestant Churches," *American Journal of Sociology,* Vol. 52 (May, 1947), pp. 517-22.

changes, as a depression, are reflected in marriage rates, divorce rates, suicides, welfare contributions, educational policy, and crime rates. The tracing of the endless chain of cause and effect can be terminated only by the exhaustion of the tracer. Religion is no exception to this truism. Although intellectually some Americans may compartmentalize their religion, this separation does not exist in fact. Since there are many different phases of these interrelationships, only two will be discussed here. First, the relation between religious and economic institutions and the resulting stratification of religious groups in the urban areas will be investigated. Second, the relation between religious groups and power will be considered. The selection of these particular aspects from the many possibilities is arbitrary but can be justified by their importance in urban life.

1. *Organized religion and social stratification.* Some type of differentiation and stratification is found in every kind of community.[20] One can view a city as being composed of layers of differential prestige called social classes. In some societies, as India, religious function provides a basis for stratification, while in America socio-economic factors, and particularly occupation, seem to provide the main source of prestige. While the stratification system in the United States possesses a great deal of fluidity and the lines are rather deceptive, these prestige differences point to real differences in behavior. Organized religion, as a part of the society, is caught up in the stratification system in the following ways.

(a) *Nationally, different denominations tend to attract a particular range of socio-economic groups.* Table XXX shows the class composi-

TABLE XXX

PERCENTAGE OF MEMBERSHIP OF RELIGIOUS GROUPS BY "CLASS"
(N-12,019)

Religious Group	Upper	Middle	Lower
Entire sample	13	31	56
Catholic	9	25	66
Jewish	22	32	46
Methodist	13	35	52
Baptist	8	24	68
Presbyterian	22	40	38
Lutheran	11	36	53
Episcopal	24	34	42
Congregational	24	43	33
Christian Science	25	36	39

Source: Information Service, National Council of the Churches of Christ in the United States of America. Vol. XXVII, No. 20, Table II.

---

[20] See Reinhard Bendix and Seymour Martin Lipset, *Class Status and Power* (Glencoe, Illinois: The Free Press, 1953).

tion of the members from particular religious groups which was derived from a nation-wide study. The "class" designation was made by the interviewer and the person was placed by certain status traits and possessions, using the specific local community as the basis for comparison. Using the total percentages of the national sample as a base, it can be seen that the Roman Catholics and the Baptists exceed their quota in the lower "class." The Jewish, Methodist, Presbyterian, Lutheran, Episcopal, Congregational, and Christian Science groups exceed their middle "class" quotas. The Jewish Presbyterian, Congregational and Christian Science also exceed their upper "class" quota.

(b) *In specific cities, individual churches attract persons from similar socio-economic strata.* Any community study which has investigated the role of stratification in specific cities describes a hierarchy of churches. There are "class" churches—churches of the lower class, churches of the middle class, and churches of the upper class. Some churches appeal only to the old families; others serve the migrants who find little in common, religiously and economically, with the "pillars" of the community. Generally, the ranking within a specific community follows the distribution of the denomination on the national scale. In some cases, a church which is a part of a predominantly middle class denomination nationally will function as an upper class, or perhaps a lower class church in a specific city. In cities where one denomination has many churches, these churches may serve somewhat different socio-economic groups. It is rare, however, to find one denomination in a city which covers the whole range of socio-economic difference from top to bottom. A church becomes identified with one particular group and other groups do not accept or are not accepted by this group. If the denomination is not flexible enough to encompass them in other churches, new denominations arise.

(c) *When a church cuts across "class" lines, church policy is formulated by the higher socio-economic group.*[21] Since there is no perfect relationship between a specific socio-economic level and a particular church, some churches do encompass a narrow range of differences. When this happens, the "best" people are usually selected and perhaps are "more readily available" to "run" the church. Of course, this is more characteristic within Protestantism and more specifically within denominations with congregational autonomy. However, even in Catholicism and in Protestant groups with Episcopal church organization, lay leadership tends to be assumed by "respectable people." "Respectable" people are usually, by definition, those who are successful economically. This often means that the values of one specific group are incorporated into church policy at the expense of the values of

---

[21] Jerome Davis, "A Study of Protestant Church Boards of Control," *American Journal of Sociology*, Vol. 38 (November, 1932), pp. 418-431.

another group. The process may have the end result of the alienation of the group that is slighted or ignored.

(d) *In the urban Negro community, a parallel stratification of religious groups exists.* The brotherhood of man sometimes stops at the church door, even though there are sermons about it given inside to a restricted audience. Possibly less than 1 per cent of white congregations have Negro members. Even in these mixed churches, the proportion is hardly equal—about one Negro to every 1,000 whites. The Negro church, in effect, is a separate unit from the white church in the city. About 95 per cent of Negro church members belong to Protestant groups, but 90 per cent of these Protestants belong to separate Negro denominations.[22] With urban migration, Catholicism has made some gains among the Negro population. Although the status system of the Negro and the white is distinct in the city, Negro churches follow a similar pattern of elaboration.[23] Specific denominations attract a certain socio-economic level and individual churches draw a restricted membership, economically as well as racially.

(e) *The socio-economic values of the religious groups are expressed ecologically by their spatial distribution in the city.* It should be apparent that the churches which draw their congregation from the higher socio-economic groups would be located in the "well-to-do" areas of the city. In Los Angeles and Indianapolis, it was found that the denominations which had greater wealth on a national scale could be found in the "best" areas in the specific city.[24] Conversely, those with a low national wealth were found in the "poor" areas of these specific cities. This gives some indication of how national patterns are expressed in the local community. It also indicates that if a denomination serves one segment of the population its religious interest tends to become identified with its "class" interests. This economic inbreeding, aided by ecological similarity, may turn religious values into economic ethics.

(f) *Within Protestantism, the socio-economic level of the congregation is reflected in ritual, sermon topics, escathology, and types of music within the church.* In general, the higher the socio-economic status of the church members, the more ritualized a church will be. This generalization, of course, excludes Catholicism and, to a certain extent, Lutheranism. Generally, as one moves up the social ladder, the following things happen. Church services shift from congregational participation to the responsibility of its conduct being assumed by a group of paid

---

[22] Liston Pope, "Caste in the Church," *Survey Graphic*, Vol. 36 (January, 1947), p. 59; also, Liston Pope, "Religion and the Class Structure," *The Annals of the American Academy of Political and Social Science*, Vol. 257 (March, 1948), pp. 84-91.
[23] Vallel Daniel, "Ritual and Stratification in Chicago Negro Churches," *American Sociological Review*, Vol. 7 (June, 1942) pp. 352-361.
[24] Thomas F. Hoult, "Economic Class Consciousness in American Protestantism," *American Sociological Review*, Vol. 15 (February, 1950), pp. 97-100.

specialists—ministers, educators, and musicians. Spontaniety is replaced by a fixed pattern of worship. Evangelism is replaced by religious education. Hymn forms and topics shift from emotionalized "folksongs" to those of the stately liturgical tradition. Recruitment of the clergy changes from a dependence upon "calling" to a dependence on the channels of education. For some, "the temple is in the heart," but to others the physical plant of the church becomes a symbol of religious affluence. Sermon topics shift from the glories of some future world to practical guides for successful living in this world. Those who possess worldly status find solace in giving it religious significance. Those who are without worldly status find consolation in the fact that these things are of little use in final salvation.

2. *The dilemma of power—church and sect.* Religious ideas are intended to have application in behavior. Historically, an important phase of religion has been in setting goals for man and pointing out the ultimate values in life. What should man and society be? What can they be? How should man conduct himself in this world? To these and other questions religion has sought to supply direction. Most religious groups assume that their answers to these problems are the best ones, although they may not make the assumption that their answers are the only possible ones.

With their answers and modes of behavior which they assume to be best, how can they insure the existence and acceptance of their ideas? To exert an influence, religion must demand certain allegiances of its adherents. If these allegiances are far different from those of the secular order, the society may be a hostile audience. The groups holding the power in the society will not be inclined to look with favor upon those who challenge the status quo.

Two paths are open to religious groups.[25] There may be combinations of these in specific instances, but these ideal types highlight the differences. One path to insure the continuity of their religious ideals is for the group, in effect, to secede from the society. They become a *sect*. The other path is to seek to convince the secular order that their religious doctrines are correct and should be incorporated into the total life pattern of the society. They become a *church*.

The *sect* sets itself apart and becomes a community bound by belief. The members have little stake in "this world" so they turn their attention to a future life. They have little influence in the power structure and they deny that temporal things are important. They exact rigid discipline over the religious behavior of their members, as they consider religious conformity more important than social conformity. They reject and distrust a hierarchy of church officials, trusting their own feelings. The dominant religious groups in the society, at best,

_____
[25] See Chapter 19 for suggestions on urban church organizational improvement.

pity the sect. The sect criticizes these dominant groups because they have, in the eyes of the sectarian, moved away from the "real" religion. The sect is sufficiently marginal to the dominant value system to be a perceptive critic. They have little vested interest in the status quo and, because of this, they can do little to change it. If they demand too much allegiance from their members, this may involve sacrifices the members are not willing to make, or, if their sacrifices conflict too greatly with those of the society around them, they may be persecuted. Since the members are peripheral to the power structure, their ideas and demands have little influence outside the community of believers. The *sect* would be typified by the store-front churches in the city.

All sects are not content to remain separate. If their ideas are correct, why not convince the total society of the correctness? It may become a religious imperative to convert the "heathen." They wish to permeate all life with their views. Instead of seceding from society, this group tries to exert dominance. They wish to become a *church*. To be dominant they must utilize the existing political and economic institutions. The power structure must be aligned on their side and organizations have to be erected in order to make the religious values effective. In building and maintaining these organizations the religious group must compromise many of their religious values. The plan of conquest is passed to a group of professionals and specialists rather than resting in the emotionality of the believer. The precedent of tradition becomes a guide rather than precedent of emotion. Salvation is found on this earth rather than in some future life. Religious success is measured by impressive buildings and a large staff, not by inner feelings. Instead of challenging the status quo, the church is the status quo. The group now has power but, in achieving it, it has reinterpreted its ideals. The radical ideas that initiated the conquest are compromised, and the values of the church and the values of the society become one and the same. The church is part and parcel of the social order. It accepts what the society accepts and it denies what the society denies. It cannot be an effective critic of the society since it would be criticizing itself. The *church* would be typified by the large, "successful" congregations in the impressive cathedrals of the city.

Such is the dilemma of the religious group. If it adheres rigidly to unique ideals, it risks both the loss of its members and the wrath of the power structure. In order to gain acceptance and ascendancy, it changes its values. Its unique ideals are compromised and reinterpreted as it climbs the ladder of acceptability. It is faced with a rather hollow choice between religious idealism without power or power without religious idealism.

Religion came to America, and came to the city, with the imprint

of the past. Our religious tradition was a part, perhaps the core, of
our cultural tradition. The parallelism of interest and experience of
the rural settlers gave rise to a similarity of religious expression. The
growth of the city provided differential life experiences and new complexities of life for its inhabitants. Immigrants brought conflicting
religious beliefs into the new environment of the city. The religious
organization which served most group needs well in rural areas becomes only one of many groups in urban areas. The different life
experiences in the city give rise to different life chances and opportunities, and consequently to a myriad of religious groups. New
ideologies, principally nationalism, become substitutes for religious
experience. The dependence of the religious guides of the past weakened in the presence of the new, as social change waits for neither man
nor institution. Urban living is a relatively new experience for man,
and no social institution has made an easy adjustment to it.

It is not easy to determine the influence of religion in the city.
Church membership and church attendance are still very much a part
of urban life. An unknown number of urbanites participate marginally
in the values and activities of organized religion. Church related
groups still satisfy many of the needs of participation for the urbanite.
Since unique religious ideas stand exposed in the city, they are more
susceptible to change. Religious values and attitudes then merge into
the total complex pattern of the city, not as a separate part but as an
interweaving thread. Because of this, it is difficult to isolate the effect
of religion in creating integration and social well-being in a specific city.

Religion, then, is not an isolated part of this community called the
city. It is intimately bound up with the totality of the urban development. Religious groups show the same divisions as any other group.
Race and class, which separate the city, also divide religious adherents.
The unique ideals of many groups, religious or non-religious, face the
alternatives of changing their ideals or risk being isolated from the
rest of society. Even with all its difficulties in achieving an urban
adaptation, religion cannot be dismissed as simply an outmoded survival from the rural past.

WORKSHOP AND PROBLEMS

1. Why would you say that the city has been frequently criticized as
immoral?

2. What are some of the more important historical factors in urban
religion?

3. What are the most important urban religious groups?

4. What are the more important functions of religion in urban
society? How adequate are our data on these roles?

5. Why do we say that religion is a part of the social structure?

6. Show how different denominations tend to attract a particular
range of economic groups or socio-economic strata.

7. In the struggle for power, what is the dilemma faced by the church? Do you agree with the position the author takes on this subject?

8. How would you characterize the future for urban religions?

BIBLIOGRAPHY

Abell, Aaron I., *The Urban Impact on American Protestantism 1865-1900* (Cambridge: Harvard University Press, 1943).

Abrams, Ray H., (editor), "Organized Religion in the United States," *The Annals*, Vol. 257 (March, 1948), pp. 1-62.

Bendix, Reinhard, and Lipset, Seymour Martin, *Class, Status and Power* (Glencoe, Illinois: The Free Press, 1953).

Fichter, Joseph, *Southern Parish, The Dynamics of A City Church* (Chicago: The University of Chicago Press, 1951).

Leiffer, Murray, *City and Church in Transition* (Chicago: Willett, Clark and Co., 1938).

————————————, *The Effective City Church* (New York: Abingdon-Cokesbury Press, 1949).

Mays, Benjamin E., and Nicholson, Joseph W., *The Negro's Church* (New York: Harper and Brothers, 1933).

Nuesse, C. J., and Harte, Thomas J. (editors), *The Sociology of the Parish* (Milwaukee: The Bruce Publishing Company, 1951).

Sears, Charles, *City Man* (New York: Harper and Brothers, 1936).

Sperry, Willard L., *Religion in America* (New York: The Macmillan Company, 1946).

Sweet, William W., *The Story of Religions in America* (New York: Harper and Brothers, 1930).

Yinger, J. Milton, *Religion in the Struggle for Power* (Durham: Duke University Press, 1946).

CHAPTER 11

Developing and Coordinating Urban Welfare Services

By ROBERT L. WESTON

Every American community has many welfare institutions and services which have been organized to bring about community betterment. These institutions and services are concerned with health, recreation, youth, and child and family care. They are financed by gifts, by income from investments, by tax funds, by fees for services, or, in some few instances, by a combination of the four sources of income. Generally the agencies which receive their support from gifts, fees, and income from investments provide preventive services, whereas, tax-supported agencies provide remedial services.

Welfare agencies were originally established to serve the under-privileged. In recent years, a great change has occurred in this concept of the availability of welfare services. Today, most of us at some time during our lives, make use of the services of welfare agencies. For example, such agencies as the Boy Scouts, Girl Scouts, visiting nurse associations, and the mental health clinics serve all income groups.

Our public welfare, or tax-supported agencies, serve the most people and spend the most money. These programs are financed by local, state, and federal funds. They include categorical assistance, general assistance, insurance programs, child welfare, mental health, and correction care.

Categorical assistance, such as assistance for the needy aged and dependent children, became a reality following the enactment of the Social Security Act in 1935. These programs are financed by federal and state governments, and are administered by the states. Care is provided for those who are in need, who are sixty-five years of age or older, the blind, dependent children, and the disabled.

General assistance is financed and sponsored by state and local governments. This program provides care for those who are ineligible for categorical assistance, or those who are waiting to be placed on the categorical assistance rolls. Standards and eligibility requirements for general assistance vary greatly between states, and, in many instances, between localities. One explanation for this is that the federal government is not able to exercise its influence to bring about standardization through the distribution of its funds.

Agencies which are responsible for the categorical and general assistance programs follow several administrative patterns. In some states, these activities are administered by one state agency which delegates local administration to county units. In other states, categorical assistance is the responsibility of a state agency and its county units, and general assistance is the responsibility of separate county welfare departments, or in some areas, of independent county and city welfare departments within the same county.

The old age and survivors insurance, and the unemployment insurance programs of the Social Security Act are important welfare services in American communities. These programs differ from the categorical services in that beneficiaries receive benefits because of financial participation, whereas, categorical grants are given to those who are able to establish that they are in need of assistance. Old age and survivors insurance is administered by the federal government and provides grants for those who participate through payroll deductions. Benefits are available for individuals sixty-five years of age and older, and for the survivors of covered workers. Unemployment insurance is financed by federal and state governments, and is administered largely by the states. The unemployed receive weekly benefits. The amount of the allotments and duration of weekly payments vary from state to state. In addition to the program previously outlined, the Social Security Act provides grants to states for services for crippled children and for maternity and child health care in areas where the need is urgent. These programs are usually supervised by state health departments.

Mental Health Services. A recent public welfare development is in the field of mental health. In 1946, Congress passed the National Mental Health Act which makes funds available for research, for training of personnel, and for local mental health services. On the local level there has been an improvement in diagnostic and training facilities, and an increase in the number of personnel trained in psychiatry, psychiatric social work, and in psychology.

Services for the Offender. The average American community has developed services to deal with the juvenile and adult offender. For the adult offender there are probation and parole services which are usually financed by state funds. For the juvenile offender, usually under eighteen years of age, there is provision in every state for either separate juvenile courts, or for specialized jurisdiction or procedure. In some communities the court is responsible for dependent and neglected children. Juvenile court procedure differs from other courts in that the hearings are generally private and informal. Cases are usually initiated by petition, instead of by complaint or indictment as occurs when adult offenders are cited for violations of the law. Most juvenile courts are authorized to appoint probation officers, who work with the judge, and who generally have the following responsibilities:

(A) preliminary investigation to determine whether the child can safely remain in his own home pending further study and court action; (B) arrangement for detention care if endorsed by the court, or other temporary care if needed; (C) social study of the child's situation for the aid of the judge in deciding what action to take; and, (D) helping the child, who has been placed on probation or under supervision by the court, and his family to understand and face the situation and to take the steps necessary to arrive at a solution of the problem, or to modify or change the behavior or conditions which were responsible for bringing the child to the attention of the court.[1]

Child Welfare Services. There are many child welfare services, some of which have been described briefly earlier in this chapter. They are either operated by state funds or by voluntary organizations which are licensed to operate in the field by the state. Those with which most of us are familiar are the adoption and foster care services. Foster care for children is a term used to designate children who are reared away from the natural family, in institutions or in foster family homes. However, foster care, according to the popular conception, is generally considered to be a service for children who are reared only in foster family homes.

On the assumption that the best place for a child is in its maternal and paternal home, most child welfare agencies hesitate to remove a child from a home, even though they recognize that it is necessary under certain circumstances. The parents develop feelings of inadequacy, and the child is in danger of serious emotional disturbances when the parents are unable to provide an adequate home. Generally, foster care is used when there are serious marital problems, disturbed parent-child relationships, or other situations where the parents are unable to provide a home.

Foster care agencies usually provide adoption services. An adoption is a legal step which creates a parent-child legal relationship which is the same as if the child had been born to the parents. Adoption practices are regulated by the states and vary widely throughout the United States. In general, they provide safeguards for the child, the natural parents, and the adopting parents. Agencies in this field are concerned with seeing that the child is placed in a family where it will have a secure and satisfying life; they are concerned with seeing that the natural parents understand what the step means to them, and

---

[1] Alice Scott Nutt, "Juvenile and Domestic Relations Courts," *Social Work Yearbook, 1949* (New York: Russell Sage Foundation, 1949), p. 273. See also, U. S. Children's Bureau, *Juvenile-Court Standards,* Publication No. 121 (1937), Washington, D. C.

what it may mean to their child or children; and, they are also concerned with seeing that the adopting parents give thoughtful consideration to what such a step means in terms of their future and the future of the child.

Services have developed in American communities where children whose parents lack concern, and are unwilling to make an effort to change bad situations, are given help. These are known as protective services, in that they are organized to protect the interests of children. Such services are usually supported by private funds and deal with two types of problems as they relate to the needs of children: (a) the individual; and, (b) the community. In regard to the individual such agencies are concerned with the failure of parents to assume their normal responsibilities, and in regard to the community, they are concerned with bringing about an improvement in community life through study and legislation as it affects children.

Other services for children are those which deal with the handicapped, the retarded, health, day care for children of working parents, or for those who need special care, maternity homes which provide care and promote preventive and protective activities for unmarried mothers and their children, and group foster care institutions such as orphanages and homes for children under observation prior to more permanent placement.

Family Welfare Services. One of the most important services in the basic welfare structure of the average American community is family social work, a casework service which focuses on family life and family relationships. The broad field of family service includes the public assistance programs which were discussed earlier in this chapter, and the privately supported services. The family welfare agency:

> Helps troubled individuals find the best possible social and personal solution to their difficulties through development of opportunity and capacity for satisfying and useful lives. Recognizing that the maximum happiness for the individual springs from healthy family ties, the family social worker seeks to strengthen family unity. He may work with an individual member of the family, with several members of the family group, or with a single, unattached person, but his emphasis is on helping people with problems which affect the unity and stability of the entire family. Family social work also operates both locally and nationally to improve conditions essential for good family life and to increase understanding of what these conditions are.[2]

In addition to providing service to residents of local communities, services are available for the transient or migrant, and for the traveler who

---

[2] Frank J. Hertel, "Family Social Work," *Social Work Yearbook, 1949* (New York: Russell Sage Foundation, 1949), pp. 190-191. See also, Ann W. Shyne, *Handbook on Statistical Recording and Reporting in Family Service Agencies* (New York: Family Service Association of America, 1949).

has encountered problems which cause him to need the help of a local social agency, and legal advice and assistance is available for persons of inadequate income who are unable to afford legal counsel. Typical agencies are Family Services Society, Travelers Aid Society, Salvation Army, Volunteers of America, and the Legal Aid Society. These agencies generally receive their support from contributed funds, and are either sectarian or non-sectarian.

Leisure Time Services. Leisure time services for youths and adults have been taking a large share of the community welfare dollar during recent years. Many different organizations provide these services. Some are sponsored by religious groups as, for example, The Catholic Youth Association and the Young Men's Hebrew Association; some are sponsored by governmental bodies; some have community-wide sponsorship. The objectives, scope, and facilities which implement the programs of these agencies are set forth as follows: some organizations are primarily concerned with citizenship training and character building, and others are organized around a specific interest; some programs are community-wide, building-centered, such as the Y. W. C. A.'s; some are neighborhood building-centered programs such as settlement houses; others are community-wide, non-building centered programs such as the Boy Scouts or Girl Scouts; some cater to boys, some to girls, some to both—and, some, such as the public recreation agencies, to everyone in the community.

All leisure time programs, whether sponsored by a church group, by an independent agency, or by a government-sponsored organization, are interested in channeling our desires for normal leisure time activities into constructive channels. Games, hobbies, handicrafts, sharing through play or teamwork, are typical activities.

Health Services. A general discussion of welfare services must include a section on health services, including public health services, voluntary health services, and public health nursing. According to Leonard A. Scheel, public health is:

A term generally applied to the administration by governments of regulatory laws, services, and facilities designed to protect and improve the health of the civilian population. The basic assumption of public health agencies is that protection and improvement of health depend upon prevention of disease (or the serious consequences thereof) and elimination of hazards to human health in the environment.[3]

Local public health departments generally provide the following services: (a) maternity and child health services, (b) laboratory serv-

[3] Leonard A. Scheel, "Public Health," *Social Work Yearbook, 1949* (New York: Russell Sage Foundation, 1949), p. 38. See also, Leonard A. Scheel, *A Philosophy of Modern Health Services* (Ann Arbor, Michigan: School of Public Health, University of Michigan, 1950).

ices, (c) vital statistics, (d) public health education, (e) sanitation, (f) control of communicable diseases, and (g) inspection services.

Voluntary health agencies can be given credit for much of the development in public health work. They demonstrate the value of health programs and bring about their adoption as part of the official health program. They carry on health education programs aimed at developing an informed public opinion. This often results in the enactment of sound health laws and regulations. An outstanding example of this process is illustrated by the work of the National Tuberculosis Association. This agency, through its health education program, developed an awareness of the need for public responsibility in this area. As a consequence, public health programs have been established which have brought about a great reduction in the incidence of tuberculosis. In fact, so great a reduction, that some of the local chapters, by special permission of the National Tuberculosis Association, have undertaken responsibilities in other health fields. In addition to the National Tuberculosis Association, many other voluntary health agencies operate on a national basis with local affiliates. Services of these agencies include direct health services to the local community, research in special fields, and prevention or control of a specific health problem. Examples of agencies operating in this field, in addition to the National Tuberculosis Association, are: National Foundation for Infantile Paralysis, American Cancer Society, American Heart Association, and American Social Hygiene Association.

Public health nursing is one of the most important community health services. The public health nurse provides:

> Nursing care and guidance to individuals and families; participates in educational programs for nurses, allied professional workers, and community groups; and, cooperates with other professions and groups of citizens in studying, planning, and putting into action the community health program. Public health nursing may be supported through voluntary contributions, tax funds, or a combination of both.[4]

Community Trusts. In recent years there has been a large growth in American communities in the community trust, with interests in the broad field of social welfare. These trusts receive capital gifts or bequests which are invested through banks. The income, and in some instances, the principal, is distributed by a citizens' committee. They differ from the usual foundation in that they accept gifts from many individuals, rather than from one person. Also, they usually give the citizens' committee power to change the beneficiaries if the original

---

[4] Anna Fillmore, "Public Health Nursing," *Social Work Yearbook, 1949* (New York: Russell Sage Foundation, 1949), p. 393. See also, Ruth Fisher and Margaret L. Plumley, *Desirable Organization for Public Health Nursing for Family Service and Development of Combination Agency* (New York: National Organization for Public Health Nursing, 1946).

purpose for which the funds were given becomes undesirable through the passage of time.

Community Chests. In more than 1,600 communities throughout the United States, the majority of the voluntary agencies have united to raise their funds in one united fund raising appeal each year. Denver, Colorado, sponsored the first united appeal for funds in 1887, when ten agencies combined their appeals and raised more money than they had raised in separate campaigns. In 1913, Cleveland, Ohio, organized the first Community Chest. It is recognized as the first modern Community Chest, in that the principle of budgeting was adopted in connection with fund raising. The Cleveland leaders realized that agency goals must reflect agency needs, and that they must be related to community needs. The next step in the growth of united fund raising was the organization of War Chests in World War I. These Chests were organized to raise funds for local agencies as well as for war related agencies. The principle of united fund raising was so well received that they continued to operate at the end of the war, to raise funds for local services. The name "Community Chest" was adopted by Rochester, New York, in 1919.

It is interesting to note that the raising of funds the united way has grown fastest during periods of stress: during World War I, as set forth above; during the depression of 1930's when there was a scaling down in the size of gifts, but an overall increase in the number of contributions; and, during World War II, when war funds were organized to finance local and war-related services.

We are currently passing through a period of stress in which American communities have been organizing to eliminate multiple appeals for funds. In 1952, more than 300 local communities united their efforts in one campaign. These united campaigns included such agencies as the Community Chest, American Red Cross, American Heart Association, American Cancer Society, United Defense Fund, and others— each of which had conducted separate campaigns. Campaign results indicated that the united campaigns were more successful than the regular Community Chest campaigns. A study of agency budgeting for eight cities conducting United Funds showed that the regular Chest agencies received 11 per cent more for 1952 than for 1951, and that the major national fund-raising agencies, excluding the United Defense Fund, received 5.7 per cent more than the same organizations raised the previous year in separate campaigns. These figures do not indicate the saving which was made in campaign costs from federation of appeals.

The Community Council. It is inevitable that a United Fund or Community Chest must engage in the following activities: (a) financing, (b) fund raising, and (c) budgeting and planning of health and welfare services. In most communities the planning function is delegated to the Community Welfare Council by the fund raising organization because of the Council's interest in the total community health and welfare program. As indicated by the summary which precedes this portion of the chapter, every American city has many health, welfare, and recreation agencies devoted to community betterment. It is important that these agencies work together to insure efficient and adequate services. The Community Welfare Council is the organization which provides the machinery through which agencies work and plan together.

The first health and welfare planning organizations were organized in Pittsburgh, Pennsylvania, and Milwaukee, Wisconsin, in 1909. Currently there are more than 450 in operation in the United States and Canada. Councils include in their membership, individuals, both lay and professional, tax and voluntary supported agencies, civic groups, labor unions, and many other organizations interested in community improvement. In most Councils, the membership or delegate body selects a Board of Directors which formulates policy and decides which projects should be undertaken by the Council. Its projects are assigned to standing committees or divisions, or to project committees, which are composed of representatives from the operating agencies and the community. Councils are generally concerned with the following types of activities: (a) coordination of services, the process through which agency staffs and volunteers work together, sharing their experiences and understanding each other's viewpoints; (b) collection of facts about the community needs and the manner in which the agencies meet those needs; (c) joint action through the Council by interested citizens and organizations to see that improvements in community health and welfare services are put into effect; such improvements may be the elimination of the service, development of a new service or a major program change; (d) improvement of the quality of existing health and welfare services through such activities as training institutions and personnel studies; (e) the operation of common services for member agencies; examples of such services are the Social Service Exchange, which enables the agencies to work together in serving families, the operation of a committee to help the agencies train, recruit and use volunteers, and the operation of a Christmas Bureau to coordinate Christmas giving; and (f) development of community understanding of community problems, and an understanding of how agencies deal with such problems.

Workshop and Problems

1. How has categorical assistance changed the welfare programs of cities?

2. What welfare services are now usually provided through state departments of public welfare?

3. What services are usually provided by local urban public health departments?

4. If possible visit a juvenile court to observe its work.

5. If possible visit a public health department and laboratory for purpose of acquiring knowledge of its organization and work.

6. Explain the difference between a Community Chest and a United Fund. What are the arguments for a United Fund?

7. Explain carefully the service of a Community Welfare Council.

BIBLIOGRAPHY

Baker, Helen C., and Routzahn, Mary B., *How To Interpret Social Work* (New York: Russell Sage Foundation, 1947).

Community Chest and Councils, *Health and Welfare Planning in the Smaller Community* (New York 1945).

Fisher, Ruth, and Plumley, Margaret L., *Desirable Organization for Public Health Nursing for Family Service and Development of Combination Agency* (New York: National Organization for Public Health Nursing, 1946).

French, David G., *An Approach to Measuring Results in Social Work* (New York: Columbia University Press, 1952).

Hillman, Arthur, *Community Organization and Planning* (New York: The Macmillan Co., 1949).

King, Clarence, *Organizing for Community Action* (New York: Harper & Brothers, 1948).

McMillen, Wayne, *Community Organization for Social Welfare* (Chicago: University of Chicago Press: 1945).

Scheel, Leonard A., *A Philosophy of Modern Health Services* (Ann Arbor, Michigan: School of Public Health, University of Michigan, 1950).

Shyne, Ann W., *Handbook on Statistical Recording and Reporting in Family Service Agencies* (New York: Family Service Association of America, 1949).

Social Work Yearbook for various years (New York: Russell Sage Foundation and, recently, The American Association of Social Workers).

Stroup, Herbert Hewitt, *Social Work: An Introduction to the Field* (New York: American Book Co., 1948).

U. S. Children's Bureau, *Juvenile-Court Standards*, Publication No. 121 (1937), Washington, D. C.

CHAPTER 12

Some Problems and Trends In Urban Government

By William E. Cole

The Problems. The rapid urbanization of the population of the United States and the great growth of individual cities have brought with them a complicated set of governmental problems to add to those that are almost as old as cities themselves. Graft, for example, has been an old problem in city government extending deep into history.

High on the priority lists of urban governmental problems are the following.

1. *Weak citizen interest in urban government.* The extent of citizen concern in urban government is difficult to measure. About the only reliable index is the analysis of voting results. The per cent of those eligible to vote who vote show wide variations between wards within a given city, show wide variation between cities, and also vary between years in which elections are local, state and local, or national. Thus Queen and Carpenter report data showing that the percentage of adults who were registered to vote and who voted varied from 20 to 46 per cent in St. Louis wards in 1945, and between 42 and 71 per cent in 1944.[1]

2. *The complicated web of urban government.* As individual cities have expanded their boundaries, and as metropolitan areas have developed, urban people have found themselves living under and being influenced by a complicated web of layers of governmental units—national, state and local. This maze of units complicates not only the machinery of government, but also citizen understanding of and participation in government. A man may own property in one unit and not be permitted to vote in that unit or to hold public office from that unit. In 1950, for example, Chicago had 821 governmental units within the metropolitan district, whereas the New York-New Jersey metropolitan district contained 1,039 units.[2]

Table XXXI reveals the governmental units in the United States in 1952 as contrasted with 1942.

---

[1] Stuart A. Queen and David B. Carpenter, *The American City* (New York: McGraw-Hill Co., 1953), p. 306.

[2] *Ibid.,* p. 307, 1953.

TABLE XXXI

TYPES OF GOVERNMENTAL UNITS IN THE UNITED STATES: 1942 AND 1952 [a]

Type of Government	Number of Units 1952	Number of Units 1942	Per Cent Change
U. S. Government	1	1	0.0
States	48	48	0.0
Counties	3,049	3,050	(1)
Municipalities	16,778	16,220	3.4
Townships	17,202	18,919	— 9.1
School districts	67,442	108,579	—37.9
Special districts	12,319	8,299	48.4
Total	116,839	155,116	—24.7

(1) Less than .05 per cent.

[a] Source: *The Municipal Year Book, 1952* (Chicago: The International City Managers' Association, 1952), p. 15.

Table XXXI shows the striking decline in school districts and a striking increase in special districts. The number of municipalities increased by 558 or 3.4 per cent. The term "municipalities" as used here includes new incorporations whether they be cities, villages, boroughs or towns, except in New England, New York and Wisconsin, where the term town has another meaning.

Many of the special districts developed between 1942 and 1952 were designed to accomplish, through government, a single purpose, as for example drainage or sewerage, although some provide a variety of service. A special district may provide water, fire protection, or electricity to an area and some may provide all the utility services.

Figure 13 shows the number of governmental units per county in the United States in 1952.

Greene and others found that in the Nashville metropolitan area public water supply was provided by the City of Nashville and four utility districts. Refuse disposal was furnished by two governmental bodies, and a wide variety of private collectors. Fire protection was provided by the City of Nashville and ten private fire stations owned by eight different concerns.[3] Figure 14 shows the special utility districts in Davidson County, where the City of Nashville is located.

3. *The need for area adjustments.* Cities expanding horizontally frequently face the need for area adjustments. This problem has increased with the use of the motor vehicle for transportation and may increase further with new modes of transportation. The shorter work day, the congestion of central cities, and the shorter work week have also been factors in horizontal expansion, as have also the high tax

[3] Community Services Commission for Davidson County and the City of Nashville (Lee S. Greene, Executive Director), *A Future for Nashville* (Summary of Findings) (Nashville: The Commission, 1952).

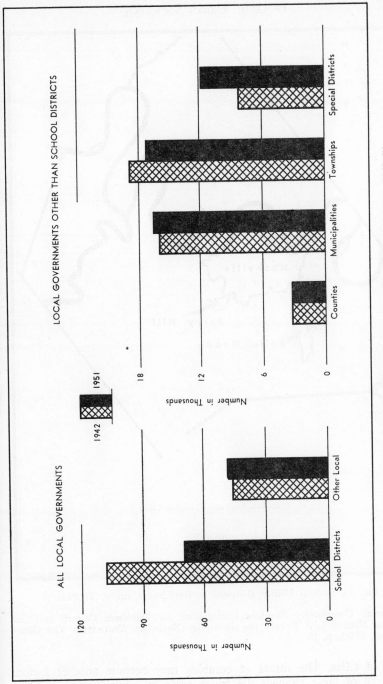

FIG. 13. Number of Governmental Units In The United States, 1942-51.
Source: The Municipal Yearbook, 1952 (Chicago: The International City
Managers' Association, 1953), p. 19.

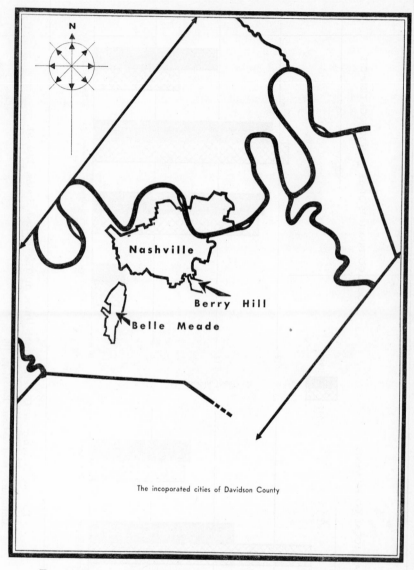

FIG. 14. Special Utility Districts in Davidson County, Tennessee.

Source: Community Services Commission for Davidson County and the
City of Nashville, *A Future for Nashville* (Nashville, Tennessee: The Commission, 1952), p. 18.

rates of cities. The threat of bombing may become another factor.
With all of these changes the fringe areas in urban government are
becoming increasingly important.

Since we have discussed the regional authority as a governmental vehicle for attacking some of the problems of the metropolitan area as such, we will discuss specifically only two proposed solutions for urban area adjustments, although we are not unmindful of special assessments for fire protection, water, sewage and police protection levied against fringe residents who live outside incorporated places. Also the theory of city-county consolidation is still worth keeping alive although it has yielded us little in the way of area adjustments during fifty years of theory and effort.

a. *Functional consolidation.* The consolidation of certain governmental functions of counties and cities, and of cities, has been a profitable movement toward area adjustment. Two, three or sometimes more cities have come together in the building of airports. City-county consolidations of health departments, hospital services, library services, and educational services are not uncommon. With the growth of public welfare services administered through county or parish welfare departments, and supervised by the states, there is little need for town and municipal departments of welfare in most of the smaller cities where at least the services could be combined with county units. In the Nashville study, which we have made reference to, the Community Services Commission recommended that the county assume responsibility for functions which were clearly county-wide—among these were public schools, public welfare, hospital care for the medically indigent, and the public health services. Through state legislation the county court would be subject to redistricting and the county would be permitted a larger element of home rule to enable it to provide these services.

b. *Annexation.* We have discussed annexation to some degree in the chapter on the metropolitan area. Historically, the most common type of urban area adjustment has been annexation of territory by the city. Annexation trends apparently fluctuate considerably from year to year. Some cities find that it creates as many problems in increased costs of urban service extensions and citizens' demands as it achieves in increased revenues. Table XXXII shows annexation trends since 1945.

Available data indicate that 402 municipalities added 276.3 square miles of territory through annexation in 1952.[4]

One of the most significant annexations in the last century is one completed by San Antonio, Texas, in 1952. This annexation involved 79.88 square miles, which compares with the Atlanta annexation of 82 square miles in 1951, and the Houston, Texas, annexation of 79 square miles in 1949.[5]

---

[4] *The Municipal Yearbook, 1953* (Chicago: The International City Managers' Association, 1953), p. 39.

[5] *Ibid.,* p. 39.

TABLE XXXII
ANNEXATION TRENDS, 1945-52 [a]

	All Cities Over 5,000	
Year	Total Number Annexing Cities	Number of Cities Annexing ½ Square Mile or Over
1952	402	75
1951	309	55
1950	382	60
1949	301	56
1948	288	59
1947	298	68
1946	259	43
1945	152	25

[a] Source: *The Municipal Yearbook, 1953*, p. 39.

After some twelve years of fragmentary annexation the San Antonio city government, under its city manager, began a study of the fringe area problems of the city, with a view to developing a sound, and somewhat bold, measure or measures to solve them. On the basis of this study, a proposal was made to city council that the best solution to the city's fringe problems would be to annex to the city 120 square miles of territory. The city council gave the ordinance a first reading and referred it back to the planning and zoning commission for further study and for feeling out citizen support and protest. Later, public meetings were held by the council, at which time support and grievances were heard. After hearings, the area to be annexed was fixed at approximately eighty miles. Annexation procedures for Texas home-rule cities are liberal, hence only council action by the annexing city is necessary.[6] In commenting upon the San Antonio annexation, John C. Rollins, writing in *The Municipal Yearbook, 1953,* comments: "San Antonio offers an excellent case study of the various elements of a sound annexation program. It similarly furnishes an outstanding example of a new city government studying deliberately and acting courageously on its convictions."[7]

4. *The lack of home rule.* The cities of many states are still the governmental victims of the states which legislatively created them. It is not unusual that the legislature from a given county may change the form of government, or the pay scales of the city employees. At the same time, such a delegation, through special legislation, may be able to legislate Sunday movies in or out, or change the bonded indebtedness, or provide for the recall of an official, all of these things being done without submission of the issues to the urban residents themselves through referendum. Frequently the attempt to make constitutional

---

[6] For a complete description of the San Antonio annexation see *Ibid.,* p. 35
[7] *Ibid.,* p. 35.

changes or to amend state laws to provide for a larger element of home rule to cities is bitterly fought by rural blocs in the legislatures.

5. *The cost of urban government.* The mounting cost of urban government, frequently accompanied by high tax rates, poses a tremendous problem to many cities. The extent of municipal debt is not exactly known. However, state and municipal debt was placed at $29.6 billion as of June 30, 1952.[8] For the first time in history, in 1952 the sale of municipal bonds exceeded $4 billion during the year. Total expenditures of 481 cities exceeded $6 billion in 1950 and 1951.[9]

Cities frequently find themselves in a vicious circle of financial tangles. Taxes being high, with a large percentage of new revenue going for bonded indebtedness, revenues frequently are scarce in accordance with need. Some cities experience a dismantling of property due to high taxes, and an outward movement of business from the central business section and an outward movement of industry from the city, plus the failure of new industry to come in because of high taxes. As a result, one financial headache adds to another. Some cities also face the problem of limitation of indebtedness by state legislative acts from which they are obliged to seek court and legislative relief.[10]

Cities attempt many things to relieve themselves of their financial administration. The refinancing of bonded indebtedness, raising legal limits on indebtedness, in-service training of assessors, improved assessment procedures, seeking a greater share of state revenue, especially gasoline taxes, and the seeking of municipal non-property taxes, in the form of service charges, municipal income taxes and sales taxes are among the attempts lately made to improve urban financing.

Some Trends in Urban Government. In our discussion of urban problems some trends of government are indicated. However, certain trends merit more detailed consideration:

1. *Increasing economic operations of urban governments.* One of the trends in urban government has been the increase in economic operations of cities. Some of these trends have been spotty. For instance, the distribution of electrical energy through municipally owned and operated utility boards piles up strongly in the power area of the Tennessee Valley Authority, whereas in New England private power distribution would continue to prevail without any trend toward municipal ownership.

Some reverse trends are noticeable. For instance, few cities own their bus or trolley systems today.

Intercity arrangements are common in the ownership and operation of utilities, especially water supply systems and sewerage systems.[11] (Table XXIII)

---

[8] *Ibid.*, pp. 193, 228.
[9] *Ibid.*, p. 193.
[10] For a recent record of these actions see the article on "Finance Administration," by Joseph F. Clark in *Ibid.*, pp. 193-198.
[11] On this point see *Ibid.*, 1953, p. 68.

TABLE XXXIII

OWNERSHIP AND OPERATION OF UTILITIES IN CITIES OF OVER 5,000,
OWNERSHIP AND OPERATION OF UTILITIES
IN CITIES OF OVER 5,000, 1953[a]

Type of Utility	All Cities Over 5,000	
	Number	Per Cent Reporting
Auditorium	406	16.6
Bus or trolley bus system	38	1.6
Electric generation and distribution	290	11.9
Electric distribution only	212	8.7
Gas manufacturing and distribution	42	1.7
Gas distribution only	66	2.7
Incinerator	421	17.2
Port facilities	78	3.2
Street railway	9	0.4
Sewage treatment plant	1,203	49.3
Slaughterhouse	26	1.1
Water supply and distribution	1,648	67.5
Water distribution only	151	6.2
Airport	510	20.9
Cities having none of the above	300	12.3
Cities not reporting	87	....

[a] Adapted from *The Municipal Yearbook, 1953* (Chicago: The International City Managers' Association, 1953), p. 67.

2. *The professionalization of city management.* The professionalization of all aspects of urban governmental services is a trend as exemplified, in part, by the growth of urban civil service or merit systems. The trend toward the growth of city managership as a profession is indicated by the fact that in 1952, 49 per cent of all persons appointed to city manager posts had been managers in other cities, whereas in 1939 this figure was 23 per cent, and between 1940 and 1949 34 per cent.[12] The trend toward appointing city managers from outside the city is another index of professionalization. In 1951, 74 per cent, and in 1952 71 per cent of persons appointed to managerial positions were from outside the cities to which they were appointed.[13]

The professionalization of the city managership is also indicated by the large number of in-service training provisions as well as professionalized programs of training in city managerships established in the universities.

3. *The growth of municipal leagues and associations.* Another trend in urban government, or at least affecting urban government, has been the growth of municipal leagues or associations of municipalities. Frequently faced by rural blocs in legislatures, and with the necessary and desired degree of urban home-rule lacking in many states,

---

[12] *Ibid.*, p. 517.
[13] *Ibid.*, p. 517.

cities have had to develop municipal associations as pressure groups, as well as to serve as a means of exchange of views and practices, and also as a source of technical assistance. Technical advisory services have been established by some of these bodies as in Tennessee, where a Municipal Technical Advisory Service is maintained by the Tennessee Municipal League in cooperation with the University of Tennessee. As of 1952 some 11,336 cities, towns and villages are now enrolled in these municipal associations which are now found in some forty-two states.[14]

The Future. In commenting upon future trends in urban government, Edward W. Weidner has this to say of the future:

> It is apparent that we have not heard the last of the attacks on freedom, and the next few years are likely to bring crucial issues of civil liberties to the attention of local governments for appropriate action. Urbanization of our society and professionalization of local government personnel and procedures also will undoubtedly continue and be extended. The services of municipal governments have not shown a substantial decline for over half a century, and there seems every reason to believe that services will continue to expand and be redefined, although on a modest scale.
>
> While problems of intergovernmental relations and finance will always be with us, it seems unlikely that either will take the center of the stage as the number one problem for local government during the next few years, except as they affect metropolitan areas. There is reason to believe that metropolitan problems will be considered the most striking phenomenon of local government in the 1950's, replacing the controversy over institutionalization of political and administrative leadership, so prevalent in recent years. Consensus seems to have been reached on local leadership, with both the council-manager and mayor-council plan being modified, the former to make room for the manager as a leader of policy, the latter to make room for an appointive administrative expert under control of the mayor.[15] Such are some projected trends for the future.

Workshop and Problems

1. What are the more crucial problems in urban government?
2. What is being done toward the solution of each of these problems?
3. What are some of the current trends in urban government? Evaluate each in terms of improvement of the city.

---

[14] See Carl H. Chatters, "State Municipal Leagues in 1952," *The Municipal Yearbook, 1953* (Chicago: The International City Managers' Association, 1953), p. 121.

[15] Edward W. Weidner, "Municipal Highlights of 1952," *The Municipal Yearbook, 1953,* p. 7.

4. What do you predict for future trends in urban government?

5. If possible spend some time in a city manager's or mayor's office in order to get some first hand information on urban government.

BIBLIOGRAPHY

Anderson, William, and Weidner, Edward W., *American City Government* (New York: Henry Holt & Co., 1950).

Bromage, Arthur W., *Introduction to Municipal Government and Administration* (New York: Appleton-Century-Crofts, 1949).

MacDonald, Austin F., *American City Government and Administration* (New York: Thomas Y. Crowell Co., 1951).

Mott, Rodney L., *Home Rule for America's Cities* (Chicago: American Municipal Association, 1949).

Municipal Yearbook, 1953 (Chicago: The International City Managers' Association, 1953).

Nolting, Orin F., *Management Methods in City Government* (Chicago: International City Managers' Association, 1942).

Queen, Stuart A., and Carpenter, David B., *The American City* (New York: McGraw-Hill Book Co., 1953).

Reed, Thomas H., *Municipal Management* (New York: McGraw-Hill Book Co., 1941).

Reimer, Svend, *The Modern City* (New York: Prentice-Hall, Inc., 1953).

U. S. Bureau of the Census, *Checklist of Basic Municipal Documents* (Washington, D. C.: Government Printing Office, 1948).

CHAPTER 13

Ecological Bases of Urban Problems

By WILLIAM E. COLE

The Thesis. Long before the time of reputable social science research, observing people saw the relationship between occupations and social problems and where people lived and certain problems of the population. For example, Pierre Clerget, writing of cities of the ancient and medieval periods, spoke of the grouping of trades into certain areas of the cities. These groupings were defined, in part, by practical considerations—economic and hygienic. Tanners and dyers worked near bodies of water. Rope-makers sought areas near the walls of cities.[1]

European scholars of the late nineteenth and early twentieth centuries developed studies showing the relationship between certain areas of cities and the existence of social and economic problems. Frédéric LePlay, "regarded as the founder of the social survey method of investigation," [2] made community studies, aspects of which dealt with the ecological structure of urban communities, as it related to standards of living of families.[3] Emile Durkheim did studies relating to the division of labor in industrial communities.[4] Many American studies have substantiated many of the observations established by the European scholars. Roderick McKenzie, in an early study of "natural areas" in the city of Columbus, Ohio, showed the relation between physical areas and dependency, delinquency, mobility and insanity.[5]

The thesis is that the total social configuration of a city breaks up into many sub-areas, some of which are given stability by zoning, but many of which exist as natural areas. The total impact of these sub-areas upon the population produces certain cultural characteristics and problems which may be different from those of other areas. Each area,

---

[1] Pierre Clerget, "Urbanism: A Historic, Geographic and Economic Study," *Annual Report of the Board of Regents of the Smithsonian Institution, 1912* (Washington, D. C.: Government Printing Office, 1913), pp. 653-659.

[2] Harry Elmer Barnes, Howard Becker and Frances Bennett Becker, *Contemporary Social Theory* (New York: D. Appleton Century Co., 1949), p. 161.

[3] Frédéric LePlay, *Les Ouvriers Europeens,,* 1855.

[4] Emile Durkheim, *De La Division Du Travail Social,* 1893.

[5] Roderick D. McKenzie, "The Neighborhood: A Study of Local Life in the City of Columbus, Ohio," *American Journal of Sociology,* Vol. 27, pp. 145-168, 344-363, 486-508, 588-610, 780-899, 1921-1922.

in turn, may attract people of different cultural backgrounds and characteristics or may attract enterprises of specific kinds which, in turn, add to the distinctiveness of the sub-area. A further aspect of our thesis is that as people change in cultural characteristics, or economic standing, they may shift from one section of a city to another in an attempt to better satisfy their value systems or in order to compete better with their competitors. The thesis also holds that ecological areas may be physically changed and that the problems growing out of them may be greatly reduced by changing the physical arrangements and by developing social, religious, health, economic and recreational programs in the areas.

Ecology and Its Processes. Ecology developed as a phase of the biological sciences, the term having been credited to Ernst Haeckel, who used it in a study of plants which was published in 1868.[6] Ecology is usually considered as the study of "the relation of organisms or groups of organisms to their environment."[7] A slightly different concept frequently used in urban sociology is that it has to do with the spatial patterning and adjustment of people and their social systems and activities to the social and physical environment of the city and the processes which give rise to these spatial patterns and adjustments.

The more important ecological processes are:

1. *Centralization.* The movement of population into a city and the tendency of population and activities of general or specific types to centralize in a definite locality for specific purposes is known as centralization. Centralization may eventually lead to concentration.

2. *Concentration.* The continuation of centralization may result in concentration which is the increased tendency for people or their enterprises to settle in a given area, thus resulting in a high density factor of both people or enterprise. Specialization and division of labor are frequently factors in economic or professional concentration. A medical center may begin and increasingly attract a large proportion of doctors of the city into the medical center area. Here the advantage may be largely special quarters suited to the needs of doctors and nearness to other physicians, especially specialists.

One frequently finds "automobile rows" in cities. Here one finds a concentration of sales, repair and parts facilities. Such concentration is no doubt due to the mutual helpfulness of one aspect of the automobile industry to another.

On the periphery of cities one invariably finds shopping centers where various business and service enterprises have located.

3. *Segregation.* Some areas of concentration in cities become so distinctive and differentiated from other areas in characteristics that

---

[6] Ernst Haeckel, *History of Creation*, 1868. See Amos H. Hawley, *Human Ecology* (New York: The Ronald Press Co., 1950), for a lengthy discussion of the development of ecology as a science.

[7] *Encyclopaedia Britannica*, Vol. 10, 14th Edition, p. 152.

they may to great degree be segregated from other areas. Sometimes through zoning commercial segregation may be favored. Price floors on new construction in residential areas may also favor segregation as do also various social and pseudo legal sanctions like provisions in deeds or in ordinances favoring certain religious or racial groups and discriminating against others. While the constitutionality of many of these measures is invalid, in many communities they do for practical purposes operate no matter what the legal theory or the legal situation is.

4. *Invasion.* Invasion is without a doubt the most spectacular ecological process found in a city. It is a process of group displacement whereby the territory occupied by one kind of group is invaded by a dissimilar group.

Common forms of invasion are the invasion of residential areas by commercial enterprises; the invasion of wholesale areas by retail businesses, or the invasion of an area occupied by one race or nationality by another race or nationality.

Lack of adequate zoning laws in the smaller urban centers and the willingness of urban governing bodies to rezone areas for commercial purposes are frequent causes of invasion. The economic rise of a segment of the population also may be a cause of invasion. Desire for prestige or for better living conditions, the shift of industries or commercial establishment, population pressure and changes in transportation routes and facilities also enter into causes favoring invasion.[8] Legal decisions against zoning laws and restrictive covenants against racial and religious groups have strengthened the courage of another culture or race to resort to invasion.

5. *Succession.* The displacement of one population element by an invading group or the development of one land use system by another is called succession.[9] In some cities one finds the areas at first occupied by single family dwellings, and at a later date by commercial establishments, now occupied by multiple family dwellings, especially apartments.

6. *Decentralization.* Decentralization is regarded as including two types of redistribution of population according to Bogue:

> *Diffusion,* or the outward flow of population from a central city into adjacent areas, and *Dispersion,* or the scattering of the population more evenly over the entire land area of the nation.[10]

[8] See Paul F. Cressy, "Population Succession in Chicago," *American Journal of Sociology,* Vol. 44 (July, 1938), pp. 59-69.

[9] See Andrew W. Lind, *An Island Community: Ecological Succession in Hawaii* (Chicago: University of Chicago Press, 1938). Also Harold Gibbard, *Residential Succession,* unpublished doctor's dissertation, University of Michigan, 1938.

[10] Donald J. Bogue, *Metropolitan Decentralization: A Study of Differential Growth* (Miami, Ohio: Scripps Foundation Studies in Population Distribution), Number 2, August, 1950, p. 2. See also Daniel Creamer, *Is Industry Decentralizing?* (Philadelphia: University of Pennsylvania Press, 1939), pp. 4-5.

Suburbanization is the most extensive diffusion trend. The suburban trend which followed World War I, and has paralleled the use of the automobile and other improved means of transportation, has become a well defined ecological trend growing out of the attempts of people to make a better adjustment to their urban environment. New York City grew 5.9 per cent between 1940-1950 but the remainder of the metropolitan area grew 19.4 per cent; the city of Detroit grew 13.9 per cent but the remainder of the metropolitan area grew 54.8 per cent. Around Los Angeles the increase was 69.8 per cent.[11]

William Whyte refers to the suburban trend as the "second melting pot" and holds that the values being formed as a result of suburbanization may become a dominant influence in America.[12] He says:

> The most striking phenomenon in the suburbs is that people's friendships, even their most intimate ones seem pretended; less on personality do friendships depend than on such seemingly inconsequential matters as the placement of a sidewalk, the view of a picture window, the height of a fence, or the width of a street.

While there are instances of friction in suburban communities and neighborhoods:

> It is the accommodation of people with each other, however, that is more significant. That people can find so much in common with one another that most of them need go no further, literally, than a stone's throw for their friendships is, to be sure, not altogether cheering; it is, however, a striking demonstration of how very deeply mass media and education have ironed out the regional and religious differences and prejudices that have separated people.[13]

Whyte holds that:

> The fact that these different kinds of people can mix so easily is due largely to the great spread of American middle class values. But it is also due to an active effort the people make to meet one another half-way. . . .[14] The seeking of common values applies markedly to religion. The neighborhood friendship patterns would be impossible unless religious beliefs had lost much of their segregating effect.[15]

Whyte discusses the design of superblocks in the Park Forest, Illinois, development as "the prototype of the new suburb." Here an attempt is

[11] Metropolitan Life Insurance Co., *Statistical Bulletin*, Vol. 33, Number 7 (July, 1952), p. 3.

[12] William H. Whyte, Jr., "How the New Suburbia Socializes," *Fortune*, Vol. XLVIII (August, 1953), pp. 120-122, 186, 188-190.

[13] *Ibid.*, p. 121.

[14] *Ibid.*, p. 186.

[15] *Ibid.*, p. 186.

made to group the apartments and rental courts to provide a "natural unit whose limit everyone understands." [16]

Bogue states that:

> Suburbanization has not been a flight to open country, but is distinctly a nucleated process. It appears to have begun in those satellite areas which contain large satellite cities and has spread rapidly into less urban areas. Thus, even though the large satellite cities were hard hit by the turning of the diffusive movement toward rural territory in the 1930's, these same cities are the nuclei for suburban settlement in this broader zone of diffusion. It appears as if not only central cities, but large satellite cities as well, are being diffusively decentralized.[17]

Bogue detects, from his research, three characteristics of the diffusive movement, namely,

> . . . the broader scope of its action than is generally recognized, the outward diffusion from large satellite cities, and a marked tendency toward rural farm as well as rural-non-farm residence . . . indicate that the growth which has occurred in the immediate environs of the metropolis is tending to a more "open pattern of land settlement." [18]

In August 1951, the President of the United States announced a national policy for industrial dispersion in order to enhance the nation's security and to protect its industrial production capacity from attack by aerial borne or submarine borne atomic weapons. A central feature of the policy was the provision that new defense installations be located ten or more miles from highly industrialized and centralized population areas.[19] In 1951, 1952, and 1953, the policy was attacked bitterly by politicians from the heavily industrialized areas. It is difficult at present writing to see to what extent such a policy would be a factor in decentralization, although it is known that some defense plant locations have been influenced by the policy the national government has tried to achieve.

One of the decentralizing ecological trends in urban areas is the trend toward polynucleation in urban areas. This is the trend toward special shopping districts and other type nuclear developments which have developed away from where the older central business areas of the cities are located. New towns and cities are frequently developed on a neighborhood basis with multiple shopping areas and with an elementary

---

[16] In connection with the topic of socialization—small groups see Leon Festinger, Stanley Schacter and Kurt Back, *Social Pressure in Informal Groups* (New York: Harper and Brothers, 1950).

[17] Bogue, *op. cit.*, p. 15.

[18] *Ibid.*, p. 15.

[19] See U. S. Department of Commerce, *Industrial Dispersion Handbook for Communities* (Washington, D. C.: Government Printing Office, 1952).

school and one or more churches in each neighborhood area. (See the accompanying diagram.)

Some Causes of Ecological Patterning. We have already hinted at a number of causes of ecological patterning. More specifically, some of the major causes are:

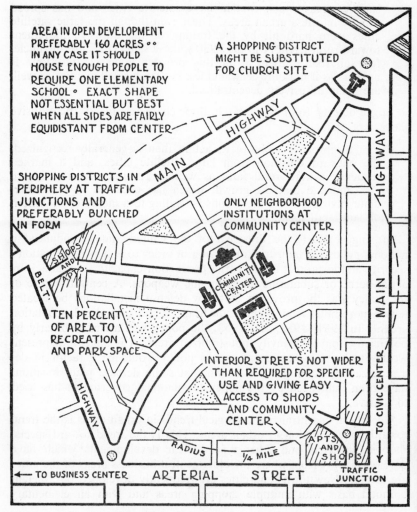

AREA IN OPEN DEVELOPMENT PREFERABLY 160 ACRES °° IN ANY CASE IT SHOULD HOUSE ENOUGH PEOPLE TO REQUIRE ONE ELEMENTARY SCHOOL ° EXACT SHAPE NOT ESSENTIAL BUT BEST WHEN ALL SIDES ARE FAIRLY EQUIDISTANT FROM CENTER

A SHOPPING DISTRICT MIGHT BE SUBSTITUTED FOR CHURCH SITE

HIGHWAY

MAIN

HIGHWAY

SHOPPING DISTRICTS IN PERIPHERY AT TRAFFIC JUNCTIONS AND PREFERABLY BUNCHED IN FORM

ONLY NEIGHBORHOOD INSTITUTIONS AT COMMUNITY CENTER

BELT

SHOPS AND APTS

COMMUNITY CENTER

MAIN

TEN PERCENT OF AREA TO RECREATION AND PARK SPACE

INTERIOR STREETS NOT WIDER THAN REQUIRED FOR SPECIFIC USE AND GIVING EASY ACCESS TO SHOPS AND COMMUNITY CENTER

HIGHWAY

TO CIVIC CENTER

RADIUS   ¼ MILE

APTS AND SHOPS

← TO BUSINESS CENTER   ARTERIAL   STREET   TRAFFIC JUNCTION

FIGURE 15. The Neighborhood Unit Plan as Visualized by Clarence Perry
Source: James Dahir, *The Neighborhood Unit Plan: Its Spread and Acceptance* (New York: Russell Sage Foundation, 1947).

1. *Competition for economic and social status and survival.*

2. *Complementary economic and social relationships*—what the plant and animal ecologists have sometimes called symbiotic relation-

ships or commensalism.[20] A good illustration of such complementary relationships is that found between retail stores, restaurants, hotels and theatres where the service of one contributes to the service of the other.

3. *Specialization as a factor in ecological patterning.* Its influence is noticeable in the symbiotic relationships established in businesses and professions. The growth of medical centers is an excellent illustration, where the services of one specialist may bear a complementary relationship to another and where the services of many specialists may complement the services of the general practitioner. The publishing and printing industry "districts" in the larger cities, especially New York and Chicago, reflect the influence of specialization upon ecological patterning.

4. *Legal and social controls* are influences on ecological patterning in that they may restrict freedom of movement of people and institutions and may restrict the purposes to which land-use may be put.

"Negro belts" may be fairly restricted to certain areas because of various restrictive covenants in deeds and social pressures. Property building restrictions may favor certain economic classes, and zoning restrictions may restrict against certain types of economic activity in favor of another type.

The price of property, either for sale or rental, may also restrict property to certain usage and accordingly favor one type of occupancy and discriminate against another type.

5. *Prestige factors* also enter into ecological patterning. Certain residential areas become prestige areas and land values rise accordingly. Certain business streets or areas have prestige value in trade over other areas hence attract certain types of trade to these areas. Competition in these instances intensifies the struggle for space and this, in turn, establishes an ecological position.

Relation to Problems. There is a wide range of problems that relate to ecological processes and ecological areas in cities. We shall mention only a few. Others are discussed in the chapters on undeveloped areas and urban deviates.

1. *The stabilizing of transitional areas.* One of the acute problems that many cities have is the stabilizing of areas which are in process of transition from one type of land use to another. One of these areas is the "zone in transition" described by Ernest W. Burgess, which surrounds the central business district in many cities.

In 1923, Burgess, in an article on "The Growth of the City," described the central section of the typical city as being made up of a series of concentric zones.[21] Beginning at the center and extending

---

[20] For a good discussion of these relationships in the field see Amos H. Hawley, *Human Ecology*, Chapter 3, "Interrelatedness of Life" (New York: The Ronald Press Co., 1950).

[21] Ernest W. Burgess, "The Growth of the City," *Proceedings of the American Sociological Society*, Vol. 18 (1923), pp. 85-89.

outward, these zones were: (1) the central business district; (2) the zone in transition; (3) the zone of working men's homes; (4) the zone of middle class dwellings, and (5) the zone of commuters' residences.

The zone in transition, which surrounds the central business district, is characterized as a zone in process of deterioration into which the central business district would later expand. Because the land is being held for central business expansion it is usually high in price even though many of the structures on it are obsolete and of low economic worth as structures. The tax monies spent on these areas are frequently large as compared to the revenue derived from them.

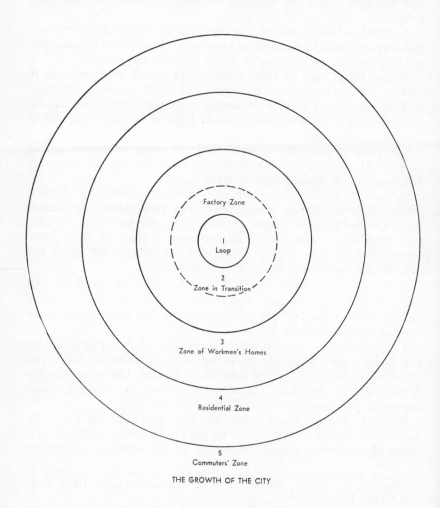

THE GROWTH OF THE CITY

FIGURE 16. Diagrammatic Ilustration of Burgess' Concentric Zone Theory

Some of the worst slum conditions in cities are to be found in zones in transition.

In a study of the Riverfront-First Creek area in Knoxville, Tennessee, which is in a zone in transition, adjacent to the central business district, it was found that the area contained 8,416 persons, or 6 per cent of the total population. This area required, in 1951, 16 per cent of the fire calls, provided 21 per cent of the adult crime, and 12 per cent of the juvenile delinquency. One out of 70 persons in the area had tuberculosis as contrasted to one case per 160 persons in the remainder of the city. While the area contained 6 per cent of the total population it provided only 3.6 per cent of total property revenue.[22]

In this transitional area several things are being done to stabilize the area. We shall use these to illustrate how areas in transition may be stabilized. A careful land use study of the area has been made. Some of the riverfront area is being used for a park and museum area. Adjacent to the central business area a civic auditorium site is being designated and several blocks are being utilized for down-town parking. Some areas are being zoned for new industrial and commercial development and others for recreation areas and athletic fields. The people who will be removed from the area to be developed are to be housed, when their income status is low enough, in public low rental housing projects. As in the Knoxville area, land use studies and land use plans for the city as a whole appear to be necessary for stabilizing areas in transition from one use to another. Some city governing bodies also encourage transitional developments by rezoning areas of the city without adequate technical advice.

2. *Delinquency areas.* No fact is better established in urban sociology than the one pointing to the relationship between juvenile delinquency and certain areas in cities. Most every city of any consequence has, at one time or another, noted this relationship. Of all American studies, perhaps those of Shaw and his associates are the most classic, in part, because of the date in which they appeared. Shaw[23] looks upon delinquency areas as disorganized communities. High rates of juvenile delinquency exist largely because the urban communities have not taken the measures they should to mitigate delinquency. This point of view is stressed by Elliott who, in speaking about these disorganized areas, says:

> They are communities in which patterns of conduct which are opposed to social well being have developed and been allowed to remain, chiefly because the members of the community have not taken constructive measures to build law abiding attitudes. Nor have they provided wholesome patterns of recreation in which

[22] G. T. Jones and L. A. Schoolcraft, *A Case Study: Cost of City Services in the Riverfront-First Creek Basin Area, Knoxville, Tennessee* (University of Tennessee, Knoxville: Department of Sociology, March 1952), unpublishd.
[23] Clifford R. Shaw and Henry D. McKay, *Juvenile Delinquency in Urban Areas* (Chicago: University of Chicago Press, 1942).

the children could be directed toward any appreciation of the desirability of law-abiding behavior. Moreover the small group with which the child or the adult criminal associates often promote the type of conduct called delinquency and crime.[24]

Settlement house programs, and other programs, as we shall see in subsequent chapters, are peculiarly adaptable to improving the conditions of high delinquency areas as is also slum clearance and urban redevelopment, with ample facilities for organized recreation programs being built into the development.

3. *Other areas of pathology.* Slums, rooming house areas and other "islands" in cities show high pathology rates. Slums and rooming house areas show high rates of vice and drug addiction [25] and other forms of personal disorganization.[26] "Islands" are also found in cities where other forms of deviation are found, the pathological classification of which would be difficult.[27]

In an interesting study August B. Hollingshead and Frederich C. Redlich tested the relationship between social stratification and psychiatric disorders.[28] This study is doubly significant because social strata are related to ecological areas in urban communities.

TABLE XXXIV

DISTRIBUTION OF NORMAL AND PSYCHIATRIC POPULATION
BY SOCIAL CLASS

Social Class	Normal Population *		Psychiatric Population	
	Number	Per Cent	Number	Per Cent
I	358	3.1	19	1.0
II	926	8.1	131	6.7
III	2,500	22.0	260	13.2
IV	5,256	46.0	758	38.6
V	2,037	17.8	723	36.8
Unknown **	345	3.0	72	3.7
Total	11,422	100.0	1,963	100.0

Chi square = 408.16, p less than .001.

* These figures are preliminary. They do not include Yale students, transients, institutionalized persons, and refusals.

** The unknown cases are not used in the calculation of chi square. They are individuals drawn in the sample, and psychiatric cases whose class level could not be determined because of paucity of data.

[24] Mabel A. Elliott, *Crime in Modern Society* (New York: Harper and Brothers, 1952), pp. 390-391.

[25] Alfred R. Lindesmith, *Addiction* (Bloomington, Indiana: Principia Press, 1947).

[26] Harvey W. Zorbaugh, *The Gold Coast and the Slum* (Chicago: University of Chicago Press, 1929).

[27] Caroline F. Ware, *Greenwich Village 1920-1930* (Boston: Houghton Mifflin Co., 1935).

[28] August B. Hollingshead and Frederick C. Redlich, "Social Stratification and Psychiatric Disorders," *American Sociological Review*, Vol. 18 (April, 1953), pp. 163-169.

Hollingshead and Redlich found a significant relationship between social class and *treated* prevalence of psychiatric disorders. They indicate, however, that these data need to be substantiated by more research. The relationships are shown in Table XXXIV.

Hollingshead and Redlich show a concentration of neurosis in the higher social classes and psychosis at the lower end of the social scale (Table XXXV).

TABLE XXXV

DISTRIBUTION OF NEUROSIS AND PSYCHOSIS BY SOCIAL CLASS

Social Class	Neurosis		Psychosis	
	Number	Per Cent	Number	Per Cent
I	10	52.6	9	47.4
II	88	67.2	43	32.8
III	115	44.2	145	55.8
IV	175	23.1	583	76.9
V	61	8.4	662	91.6
Total	449		1,442	

Chi square $=$ 296.45, p less than .001.

While the distribution in Table XXXV may be influenced by social distance between psychiatrist and patient and a class reaction to cost of psychiatric treatment, the authors believe there is a close relationship involved. In order to test further this relationship, Hollingshead studied schizophrenics in relation to class. He found that the index to prevalence in Class I, the highest was 22 and in Class V, the lowest, 246.[29]

WORKSHOP AND PROBLEMS

1. What is ecology?

2. What are the major ecological processes found in urban areas?

3. What are some of the important causes of urban ecological patterning?

4. Evaluate Whyte's appraisal of suburbanization.

5. Study at first hand examples of invasion.

6. What may be done to stabilize urban transitional areas?

7. What particular social problems tend to cling to certain ecological areas?

8. What may be done toward the redevelopment of urban "problem areas?"

9. Make an ecological map of some town or city with which you are acquainted.

---

[29] *Ibid.,* p. 168.

BIBLIOGRAPHY

Bogue, Donald J., *Metropolitan Decentralization, A Study of Differential Growth* (Miami, Ohio: Scripps Foundation, 1950).

Burgess, Ernest W., "The Growth of the City," *Proceedings of the American Sociological Society,* Vol. 18 (1923), pp. 85-89.

Cressy, Paul F., "Population Succession in Chicago," *American Journal of Sociology,* Vol. 44 (July, 1938), pp. 59-69.

Dahir, James, *The Neighborhood Unit Plan: Its Spread and Acceptance* (New York: Russell Sage Foundation, 1947).

Drake, St. Clair and Cayton, Horace R., *Black Metropolis: A Study of Negro Life in a Northern City* (New York: Harcourt Brace & Co., 1945).

Elliott, Mabel A., *Crime in Modern Society* (New York: Harper & Brothers, 1952).

Hawley, Amos H., *Human Ecology* (New York: The Ronald Press Co., 1950).

Hollingshead, August B. and Redlich, Frederick C., "Social Stratification and Psychiatric Disorders," *American Sociological Review,* Vol. 18, pp. 163-169, April 1953.

Lindesmith, Alfred R., *Addiction* (Bloomington, Indiana: Principia Press, 1947).

McKenzie, R. D., "The Neighborhood: A Study of Local Life in the City of Columbus, Ohio," *American Journal of Sociology,* Vol. 27, pp. 145-168, 344-363, 486-508, 588-610, 780-899, 1921-1922.

Shaw, Clifford R., and McKay, Henry D., *Juvenile Delinquency in Urban Areas* (Chicago: University of Chicago Press, 1942).

Ware, Caroline F., *Greenwich Village 1920-1930* (Boston: Houghton Mifflin Co., 1935).

Zorbaugh, Harvey W., *The Gold Coast and the Slum* (Chicago: University of Chicago Press, 1929).

CHAPTER 14

Developing An Economic Base

By WILLIAM E. COLE

The Great Contribution and the Great Blight. One of the great contributions which the city has made has been the volume and variety of jobs which it has made available. The significance of this contribution is more than economic—it strikes deeply at democratic theory and practice. The democratic theory says that people are different. They are born with different characteristics and the impact of social conditioning adds to this difference. The democratic theory holds also that they should be schooled and trained in accordance with these individual differences and then that they should have an opportunity, on the labor market, to exchange their developed skills or capacities for cash or kind. The city, therefore, through making available a wide range of jobs and services at all skill levels, is making contributions not only to a sound economy but also is effectively implementing democratic ideology and democratic practice.

The great blight, and the fear of the great blight, that hovers over cities is the spectre of unemployment in urban life. The fears of the thirties are still present in the minds of the adult generation. At that time more than 12 million adults were unemployed in the nation. This fear is present because it is true that urban people do not till the fields, fell the trees or dig the minerals or net the streams and the ocean, but make their living by working with other people, i. e., selling goods or services, transporting people or moving goods for them, or manufacturing goods to be sold on the competitive market. This means that urban people are mutually interdependent. They do not, mostly, work for themselves but for someone else. They are, in short, dependent upon jobs. When anything happens to the availability of jobs, unemployment mounts and economic distress follows. There is no land to fall back upon, even though the people knew how to till it. While unemployment compensation is available now, as it was not during the depression of the thirties, such compensation is designed to cushion only the impact of short periods of unemployment rather than periods of long range unemployment.

Some Long Range Trends in the Labor Force. There are a number of

243

long range trends in the labor force pertinent to our discussion of an urban economic base. Others have been discussed in the chapters on urban growth. Some of these trends are:

1. *The decline of the labor force in agriculture.* This decline is indicated in Table XXXVI and has, of course, been followed by an accompanying increase of the per cent of the total labor force employed in non-agricultural pursuits.

As indicated in Table XXXVI, in 1820 31.8 per cent of the population, ten years of age and over, were engaged in agricultural pursuits, and 12.5 per cent in non-agricultural pursuits. By 1940 this per cent had changed to 8.3 per cent of those ten years of age and over who were employed in agriculture and 38.9 per cent employed in non-

TABLE XXXVI

EMPLOYMENT IN AGRICULTURAL AND NON-AGRICULTURAL
PURSUITS, 1820-1940, 1953

	All Persons 10 Years and Over				
		Employed in Agricultural Pursuits		Employed in Non-Agricultural Pursuits	
Year	In the Total Population	Number	Per Cent	Number	Per Cent
1820	6,487,815	2,068,958	31.8	812,042	12.5
1830	8,639,412	2,772,453	32.0	1,159,084	13.4
1840	11,629,006	3,719,951	31.9	1,700,049	14.6
1850	16,452,835	4,901,882	29.7	2,795,314	16.9
1860	22,429,625	6,207,634	27.6	4,325,116	19.2
1870	29,123,683	6,849,772	23.5	6,075,179	20.8
1880	36,761,607	8,584,810	23.3	8,807,289	23.9
1890	47,413,559	9,938,373	20.9	13,379,810	28.2
1900	57,949,824	10,911,998	18.8	18,161,235	31.3
1910	71,580,270	11,591,767	16.1	25,779,027	36.0
1920	82,739,315	11,448,770	13.8	30,984,765	37.4
1930	98,723,047	10,471,998	10.6	38,357,922	38.8
1940	110,443,129	9,162,547	8.3	42,985,704	38.9
1953*	111,300,000	6,070,000	5.0	55,158,000	49.5

* The 1953 (April) data are for 14 years of age and older but they are roughly indicative of the trend.

Source: Adapted from U. S. Bureau of the Census, *Statistical Abstract of the United States: 1952* (Seventy-third edition) (Washington, D. C.: 1952), p. 175. The data for 1953 are from "The Monthly Report on the Labor Force: May 1953," *Current Population Reports, Labor Force,* Series P-57, No. 131, June 5, 1953.

agricultural pursuits. In April 1953, of those fourteen years of age and older in the population, only 5.0 per cent were engaged in agriculture and 49.5 per cent in non-agricultural pursuits.

Specifically, in field types of occupations in which there have been declines are forestry, mining and fishing. Some of this decline in employment has been due to the increase in mechanization of these pursuits.

2. *An increase in the services and in the professions.* Urbanization has speeded the increase in services and the professions. Much of this increase is due to the division of labor, the increased specialization and increasingly complex occupational structure of urban communities which has grown out of the demand for goods and services by urban dwellers. Some examples of increases in the services and professions are the services which have developed around the sale and use of the automobile, the increase in personal services such as beauty salons, and the great specialization that has taken place in the medical profession in the last thirty years.

3. *Increase in transportation and communication.* An important phase of technological change has been in transportation and communication. A steady increase in employment in these fields is noticeable. The sizable increase in the trucking industry and in employment in broadcasting, telecasting, and advertising are aspects of this increase.

4. *An increase in governmental employment.* One of the noticeable trends in employment has been the long range increase in personnel in government service. The national and state capitals have grown as a result of expansion in government operations. To lesser degree, this has also been true of local centers of government. Many political capitals have also grown as manufacturing centers or centers for trade and other services.

5. *An increase in unionized employment.* At one time the urban worker was not unionized and was in a real sense his own bargainer. That day is past. He is today largely a unionized worker with various officials carrying on the representation and the bargaining process for him. This means in part certain mass privileges such as the forty hour week and vacation privileges. While no doubt many gains have been made through unionization, it is also true that the unionized worker has lost certain rights and privileges which he once had, one of which is the right of bargaining on an individual basis.

What Business and Industrial Enterprises Expect of a Community. Business enterprises are not and cannot be in business for their health—they are in business to make money. They may be in business for a variety of reasons but a primary goal is profit.

There are likely to be many urban communities in which an industry could make a profit, therefore, we have to look to other factors which industry expects from urban communities. One is nearness to markets and another may be nearness to raw products, if the raw products are heavy in weight or bulky, thus entailing high costs in transportation. Business interests are also concerned with good factory sites, good sites for stores or other forms of commercial buildings. Cities interested in obtaining industries or new commercial enterprises should try to see that sites are available at all times. Business enterprises want to know how existing business and industry is being treated by the local community.

Business is suspicious of poor urban government and, no doubt, some cities are passed up by prospective industries and other new businesses because of the poor government of the city.

New industry wants a potential labor supply comparable to its needs. Economic enterprises want a community which ranks high in the elements making up a good community. They are anxious that the community provide good schools, churches and adequate recreation facilities and direction. They want also a community whose class structure is such that their employees will fit well into the community class structure without great friction or class frustration.

Industry seeks reasonable taxation and fair tax systems. Most substantial industries are willing to pay a fair share of the tax bill. This is true, if for no other reason, than that industry desires a voice in government, and being a taxpayer gives it a right to a voice in government. Elsewhere we will discuss subsidization in more detail.

Industrial Planning for Cities. In addition to planning for industrial sites and commercial areas as part of comprehensive urban land planning, there are many things that cities are doing specifically related to the development of a more adequate economic base.

1. *The development of economic base studies.* As a phase of master plan development, some of the larger cities are developing economic base studies. These studies are highly variable in content, being tailored especially to the unique economic features and situations of the city.

One of the finer earlier economic base studies was made in Detroit.[1] This report stressed the geographic and historical setting of Detroit; the economic function of the Detroit community; manufacturing employment; secondary employment in the trades and services; future employment in the Detroit area; Detroit's potential for new economic activity and the possible impact of the St. Lawrence Waterway, long under discussion, and now about to get underway, upon the economy of Detroit. In a section on "Employment Factors in the Living Pattern," the major occupational groups are analyzed; employment instability and the peculiar lack of secondary workers in the Detroit community is discussed. Finally, employment stability and the future city is dealt with in some detail.

It must be stressed at this point that economic base plans or studies are not to be confused with financial plans for the financing of a program of physical development such as those sometimes set forth in a comprehensive city plan.

2. *Industrial development staffs.* The traditional local Chamber of Commerce organization is so well known that it need not be discussed at this point. However, some chambers are developing industrial divisions, designed especially to seek new industries and expand existing

---

[1] City Plan Commission, City of Detroit, *Economic Base of Detroit* (Detroit: The Commission, 1944).

ones. Some cities are setting up industrial development bodies and committees outside of the chamber of commerce structures to push their respective committees in the quest for new economic enterprise. Some of these are quite successful in attracting new industries.

3. *Community inventories of industrial advantages.* One of the problems faced by small urban communities is the lack of information concerning them in the hands of out-of-community firms contemplating new enterprises, or the expansion of existing enterprises. To help overcome this problem, the Tennessee State Planning Commission, to use an example, has asked all the towns and cities of the state to make an inventory of their industrial advantages. This information is then filed under various systems of cross indexing in all the regional offices of the State Planning Commission, in the state office of the Commission, and in the offices of the Tennessee Valley Authority, for use by the representatives of companies seeking new industrial and commercial locations. The Tennessee inventory covers the following items for each community.

A. *Natural Resources:*[2]
   1. Geography
   2. Climate
   3. Local raw materials.

B. *General Economy:*
   1. Population [3]
   2. Labor
   3. Market
   4. Existing manufacturing industries in community
   5. Transportation facilities:
      a. Railroads
      b. Bus and truck systems
      c. Waterways
      d. Airport
   6. Power
   7. Fuel
   8. Sewage and waste disposal
   9. Water supply
   10. Communication facilities.

C. *Government:*
   1. Administration

---

[2] See also Victor Roterus, *The Geographic Basis of Urban Planning* (Washington, D. C.: Department of Commerce, June 1950).

[3] See Van Buren Stanbery, *Better Population Forecasting for Areas and Communities* (Washington, D. C.: U. S. Department of Commerce, September 1952), and also *Population Analysis of Small Areas* (Washington, D. C.: U. S. Department of Commerce, May 1950).

    2. Finances
    3. Special inducements to new industry.
D. *Community Facilities:*
    1. Existing data, maps, etc., on the community
    2. Educational facilities
    3. Health facilities
    4. Recreation facilities
    5. Police protection facilities
    6. Fire protection facilities
    7. City streets
    8. Banking facilities
    9. Construction and service facilities
   10. Retail facilities
   11. Housing conditions
   12. Hotels and restaurants
   13. Newspapers
   14. Laundries and dry cleaners
   15. Civic organizations
   16. Community leaders.

Many firms have located commercial, service, and industrial enterprises in Tennessee as a result of the use of the community inventories.

4. *Incentive plans.* Some cities and some states, as a policy offer various types of incentives to new economic enterprises. Among such incentives are: freedom from taxation for a period, or special tax privileges; factory or commercial sites or buildings; special provision of utilities as roads, water, sewage or power connections; special utility rates, and so on.

According to the records:

> Mississippi was the first state to authorize issuing municipal bonds to construct buildings to be leased to industry under a "balance-industry-with-agriculture" program.
> States in which municipalities may issue such bonds now (1952) include Alabama, Illinois, Kentucky, Louisiana, Mississippi and Tennessee. Legislatures in Maryland, Massachusetts, Rhode Island and Virginia have refused to enact legislation permitting issuance of such industrial plant bonds.[4]
> The Mississippi legislature in 1952 passed a statute authorizing municipalities to exempt ad valorem taxes for limited periods on real and personal property to new industrial plants.[5]

Frequently incentive plans are of doubtful wisdom and sometimes prove a genuine handicap to a community. One or two instances are

---

[4] *The Municipal Yearbook, 1953* (Chicago: The International City Managers' Association, 1953), p. 195.
[5] *Ibid.,* 1953, p. 195.

sufficient to indicate this. One town of 5,000 population, anxious to add to its payroll, offered at the town's expense a building to a firm as a shirt factory. The county court also granted the firm immunity from taxation for five years. At the end of the free-tax period, the county placed an assessment on the plant only to have the company remove its machinery to another town in another county which also offered it a building and freedom from taxation. Another large firm was granted tax immunity by the county for five years. In the meantime the county needed funds and proceeded to tax the industry. A law suit resulted with the corporation being upheld. As a matter of good-will the corporation made a $40,000 contribution to the county to be used as it saw fit.

Seward B. Snell indicated three criteria, according to tax theorists, which should all be met to establish a valid case of tax exemption:

> (1) The property seeking exemption should be used in rendering a service affected with a bona fide public interest; (2) the service must be capable of being fostered adequately on a purely commercial basis, without additional assistance in the form of grants-in-aid, free supplies, etc.; and (3) the exemption should not be granted unless it can be done without serious disproportion between the benefit and the cost of the municipality concerned.[6]

Increasingly, the human factor is entering into the economic development of cities. Where groups of men get together intent on developing the economic life of their communities progress is made. Akron, Ohio, stands as symbol of such initiative as well as do some of the smaller communities, like Kingsport, Tennessee. Aggressiveness of a business group in quest for new enterprise will at times overcome some of the physical and institutional handicaps of a city. It certainly is also needed to sell the potentialities of a community to a prospective client.

WORKSHOP AND PROBLEMS

1. What has been the great contribution the city has made to the economic well-being of people?
2. What have been the long range trends in the labor force?
3. What does industry expect of a community?
4. What is being done by communities to more intelligently attract industry?
5. What is your community doing to attract industry?

BIBLIOGRAPHY

Area Development Division, U. S. Chamber of Commerce, *Basic Industrial Location Factors* (Washington, D. C.: U. S. Government Printing Office).
Bureau of Research, University of Santa Clara, *Bidding for Industrial*

---

[6] Seward B. Snell, "Tax Exemptions to Encourage Industry," *Taxes: The Tax Magazine* (May 1951).

Payrolls: A Study of Current Methods and Results in Community Advertising (Santa Clara, California: November, 1951).

Economic plans or economic base reports of various cities.

Queen, Stuart Alfred, and Carpenter, David Bailey, *The American City* (revised edition) (New York: The McGraw-Hill Book Co., 1953).

Snell, Seward B., "Tax Exemptions to Encourage Industry," *Taxes: The Tax Magazine,* May, 1951.

Stanbery, Van Buren, *Better Population Forecasting for Areas and Communities* (Washington, D. C.: U. S. Department of Commerce, 1950).

U. S. Department of Commerce, *The Geographic Basis of Urban Planning* (Washington, D. C.: June, 1950).

————————————————, *Population Analysis of Small Areas* (Washington, D. C.: May, 1950).

Chapter 15

Housing the Urban Population

By William E. Cole

The Chief Problems. Housing; along with food and clothing, constitutes one of the primary needs of man. Its provision in urban societies is much more complex than in rural areas, although certain aids in providing housing may be found in cities that are not available for rural peoples.

The problems in urban housing are many. We will treat several of these briefly and then devote considerable attention to the major problem which is providing adequate housing for low income families.

1. *Providing an adequate number of dwelling units.* The mere physical task of providing a sufficient volume of housing to take care of new families in a growing population, which is at the same time undergoing urbanization, and to provide for those being abandoned and dismantled because of obsolescence, is within itself a big problem. To add to this acuteness over the past two decades was the slump in housing in the depression of the 30's and the restrictions placed upon housing during World War II and the early period of the Korean conflict. To further aggravate the situation was the great increase in marriages of the war and post-war period and the high birth rates following World War II.

> For the fifteen year period 1946-1960, it is estimated that an average of 1,070,000 new urban dwelling units would be demanded annually, at an average construction cost slightly in excess of $3,800 per unit at 1940 prices.[1]

When we compare this demand with the total volume of new urban and rural non-farm dwellings built between 1920 and 1951, the magnitude of the task is great. Only in 1948, 1949, 1950 and 1951 did we start more than a million urban and rural non-farm dwelling units (see Table XXXVII).

Between April 1947 and April 1948, families increased by 1,040,000 and households increased 1,582,000 in number. Between April 1948

---

[1] J. Frederick Dewhurst and Associates, *America's Needs and Resources* (New York: The Twentieth Century Fund, 1947), p. 155.

and April 1949 families increased 1,257,000 in number and households 1,387,000. In April 1952 there were 45,464,000 households in the United States. A median estimate is that there will be 47,701,000 households by July 1955, and by 1960, 50,822,000 households.[2] These data reflect the tremendous task in home building if the great increases in households and families are to be serviced. To add to the problem an unknown volume of housing will become dilapidated between now and 1960.

2. *The problem of inadequacy of existing housing.* It is difficult to appraise the adequacy of existing housing. The 1950 Census of Housing indicated 3,263,000 vacant dwelling units of which 1,238,000 were seasonal housing. Non-seasonal dilapidated dwelling units amounted to 266,000 units, of which 115,000 were in urban areas and 151,000 in rural non-farm areas.[3] In an inventory of non-farm housing made

TABLE XXXVII

NON-FARM DWELLING UNITS STARTED IN URBAN AND RURAL
NON-FARM AREAS, 1920-1951

Year	Urban	Rural Non-Farm
1920	196,000	51,000
1925	752,000	185,000
1930	236,000	94,000
1935	117,000	104,000
1940	397,000	206,000
1942	227,400	128,600
1943	66,600	143,600
1944	45,700	117,700
1945	133,900	75,400
1946	403,600	266,900
1947	479,800	309,200
1948	624,000	406,700
1949	588,800	436,300
1950	827,800	568,200•
1951	595,300	496,000

Source: U. S. Bureau of the Census, *Statistical Abstract of the United States, 1952* (Seventy-third Edition) (Washington, D. C.: 1952), p. 726.

in April 1947, the U. S. Housing and Home Finance Agency, using the categories "standard" and "substandard" indicated some 6,104,000 slum dwellings which needed either extensive repairs or replacement. Out of 34,133,000 non-farm units, 2,703,000 were definitely sub-

[2] Bureau of the Census, Current Population Reports, *Population Characteristics,* Series P-201, No. 42 (December 28, 1952), p. 1.
[3] Bureau of the Census, "Housing Characteristics of the United States, April 1, 1950," *1950 Census of Housing, Preliminary Reports,* Series HC-5, No. 1 (February 17, 1951), p. 1.

standard and in need of major repairs and 6,389,000 units were in good condition but lacked private bath and toilet (Table XXXVIII). One of the reasons for inadequacy is the age of dwellings. Data collected in 1950 indicate that 46.4 per cent urban dwelling units were built prior to 1919, whereas another 22.2 per cent were built between 1920 and 1929 (Table XXXIX). The Federal Housing and Home Finance Agency estimates that the total number of non-farm houses in need of replacement or rehabilitation between 1947 and 1960 will be 8,470,000 (Table XL).

While rural-farm housing has much less adequate facilities than urban housing (Table XLI), data on facilities in urban dwellings indicate many substandard factors. In 1950, 5.5 per cent of dwelling units shared an indoor flush toilet with another family, whereas 7.1 per cent had no inside flush toilet. No bath tub or shower was found in 11.3 urban dwellings, while 10.9 per cent had only cold water inside the dwelling structure.

3. *The problem of blighting and the creation of slums.* Blighting is a term that has been applied to the gradual but progressive deterioration of an area. Professor Mackintosh develops four factors in the creation of slums, two of which are environmental and two of which are personal, namely:

TABLE XXXVIII

QUALITY OF THE NON-FARM HOUSING INVENTORY, APRIL 1947
(In Thousands)

Condition	Total Non-Farm	Urban	Rural Non-Farm
Total units	34,133	24,430	9,703
In need of major repair	2,703	1,658	1,045
Standard	0	0	0
Sub-Standard	2,703	1,658	1,045
In good condition but lacking private bath and toilet	6,389	2,903	3,486
Standard	2,988	0	2,988
Sub-standard	3,401	2,903	498
In good condition and having private bath and toilet	25,041	19,869	5,172

ᵃ Excludes 115,000 other dwellings—tents, caves, houseboats, etc.

Source: Housing and Home Finance Agency, *How Big Is the Housing Job?* (Washington, D. C.: Housing and Home Finance Agency, (September 1949), p. 16.

TABLE XXXIX

URBAN DWELLING UNITS—YEAR BUILT, 1950

Year Built	Number (Thousands)	Per Cent
Number reporting	28.292	100.0
1919 or earlier	13,137	46.5
1920-1929	6,267	22.2
1930-1939	3,351	11.8
1940-1944	2,186	7.7
1945 or later	3,351	11.8

Source: U. S. Bureau of the Census, *Statistical Abstract of the United States, 1952* (Seventy-third Edition) (Washington, D. C.: 1952), p. 739.

TABLE XL

RURAL NON-FARM DWELLING UNITS NEEDING REPLACEMENT OR REHABILITATION (1947-1960)

Condition	Number
Urban and rural non-farm units which were in need of major repairs and urban units which lacked private bath and toilet in April 1947	5,600,000
Current standard non-farm units which will deteriorate by 1960	1,500,000
Suburban units lacking private bath and toilet	500,000
Estimated losses through disaster, demolition, etc.	520,000
Losses through removal of temporary housing	350,000
Total replacement and rehabilitation need	8,470,000

Source: U. S. Bureau of the Census, *Housing Characteristics of the United States,* Series P.70 (April 1947).

TABLE XLI

DWELLING FACILITIES, URBAN, RURAL NON-FARM AND RURAL FARM, 1950

Facility	Urban	Rural Non-Farm	Rural-Farm
With electric lights	98.9	90.4	77.7
No electric lights	1.1	9.6	22.3
Flush toilet inside structure, exclusive use	86.7	54.7	27.3
Flush toilet inside structure, shared ...	5.5	2.0	0.4
Other toilet facilities (including privy)	7.1	39.9	65.4
No toilet	0.7	3.4	6.9
Installed bathtub or shower, exclusive use	83.5	53.3	29.1
Installed bathtub or shower, shared ...	5.1	1.9	0.3
No bathtub or shower	11.3	44.8	70.6
Hot and cold piped running water inside structure	85.2	50.9	27.2
Only cold water inside structure	10.9	17.2	14.6
Piped running water outside structure	1.8	3.6	2.7
No piped running water	2.0	28.2	55.5

Source: Bureau of the Census, *Statistical Abstract of the United States, 1952* (Seventy-third Edition) (Washington, D. C.: 1952), pp. 738-739.

1. The physical surroundings of the house
2. The physical condition of the house
3. The owner
4. The tenant.[4]

A simple test of environment, according to Mackintosh, is this:

> Would a new house on the same site satisfy the needs of comfort and reasonable amenity, or merely perpetuate the defects—of lack of light and air, for example—against which the progressive authority is striving?[5]

Poor drainage, poor use of sloping land, land overcrowding, inadequate original construction are causes of blighting. Smoke is also an important cause of blighting, making upkeep of houses, especially wooden, painted houses difficult. The change in use of a house, say from residence to shop, and frequently the rezoning of an area from residential to commercial use, is likely to cause the deterioration of an area for residential purposes. The conversion of a single family dwelling into apartments or the invasion of industry or commercial establishments into a residential area frequently leads to the beginnings of blighting. The change from owner to tenant occupancy may mean that standards are not maintained. Many cities do not have occupancy standards other than a requirement that sewage connections be made,* and, therefore, houses may be permitted to deteriorate to a point where they are not suitable for habitation. Finally, the quality of housekeeping that goes on in a housing unit may hasten or impede its deterioration. This has been a problem in public housing. When poor housekeeping, combined with adverse environmental factors, is added to a poorly built structure, which houses an economically marginal or submarginal population, then the stage is set for the process of deterioration we call blighting in which we find individual units of what Mackintosh calls "sordid houses."[6]

5. *The cost of slums.* Many studies have been made of the cost of slum areas, showing the inflow of public monies and services into slum areas as compared to what comes out of them. One study in Louisville, Kentucky, indicating the inflow of services into a standard and substandard area of approximately the same population, shows that the substandard area cost in relief and administrative services over $43 thousand as compared to slightly over $3 thousand in the standard area (Table XLII).[7]

[4] J. M. Mackintosh, *Housing and Family Life* (London: Cassell and Co., Ltd., 1952), p. 16.
[5] *Ibid.*, p. 16.
*In some cities such connections do not have to be made if the foundation of the house is below street level.
[6] *Ibid.*, pp. 30-41.
[7] *Public Services and Blighted Areas* (A Joint Report of the Louisville and Jefferson County Planning and Zoning Commission and the City of Louisville Municipal Housing Commission, April 1951).

TABLE XLII

COMPARISON OF SERVICES IN STANDARD AND SUBSTANDARD
AREA OF LOUISVILLE, KENTUCKY, 1949

Item	Substandard Area	Standard Area
Per cent of total city population in area	4.7	4.3
Residential acres	400	660
Housing (per cent)		
Slum	68.0	3.5
Substandard	27.0	19.0
Acceptable	5.0	77.5
Per cent of city arrests	6.0	2.2
Patrol calls	2,048	1,091
Ambulance calls	137	73
Cases referred to Criminal Court	300	95
Delinquents appearing in Juvenile Court (1948-1950)	268	73
Residential fire calls	146	100
Number of families receiving assistance from Municipal Bureau of Social Services	91	6
Relief expenditure—one month	$3,194.86	$225.52
Relief and administration expenditures for year 1950 (estimated)	$43,138.32	$3,126.24
Number of social service cases residing in study areas as revealed by nine agencies	1,147	341
Tuberculosis death rate, 1949-1950 (per 100,000 population)	40.6	25.3
Infant mortality rate, 1949-1950 (per 1,000 live births)	39.6	34.2

The Louisville data speak for themselves. They reflect a substandard area requiring a wide variety of services out of proportion to its size and area and reflect a high incidence of social pathology.

In a study of a similar substandard area in Knoxville, Tennessee, Jones and Schoolcraft found a similar situation.[8]

The unmeasurable human results of having to live in slum areas—the frustrations, the blighted personalities, lack of privacy, low idealism, etc.—are perhaps the most crucial costs and cannot be measured in dollars.

6. *The problem of housing special groups.* In addition to the general problem of housing of families, there are a number of special groups in urban communities that need housing. First, are the needs of the *single* person. Here the needs are highly variable ranging from one room desired by many persons to efficiency apartments desired for light housekeeping. YMCA, YWCA, YWHA, and YMHA organizations support residence facilities in most cities. The Mills hotels

[8] G. T. Jones and L. A. Schoolcraft, *A Case Study: Cost of City Services in the Riverfront-First Creek Basin Area* (unpublished) (Knoxville: The University of Tennessee, Department of Sociology, March 1952).

in New York City constituted an early attempt through philanthropic subsidy to provide housing for working men. A number of foreign cities and countries, for example Glasgow, Scotland, have promoted the provision of municipal lodging houses and hotel facilities for single folks.[9]

The *aged* comprise a neglected group in housing. To add to the difficulty are the several different physical conditions of aged folk in need of housing. There are those who are well and those bedridden, with various in-between classes. There is the aged single person and the aged couple. Some provision for aged couples should be provided in every public housing project, preferably on the ground floor. Special hospital facilities for the bedridden and senile aged are often necessary to keep them out of mental hospitals, almshouses and general hospitals. Such specialized geriatric institutions may be developed and maintained by municipalities, or at county, parish or state expense. It would also seem that boarding homes for aged persons, with funds available through themselves or through relatives, could be provided at a fair rate of income on investment by private enterprise. The state of Florida is now promoting the development of villages for retired persons where certain physical features, such as handrails and ramps to replace stairways and steps, would be built into the structures and where special provisions would be made for recreation and physical treatment.[10]

In England the National Corporation for the Care of Old People has placed in high priority on its list of activities the making of grants toward the establishment of homes for the aged. The work of the Corporation is designed to supplement the work of establishing residential homes for the aged carried out by many church and philanthropic groups. The Corporation has also been instrumental in developing facilities for the aged in housing projects and has also been instrumental in promoting complete housing units for aged people.[11] A number of organizations in England have given attention to making available mobile meal service, visitation services and medical care and housekeeping services for aged people, as well as the development of occupational pursuits and recreational activities.[12] Such planning approaches the provision of what is needed in the way of housing and associated services if the needs of the aged are to be met.

Another special group that must be countered with in housing is the *undesirable tenant,* frequently a family of low ability and low standards

[9] See Maurice Davie, *Problems of City Life* (New York: John Wiley and Sons, 1932), pp. 128-143.

[10] J. M. Mackintosh in his *Housing and Family Life* (London: Cassell and Co., Ltd., 1952), pp. 185-190, devotes considerable space to the housing of the aged and the physical features which should be built into the structures. His treatise of course is designed to fit English conditions.

[11] See: National Old People's Welfare Committee, *Age Is Opportunity* (London: National Council of Social Service, 1949).

[12] See *Ibid.* for detailed statements on these services.

who have never known adequate housing and who would probably be destructive of adequate housing maintenance once it was provided for them. If the facts were known, we, no doubt, have tried to keep these families out of housing projects through a selective process. Housing supervisors have also tried to deal with low standard tenants through education in housekeeping before and after such families were moved into housing projects. This is done on the assumption that families can be taught to care for and to have respect for property. Holland, according to Mackintosh, has developed a plan for caring for such families. Under constant supervision they are placed in simple, low cost houses where the floors and walls are of concrete or other masonry and where the doors and window frames are of metal; where all hardware and electric fixtures are exceptionally strong; where the stove is simple and the heat is from a central heating unit. Monetary rewards are then made for good conduct, and after a period of good housekeeping the families may be graduated to a higher standard housing project.[13]

7. *The big problem—adequate housing for low income classes.* The biggest problem in housing is the problem of providing adequate low cost housing for perhaps the lowest 20 per cent of families on the economic scale.

Out of his experience as teacher and as a member of a local housing authority, it has never been clear to the writer that adequate housing could be provided for this element in the population by private enterprise, and that some form of public subsidy is necessary if adequate housing is to be provided. Above this group, it may be possible for private enterprise to do most of the housing job, and should have only the implementation of government through the underwriting of private financing. Suggestions have been made to private industry as to how it can implement low cost housing.[14]

Desirable Standards in Housing. It is not possible in this volume to develop in any detail all the standards desired in housing as there are a large number of standards desirable for site selection, utilities, traffic ways, neighborhood density and room occupancy.[15]

Dewhurst and his associates have stated briefly and simply the minimum characteristics which any house should possess:

1. Adequate protection against the elements and such threats to health and safety as are encountered in the particular locality. . . .

---

[13] See J. M. Mackintosh, *Housing and Family Life* (London: Cassell and Co., Ltd., 1952), pp. 191-199.

[14] U. S. Federal Housing Administration, *Low Rental Housing for Private Investment* (Washington, D. C.: U. S. Government Printing Office, 1940).

[15] See: American Public Health Association, Committee on Hygiene of Housing, *Planning the Neighborhood* (Chicago: Public Administration Service, 1948); and American Public Health Association, Committee on Hygiene of Housing, *Basic Principles of Healthful Housing* (2nd Edition) (New York: The Association, 1931).

2. Heating of rooms sufficient for the lowest temperature encountered. . . .
3. Pure water supply, and toilet and bathing facilities consistent with local problems of waste and sewage disposal. . . .
4. Adequate light and ventilation. . . .
5. Adequate fire resistance. . . .
6. Floor area to ensure sufficient storage space and placement of minimum furniture without interference with free movement. . . .
7. Enough rooms, adequate in size, to prevent overcrowding, to ensure decent sleeping arrangements, and for cooking and eating. . . .
8. Environmental conditions conducive to quiet, safety and health.[16]

The Committee on the Hygiene of Housing of the American Public Health Association has designed certain fundamental minimum standards housing should have if the fundamental needs of families are to be met. These are as follows:

A. Fundamental Physiological Needs
   1. Maintenance of a thermal environment which will avoid undue heat loss from the human body.
   2. Maintenance of a thermal environment which will permit adequate heat loss from the human body.
   3. Provision of an atmosphere of reasonable chemical purity.
   4. Provision of adequate daylight illumination and avoidance of undue daylight glare.
   5. Provision for admission of direct sunlight.
   6. Provision of adequate artificial illumination and avoidance of glare.
   7. Protection against excessive noise.
   8. Provision of adequate space for exercise and for play of children.

B. Fundamental Psychological Needs
   9. Provision of adequate privacy for the individual.
   10. Provision of opportunities for normal family life.
   11. Provision of opportunities for normal community life.
   12. Provision of facilities which make possible the performance of the tasks of the household without undue physical and mental fatigue.
   13. Provision of facilities for maintenance of cleanliness of the dwelling and of the person.
   14. Provision of possibilities for esthetic satisfaction in the home and its surroundings.
   15. Concordance with prevailing social standards of the local community.

---

[16] Frederic Dewhurst and Associates, *America's Needs and Resources* (New York: The Twentieth Century Fund, 1947), p. 158.

C. Protection against Contagion
16. Provision of a water supply of safe sanitary quality, available to the dwelling.
17. Protection of the water-supply system against pollution within the dwelling.
18. Provision of toilet facilities of such a character as to minimize the danger of transmitting disease.
19. Protection against sewage contamination of the interior surfaces of the dwelling.
20. Avoidance of insanitary conditions in the vicinity of the dwelling.
21. Exclusion from the dwelling of vermin which may play a part in the transmission of disease.
22. Provision of facilities for keeping milk and food undecomposed.
23. Provision of sufficient space in sleeping rooms to minimize the danger of contact infection.

D. Protection against Accidents
24. Erection of the dwelling with such materials and methods of construction as to minimize danger of accidents due to collapse of any part of the structure.
25. Control of conditions likely to cause fires or to promote their spread.
26. Provision of adequate facilities for escape in case of fire.
27. Protection against danger of electrical shocks and burns.
28. Protection against gas poisonings.
29. Protection against falls and other mechanical injuries in the home.
30. Protection of the neighborhood against the hazards of automobile traffic.[17]

Certain criteria are, of course, set up for judging substandard housing. Housing, which the Census Bureau says is "in major need of repairs," is looked upon as "substandard" as well as are houses in cities and towns without private baths and flush toilets. Non-farm houses located in open country may not be considered substandard if they do not have a private bath or flush toilet.[18]

Sources of Improved Housing. There are many sources of improved housing, some of which reside in the education and the self-policing of the home construction industry itself. There is no substitute for this and our only purpose at this time is to merely mention the importance of high standards in building as set by builders themselves through their various trade associations.

1. *Adequate building codes and better design.* Dwelling construction

[17] American Public Health Association, Committee on the Hygiene of Housing, *Basic Principles of Healthful Housing* (2nd Edition) (New York: The Association, 1939).

[18] For a discussion of what are substandard dwellings see the Census designations or consult *How Big Is the Housing Job?* (Washington, D. C.: Housing and Home Finance Agency, September 1949).

may be greatly improved through adequate building codes covering residential construction. Such codes, as they relate to single family dwellings, are frequently inadequate, providing only for a building permit and the inspection of electrical and sewage installations. As a consequence, a great deal of cheap construction or "jerry building" goes on in urban communities. F. H. A. building standards have greatly improved standards in residential construction generally, but many cities are in need of revamped building codes especially for residential construction.

2. *Occupancy standards.* Many towns and cities have no occupancy standards for building apart from those relating to sewage connections and even these are frequently inadequate. Under police powers, buildings may be condemned if dangerous but in many cities condemnation powers are infrequently invoked except in public-use buildings or apartment buildings.

As a result of lack of occupancy standards stating certain minimum standards below which buildings may not be inhabited, buildings frequently deteriorate to as low a level as they can be rented. The lack of such standards encourages blighting and encourages slum making.

3. *Building and loan associations.* The building and loan association has been an important source of improved residential construction,

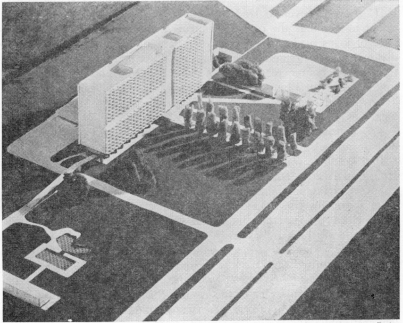

Courtesy of The Institute of Contemporary Art, Boston

FIGURE 17. Apartment House Authorized by the Ministry of Reconstruction 1947, for Marseilles, France—A La Corbusier Apartment for 1600 Persons.

largely through making available long term loans for residential construction. These associations have also been important as a means of encouraging private investment in housing. The building and loan association is reputed to have started in Birmingham, England, in 1798. The first association in this country was established at Frankford, Pennsylvania, in 1831. By 1935 there were more than ten thousand associations with more than seven million lending and borrowing members and with mortgages held amounting to almost four billion. Building and loan associations were loosely regulated even up to the middle 1930's. As a result of this, plus the inroads of the depression of that period, many loan associations closed and many lending customers lost heavily in these enterprises. As a result of the work of the Federal Deposit and Insurance Corporation, created in 1934, investors in approved associations were insured up to $5,000 of investment. This has since been increased to $10,000 which is an important factor in encouraging the lending of funds to building and loan associations. The provision, plus better state and federal regulations, has added stability to these organizations.

4. *F. H. A.* The Federal Housing Administration was established in 1934 by the National Housing Act. Although the organization has been changed in name from time to time, the F. H. A. secured loan became almost a household word in home financing. The purpose of F. H. A. was never to lend money for the financing of housing but rather to stimulate the private financing of housing through the insurance of loans made for repairs, alterations or new construction of individual homes or multiple housing units. As a result of this activity, there has been an increased flow of individual funds, insurance company funds and savings and loan association funds into housing.

5. *Federal construction of housing projects.* The federal government has at intervals engaged in what is called "defense" housing or "war" housing in order to care for workers employed on or near defense projects. These projects we need not discuss.

In 1933 there was established in the Public Works Administration a Housing Division. This Division developed, as part of an employment policy, a highly centralized slum clearance and low rent housing program and finally constructed fifty-one slum clearance projects in thirty-seven cities. At least one important greenbelt community, Greenbelt, Maryland, was built by PWA.

Most of the housing projects built by PWA have been sold to local housing authorities and are now managed by these authorities.

6. *Federal local low-income housing, Act of 1937.* One may say that the President's signing of the Wagner-Steagall Housing Bill in 1937 constitutes the beginning of a permanent national policy of subsidized low cost public housing in the United States.[19]

---

[19] William F. Larsen, *New Homes for Old* (Knoxville, Tennessee: The Bureau of Public Administration, The University of Tennessee, 1948), p. 17.

The first section of the United States Housing Act of 1937 makes the following significant declaration:

> It is hereby declared to be the policy of the United States to promote the general welfare of the Nation by employing its funds and credit, as provided in this Act, to assist the several states and their political subdivisions to alleviate present and recurring unemployment and to remedy the unsafe and insanitary housing conditions and the acute shortage of decent, safe and sanitary dwellings for families of low income, in rural or urban communities, that are injurious to the health, safety, and morals of the citizens of the Nation.[20]

It has been under authority of the U. S. Housing Act of 1937, and the subsequent amendments to this act, that the bulk of low rent public housing units have been completed (see Table XLIII), these numbering some 181,888 units out of 212,215 low rent units completed between 1935 and 1951. The title of the United States Housing Authority has changed from time to time, being called at one time the Federal Public Housing Authority and later the Housing and Home Finance Agency,

FIGURE 18. Low Cost Housing Project—Apartment Type.

Source: Housing and Home Financing Agency.

---

[20] 50 Stat. 888.

TABLE XLIII

TOTAL NUMBER OF PUBLIC HOUSING UNITS
COMPLETED FOR OCCUPANCY, 1935-1951

Year	All Public Housing [a]	Total [b]	Low Rent U.S. Housing Act [c]	Low Rent All Other	War Housing	Veterans Re-use Housing
Total ..	1,201,921	212,251	181,888	30,363	724,018	265,652
1935	3,932	3,932	....	3,932	....	....
1936	1,213	1,213	....	1,213	....	....
1937	7,849	7,849	....	7,849	....	....
1938	17,319	17,319	....	17,319	....	....
1939	3,858	3,858	3,858	....	....	....
1940	31,940	31,940	31,940	....	....	....
1941	119,634	59,848	59,848	....	59,786	....
1942	158,266	37,537	37,537	....	120,729	....
1943	374,729	27,325	27,325	....	347,404	....
1944	153,158	2,831	2,831	....	150,327	....
1945	45,026	2,949	2,949	....	1,906	....
1946	134,726	1,804	1,804	....	128,871	....
1947	107,097	466	466	....	106,631	....
1948	30,054	1,336	1,336	....	27,168	....
1949	1,242	547	547	....	695	....
1950	1,582	1,201	1,201	....	381	....
1951	10,246	10,246	10,246	....	....	....

[a] Includes PWA, Subsistence Homestead and Greenbelt Town Projects.
[b] Includes fifty PWA units built in 1934.
[c] Includes 60,489 units completed as war housing, of which all but 3,098 have been returned to low-rent use.

Source: U. S. Bureau of the Census, *Statistical Abstract of the United States, 1952* (Seventy-third Edition) (Washington, D. C.: 1952), p. 736.

but its functions have been largely loans to local housing bodies and small subsidies. The usual procedure which a community will follow in getting a public housing loan for low rent housing is as follows:

1. The establishment of a local housing authority.

2. Application to the Federal Housing Agency for a loan to make an investigation of the need for a housing project.

3. Application to federal agency showing the housing proposal, together with evidence that the local governing body approves the project. The application should show need for the project and the inability of private capital to do the job. Rather complete data on the population to be rehoused, rent schedules proposed and other supporting data, along with preliminary architectural plans.

The above information becomes the basis for a loan. In the law of 1937, the federal government could make annual contributions up to 20 per cent of the annual operation of the project.

7. *Housing Act of 1949.* Title I of the Housing Act of 1949 provided for the first time in American history comprehensive provisions for slum clearance and urban redevelopment, based upon local responsibility, initiative and operation, by making available assistance to local urban housing or redevelopment bodies for the development and com-

pletion of slum clearance and urban redevelopment projects. Over a five year period one billion dollars could be borrowed by the Administrator of the Housing and Home Finance Agency from the Federal Treasury for purposes of assisting in such projects. The Act also provided that private funds for such projects could be secured through a pledge of federal contract.

Areas which may be acquired under the 1949 Act are in general of four types:[21]

1. A slum area or deteriorated or deteriorating area which is predominantly residential in character.

2. Any other deteriorated or deteriorating area which is to be developed or redeveloped for predominately residential uses.

3. Land which is predominately open and which because of obsolete plotting, diversity of ownership, deterioration of structures or of site improvements, or otherwise, substantially impairs or arrests the sound growth of the community and which is to be developed for predominately residential uses.

Figure 19. Low Cost Housing Project—Garden Tpye.

Source: Ford Foundation, Dearborn, Michigan (Garden-type Apartments).

---

[21] Housing and Home Finance Agency, *A Guide to Slum Clearance and Urban Redevelopment* (Washington, D. C.: The Agency, February 1950), p. 6.

4. Open land necessary for sound community growth which is to be developed for predominately residential uses.

Preliminary loan advances may be made for surveys to determine the feasibility of projects, and for the general preparation of the area for redevelopment after which long term loans may be made for the project itself. While residential development is held to be a central function of the Act, fairly liberal provisions make it possible to carry on street widening, certain open space development and the preparation of sites for the schools, utilities and services which may be needed by the families living in the area. Families removed have to be provided for in either temporary or permanent housing and some of the lands acquired may be leased or sold to private enterprise if this facilitates the development of the area or at least does not hinder it. The comprehensiveness of the Act provides a legislative vehicle which makes it possible for many cities to redevelop extensive slum area.

WORKSHOP AND PROBLEMS

1. What are the chief housing problems?
2. What is the projected need for housing?
3. What are the main roads to improved housing?
4. What are the pro and con arguments for public housing?
5. What is your community doing to obtain improved housing?
6. Review critically recent federal housing legislation.

BIBLIOGRAPHY

American Public Health Association, Committee on the Hygiene of Housing, *Basic Principles of Healthful Housing* (2nd edition) (New York: The Association, 1939).

Bureau of the Census, the various reports on housing, some of which are indicated at the bottom of the tables in this chapter.

Davie, Maurice, *Problems of City Life* (New·York: John Wiley and Sons, 1932).

Dean, John P., "The Myths of Housing Reform," *American Sociological Review*, Vol. 14 (April, 1949), pp. 281-288.

Dewhurst, Frederic, and Associates, *America's Needs and Resources* (New York: The Twentieth Century Fund, 1947).

Housing and Home Finance Agency, *How Big Is the Housing Job?* (Washington, D. C.: The Agency, September, 1949).

——————, *A Guide to Slum Clearance and Urban Redevelopment* (Washington, D. C.: The Agency, February, 1950).

Larsen, William F., *New Homes for Old* (Knoxville, Tennessee: The Bureau of Public Administration, The University of Tennessee, 1948).

Mackintosh, J. M., *Housing and Family Life* (London: Cassell and Co., Ltd., 1952).

National Old People's Welfare Committee, *Age Is Opportunity* (London: National Council of Social Service, 1949).

Public Services and Blighted Areas (A joint report of the Louisville and Jefferson County Planning and Zoning Commission and the City of Louisville Housing Commission) (Louisville, Kentucky: Louisville Housing Commission, April, 1951).

CHAPTER 16

Social Programs In Underdeveloped Areas

By CLARENCE W. BOEBEL

The term underdeveloped, as used here, signifies a geographic location; city, section, neighborhood, or any combination, where the people populating it cannot fully satisfy their socially acceptable desires. To those people, such areas are underdeveloped. A group of families living in Buffalo, New York, considered their area underdeveloped not because they did not have recreation, sound housing, or good living standards, but because they could not read the city newspaper. A great many people living in their neighborhood were foreign born and to be able to read the evening paper was at that time their most important social need. Their ability to satisfy their desire in this case depended on the formation of special classes to teach them to read English. A group of socially prominent and financially well-to-do young women felt that their upper-class section of town was underdeveloped. They were unable to fully satisfy their desire to profitably use their abilities, education, and leisure time. The Junior League of America was an outgrowth of that feeling. Underdeveloped areas in upper class society in many cities today are sensing the same inadequacy in their communities and new programs are being developed. Underdevelopment is a state of being, dependent on the awareness of the people affected, and is not a static entity which has a predetermined set of criteria which asserts that one section of the city is positive, while the other is negative.

Some Historical Considerations. Social programing for local communities was at the time of the landing of the Pilgrims primarily the job of the local church or parish. Discussions, meetings, socials, suppers, outings, sewing, and many other areas of interest were satisfied by the church. Those interests not so satisfied were often considered by the church of the time to be unhealthy, morally degrading, or un-Christian. As the communities became more complex and the population more heterogeneous, social programming for all by the church became more and more difficult. Private societies developed in many communities. These were formed by the whim and vigor of those citizens in various localities who were drawn together by a common interest. Debating societies, sewing clubs, political clubs, sporting clubs,

267

sprang up in every sizable town. Many of these had extremely short histories while others continue to the present time.

Urban living became more complex as a result of the Industrial Revolution. The impact of political strife and economic development that followed the Civil War stifled whole areas of our larger cities. Social programs in many of these sections no longer existed for a large share of the population. Christian societies were on the whole unable to cope with the situation but Christian-thinking men pursued the problem.

The first organized service in the United States to provide social programs for underdeveloped areas was started in 1851. The Boston sea captain J. V. Sullivan was so impressed with what he saw of the Young Men's Christian Association in London, England, that he urged the formation of a similiar society in Boston. Later, the Dashaway Club was organized by three women at Hartford, Connecticut, in 1860. It was a self governing organization which later became known as "Boy's Club." Their social programs included games, music, theatricals, and dancing. Boston was also the birthplace of the Young Women's Christian Association, formed in 1866.

The first American settlement house was established by Stanton Coit, who after living with Canon Barnett at Toynbee Hall in London, decided that New York City needed a similiar program. By the winter of 1887 five clubs were holding regular meetings and a federation of young people's clubs was organized calling themselves the "Neighborhood Guild." Supervised playgrounds are thought to have developed in the United States from a Sand Garden organized in Boston by the Massachusetts Emergency and Hygiene Association in 1886. New York City pioneered the use of school plants for evening recreational activities in 1906. The "Daily Good Turn" principle of scouting practiced by Baden-Powell's Boy Scouts was brought from London by W. D. Boyce and the Boy Scouts of America was incorporated under the laws of the District of Columbia in 1910 by Boyce, Edward S. Stewart, and Stanley Willis. The Camp Fire Girls program was formulated by a group of educators in 1911, and the Girl Scout movement was founded in Savannah, Georgia, in 1912 by Mrs. Juliette Low as an outgrowth of the Girl Guides of Great Britain.

This surge of interest and concern about the social welfare of people living in crowded cities created an entirely new approach to the problem of serving underdeveloped areas. In typical American fashion new agencies and societies were created. Experimentation by trial and error became the means for establishing techniques and programs. The total movement during this period covered not only the recreation field but also Adult Education and religious education. The movement for free public libraries, the organization of the Chautauqua Institution, educational services in museums and art galleries, and the development of extension systems in universities got underway in the 1870's and 1880's. In the period following World War I new and more diversified programs developed from these early concepts. The increased leisure time afforded the working man helped develop the trend towards more and more voluntary education. Workers' education programs to provide basic courses for the foreign born and to eliminate adult illiteracy expanded in ever increasing proportions.

During this same period of the late 1800's every large Protestant denomination developed a youth movement of its own. The Baptist Young Peoples Union, the Epworth Leagues, the King's Daughters all served to develop social programs based on sound Christian ideals. Catholic programs have steadily advanced since 1915 with the development of new organizations to provide the much needed Christian recreation for the youth of its churches. At approximately the same time Jewish youth groups emerged representing various affiliations with temples and synagogues and other ideological interests. All three major religious groups felt the need of the times to provide socially acceptable programs for the growing needs of their followers.

Residual Social Programs. A third area of organized social programing in American communities developed as a secondary goal of organizations whose primary function was something else. These included the programs sponsored by industrial plants, churches, unions, politically oriented groups, and governmental bodies. In some cases these programs developed because the people who formed the particular group developed relationships which made social programs a natural additional step. In other instances the organization made use of social programing as a means of attracting and holding its members. In several cases the federal government in creating new communities for the production of vital defense material provided a wealth of social programing in order to maintain the community at a socially healthy level and make it inviting to discriminating people.

Perhaps the most recent development in the social program area is the development of programs for therapeutic reasons. These programs are developed by specialized health and welfare agencies that are providing a new interest area for hospital patients, psychiatric clinics, children's institutions, cardiac patients, tuberculosis sanitoriums, and to an ever increasing group of people afflicted with physical and mental handicaps.

The rapid growth of organizations, societies and national institutions that have developed over the past seventy-five years might on the surface indicate that the needs of under-developed areas are now being met by the wealth of agencies that promote social programs. However, the reality of the situation is that service is neither complete nor adequate. Certain segments of the urban population receive social program service out of proportion to their needs. Certain racial and religious groups are slighted. Vested interests, in some communities, secure more than their share. Duplication and poor programming affect other areas.

The past seventy-five years established the public concern for social programs. The growth of both public and private agencies providing these community services has been rapid and their ability to service the real needs of specific areas has continually developed through experimentation and study. It is primarily from a companionship between public and private welfare effort that the future hope for adequate services of social programs will mature.

Community Welfare Councils developed slowly. By 1923, councils were functioning in only twenty of America's larger cities. Today, almost every city over 100,000 in population has some type of community council for planning and coordinating its health and social welfare services. The two areas of financing and planning in a coordinated way have produced problems of importance in modern communities. Where in the past agency functions and services were clear cut they are now diversified and often overlapping. The fact that large segments of the population are receiving insufficient programming while others are receiving more than their share is due, in many instances, to historical preferences or traditions which are no longer adequate in modern day society. This, then, is becoming one of the problems facing the present day city dweller. Social programming through public and private social welfare agencies is maturing. It has reached the seventy-five-year-old adolescent period and has developed growing pains. The cure for the growing pains as well as the salvation of social programming for urban living lies in an enlightened public and the development of socially mature boards of directors and administrators in the various public and private agencies.

Social Programs—Traditional and Experimental. One of the dangerous by-products of urban living is the destruction of neighborhoods, not so much in the physical sense but by the limitations it places on developing personal contacts, securing binding relationships and the development of personality. It was in this area that the settlements traditionally made their mark. The National Federation of Settlements and Neighborhood Centers published a statement in 1953 indicating that the traditional function was still the primary concern:

> Settlements and neighborhood houses are social welfare agencies which work with people in learning how to live together harmoniously and how to secure good living conditions. Their two major concerns are the strengthening of family life and the development of better neighborhoods.

Too often the immediate pressure for recreation clubs and activities within the neighborhood drained all the agency's resources. In a great many instances the general public looked to the settlements as a recreation agency.

Dale Avenue Settlement House, a United Fund Agency in Knoxville, Tennessee, was vexed by this same chain of circumstances. Programs for teen-agers, young adults, old-age groups, children, and kindergarten along with a wide variety of cultural and educational activities were offered to the neighborhood. But there remained a large gap in the scheduled programming. Adults came only to bring their children or to share particular problems with the trained staff. As there was no formal program for adults the agency decided that they were not serving the total neighborhood and therefore were not carrying out their function.

Discussions were held with other local agencies and a stimulating program of interest to adults was prepared by the agency staff. Arrangements were made to turn the entire building over to the group one evening a week and attractive publicity was sent out. The program was a failure. After four months of stimulation the agency found that there were less than four women who came with any degree of regularity. The only evening with an attendance greater than eight had been the first one and not once did a man set foot in the building on Adult Night.

Three years later, in 1951, the Settlement House, through its staff and board of directors, became concerned, along with the people of the neighborhood, about a proposed super highway which was to be routed through the neighborhood. This time the trained staff went out into the neighborhood and discussed the mutual problem with the adults in their homes, shops, and places of business. One short strip of highway was completed; there had been little warning. Homes were condemned and torn down; no provisions for low cost housing for the displaced were considered. Then work on the highway stopped. A year passed, bringing changes in the local government, and during that time the neighborhood was working itself into a state of confusion. Landlords refused to improve premises which had not seen improvement first because of the depression, then because of the war, and now because of the highway. Home and shop owners were in the same predicament.

It was at this point that the hours of conversation and study began paying off in terms of neighborhood cooperation. The agency proposed an open meeting at which it would invite the Mayor and other officials who should know some of the answers, if the neighborhood people wanted it. At that first meeting there were over 200 adults who listened attentively to the officials and then asked the questions that had been piling up for almost two years. This was the start of a series of meetings which reached a climax when a committee of neighbors appeared before the city council to present the views of the neighborhood. This was also the first step towards the formation of a civic club which helped to bring about some important changes in the local highway planning.

The first program had been superimposed upon the adults of the neighborhood. They should have been interested but it did not bring them into the planning nor did it take several important factors into consideration. This was a lower economic community where most of the adults worked long hard hours. Families were large and the adults retired at a very early hour. The churches played a very strong part in their lives with regular prayer meetings on Wednesday and special meetings during the week. Union meetings and family affairs used whatever spare time was available. The settlement house had for years been a Day Nursery and many parents considered it a place for children but not for grown men and women. This was a hard working society where recreation had to have more to it than just "playing around."

The second program was successful because it was basically the neighbors' program; it was what they wanted. This was the area in which they considered themselves underdeveloped. They did not see a need for developing interpersonal relationships but they did see a need for finding out about the highway. Interpersonal relationships did develop as a result of the meetings and committee work and these secondary outcomes began to have increasing value for them.

Glenville was a fashionable resort and boasted a famous race track when it was annexed by the City of Cleveland in 1900. After annexation Glenville expanded rapidly and shopping centers and institutions grew with it to serve the growing community. It is the population changes, however, more than the commercial changes that make Glenville an underdeveloped area.

Prior to the first World War its population was primarily Scotch, Irish, English with a few German farmers and New England immigrants. After 1920 many Jewish people began to move into the Glenville area from greater Cleveland. Along with them came Jewish people in Cleveland. With the increased economic security brought about by the second World War many of the home owners in Glenville moved further east to the suburbs. At that time Negroes who were working in Cleveland and living in overcrowded neighborhoods were seeking better homes. The push of the overcrowded neighborhoods and the pull of better housing helped to bring to Glenville a large increase in its small Negro population. Thus in less than fifty years a rural village was transformed into a heavily populated interracial area of Cleveland.

This large population shift brought about severe inadequacies in much of the social programming. Housing and real estate problems were created, recreation facilities for all groups were limited, and racial tensions in the area were increasing at an alarming rate. Several studies were made by Western Reserve University's School of Applied Social Sciences and the Welfare Federation of Cleveland. Through the stimulation of an Independent Voters Committee, the Council Educational Alliance and the Civilian Defense Block Plan a meeting was held in 1945 which was the guiding force behind the formation of the Glenville Area Community Council.

The Young Men's Christian Association has a long and outstanding history of service in the Cleveland area. Its many branches have in recent years spread out in a decentralized program giving service to almost all of greater Cleveland. Traditionally its services have been to the middle and upper middle economic classes and tradition had also fostered separate agencies for Negro and white as it does for most YMCA's throughout the country. It was with considerable concern that the YMCA started an experimental program in this Glenville area. Its aims were still those of providing a stronger Christian brotherhood programs were desperately needed but of greater concern was the mounting racial tensions.

In a rented store front on one of Glenville's main streets one professional worker, a secretary, and a few part time workers attempted to relieve some of the pressures from an underdeveloped area. The agency was opened in 1949 and the young boys in the neighborhood signed up for membership. There were no new or startling programs, just the traditional healthy creative activities that younger boys enjoy. What the boys did not observe was the work that the staff had done before the doors of the "Y" had opened, and continued throughout the experiment.

The professional social group worker had laid his plans well. Days and weeks had been spent in discussing the problem of Glenville's youth needs with everyone who would discuss them with him. Jew, Protestant, Catholic, Negro, worker, merchant, banker, real estate agent, teacher, and housewife were interested. This was their problem and whenever the opportunity presented itself the merchant, the teacher, the worker were asked to serve on a committee—one where their particular skill had real meaning. If committee work wasn't meaningful there were endless projects that needed starting: posters had to be made, additional funds had to be raised, volunteer leaders had to be trained. The long list of jobs started to be filled by the men and women who lived in the community and who knew and cared about Glenville.

As the adults saw the program taking shape and saw the boys finding deep satisfactions in their clubs, projects and activities they intensified their efforts. There were many ups and downs, almost as many defeats as victories, but the "almosts" overbalanced the scale and a meaningful inter-racial program developed. Adults were involved in the program from the beginning and the neighborhood, along with trained leadership, helped make it a successful venture.

How successful is difficult to determine. In three years' time the staff doubled in size. A building fund was well under way and the central branch had promised help for their campaign for a modern community center YMCA. Teachers, ministers, police, reported small but important changes in attitudes. Of greatest importance, the men, women, and boys working together were even more enthused than they had been during the first flush of victory. A small group of the Negro and white population had found a partial solution to their problems in Glenville.

In 1952 the Savannah River Atomic Energy Project had created in its wake a whole series of welfare problems. Work units of population were moved, the new communities sprang up almost over night. Near Augusta, Georgia, 5,000 graves and 7,000 live people were moved simultaneously. In Akin, South Carolina, land owners were making unwarranted profits. Trailer camps sprang up behind row after row of garbage cans on the hot flat dusty plains. There were little or no provisions for sanitation. Recreational facilities were meager. In the Huntsville area 200 German scientists were brought into the community. The local leadership had made intelligent plans before their arrival but several tense situations developed. Surveys made showed that problems like traveling 180 miles to the nearest maternity hospital needed immediate attention. The government was slow in meeting needs. As a result of the delays and the neglect of human interests many workers left at Christmas and didn't come back.

Warner Robins, Georgia, eighteen miles south of Macon, was a ten-year-old town close to a storage base for airplane parts. The needs of the atomic energy project brought an influx of over 14,000 employees into the small community. The government bought buildings quickly and the housing provisions for 16,000 people occupied a space of one square mile. There were little or no public health or recreation facilities. There was one road owned by the town and paved. Three individuals owned the whole housing area and were on the City Council. The owners had threatened to turn off the water supply if the tenants did anything they didn't like. Some 3,000 Negroes worked at Warner Robins but had no place to live so they had to commute from Macon.

A large shift in income had developed for most of the 60 per cent of the new population who came from the rural South. Some had earnings previously of $500 a year, while at present one family with two members working was earning $500 a month. Forty per cent of the workers came from all over the USA. All of them needed to be made aware of their role as part of the local community and of their relations to their neighbors.

The federal government had made little or no provisions for funds to augment or create needed social programing or other basic welfare needs. The United Community Defense Service had surveyed the area and considered it a critical defense area. It asked the National Federation of Settlements and Neighborhood Centers to start a local operation in Warner Robins. The local Community Chest was in favor of the plan and the UCDS proposed $6,000 for the first four months experimental operation.

Three steps were taken before operations began. First, an expert public administrator was consulted. Secondly, it was necessary to secure the advice of a trained city planner, and thirdly, the water problem had to be solved. The City Council voted $7,000 and employed a qualified firm from Atlanta to do the job.

Two experts were sent into the community by the National Federation of Settlements and Neighborhood Centers. One was trained in community organization and the other skilled in program activities. Two barracks of the Air Force with a lounge section and dining room area were offered for headquarters. The recreational needs were so great that a program was started immediately. This was what the population had expected, and to have done otherwise would have been disastrous. A successful day-camp experience was developed with the existing community agencies participating, and several adult activities were provided.

With this under way the two trained staff members seemingly moved in all directions at the same time. They were never too busy to talk over common problems with any one who wanted to discuss them. Glaring inadequacies were found in some of the living quarters. The headquarters space provided was almost useless. But with professional skill and hard work they overcame the fears of the city council and local community chest. They were there to help the community do the things that the community wanted accomplished. The staff worked with the Community Chest and helped plan the current campaign which successfully raised several times the amount of money it had the year previously. Volunteer training programs were started and the number of volunteer workers increased immediately. Public health agencies moved in to help, some of the housing problems were improved, and the total recreation and welfare picture changed in a little over a year's time.

The operation is in process, the professional staff has increased slightly in size, but the volunteer staff is large. Not only have most concerned been pleased with the project, but of greater importance, the community is proud of their accomplishment. They literally lifted themselves up by their boot straps with the help of a few professionals and a limited amount of outside money. There is still room for considerable improvement, but Warner Robins is now a place where the families want to improve their living conditions rather than move away as soon as an opportunity arises.

Some Elements in Sound Social Programming. Each of the three situations described was in an underdeveloped area. The first occurred in an upper-lower economic area, the second in a lower middle, and the third in an area so new that no sound base could be established but where employment was at a peak and total incomes were extremely high. All three locales needed social programming and in each case the form of programming was different. The factor which each shared was the need for the development of the human relationships within the area. The basic method in each case was the same, each made use of a skilled professional social worker, and in each case the processes of developing the social programs were the same, yet the agencies involved were different.

In each of the three areas it would have been possible to state that it was essential that the "needs" of the people being served had to be known in order to develop sound social programs. Yet social needs are difficult to determine. Social needs and social desires of a group of people are quite often dissimiliar. Needs in a psychological sense refer to the striving for certain personality characteristics, satisfying human experiences and meaningful relationships with fellow beings. Therefore it is not a simple problem of surveying a group of people or of asking them what they want. The only sound approach to discovering human social needs is in creating social programs flexible enough to help the people express themselves, having trained staff sensitive enough to hear the expressions, and then moving into those new areas if and when the people are ready to move.

Social programs for our underdeveloped urban areas are provided by a vast network of organizations and agencies. These can briefly be grouped into four divisions: first, the vast empire of commercial entertainment; second, those programs provided through the many voluntary associations which people organize for their own pleasure as well as the various civic clubs and social action groups; third, private organizations and agencies where social programs for specific sections of the population are provided and are financed by those interested; and, fourth, the public recreation and educational organizations supported by governmental bodies. This chapter has dealt primarily with those agencies in the last two divisions. These are the agencies which commonly come within the scope of the Community Welfare Councils or Councils of Social Agencies in the larger cities in America today.

Social programming is gradually growing into a new and ever widening area. A new concept of total coverage of specific areas or communities is being pursued. With this pursuit comes an even greater challenge to clarify the functions of social program agencies. It is no longer claimed that recreation facilities alone will prevent social evils, but it is claimed that adequate recreation facilities along with efforts to provide adequate housing, raise wages, improve public health, abolish segregation and provide psychiatric services can be effective in a total approach.

One of the dilemmas of our present society in planning adequate social programs for specific areas is the overlapping of functions and services provided by the many health and welfare agencies. It is part of the American democratic heritage to organize, experiment and promote. But the point has been reached where social welfare agencies so conceived must make a concerted effort to clarify their functions. This does not infer that tradition must be discarded. It means that thinking must be in terms of the total needs of the community in relation to what each of the interrelated organizations is best equipped to provide. Planning organizations can no longer think in terms of social services to the needy, to the boys, to the aged, but must strive to plan for the total. That requires concentrated effort and a fresh approach to thinking through each individual community's need in terms of its location, mores, history, and its people. It is difficult but important that the sights remain on helping people of a community secure what they want and not provide them what a particular pressure group, council, agency, or government body thinks best.

To maintain, preserve, and strengthen our democratic way of life it is necessary to have enlightened citizens, it is necessary to be concerned with the dignity and rights of each person as an individual, it is necessary to relieve underdeveloped areas. But democracy can only be served by democracy. The processes of serving, promoting, and maintaining social programs are as important as the programs themselves. The end to be reached is not a swimming pool in each neighborhood, or a chicken in every pot. But rather, a community where its citizens have the strength and warmth of relationships to help one another solve their own problems of inadequacy.

WORKSHOP AND PROBLEMS

1. What is the meaning of the term underdeveloped areas? How does the public refer to such areas?
2. Trace the growth of settlement houses in this country.
3. What is the basic purpose of a settlement house?
4. As a group project study an underdeveloped area, preferably an urban one, and develop a program of services for it.
5. If available, spend some time working in a settlement house.
6. What relationship exists between social programming for underdeveloped areas and the physical restoration of these areas through city planning and development?

BIBLIOGRAPHY

Addams, Jane, *Forty Years at Hull House* (New York: The Macmillan Co., 1935).

Baxter, Bernice, and Cassidy, R. F., *Group Experience: The Democratic Way* (New York: Harper & Brothers, 1943).

Ellis, Lionel F., "Toynbee Hall and the Settlements," *Social Service: A Quarterly Survey* (June—August, 1948).

Hillman, Arthur, *Community Organization and Planning* (New York: The Macmillan Co., 1950).

Lieberman, Joshua (Editor), *New Trends in Group Work* (New York: The Association Press, 1938).

McDowell, John, "Settlements and Neighborhood Centers," *Social Work Yearbook, 1951* (New York: The American Association of Social Workers, 1951).

Slavson, S. R., *Creative Group Education* (New York: The Association Press, 1937).

Taylor, Graham, *Pioneering on Social Frontiers* (Chicago: University of Chicago Press, 1930).

CHAPTER 17

Urban Delinquency and Crime

By LUKE EBERSOLE

In the present chapter we are concerned with the more distinctly urban manifestations of delinquency and crime. In many respects, of course, urban offenders against the law are like offenders elsewhere. When the quest for causes is pushed as far in the direction of original causes as it seems possible to go, the motives that impel individuals to violate the codes of society appear not to be dissimilar from one place to another. Nevertheless, the incidence of crime varies from country to city and within cities. There are differences in the frequency with which some offenses occur. The city has produced a number of typically urban forms of criminal organization. In short, the pattern of crime in cities is not the same as everywhere; and the understanding, prevention, and treatment of crime in cities must be with reference to the urban pattern.

THE URBAN PATTERN OF CRIME

Extent of Crime. Existing evidence, although hardly conclusive, seems to indicate that crime rates are higher in urban areas than in rural areas. In a study of commitment rates in Iowa, Burrows found that "the relation seems to be in almost direct ratio to the extent of urban conditions."[1] Rates were lowest in the rural counties and highest in the urban counties. Counties that were in the middle with respect to degree of urbanization had crime rates that fell midway between the rates for the urban and the rural counties.

The relation between urbanization and higher crime rates appears further to be indicated by the fact that rates are higher in large towns than in small towns, and higher in big cities than in little cities. In another study made in Iowa, Mounts reported that commitment rates for juvenile delinquents increased with the size of the town.[2] Throughout the United States in the first half of 1948 the complaint rate for

[1] Charles N. Burrows, "Criminal Statistics in Iowa," *University of Iowa Studies in the Social Sciences,* Vol. 9, No. 2 (1921), Iowa City, p. 110.
[2] L. H. Mounts, "Dependents, Defectives and Delinquents in Iowa; a Study of the Sources of Social Infection," *University of Iowa Studies in the Social Sciences,* Vol. 7, No. 2 (1919), Iowa City.

279

robbery in the largest cities was 43.5, whereas in cities of between 10,000 and 25,000 population the rate was 10.5.

Although it is generally agreed that crime rates are higher in urban areas than in rural areas, the evidence must be treated with caution. It is possible that the difference in rates reflects, in part, the differential apprehension, sentencing, and commitment of offenders in rural and in urban areas. Offenses which under the watchful eye of more highly organized law enforcement agencies are dealt with as crimes may go unnoticed in places in which law enforcement is less well organized. Also, crime reporting is more highly developed in urban areas than in rural areas. To a certain extent differences in crime rates may be attributed to differences in reporting. Rural-urban and little-city and big-city comparisons are further made difficult by the mobility of criminals. City criminals do not always operate within the city. Thus, crimes having an urban source may be under-counted.

Distribution of Crime. Crime rates vary significantly within urban areas. In a study of delinquency rates in Chicago, Shaw and his colleagues spotted on maps the addresses of at least 55,998 offenders including school truants, juvenile delinquents and adult criminals. Crime rates for square-mile areas were computed for the entire city. Male delinquency rates for these areas were found to vary from 0.8 to 19.4. Female delinquency rates varied from 0.1 to 9.0. Areas that had high rates for one group of offenders frequently had high rates for other groups.

Thus, high rates for school truancy, male delinquency, female delinquency, and adult criminality tended to be found in the same area. Delinquency and crime rates were high near the central business district and lower in the outlying areas. Radials were drawn extending from the heart of the city outward and rates were indicated every two miles along these lines. Also, rates were calculated for concentric zones spreading outward from the central business area. In general, delinquency rates increased gradually with distance from the center.[3]

In another study, Shaw and McKay attempted to discover what social conditions exist in areas in which delinquency rates are highest. Areas of physical deterioration, industrial concentration, population decline, residential mobility, foreign-born and Negro population concentration, and economic dependency had the highest delinquency rates. In some areas delinquency rates had remained high even though the composition of the population had changed. The characteristics of low-delinquency areas were, in general, in contrast with those of high-delinquency areas.[4]

---

[3] Clifford R. Shaw, *Delinquency Areas* (Chicago: University of Chicago Press, 1929).

[4] C. R. Shaw and H. D. McKay, "Social Factors in Juvenile Delinquency." *National Commission of Law Observance and Enforcement, Report on the Causes of Crime* (Washington, D. C.: 1931), Vol. 2, No. 13, pp. 60–108.

In other cities, Shaw and McKay found the distribution of crime to be much the same as in Chicago. Studies by other researchers have produced similar findings. In Seattle, Schmid found that for the period from 1915 to 1923, 25 per cent of the homicides were committed in an area ten blocks long and four blocks wide near the center of the city. The homicide rate in this area was 5.8 per 100,000 as contrasted to 1.5 per 100,000 in the outer residential area.[5] In Indianapolis, White divided the city into five zones by drawing concentric circles at one mile intervals from the center. From 1930 court records the residences of felons and the places in which felonies were committed were located. Starting in the center zone and going outward, the number of felons per 1,000 males fifteen to seventy-four years of age residing in each zone was 10.1, 5.1, 3.0, 1.9 and 1.5. For the same group and also starting in the center the number of felonies committed in each zone was 15.0, 3.5, 2.9, 2.5 and 2.7.

It appears to be clear that the distribution of crime throughout the city is not uniform and that certain areas rather consistently show a concentration of crime. But these statistics, like those used in making rural-urban comparisons, must be used with care. Again the factor of differential reporting and treatment is involved.

Six types of urban areas in which delinquency is especially prevalent have been identified by Taft:

1. The first is the simple area of poverty and fairly normal family organization relatively uncomplicated by other influences. The great bulk of poor people are by no means delinquent, but petty stealing is relatively prevalent in such areas.

2. A second type of neighborhood is the slum. Here poverty is complicated by heterogeneity of population and other factors. . . . The people have little or nothing to lose and no pride in the past which has seen their failure. . . .

3. The term "interstitial area" is somewhat useful, but it overlaps with the concept of the slum. An interstitial area is one that is shut off from conventional society by some physical or social barrier, perhaps a mass of railroad tracks, a river or canal, or a large industrial area, or, just as often by a color line or the animosities of rival nationalities. . . . Any such marginal region is a battleground of conflicting cultures and at times a literal battleground of gangs representing them. . . .

4. The rooming-house area is a goodly portion of the slum but not all of it, and the higher type rooming houses are outside the slum. . . . It is a region of impersonal relations. . . . There is no community tradition, no common definition of situations or generally accepted morals, no public opinion. . . .

---

[5] Calvin F. Schmid, "A Study of Homicides in Seattle." *Social Forces*, Vol. 4 (June, 1926), pp. 745-756.

5. A certain type of ghetto—or neighborhood inhabited by any single foreign group—may also be a center of crime, although . . . the ghetto . . . is usually far less delinquent than the heterogeneous slum. . . .

6. Vice areas are usually slums, but not all slums are vice areas. These areas are characterized by police-protected commercialized vice such as prostitution and gambling. Not only do these violations of law center there, but they attract more dangerous criminal exploiters. . . .[6]

Types of Crime. The urban setting and culture have been particularly conducive to the occurrence of certain types of crime. Comparisons for eight major offenses may be made on the basis of the Federal Bureau of Investigation 1948 report of crimes known to the police. Rates per 100,000 were as follows: murder—6.15 in rural areas, 5.99 in cities of all sizes, 7.28 in large cities (over 250,000 population), 3.98 in small cities (under 10,000 population); manslaughter—4.26 in rural areas, 3.96 in all cities, 5.11 in large cities, 2.14 in small cities; rape—12.23 in rural areas, 12.33 in all cities, 16.81 in large cities, 9.11 in small cities; robbery—18.4 in rural areas, 56.2 in all cities, 82.4 in large cities, 23.1 in small cities; aggravated assault—36.5 in rural areas. 75.8 in all cities, 97.3 in large cities, 35.3 in small cities; burglary—149.98 in rural areas, 392.2 in all cities, 464.9 in large cities, 245.4 in small cities; larceny—220.3 in rural areas, 975.2 in all cities, 1037.8 in large cities, 650.8 in small cities; auto theft—54.0 in rural areas, 165.5 in all cities, 184.0 in large cities, 100.0 in small cities.[7]

If the eight offenses listed above are divided into crimes against the person and crimes against property, it is in the second category that the difference between country and city is conspicuously evident. City rates are three times higher than rural rates for robbery, about two and a half times higher for burglary, almost four and a half times higher for larceny and three times higher for auto theft.

Of the various sex offenses, prostitution has usually been associated with population centers. Prostitution has by no means been limited to the city, but it is in urban areas that the commercial exploitation of sex has been most common.

Organized prostitutes and semi-independent and independent operators have found that the urban environment provides the most convenient and the most profitable circumstances in which to carry on their activities. A few decades ago much of the prostitution in the city was concentrated in the "red light" district near the center of the city. In many cities these districts have almost disappeared. Houses

---

[6] Donald R. Taft, *Criminology* (New York: The Macmillan Co., 1950), pp. 168-170. By permission of the publishers.

[7] Federal Bureau of Investigation, *Uniform Crime Reports*, Vol. 19, No. 2 (1948), pp. 78, 106.

of prostitution are more widely scattered and more carefully disguised. At the same time prostitution carried on in hotels, apartments and tourist camps has increased. Tourist camp prostitution has increased rapidly in recent decades and reflects the general dispersion of commercialized sex services. Although "motels" are usually outside the city, the practice of prostitution in them is essentially an urban phenomenon.

Much of the illegal sale and purchase of drugs is carried on in cities. The extent of this activity in the United States is not known, but in 1947 the United States Bureau of Narcotics estimated that there was one drug addict for every 3,000 population. In cities drug users appear to be found most frequently in unattached and mobile groups. In Chicago, Faris and Dunham after classifying drug users committed to mental institutions, reported highest rates for hobo and rooming-house districts, and some high rates also for apartment and apartment-hotel districts.[8]

In the study, *Opium Addiction in Chicago,* Dai found high proportions of drug addicts living in areas having an excess of male population, areas of mobility, and areas characterized by family disorganization and general social disorganization.[9]

Drug addiction itself is not a crime, but in view of the laws concerning the sale and purchase of drugs it is obvious that widespread addiction is impossible without considerable violation of the law by users and their suppliers. Drug addicts and drug peddlers are found in the same place, for the drug addict can never be too far from his source of supply.

Urban areas have been the chief base of operation for the promoters of illegal gambling. Not all gambling is illegal, and much illegal gambling is disregarded by law enforcement agencies. When the legal suppression of gambling is attempted it is often not the gamblers but those who create opportunities for illegal gambling who feel the force of the law. None the less because of the indifference of law enforcement agencies, and not infrequently with their cooperation, it is possible for illegal gambling to flourish. Thus, there has developed a group of criminals who make it their business to promote illegal gambling and to systematically evade law enforcement agencies. Such criminals have tended to concentrate in urban areas.

URBAN OFFENDERS

Most urban offenders fall into one of the following classes: juvenile delinquents, occasional criminals, career criminals, professional criminals, and organized criminals.

[8] R. E. L. Faris and H. W. Dunham, *Mental Disorders in Urban Areas* (Chicago: University of Chicago Press, 1939), pp. 121-123.

[9] Bingham Dai, *Opium Addiction in Chicago* (Shanghai, China: The Commercial Press, 1937).

Juvenile Delinquents. Juvenile delinquents in the United States are not criminals. They are children whose offenses come under the jurisdiction of the juvenile court. In most of the states having juvenile-court laws, offenders do not come under the jurisdiction of adult courts and are not defined as criminal until they pass the age of sixteen, and in some states not until they have passed eighteen. Some of the codes that they violate apply only to children and not to adults. But in certain respects juvenile offenders are not unlike adult criminals. They are violators of legal codes and are subject to treatment by official agencies.

The ratio of boys and girls who come before juvenile courts is about five or six to one. A disproportionate number of the persons who are brought to juvenile courts are from the lower income classes. They are children who are surrounded by demoralizing conditions, culture conflict, and weak social control. In the period since World War II there appears to have been an increase in the number of juvenile delinquents coming from the middle income groups. The delinquency pattern is not so widespread in these groups, but it is evident that social disorganization as it affects the behavior of children is not limited to the groups that we have been accustomed to thinking of as disorganized. The full extent of juvenile delinquency in the more privileged groups is, of course, not known inasmuch as middle- and upper-class child offenders are frequently dealt with other than through juvenile courts.

Occasional Criminals. Criminals who fall in this category have not settled down to a life of crime, but under particular circumstances they become involved in criminal activity. As a result of economic problems, emotional disturbances, mental disease, drinking and fortuitous circumstances they commit acts of crime. Their offenses may include murder, rape, indecency, burglary, robbery, larceny, and almost every variety of crime. Their criminal behavior may occur on only a very few occasions, or it may occur a number of times in short or in long intervals. But in any case, criminal behavior is not an established part of the life pattern of the person.

There is reason to believe that a considerable proportion of the occasional offenders are never accounted for by law enforcement agencies. In their study, *Our Law Abiding Law Breakers,* Wallerstein and Wyle reported on the results of a questionnaire which they submitted to businessmen, lawyers, teachers, social workers, scientists, physicians, clergymen, sales and office workers, military and government employees, mechanics and technicians, farmers, laborers, housewives, and students. These people were asked to indicate which of forty-nine offenses they had committed. There were 1,020 men and 678 women who responded to the questionnaire. Of these, 91 per cent indicated that they had committed offenses after they were sixteen years old. A few of the violations along with the percentage of offenders were as follows: disorderly conduct, 85 per cent of the men and 76 per cent of the women; assault, 49 per cent of the men and 5 per cent of the women; indecency, 77 per cent of the men and 74 per cent of the women; auto theft, 26 per cent of the men and 8 per cent of the women; larceny, 89 per cent of the men and 83 per cent of the women; falsification and fraud, 46 per cent of the men and 34 per cent of the women.[10]

It may be that some of the persons who responded to the questionnaire were more than occasional criminals, but they had not been punished and were regarded as respectable citizens. The study demonstrates that on occasion many persons violate laws. Only a relatively limited number of these offenses come to the attention of law enforcement agencies.

Career Criminals. A career criminal is one whose criminal behavior is a definite component of his pattern of living. He is not necessarily engaged in criminal pursuits exclusively, but criminal activity is a regular and established part of his way of life. By definition "criminal careers probably must be limited to crime of gain which would represent mostly property crimes."[11] Thus habitual sex offenders, drunkards, and drug addicts are not regarded as career criminals.

The person who has a career in crime may devote most of his working time to illegal activity or he may engage in legitimate occupations and supplement his income through crime. He tends to develop criminal specialties. He stays in an environment in which he can conveniently practice his chosen crimes. If this is not his original environment he gravitates toward it. His associates are people who can be helpful or who are at least tacitly sympathetic to his criminal operations. His life organization includes values and ways of thinking which fit his patterns of behavior.

Professional Criminals. The professional criminal is a particular type of career criminal. The concept of professionalization in crime was given considerable attention by E. H. Sutherland, who wrote:

> The term "professional" when applied to a criminal refers to the following things: the pursuit of crime as a regular, day-by-day occupation, the development of skilled techniques and careful planning in that occupation, and status among criminals. The professional criminal is differentiated from the occasional criminal, the amateur criminal, the unskilled and careless criminal.[12]

---

[10] James S. Walterstein and Clement J. Wyle, *Our Law-Abiding Law-Breakers*, reprint from *Probation*, April, 1947.

[11] Walter C. Reckless, *The Crime Problem* (New York: Appleton-Century-Crofts, 1950), p. 105.

[12] Edwin H. Sutherland, *Principles of Criminology* (Philadelphia: J. B. Lippincott Co., 1939), p. 213.

Professional criminals are the more specialized and more skilled of the career criminals. They have not only been trained in the technique of their craft; they have learned the code of their profession. They know when they may and may not "talk," what their obligations are to their colleagues in crime, and how they must react to representatives of the law. The professional criminal has a status to maintain within his occupational group. He is known by other criminals and achieves recognition from them just as do members of other professions.[13]

Organized Criminals. There are several different concepts of organized crime. According to one point of view most types of association in crime are regarded as organized crime. Lindesmith defines organized crime as a form of "cooperation of several different persons or groups for its successful execution."[14] Organized crime would then include confederates or partners in crime such as pick-pockets and confidence men. To such a definition Reckless objects:

> Over and above confederacy, partnership in crime, or association in the criminal deed, it is necessary to have a more definite business organization in order to have organized crime. Syndicates, rings, or combines in the business of crime are more truly the pattern of organized crime. An organizational hierarchy, consisting of a top man with affiliates or with his lieutenants and sub-lieutenants, is likely to be the basic organizational pattern of a combine, a ring, or a syndicate in crime.[15]

It is in this sense that we here use the term "organized criminals." The chief types of activity organized in this way are traffic in drugs, prostitution, gambling, illegal manufacture and sale of liquor and various forms of racketeering.[16]

FACTORS RELATED TO URBAN CRIME

High urban rates for crime in general and for specific types of crime are not simple to account for. There are, however, a number of characteristics of urban society and culture which appear to be related to the incidence and the pattern of urban crime.

Things, Money and Status. The high urban rate for offenses against property may, in part, be attributed to the accessibility of things desired. The urban concentration of stores, distributing agencies and financial services provides a convenient area in which to acquire money and things by illegal means. Thus, within urban areas rates for most of the crimes against property are highest in the center of

---

[13] See Edwin H. Sutherland, *The Professional Thief*, as told by Chic Conwell (Chicago: University of Chicago Press, 1937).

[14] Alfred R. Lindesmith, "Organized Crime," *The Annals of the American Academy of Political and Social Science*, Vol. 217 (September, 1941), p. 119.

[15] Walter C. Reckless, *The Crime Problem* (New York: Appleton-Century-Crofts, 1950), p. 144.

[16] *Ibid.*, pp. 145-159.

the city where the opportunity to commit these offenses is at a maximum.

But high rates for crimes against property are not the result of accessibility alone. The rates reflect also the urban preoccupation with things and money. Nor is it true that city criminals are peculiarly driven to crime in order to get by economically. A high proportion of those who attempt to acquire money and things by illegal means do not do so because they lack the essentials for existence. The deprivation that motivates crimes against property is often psychological rather than physical. Money is more than a means of subsistence. In a society of impersonal and secondary contacts, money and the things that money buys are, to a singular degree, symbols of prestige. The prestige may, in reality, be somewhat illusory, or it may be limited to a very small group, but in this regard the criminal is not unlike many noncriminals. The struggle is for status as well as for survival or for comfort.

Impersonality and Anonymity. A large proportion of urban social relations are impersonal. It is impossible for an individual to know more than a small proportion of the people whom he sees. Under these circumstances the needs, ambitions and hopes of most other people are unknown to the city dweller. His relations with them are chiefly to satisfy his own needs and wants. He thinks of other people primarily as they are related to his purposes. Thus, urban social relations often become exploitative. Other people tend to be viewed as means of achieving individual ends. The degree to which the impersonal-exploitative attitude influences behavior varies with individuals and with groups. In the criminal the attitude frequently is developed in the extreme.

Further, the anonymity of the city provides protection for the criminal. He can be lost in the mass, unrecognized by his victims and by agents of the law. Who he is and what he does is of no concern to most of the people around him. The studies of the distribution of crime in the city have rather consistently shown that it tends to be concentrated in the center of the city in the areas of greatest mobility, impersonality and anonymity.

A Culture of Crime. In urban areas is found a continuity in criminal culture which is generally lacking in rural areas. Association with criminals and knowledge of tested criminal techniques prior to violation of the law is found far more frequently in urban than in rural areas. A culture of crime, consisting of ideas, attitudes, values and techniques, is transmitted by criminals to other persons. To observe that there is a culture of crime does not explain why some persons are influenced by it while others are not. But it seems inevitable that where such patterns exist, crime will be more prevalent than in other areas.

The transmission of violational patterns of behavior takes various forms. Among urban juvenile offenders, gangs are an important factor in transmitting the culture of delinquency. After one ten-year-old delinquent gave the author a detailed account of the practices, attitudes and ideas of his gang, further investigation revealed that for more than twenty years the same gang with changing membership had operated in the same area. In a study of the relation between urbanization and criminal behavior Clinard found that gangs were not important in the lives of male farm offenders, and that the age at which association with offenders occurred decreased as the degree of urbanization increased.[17]

Concerning the influence of the culture of crime in producing a criminal type, Clinard reported:

> The use of criminal argot was characteristic of the life-histories of city offenders. As compared with those from areas of slight and moderate urbanization, offenders from the cities had had extensive contacts with other deviant social types, such as prostitutes, "pimps," racketeers, and "fences." This indicated the criminal division of labor, as well as the general social disorganization permeating areas of extensive urbanization.
>
> . . . . .
>
> To develop a criminal social type there must be in existence some organized criminal culture which is at least tolerated in the area and through which deviant norms are transmitted. . . . The division of labor and heterogeneity of standards of an urban world make possible the existence of a criminal culture independent of the traditional culture.[18]

Supply and Demand. One of the reasons why certain forms of organized crime operate in the city is quite apparent. The greatest market for the things in which organized criminals deal is in the city. A ready market for sex, gambling, dope and "protection" is necessary for the existence of the leading forms of organized crime. The "demand" for "protection," of course, is created by the criminals themselves. To some degree organized criminals also help to promote the demand for the other things that they have to sell.

The existence of a demand for their services is used by organized criminals as a rationalization for their activities. When attempts are made to suppress these activities, it is usually those who are engaged in providing illegal services who are brought into court. Their clients are rarely apprehended. But the criminal frequently takes the point of view that his behavior is no more reprehensible than that of his clients. Whatever the judgment on this point it is clear that commercialized

---

[17] Marshall B. Clinard, "The Process of Urbanization and Criminal Behavior," *American Journal of Sociology,* Vol. 48 (September, 1942), pp. 202-213.

[18] *Ibid.,* p. 211.

crime could not thrive apart from the toleration of the citizenry at large and without the support of a segment of the urban population.

Social Control. Most organized crime cannot prosper without clients, nor can it prosper without either the active or the passive cooperation of law enforcement agencies. This touches on the nature of social control in cities. When social relations are primary and personal, informal controls such as social approval and disapproval are effective. When social relations are secondary and impersonal, more reliance is placed on the formal control of law and law-enforcement agencies. There arises then the problem of control of the agencies of formal control. It is evident that in many cities the control of the people over those who are supposed to enforce the law is weak. The tacit alliance of organized law violators and agents of law enforcement in many cities has been an important factor in producing an environment in which crime can flourish.

WORKSHOP AND PROBLEMS

1. Compare delinquency and crime rates in urban and rural areas. How do you account for the differences?

2. Within the city, what areas show highest crime rates? Why?

3. What areas show highest delinquency rates? Why?

4. In what types of crime do cities exceed? Do large cities exceed?

5. In what types of areas are sex offenses highest?

6. In what types of areas is drug addiction higher?

7. Who are career criminals? Professional criminals? And what is their relation to cities?

8. How do things, money, and status contribute to urban crime?

9. How does impersonality and anonymity contribute to urban crime?

10. What is a culture of crime?

11. Spend some time in an urban police station studying their records and procedures.

12. If possible, as a class project, do a delinquency or crime survey of your city.

BIBLIOGRAPHY

Burrows, Charles N., "Criminal Statistics in Iowa," *University of Iowa Studies in the Social Sciences,* Vol. 9, No. 2 (1921), Iowa City, p. 110.

Clinard, Marshall B., "The Process of Urbanization and Criminal Behavior," *American Journal of Sociology,* Vol. 48 (September, 1942), pp. 202-213.

Dai, Bingham, *Opium Addiction in Chicago* (Shanghai, China: The Commercial Press, 1937).

Federal Bureau of Investigation, *Uniform Crime Reports,* Vol. 19, No. 2 (1948).

Lindesmith, Alfred R., "Organized Crime," *The Annals,* Vol. 217 (September, 1941), p. 119.

Mounts, L. H., "Dependents, Defectives and Delinquents in Iowa; a Study of the Sources of Social Infections," *University of Iowa Studies in the Social Sciences,* Vol. 7, No. 2 (1919), Iowa City.

Reckless, Walter C., *The Crime Problem* (New York: Appleton-Century-Crofts, 1950).

Schmid, Calvin F., "A Study of Homicides in Seattle," *Social Forces,* Vol. 4 (June, 1926), pp. 745-756.

Shaw, Clifford, *Delinquency Areas* (Chicago: University of Chicago Press, 1929).

Shaw, Clifford, and McKay, H. D., "Social Factors in Juvenile Delinquency," *National Commission of Law Observance and Enforcement, Report on the Causes of Crime,* Vol. 2, No. 13 (1931), Washington, D. C., pp. 60-108.

Sutherland, Edwin H., *The Professional Thief* (Chicago: University of Chicago Press, 1937).

——————, *Principles of Criminology* (Philadelphia: J. B. Lippincott Co., 1939).

Taft, Donald R., *Criminology* (New York: The Macmillan Co., 1950).

Vedder, Clyde B., Koenig, Samuel, and Clark, Robert E., *Criminology: A Book of Readings* (New York: The Dryden Press, 1953).

Chapter 18

Toward a More Dynamic Urban Church

By Samuel W. Blizzard

The dynamics of the urban church focus on its theological orientation and community orientation. New trends in theology are likely to be seen in the urban areas before they appear in the rural areas. The newer theological values seem to be found in the city, where the clergy are more highly educated and accordingly are more aware of current theological thought. Theological values seem to be preserved in the rural areas where resistance to social change is more evident.

The innovating function of the city and the conserving function of the rural areas in matters of culture is important for an understanding of the dynamics of urban religion.[1] Urban religious leaders are more apt to espouse a new expression of religious values or a new method of religious practice than are other ecclesiastical leaders. The urban minister competes with other community leaders for response to his program. This competitive situation creates a readiness on his part to try new methods and to espouse new expressions of religious values. This has a pronounced effect on the type of religious belief and behavior that is found in the city.

A second focus in the dynamics of urban religion involves the changes that are occurring in metropolitan communities. As populations shift and neighborhoods change, churches in these communities are placed in a condition of chronic crisis. Any redistribution of population is almost certain to mean a redistribution of church members and of church resources. A shift in the number and character of churches from one area to another sets off a chain reaction that results in the readjustment of church structure and strategy. This chapter is aware of the changes in theological orientation, but it gives major attention to the dynamics of the church in the community.

In focusing attention on the community orientation of the city church, the functioning of religious systems will be observed. The variety of urban churches will be studied on a background of the cultural horizon. Parish patterns and the formal organization of a

---

[1] T. Lynn Smith and C. A. McMahan, *The Sociology of Urban Life* (New York: The Dryden Press, 1951), pp. 503-4.

church will be examined so that the structure of the city church may be described. The functions of associations in the church will be seen in an interactional approach.

Social stratification systems that operate in the community also function dynamically within the church. In many respects church members are a cross section of the inhabitants of a city because it is difficult to distinguish members from non-members. Underlying value conflicts in the larger society are reflected in church membership relations.

Urban religious dynamics require an understanding of human ecology and the distribution of church members and church edifices in relation to the geography of the city. The three major faiths have special ecological features that affect the way they serve their adherents.

Religion responds to social change more slowly than do other institutions. Factors which lead to a change in the urban church are a declining or expanding industry, ecological forces, and population shifts. There are many church strategies that are designed to bring about an adjustment to these changes in community orientation. One basis for continued church planning and adjustment is a program of research.

Church-community relations are important if a dynamic approach is to be taken to religion in the city. The complexity of social organization in the metropolis requires that many reciprocal relationships be established and maintained with other institutions and agencies.

Urban Religious Systems—The rise of the modern city and the development of social systems that make urban living possible have had an impact on organized religion.[2] Leaders of Protestant churches that have been traditionally strong in American rural and urban areas have expressed alarm over the effect of the city on the church. This is reflected in a comment by Shippey, in whose opinion, "Urban church trends since the turn of the century reveal that Protestantism is in danger of losing the city."[3] He feels that Protestant church strategists have been embarrassed by an inadequate knowledge of community life. It might be added that a functional analysis of the city parish by a theologically oriented social scientist would contribute to an understanding of the dynamics of the city church. The church administrator, as well as the minister of an urban congregation, who understands that the parish is a social system, will be better prepared to develop a religious program that is indigenous to the city.

Wide varieties of urban religious systems and behavior occur. There is no church that is typical of the city. Response to its social environment is one noticeable characteristic of religious institutions in the city. Particularly in the large city, variety of religious organizations

---

[2] Aaron I. Abell, *Urban Impact on American Protestantism* (Cambridge: Harvard University Press, 1943).

[3] Frederick A. Shippey, *Church Work in the City* (New York: Abingdon-Cokesbury Press, 1952), p. 23.

is possible. Membership may be drawn from a local neighborhood or on the basis of individual interest from widely scattered areas throughout the city. As the urban church responds to its environment and the needs of the people it reaches in its program, variety in religion occurs. The mosaic of urban neighborhoods and the numerous segments of the population make one typical urban church impossible.

Urban Protestantism, to a greater degree than Judaism or Catholicism, presents a mosaic of differing theological orientations and ecclestiastical structures. In a study of churches in twenty-three metropolitan districts in the United States in 1950, H. Paul Douglass included 8,325 Protestant churches. He made a distinction between the more regular (denominations) and the exceptional (sects) Protestant churches. Of the Protestant churches studied, one-fourth were of the exceptional variety that give a cultural expression to religion which is in conflict with the basic social structure of American society. However, these religious groups furnish only about one-fourteenth of the membership in the Protestant churches in the communities studied.[4] The sect gives substance to one of the dynamic features of urban Protestantism.

Recognizing the variety of urban churches, urban sociology is interested in the technical organization of religion in the city. The church buildings, the theological systems, the literature and the symbols all contribute to an understanding of urban religious culture. However, the human organization of the parish has more interest for the sociologist. The role of the minister, the functioning of lay leaders, the involvement of people in the program and the ways in which the church helps people realize their values, give meaning to urban religious behavior.

Parish patterns are one evidence of the way in which the religious life of a city is structured. In the Catholic tradition churches typically have an ecological orientation in the city. Roman Catholic churches are organized on a more or less rigid geographic parish system. The territory of the parish is a specific geographic area. Each parish in this religion is intended to serve all Catholics within its own area. An exception is made when nationality groups are dispersed throughout the city and are served by a language church. In the Protestant and Jewish traditions a system of voluntary identification makes it possible for parishioners or prospective parishioners to choose the church to which they wish to belong. The individual churches of these groups tend to select adherents by preference factors based on racial or ethnic identity, socio-economic class, historical precedent, type of theology, the personality of the clergymen, kinship ties, etc., rather than by area. If the selective factor that operates in the organization of a particular church is localized, then the parish may assume an

---

[4] *Information Service*, Federal Council of Churches, January 21, 1950.

areal identity. If, however, the selective factor is not localized, the parish tends to become areally indistinguishable. This free choice system usually results in a scattering of the members of Protestant churches over a wider area. Of 1,350 metropolitan Protestant churches in the 1950 Douglass study, 53 per cent had compact parishes in the sense that two-thirds or more of their people lived within a mile of the church. About one-fifth had scattered parishes in the sense that less than one-third lived within a mile of the church. The remainder of the churches had a moderate dispersal of constituents, from one-third to two-thirds living within a mile of the church. Suburbs showed the smallest proportion of scattered parishes. The majority of scattered parishes belonged to churches at or near city centers.[5]

The leadership positions and membership roles are part of the formal organization of a city church. It is possible to see this organizational chart with positions occupied by persons with authority and responsibility whether it is the minister or a trustee, a church school teacher or an officer in the youth organization. The polity of the church defines formally the role that each individual plays. This formal blueprint of the structure of a city church oversimplifies the way a parish functions. Total conformity to the table of organization is not achieved in every parish. There are strains and stresses on this formal organization. Communication systems that are supported by kinship, friendship, work groups, lodge memberships, and the contacts on the commuter train may supplement or challenge the more formal and recognized channels. The formation of informal groups and uncharted status positions within them give city parish life an often unrecognized dynamic.

The associational structure is a subsidiary of the urban Protestant parish and is an evidence of variety in urban religious systems. In the 1950 Douglass study of metropolitan churches, 1,595 churches in nine metropolitan districts reported a total of 8,150 associations in addition to the Sunday School, an average of 5.1 per church.[6] Donovan has noted the significance of the associational structure of a Roman Catholic church.[7] The Holy Name Society, the Rosary Society, the Altar Society and the Sodality are all subsidiary organizations that contribute to the total effort of the church to make Catholic religious values effective among the Catholic and non-Catholic laity in the city. The number and type of associations in the church will vary as the location and type of population served varies throughout the city. A downtown church will have a different associational structure from that of a neighborhood or suburban church.

[5] Ibid.

[6] Ibid.

[7] John D. Donovan, "The Social Structure of the Parish," C. J. Nuesse and Thomas J. Harte, The Sociology of the Parish (Milwaukee: The Bruce Publishing Co., 1950), p. 96.

Recent studies by Catholic sociologists feature an interactional approach to the parish.[8] The traditional urban church study has provided valuable data that describe the structure of the church in the city. The number of churches, clergy and members, the number and type of auxiliary organizations, the ecology of the urban church and the extent of participation in relation to other organizations are all useful data about urban religious systems. These researches, made periodically, can, at best, only alert church planners to trends. Of more significance are: the religious values and behavior as they are expressed through the church as a social structure; the leadership structure in the parish and the ways that it is functionally related to the total community life; the social processes by which solidarity is achieved in the parish and consensus is reached; the ways in which a local parish deviates from the ideal of the denomination and the means that are used to sustain these deviations. These less obvious and more informal aspects of the structure and operation of a parish in the city underline the importance of a dynamic approach to urban religion.

Social Stratification Systems. There is no sharp line between those who practice a religious faith in the city and those who do not. Fichter, in his analysis of a Southern parish, recognized that in relation to Catholicism there were at least five groups that displayed different religious behavior patterns: the nuclear group, those who are the most active participants and the most faithful believers; the modal group, the normal practicing Catholics; the marginal group, those who perform the bare minimum of expected religious behavior; the dormant group, those who have given up Catholicism but who have not espoused another faith; and the non-Catholic.[9] Cuber made a similar analysis of participation in Protestant churches.[10] He likewise conceived of religious participation in terms of marginality rather than a dichotomous classification of church people and non-church people. He reported that in one study of a metropolitan city, in four churches from 18 to 37 per cent of the persons in attendance were non-members. The sociologist looks for the relationship between these factors and the social structure of the city.

Sociological insights about urban religious behavior make it possible to see traditional denominational differences in a different perspective. Lynd found in Middletown that "there is more subtle church rivalry today than formerly, as financial and social competition, particularly

[8] Joseph H. Fichter, *Dynamics of a City Church* (Chicago: University of Chicago Press, 1951); C. J. Nuesse and Thomas J. Harte, *The Sociology of the Parish* (Milwaukee: The Bruce Publishing Co., 1950)

[9] Joseph H. Fichter, "The Marginal Catholic: An Institutional Approach," *Social Forces* (Vol. XXXII, No. II, December 1953), pp. 167-173.

[10] John F. Cuber, "Marginal Church Participants," Logan Wilson and William L. Kolb, *Sociological Analysis* (New York: Harcourt, Brace & Co., 1949), pp. 674-77.

among the business class, have tended to replace earlier doctrinal differences as lines of cleavage."[11] The interest groups in the modern urban community tend to associate their values with those of a particular church. The long established interest of the white collar segments in organized religion is now being challenged by the interest of labor leaders in the church. Some may interpret this as a renewed interest in religion, but others see it as an effort of union groups to get church approval of labor values in a community power group struggle. Religious leaders will want to be aware of these background facts as they interpret changes in urban religious behavior.

The class function of religious practices in the city has been noted in a number of researches. Lynd found that, particularly among the business class, membership in a Middletown church was taken for granted. While members of the working class participated in church activities, their belief patterns and associated values were found to differ notably from those of the white collar group.[12] The ability of religious leaders associated with different strata of the social structure to give expression to the values of those for whom they minister is essential for a dynamic approach to urban religion.

The identification of certain Protestant groups with particular social strata in the city is a well noted fact. Barry found that the distribution of Presbyterian members in the Portland (Oregon) metropolitan area, although reflecting the general population distribution, showed a definite tendency for Presbyterians to be most numerous among the 12 per cent of the Portland families who make up the upper and upper middle income groups.[13] Barry suggests that the Presbyterian church must examine its strategy to help secure its future among the groups from among whom (because of their higher birth rates) the largest proportion of Portland's future population is going to come.

The accommodation of the church to the class structure of an urban community has also been studied by Warner and Lunt. It was noted in Yankee City that the two churches with the largest proportion of members from the upper levels of the class system in the congregation devised a method for limiting the number of people in the lower levels of the class structure who might participate. Each of these churches maintained a chapel in another section of the city. These chapels functioned as a mission and were attended by many people from the lower levels of the status hierarchy.[14] It would seem that the same

[11] Robert S. Lynd and Helen Merrell Lynd, *Middletown* (New York: Harcourt, Brace & Co., 1929), p. 333.

[12] *Ibid.,* pp. 315, 329.

[13] David W. Barry, *The Presbyterian Church in the Portland (Oregon) Metropolitan District* (New York: Presbyterian Board of National Missions, 1945), p. 15 (mimeographed).

[14] W. Lloyd Warner and Paul S. Lunt, *The Social Life of a Modern Community* (New Haven: Yale University Press, 1947), pp. 356-9.

policy is practiced on the part of fashionable Fifth Avenue and Park Avenue churches in New York City.

The stratification picture may be an important factor in the success or failure of specific religious groups. The participation of the white collar groups and the lack of participation by blue collar groups in the church has been described by Pope.[15] The lack of appeal that religious organizations have for the working class in urban society is marked. In Gastonia, North Carolina, Pope found that the Protestant Episcopal and Roman Catholic Church had never secured a significant following. He observed that "They have reached almost no mill workers, chiefly because they have not adapted themselves to the mill village system."[16] The participation of mill workers in the various sects is a noticeable contrast. The coordination of the theological orientation of a church with the social systems that operate in a community would seem to hold the key to an effective religious program for the blue collar classes. In this connection an experimental strategy of the Roman Catholic Church in relation to the religious needs of a working class suburb in Paris, France is described by Abbé G. Michonneau. The traditional Roman Catholic parish is examined and re-structured in response to the community structure. It was the desire of Abbé Michonneau that "the parish must cease to be a mere parish milieu; it must become again a community."[17]

The religious organizations of the city present a variety of theological orientations that are reflected in related social values and social stratification. The dynamic of urban religious behavior inherent in these and other factors fosters relations between the adherents that are characterized by both harmony and dissonance.[18] The areas of cooperation and conflict in the religious structure are influenced by the family life, the economic values, and the educational values of the adherents. Public opinions about evolving social policy often reflect the testing of religious and other values. Recent discussions of public support for parochial education provided an opportunity for underlying religious value conflicts to break into the open. Or, the refusal of the Roman Catholic Church in New York City to participate in a coordinating council for social welfare if a Planned Parenthood group also held membership is one example. These conflicts reflect social stratification struggles that center around the varieties of religious value systems in the city.

---

[15] Liston Pope, "Religion and the Social Structure," "Organized Religion in the United States," *The Annals* of the American Academy of Political and Social Science, Vol. CCLVI (March, 1948), pp. 84-91.
[16] Liston Pope, "Patterns of Denominational Development: Church and Sects," Logan Wilson and William L. Kolb, *Sociological Analysis* (New York: Harcourt, Brace & Co., 1949), p. 663.
[17] Abbe G. Michonneau, *Revolution in a City Parish* (Westminster, Maryland: The Newman Press, 1952), p. 16.
[18] Jessie Bernard, *American Community Behavior* (New York: The Dryden Press, 1949), pp. 242-57, 356-414.

Human Ecology and Urban Religious Dynamics. A dynamic approach to urban religion would suggest that each institution attempt to locate itself advantageously with respect to the population group it seeks to serve. The ecological pattern that is established will depend on a number of factors including the time of organization and the number of constituents. In a metropolitan center the larger denominations may have sufficient adherents to maintain a church in a relatively small area. The smaller denominations may be forced to cover a greater area in order to find sufficient members to maintain the institution.

The most thorough study of human ecology in relation to religious dynamics in an American city has been made of Cincinnati by Hotchkiss.[19] It is an attempt to understand the geographical relationships of religious institutions to the dynamic organization of the Cincinnati metropolitan area. It is discussed in this section as a case study of religion and urban ecology. While generalizations may be made for other cities, it is not intended to imply that Cincinnati is typical of American metropolitan communities in this respect. The religious institutions of the Cincinnati area, it was found, are associated most directly with residential land use. However, unless the religious institutions are typed and classified, significant areal differences do not appear in Cincinnati. The pattern of residential land use is the matrix in which the religious institutions are contained.

The major Protestant denominations in Cincinnati tend to be neighborhood institutions to a greater extent than the Roman Catholic churches, mainly because their numerical strength in the population permits this type of locational pattern. Where only one church operates, there appears to be a strong tendency for these Protestant churches to function as community churches, serving almost the entire Protestant population within the neighborhood rather than being limited to a specific denomination. While Protestant churches are not organized on the geographic parish plan in Cincinnati, their location and the natural areas of the urban structure tend to produce many features of the graphically defined parish. In 1947 it was found that 56 per cent of the regular Protestant churches had compact parishes (two-thirds of their members lived within a mile of the church). Scattered Protestant parishes were more characteristic of the smaller denominations and of the churches located in the central city.

Protestant diversity does not permit a generalization about the ecology of the overall structure of Protestant churches because of the regular Protestant groups (denominations) and the irregular groups (sects). In Cincinnati this latter group has about one-fourth as many congregations as the former. The sects are not as widely scattered since they tend to serve specialized segments of the population.

---

[19] Wesley A. Hotchkiss, *Areal Pattern of Religious Institutions in Cincinnati* (Chicago: Research Paper No. 13, Department of Geography, University of Chicago, 1950). This section draws heavily on the report of Hotchkiss.

In Cincinnati the Roman Catholic Church is a community institution, and in some places, where the proportions of Roman Catholic populations are greatest, the churches are located on a neighborhood basis. Completeness and uniformity of their area coverage of the built-up residential land characterizes Roman Catholicism in Cincinnati. The total effect of this locational pattern indicates centralized planning on the part of Catholic churchmen. The concentration of Roman Catholics appears as frequently in above average socio-economic areas as it does in below average areas in Cincinnati. The distributions of regular Protestant and Roman Catholic groups tend to complement each other. The traditional strength of the Roman Catholic group in the low socio-economic areas is not found in Cincinnati. Two population groups which are characteristically non-Roman Catholic have settled in the low income areas: the Negro population and the inmigrant group from Kentucky and the Southern states.

Catholicism and Protestantism vary from area to area throughout Cincinnati, but Judaism is more localized. Two major factors operate in the locational patterns within the different types of religion: the location of the people whom the particular religion seeks to serve; and the theory of parish structure of the religion. The three major faiths, Protestantism, Roman Catholicism, and Judaism, differ in these two factors.

The Jewish community in a city will sometimes divide itself on the basis of the degree of assimilation into American culture. In an eastern Pennsylvania metropolitan city two groups of Jewish people may be found. Those who live in the old section of town attend the synagogue in greater numbers, while those who attend the temple tend to live on the hill in a neighborhood adjacent to the college. Aside from the socio-economic differences which may be observed, there are differences between the two groups in the degree to which they have held to old world ways of living and worshiping. Those who attend the temple and live on the hill are younger, are engaged in higher status occupations, and accept the values of American society more completely.

Urban Religion and Social Change. The changing features of the urban social façade are easier to observe than the response of church programs to these changes. It should be noted that religious beliefs and practices change more slowly than other life activities in the urban community. Outward changes in urban religion, as evidenced by new church structures, may be observed, but it may be questioned whether organized religion has grown in its significance in city life. In part this may be related to the conserving function of institutions, especially religion. A tendency to conserve religion may crowd out a desire to be relevant to community life. Lynd found that Middletown sermon titles before and after the depression were interchangeable. The postwar visitor in New York City finds the sermon topics on the church page in the Saturday newspaper strangely similar to those advertised

during the depression. Lynd found in *Middletown in Transition* that
". . . in ministering to material, as to spiritual needs, the church does
not appear to have extended its function during the depression years."[20]
He adds that ". . . religion . . . in Middletown is torn by conflicts as
to what its function is and whose values it shall serve."[21] These data
demonstrate the differential between social change and the response
of urban religious behavior to these changes.

Research has presented many data which show the rigid resistance
of religion to a changing social environment. In his 1950 studies of
metropolitan Protestantism Douglass concluded that:

> . . . there is very little specific adaptation on the part of the
> churches as a body to the particular needs of a given neighbor-
> hood area. Their activities, their ongoing programs, are not directed
> with any precision to meeting the local versions of common
> human needs. Whether children are many or few, whether aged
> are predominant or not, whether there are surplus single men or
> surplus single women, whether people of one race or occupation
> are massed in a single area, whether students or some other group
> are concentrated there, makes little difference with the habitual
> programs of the churches to which these conditions are adjacent.
> Pastoral ministries are not essentially different, as carried on by
> the average minister, in the socially superior or inferior zones
> of the city, though one may have tenfold more crime, delinquency
> and poverty than another. The social emphases of the church, in
> the pulpit or in religious education, are not closely concerned
> with local environmental tensions. When race and nationality
> issues are discussed, it is generally in world terms, and not in
> terms of the neighborhood.[22]

Remembering that Douglass was a religious researcher for a national
church body, these observations must be accepted as those of an informed insider and not those of a superficial, unsympathetic outsider.

Many background factors must be considered if an adequate understanding is desired for the religious lag in relation to social change.
For example, cities that were built on an industry that is now declining
face adjustments in religious life as well as other aspects of their
social structure. Scranton, Pennsylvania, because of the declining importance of anthracite coal mining in its economic structure, was
facing this type of situation when a religious survey was conducted in
1944. It was found that Scranton had considerably more than one
church for each 1,000 population in 1944. Using national averages as
standards, Douglass found that Scranton had approximately 23 per
cent more churches than the number needed to serve the population.

[20] Robert S. Lynd and Helen Merrell Lynd, *Middletown in Transition* (New
York: Harcourt, Brace & Co., 1937), p. 306.

[21] *Ibid.*, p. 309.

[22] *Information Service, op. cit.*

As an adjustment toward maintaining the effectiveness of churches, in this depressed economic area, the uniting of numerous functions and activities of groups of contiguous churches under an urban larger parish plan was proposed. Under this plan each church would maintain its own identity but would unite for special phases of work.[23] As an accommodation technique for churches in an area with a contracting, rather than an expanding, economic base, this suggestion has dynamic possibilities.

The changing of neighborhood populations, functions and structures is another background factor in the environment of the church. As neighborhoods change, so must the program of the church. The presence of a new population type or a different land use (residential apartments, business or factory) should be a cue to any church that it is time to reexamine the needs of the community in relation to the function of the church. Sometimes church leaders do not catch the cue. The aftermath is churches that are stranded or that have not changed their program. The presence of any new population groups or a change of land use is the signal for a church to re-evaluate its function in the community.

The dynamic effect of population shifts on religious institutions is traced in the history of Brooklyn, one of the five boroughs in New York City. At the turn of the century 52 per cent of the population in Brooklyn was Protestant, 34 per cent was Roman Catholic, and 14 per cent was Jewish. By 1946 the proportion of Protestants had declined to 29 per cent, while the proportion of Jewish people had increased to 37 per cent. Roman Catholic members had declined only slightly (27 per cent), and Eastern Orthodox adherents comprised 2 per cent of the population. Protestants were a minority. In the first half of the twentieth century, with the exception of Negro churches and certain Lutheran groups, Protestant groups declined sharply. Not only were there fewer Protestants in Brooklyn, but the leading members of Brooklyn Protestant churches tended to live farther from the churches to which they belonged.[24] The effect of these changes in the population structure on the Protestant religious life has not been uniform in all neighborhoods. Dramatic changes in the population structure necessitate a re-alignment of religious resources.

Shifts in the distribution and changes in the structure of the population of a city usually require the re-location of churches. This presents a recurring problem of church adjustment because of a lag that develops between church location and population distribution. Barry and Perry have observed that in Detroit in 1945 the location of Presbyterian churches was a number of years behind the process of popula-

[23] H. Paul Douglass, *Scranton and Lackawanna County Churches* (Scranton, Pennsylvania: United Churches of Lackawanna County, 1945).
[24] H. Paul Douglass, *et al.*, *Brooklyn Protestantism—1930-1945* (New York: Brooklyn Church and Mission Federation, 1946).

tion movement. The 1945 location and size of churches of that denomination reflected the distribution of a potential constituency of a decade or more ago.[25] When churches are not located conveniently for those who are potentially the constituency, it is a limitation on the type of program that may be offered and the effectiveness of the program in meeting needs. A dynamic approach to the urban church requires that this lag be kept to a minimum.

New populations in the neighborhood present another urban situation requiring church adjustment. The newcomers and the old residents may be of the same religious tradition but their cultural differences may hinder the established churches in the community from absorbing new members who speak a different language. Protestant churches ministering to the growing Puerto Rican community in New York City increased 300 per cent between 1947 and 1953. In a recently published study of the New York Puerto Rican community it was found that 55 per cent of the Protestant churches in which Spanish was spoken were of the exceptional (sect) type, and 22.5 per cent were affiliated with more typical, regular Protestant denominations. Fourteen per cent were independent churches without national Protestant affiliation.[26] Apparently the traditional Protestant churches were not accommodating the newcomers.

A dynamic urban church is concerned with the assimilation of newcomers. In a study of migrants in Pittsburgh, Pennsylvania, it was found that those with a rural background became members of churches to a lesser degree than other newcomers.[27] C. W. Mills found that Puerto Rican migrants are less likely to attend church in New York City than they were in Puerto Rico. A 1953 survey reported that the Protestant churches in the communities where Puerto Ricans are settling are doing little to welcome them and less to discover their needs and help meet them.[28] Aid in the adjustment process of the new migrant is a necessary prerequisite for a vital church program.

Frequent change of residence is typical, rather than atypical, of urban living. The feeling of transience that this gives people may result in a reluctance to join a church even though they may have been participating in religious activities at a previous residential location. Their religious values may lead them to state a denominational preference in a religious census, but their pattern of living may preclude

[25] David W. Barry and Everett L. Perry, *The Presbyterian Church in Metropolitan Detroit* (New York: Presbyterian Board of National Missions, 1946), p. 9.

[26] *The New York Times*, September 20, 1953.

[27] Samuel W. Blizzard and Machlin E. John, "Social Participation of Husbands and Wives Who Are Migrants in the City," *Journal Series*, Paper No. 1722 (State College, Pennsylvania: Agricultural Experiment Station, February, 1952).

[28] "The Puerto Rican Journey," *Information Service* (New York: National Council of Churches, November 14, 1953).

active participation in the church of their choice. The problem of the stranger consequently places certain demands on the resources of the church in relation to the urban community.

Church Strategy and Community Change. The church in the city is constantly facing a changing neighborhood or a moving constituency. The tourist, or the newcomer in the city, often does not realize that the church on the street corner may have gone through many stages and may have been located on several sites before it found its present ministry. The Riverside Church in New York City, built in 1929, and operating currently on an annual budget of nearly six hundred thousand dollars, is the successor to three previous organizations. Etched in stone in the narthex is this statement:

> This congregation,
> organized in 1841,
> Known as:
> The Norfolk Street
> Baptist Church
> until 1860;
> The Fifth Avenue
> Baptist Church
> 1860—1922;
> The Park Avenue
> Baptist Church
> 1922—1929;
> The Riverside Church
> December, 1929.

Dramatic as this historical note may be, it is typical of churches that have survived in a metropolis.

The history of religious institutions in any downtown metropolitan area points up the problem. The story of the Presbyterians in downtown Baltimore, Maryland, for example, is sprinkled with churches that faced adjustment problems. At one time there were fifteen Presbyterian churches within five square miles of downtown Baltimore. As the community changed, only four of these churches remained: First Presbyterian, Franklin Street Presbyterian, Westminster Presbyterian and McKim Memorial. Five of the churches moved to more favorable residential communities in the suburbs. Four churches were abandoned. One church was turned over to a Polish group and later was dissolved. Another building is a synogogue for a group of Jewish people. Over the years changing neighborhoods have required new strategies for this Protestant group of churches.

Developing a strategy for accommodation to an urban culture and adjustment to changing local neighborhoods within the larger metropolitan community is a major problem for the urban church. When a church faces a declining neighborhood situation, Kinchloe found that there are five alternative strategies: (1) an effort may be made to adapt the program to the social characteristics of the district; (2) a new location may be sought which will be more convenient to the membership; (3) the congregation may disband and sell the property; (4) a few of the faithful may hold on, vaguely hoping that they may be able to maintain their church; (5) a metropolitan church may be developed, if the location is favorable, the leadership is imaginative and adjustable, and the financial resources are adequate.[29]

The East Harlem Protestant Parish in New York City is an example of a religious program being adapted to its environment. It was organized to explore new ways of developing an effective religious program in an area of the city that has traditionally been a port of entry. The religious structure of the parish was developed in response to the social structures found in this area of the city. Several features of the parish program have grown out of a sociological understanding of the neighborhood. The ministers and the church are made accessible to the people through having the clergy live in the community (a unique requirement even for social workers who work in depressed areas of the city), and by holding religious services in storefront churches. Many features of the larger parish plan for rural areas have been adapted to East Harlem needs. The parish is organized on the basis of a group ministry for purposes of coordinated planning and programing as well as for supporting the morale of the clergy. The ministry of the church is designed to touch the whole life of the people in the neighborhood. The East Harlem Protestant Parish is concerned with housing as well as religious education, police practices as well as social justice, and political action as well as preaching. The needs of people shape the program of the parish as religious resources are used within the structure of the community.[30]

The foreign language churches in the city originated out of a desire of church officials and new settlers to provide a religious structure adapted to the needs of persons oriented in cultures foreign to the dominant culture of the United States. Adjustability must be maintained, however, after the program has been established. It may become a barrier to complete assimilation of the group in the larger religious community. In the assimilation process, a life cycle can be seen in the life of a foreign-speaking congregation. Sociological insights assist in recognizing when the church has completed the cycle and is assimilated into the larger American urban community. An example of this process is the history of four Slovak-American Congregational churches in metropolitan Pittsburgh. During the first half

---

[29] Samuel C. Kinchloe, "The Behavior Sequence of a Dying Church," *Journal of Religious Education*, Vol. XXIV, 1929, pp. 329-345.
[30] *The City Church*, Vol. III, No. 4, September, 1952; *Newsweek*, October 31, 1949.

of the twentieth century Congregational missionary agencies subsidized these churches to the amount of a quarter of a million dollars. A survey of these congregations in 1948 revealed ". . . practically complete integration of the constituencies of these four Congregational churches into the total American community."[31] At the time of the survey it was anticipated that mission aid would be gradually terminated.

A second strategy involves the relocation of churches. Recent population shifts to the suburban towns and the rural urban fringe dramatize this need. Sanderson found in the Bridgeport, Connecticut, metropolitan district that there were enough churches. The suburban areas needed more churches, but many areas within Bridgeport city were over-churched. The relocation of established congregations was recommended, however, rather than the establishment of new congregations.[32]

The disestablishment of a church is one adaptation strategy. Churches do not always adapt their programs to the demands of the changing city. Hallenbeck refers to the "graveyard of churches."[33] He documents his use of this dramatic phrase by citing a spot map that had at one time been prepared by the Research Department of the Chicago Church Federation. On a city map the locations at which Protestant churches had died during the life of the city were marked. Some three hundred spots, with greater density at the center of the city, were scattered over the map.

When a church organization declines in a neighborhood and cannot continue its program, some disposal must be made of the building. It is sometimes condemned and is dismantled; or it may be sold for a non-religious use. In some cases a new congregation may use the building. In 1946 in downtown Philadelphia there were a number of church buildings now used by congregations other than the group for which they were built. The Church of the Advent, where Phillips Brooks began his ministry in 1859, was a Polish Catholic Church. A Greek Catholic congregation used the building of the Second Reformed Church of Philadelphia where T. DeWitt Talmadge came as pastor in 1862.[34] An adjustment technique for a church that does not wish to continue its ministry in the downtown area is to turn over its building to a new population group.

The population characteristics of a metropolitan neighborhood often change relatively frequently. Church buildings may have a longer use-

[31] Thomas A. Tripp, *Slovak-American Congregational Churches in Pennsylvania* (New York: Congregational Church Extension Division, 1948), p. 3 (mimeographed).

[32] Ross W. Sanderson, *Toward a Church Strategy for Metropolitan Bridgeport* (New York: Board of Home Missions of the Congregational and Christian Churches, 1947), p. 56.

[33] Wilbur C. Hallenbeck, *American Urban Communities* (New York: Harper & Brothers, 1951), p. 479.

[34] *The Presbyterian*, November 7, 1946.

fulness than the tenure of a specific population group. For example, in 1950 a church building on East Eighty-Ninth Street in New York City that had been used successively by two Protestant congregations, was opened for use by a Roman Catholic congregation. Reflecting the need for a religious group indigenous to the neighborhood, the building at first housed a Protestant Episcopal congregation that later merged with another congregation of that faith. More recently a Reformed Church congregation used the edifice. This group disbanded just prior to the sale of the building to the Catholic Diocese.[35] By this adjustment technique population dynamics and religious dynamics may be coordinated.

Shifting populations may lead to the closing of old churches as well as the opening of new churches. Occasionally a church that was closed after many years of service, because of the depopulation, is opened again when new residents move into its potential service area. The Plain View Methodist Church, located near Hicksville, New York, was closed in 1925 because of population shifts. Eighteen years later it was reopened because a new housing development of 4,000 homes had been built nearby.[36] Changing population in terms of numbers or composition is an occasion for reappraising the program, location and resources of a church. A dynamic approach to the urban church requires an alert and constant checking of population changes.

The self-chosen parish system and the voluntary nature of Protestant religious organization create problems in adjusting to community changes. In many Protestant churches adjustment to a changing neighborhood is a voluntary action on the part of a specific congregation. This encourages faithful and loyal, but misguided, parishioners to select a "stick it out" strategy. The blighted transition areas are a classic illustration of this fact. At times it appears that in these areas of deterioration there is, to use Sanderson's phrase, "under-churching in the midst of over-churching."[37] The density of population and the religious preferences of the area when it was a residential area demanded more churches than the current populations of the transition area. It was found in Los Angeles that the churches that remain in transition areas are of the wrong sort to be able to do the job required by the situation as it is now. The people who move into the area have a different way of life than the previous residents.

East Boston, Massachusetts, has seen successive waves of new population take up residence in the last fifty years. Canadians, Italians, the Irish, and Russians have settled in the area since a rapid transit tunnel made quicker transportation to Boston available in 1904. Since

[35] *The New York Times*, July 10, 1950.

[36] *Ibid.*, October 17, 1953.

[37] Ross A. Sanderson, *The Churches of Los Angeles, California* (New York: Committee for Cooperative Field Work, National Council of Churches, 1945), p. 19.

the population types in a community and their way of life and means of livelihood affect institutions and their programs, the churches in East Boston have been affected by community changes. Institutions, including the church, are ultimately interdependent and are conditioned by various phenomena arising from their common social milieu.[38]

East Boston Protestant churches, some of them having a history of a century of service to the community, hardly made an adequate adjustment to the changes in their environment occasioned by new populations with Roman Catholic and Jewish backgrounds. Some churches were closed or were merged with other congregations. Others tried, with or without aid from their denomination, to adapt their program to the needs of the new residents. It was found in the survey of Protestantism in East Boston that the churches of these denominations were not generally aware of the values and cultural patterns of the foreign-speaking newcomers. This was particularly true for Italians in 1946 who are predominant almost everywhere in East Boston.[39] It would appear that Protestant churches desiring to expand their program in a neighborhood would need to be aware of and understand thoroughly the values and culture patterns of the residents.

The Downtown Church. The successful downtown church has usually survived in an area where others have failed. Sanderson suggests that ". . . a good church in a poor neighborhood has a widely scattered parish."[40] Churches that maintain themselves in a central city location draw a congregation from a wide radius through appealing to "special interest groups." The religious ministries of the downtown church are specialized. It may be the only congregation in the city of a certain denomination, or the clergymen may represent a specific theological orientation. The pastor of the central city church may have a reputation as a personal counselor, or the location of the church may place it at the crossroads to minister to the traveler or the transient guest of a downtown hotel. The willingness of the minister to discuss public policy and community issues may draw some parishioners to a downtown church. For denominations largely represented by neighborhood churches throughout the city, a downtown church may have symbolic value for the prestige of the denomination.

The downtown parish, when its history is studied, offers an insight into the various stages through which most urban churches might go as they respond to the changing community. Fosselman has sketched the life history of St. Patrick's Roman Catholic Church in Washington, D. C., with this cyclical understanding. The foundations for the parish were laid when Catholic workmen were brought to the new city of

---

[38] William J. Villaume, *Protestantism in East Boston—1920-1946* (Boston: Department of Research and Planning, Massachusetts Council of Churches, 1947).

[39] *Ibid.*

[40] Sanderson, *op. cit.*, p. 17.

Washington in the last decade of the 18th century to build head-quarters for the federal government. As the decades passed, parish schools and institutions were built. Daughter churches were established to the east, to the west, and to the north of St. Patrick's parish between 1820 and 1870. After the Civil war, St. Patrick's entered its "golden age." An unsuccessful attempt to move the church away from en-croaching business had been resisted. For the next thirty years the church held a dominant position among the churches of the nation's capital. Religious functions of city-wide significance were held there. At the turn of the century it developed into a typical downtown parish. Two-thirds of the geographic limits of the parish are occupied by business establishments. Only a handful, relatively, of the parishioners remain in the neighborhood of the parish. The program now is geared to a transient population. It may be thought of as the church of the strangers. The services are now scheduled to accommodate the ebb and flow of the city's daily traffic.[41]

The downtown church with a program that ministers to parishioners whose residences are scattered widely throughout the city, as well as to overnight guests in downtown hotels, has often developed its metro-politan character in response to many changes. The Second Presby-terian Church, of Richmond, Virginia, was established in 1845 in a neighborhood that was entirely residential. Today the church structure is tucked in between tall buildings in the downtown area. About one-fourth of the Presbyterian churches presently in Richmond were organized by former members of the Second Presbyterian Church. The mother church continues to present a religious program designed for the downtown area. The history of this church is a series of adjustment episodes.[42]

The importance of the role of the large central downtown church is demonstrated in San Francisco where over one-third of the total church membership in the churches of eleven major Protestant de-nominations belong to these churches. Forty-four per cent of member-ship of the corresponding denominations belong to churches adjacent to the centers of Oakland, Berkeley, Alameda or Richmond. There is evidence of the need for a more balanced distribution of religious resources between the central city churches and the neighborhood churches when it is recognized that some of the central churches are largely disassociated from their immediate neighborhood and that land is increasingly being devoted to business and other non-residential uses.[43]

[41] David H. Fosselman, "The Parish in Urban Communities," C. J. Nuesse and Thomas J. Harte, *The Sociology of the Parish* (Milwaukee: Bruce Pub-lishing Co., 1951), pp. 135-47.

[42] Wyndham B. Blanton, *The Making of a Downtown Church* (Richmond: John Knox Press, 1945).

[43] H. Paul Douglass, *et al.*, *The San Francisco Bay Area Church Study* (New York: Committee for Cooperative Field Research, National Council of Churches, 1945), pp. 15-17.

The Suburban Movement. The suburban movement has changed many communities from a rural and agricultural orientation to an urban and industrial outlook. The Pittsburgh Church Study analyzed the church adjustment problem in the rural-urban fringe. Because of the cultural and religious background of new residents in the fringe, Protestant churches were presented with a growth potential. It was observed, however, that old established churches with a rural orientation failed to adjust to the changing community situation. Reluctance to include urban employed and oriented newcomers in the community focused attention on the identification of these churches with rural values exclusively.[44]

New suburban areas offer Protestant churches an opportunity to work cooperatively. This is especially true when a new housing development is established as was the case in Forest Park, Illinois. The United Protestant Church was established in this new community of 19,000 population because it was recognized that the mobility of our population has made obsolete former methods of starting new churches. Forest Park residents are typically professional and business white collar workers. The average family income is $5,800 per year. Since many residents of the more than three thousand rental units are highly educated junior executives with their companies, people are always moving in and out. There is a high transiency rate. There are five Protestant denominations cooperating in the United Church. From the start the church has financed its own program.[45]

Sociological Research and Church Strategy—Sociological research may be a servant of the church. Since the community is dynamic, so must be the program of the church. Leiffer feels that ". . . if it is to be effective, the church dare not be less dynamic than the community itself."[46]

A periodic review of a church's program in the city is essential to survival. A superficial examination of the church's relation to its community will not be adequate. The survey must be rigorously and diligently executed. A periodic review of the church's program in the changing community will help a church offer a community-centered and not merely an institution-centered program.

The rapidity of community change and the mobility of the population underline the need for research and planning. Sanderson, noting that Los Angeles, California, had a population which more than trebled between 1920 and 1945, stresses the implications of this change for church strategy. The rapid growth of the city, coupled with the decentralization occurring in the Los Angeles area, presents seemingly

---

[44] H. Paul Douglass, *et al., The Metropolitan Pittsburgh Church Study* (New York: National Council of Churches, 1948).

[45] *The City Church,* Vol. IV, No. 2, April, 1953, p. 3-5.

[46] Murray H. Leiffer, *The Effective City Church* (Nashville: Abingdon Cokesbury Press, 1949), p. 69.

insurmountable problems of church administration. Knowing that the fortunes of the church are tied to the welfare of the community, Sanderson suggests that close scrutiny of new developments is essential for the continuance of a dynamic church program.[47]

Church planning and adjustment require factual data to be wisely executed. An adequate understanding of the social setting in which a church functions is required. The community cannot be understood without knowing all aspects of its social structure, including institutions and churches, population characteristics and mobility, cultural patterns, and occupational structure. The services of a technically trained social researcher are needed to adequately understand these social structures and processes. The Massachusetts Council of Churches has provided an interesting experiment in uniting action research and needs for church planning and adjustment. Religious researchers from outside the community provide technical assistance to the resident religious leadership in the community as they study their community in relation to its religious needs. The technical services of the researcher are directed toward practical results. The cooperation of the technician is available on the basis that the project will be defined, agreed upon, and carried out by the local leaders in a democratic fashion.[48]

Urban Church-Community Relations. The community functions of churches in the urban community follow a cycle. Riemer has shown that the church in the immigrant and inmigrant sections of the city serves a comprehensive community function. It is a community center and is the only institution which migrants tend to carry from the village environment to the city without noticeable changes. Foreign language churches at first brought their ministers from the old country. Preachers from the southern highlands often follow their parishioners as they migrate to an industrial city. Religious as well as social, recreational, and family activities, are tied to the church. In some cases burial societies and insurance programs have a quasi-relationship to the religious organizations.[49]

In a second stage the newcomers, or their children, begin to move to more desirable residential areas. If they move in a group, the relocation of the church may follow and a new community-centered religious program is established. More than likely, however, the people may move out family by family, but the church building will remain in the old neighborhood. In this event, their loyalty may bring them back to the old neighborhood for worship, but the broader community function of the church will be limited by the scattered distribution of its membership.

---

[47] Sanderson, *op. cit.*
[48] William J. Villaume, *Church Planning and Adjustment* (New York: Committee on Cooperative Field Research, National Council of Churches, 1949).
[49] Svend Riemer, *The Modern City* (New York: Prentice-Hall, 1952), pp. 349-51.

Or the members of the church that were ethnically oriented to a church may move to scattered sections of the city in more favored residential areas. It may not be possible for the church to follow because they are not settled in a compact homogeneous group. In this event the church may move to a location with a high membership potential even though its previous ethnic group does not predominate. In this process, the church may tend to lose its community function and gather a congregation based on individual rather than group membership.

The cycle is completed when the church moves to the peripheral areas of the city, particularly if the church is established before the new community structure is evolved.[50] Church facilities will be used for a variety of functions. In addition to worship and religious education the recreational and association life of the new community in the rural-urban fringe will center in the church. Highly urbanized suburban churches tend to build their programs around the family unit and provide a number of specialized community functions for the convenience of its membership.

Regardless of this cycle, the effective church will work out its community relations program with full cognizance of the overall community picture. The urban church is a part of the social structure of its community. Church-community relations must be viewed as a reciprocal problem with responsibility for improvement resting upon both the churches and other institutions in the city. Within its purposes it would be expected that the church would take the initiative in maintaining its good will and in establishing a cordial cooperative relationship with other agencies in the city. A survey made in the South, however, showed that ". . . neither agencies nor churches have given sufficient attention to the problem of how churches can assist in community development."[51]

The identification of an urban church with its community may be assisted by the understanding of and concern for the living problems of its parishioners. The practical issues of city living that revolve around housing and education, government and business, crime and civic improvement call for a clear voice to be heard in the church. Churches in the city at times do not seem to be interested in the daily problems of people. The politician and the social worker are more likely to devote attention to people's problems. This type of reaction is reflected in the observation made by the Lynds when they reported, "To such controversial issues—the great majority of the churches of Middletown present the negative face of the community, or are silent,

<hr/>

[50] Samuel W. Blizzard, "Churching the Rural-Urban Fringe," *The City Church*, Vol. IV, No. 3, May-June, 1953, pp. 6-7; Samuel W. Blizzard, "The Religious Situation in the Rural-Fringe," *The Christian Rural Fellowship Bulletin*, No. 185, September, 1953.

[51] Gordon W. Blackwell, *et al.*, *Church and Community in the South* (Richmond: John Knox Press, 1949), p. 158.

or talk such generalities that their position is equivocal."[52] The church that is a dynamic institution will relate its program to the problems of the community in which it functions.

Recent studies point to a need for a revitalization of the church in relation to community needs. There is an increasing emphasis upon functional Christianity that has implications for the church and the city. An urban pastor can no longer preach sermons or play the other roles that his profession has been assigned without an understanding of the community in which the church is located. The sociological orientation of the urban church is important. A dynamic approach to urban church programming requires that the social, economic, health and educational backgrounds of parishioners be seriously considered in a church's plans for serving the community.[53]

A sociological profile will assist church leaders in determining what agencies are active in the community, what needs each of these agencies is attempting to meet, how the church can cooperate by assisting these agencies to do a more effective job, and finally, what needs remain which are the distinctive function of the church. In terms of church strategy, this selective process is important if religious resources are to be used efficiently and effectively.

Social participation in the city is widely scattered among a variety of interest groups. Churches are finding that they must share their members with the lodge, the service club, the chamber of commerce, the labor union and many other associations. Churchmen are inclined to see the competitive aspects of this trend rather than the way in which it fits into the total community situation. Considered functionally, the ability of these non-church groups to present a systematic program directed toward the specialized interest and welfare of the community is a direct contrast to the typical churchman's attitude toward the community needs these associations meet. Some of these needs—recreational, economic, and benevolent—the churches aid in hit-and-miss fashion, but they are often thought to be peripheral to their theological orientation. The Rotary and other associations seem to place them at the center of their program.

In the complex urban environment the church is only one of many institutions which residents of the city have established. Religious leaders, lay and clergy, who wish to have institutions take a vital part in community life, must have a thorough understanding of the other public and private agencies that are a part of the social structure of the city. Some of these agencies are legally responsible for meeting specific needs. Their role is clearly defined and implemented by law. Other agencies are voluntary and depend on private funds to carry out their role. The church must play its role in meeting needs in terms of the total community structure.

---

[52] Lynds, *Middletown in Transition, op. cit.*, pp. 312-13.
[53] Blackwell, *et al., op. cit.*, pp. 127-173.

The tendency of the church in the city to take a more functional approach to the community poses many problems. The training of a clergy that is socially alert and skilled in participating in the social processes of the community is essential. The church's program of preaching and pastoral care, music and religious education, social activities and recreation must be geared to the needs of the community and its cultural milieu. A further requirement is that the individual congregations must be enthusiastic for an active role of the church in community affairs. A permissive attitude on the part of other community agencies must be developed toward the participation of the church in community life. Any attitude that assumes that the church has no place in this process or that the church is an intruder must be re-structured.

The community relations program of the urban church will be advanced by training community-minded clergy. The type of training that the clergy receive may produce respected scholars or effective practitioners. A thorough theological orientation and a knowledge of the Christian system of values and its meaning may be the possession of the scholar. A knowledge of and an ability to practice in a community setting, however, is important if this theological orientation is to function in religious life and behavior. Only a wedding of these foci—theological and sociological—in the training process of the clergy will produce practitioners who understand the purposive inner functions of Catholicism, Protestantism or Judaism on the basic level of the congregation itself. The next advance in church-community relations awaits clergy with this training.

A theological point of view and a community orientation are the foci for a dynamic approach to urban religion. The poignancy and variety of theological orientations are recognized, but as a sociologist, the author has placed a major focus on the community orientation of the city church.

Religion in the city is conceived as a social system. Urban culture has made an impact on the urban church. The religious behavior, the parish pattern, the organizational structure, and the associations that are affiliated with the church in the metropolis, all bear the imprint of city living.

Features of the broader social structure of the city are reflected in the church. It is difficult to distinguish church members from non-church members. The stratification system that functions in the city also operates within the church. Struggles for power and rivalries for social position occur within the church as well as in the larger community structure. The way in which the churches are accommodated to the power and prestige groups of the community largely determines their effectiveness in implementing religious values.

Diversity of religious culture in the American city gives a dynamic character to ecological factors. Variations in urban religion complicate the problem of locating churches to effectively serve the population. Freedom of religion in America presents the citizen with a choice of participation or non-participation. Religious preferences and the pattern of residential land use give substance to the ecology of the city church.

The structure of the urban community is constantly changing. Economic enterprises rise and fall, neighborhoods are built and gradually decline in status, the structure of the population shifts from one race to another or from one nationality to another, and the mobility of the community residents operate as factors for change. The urban environment in which the church ministers is a constant challenge to the adjustability of religious leadership.

Churches develop strategies to aid in adjusting to community change. When the neighborhood in which a church is located is re-structured, the program may be adapted to the new community structure, or the church may move to another neighborhood. Another strategy is to resist the forces operating in the changing neighborhood, or the church may disband. A fifth strategy is used by churches that are able to develop a city wide ministry. The strategy chosen must be selected with recognition of the goals, resources, and opportunity of the church. Sociological research will assist in the designing of a workable strategy.

A community orientation places major attention on the people that the church serves and the living problems they face. A church-community relations approach to the practical decisions of daily living gives a new dynamic to religion and makes a theological orientation relevant to the human situation.

WORKSHOP AND PROBLEMS

1. In what ways is the city important as a source of innovation in religion?

2. How would you characterize the urban religious systems?

3. What is the relation of human ecology to urban religious dynamics?

4. What is the relation between urban religion and social change?

5. In what way is church strategy related to community change?

6. What would you say are some characteristics of successful downtown churches?

7. How do suburban areas offer Protestant churches an opportunity to work cooperatively?

8. What are some of the contributions that sociological research may make to church strategy?

9. What are some community functions served by urban churches?

BIBLIOGRAPHY

Abell, Aaron L., *The Urban Impact on American Protestantism* (Cambridge: Harvard University Press, 1943).

Abrams, Ray H., Editor, "Organized Religion in the United States, *The*

Annals, American Academy of Political and Social Science. No. 256 (March. 1948).

Barry, David W., *The Presbyterian Church in the Portland (Oregon) Metropolitan District* (New York: Presbyterian Board of National Missions. 1945) (mimeographed).

Barry, David W. and Perry, Everett L., *Presbyterian Church Extension Strategy in Metropolitan Chicago* (New York: Presbyterian Board of National Missions, 1947) (mimeographed).

Barry, David W. and Perry, Everett L. *The Presbyterian Church in Metropolitan Detroit,* (New York: Presbyterian Board of National Missions, 1946) (mimeographed).

Bernard, Jessie, *American Community Behavior* (New York: The Dryden Press, 1949).

Blackwell, Gordon W., *et al. Church and Community in the South* (Richmond: John Knox Press, 1945).

Blanton, Wyndham B., *The Making of a Downtown Church* (Richmond: John Knox Press, 1945).

Bushee, Frederic A., "The Church in a Small City," *American Journal of Sociology,* Vol. XLIX (November, 1943), 223-32.

Douglass, H. Paul, et. al., *Brooklyn Protestantism—1930-45* (New York: Brooklyn Church and Mission Federation, 1946).

Douglass, H. Paul, *Church Unity Movements in the United States* (New York: Institute of Social and Religious Research, 1934).

Douglass, H. Paul, *Protestant Cooperation in American Cities* (New York: Institute of Social and Religious Research, 1930).

Douglass, H. Paul, *Scranton and Lackawanna County Churches* (Scranton: United Churches of Lackawanna County, 1945) (mimeographed).

Douglass, H. Paul, "Some Protestant Churches in Urban America," *Information Service* (Federal Council of Churches), January 21, 1950.

Douglass, H. Paul, *The Church in a Changing City* (New York: George H. Doran Co., 1937).

Douglass, H. Paul, *The City's Church* (New York: Friendship Press, 1929).

Douglass, H. Paul, *et al., The Metropolitan Pittsburgh Church Study* (New York: National Council of Churches, 1948).

Douglass, H. Paul and Brunner, Edmund deS., *The Protestant Church as a Social Institution* (New York: Harper and Brothers, 1935).

Douglass, H. Paul, *et al., The San Francisco Bay Area Church Study* (San Francisco: San Francisco and Oakland Council of Churches, 1945).

Fichter, Joseph H., *Dynamics of a City Church* (Southern Parish, Vol. I) (Chicago: University of Chicago Press, 1951).

Fichter, Joseph H., "The Marginal Catholic: An Institutional Approach," *Social Forces,* Vol. XXXII, No. 2 (December, 1953), 167-73.

Gordon, Albert I., *Jews in Transition* (Minneapolis: University of Minnesota Press, 1949).

Hallenbeck, Wilbur C., *American Urban Communities* (New York: Harper and Brothers, 1951).

Hallenbeck, Wilbur C., *Urban Organization of Protestantism* (New York: Harper and Brothers, 1934).

Hatt, Paul K. and Reiss, Albert J., Jr., *Reader in Urban Sociology* (Glencoe, Illinois: The Free Press, 1951).

Hotchkiss, Wesley Akin, *Areal Pattern of Religious Institutions in Cincinnati* (Chicago: Research Paper No. 13, Department of Geography, University of Chicago, 1950).

Kinchloe, Samuel C., *The American City and Its Church* (Chicago: Friendship Press, 1938).

Kinchloe, Samuel C., "The Behavior Sequence of a Dying Church," *Journal of Religious Education,* Vol. XXIV (1929), 329-45.

Leiffer, Murray H., *City and Church in Transition* (Des Moines: Willet and Clark, 1938).

Leiffer, Murray H., *The Effective City Church* (New York: Abingdon-Cokesbury Press, 1949).

Lynd, Robert S. and Lynd, Helen Merrell, *Middletown* (New York: Harcourt, Brace & Co., 1929).

Lynd, Robert S. and Lynd, Helen Merrell, *Middletown in Transition* (New York: Harcourt, Brace & Co., 1937).

Massarik, Fred, *The Jewish Population of Los Angeles* (Los Angeles: Los Angeles Jewish Community Council, 1953) (mimeographed).

Mays, B. E. and Nicholson, J. W., *The Negro's Church* (New York: Institute of Social and Religious Research, 1933).

Michonneau, Abbé G., *Revolution in a City Parish* (Westminster, Maryland: The Newman Press, 1952).

Nuesse, C. J. and Harte, Thomas J., *The Sociology of the Parish* (Milwaukee: The Bruce Publishing Co., 1950).

Nygaard, Norman E., *Twelve Against the Underworld* (New York: Hobson Book Press, 1947).

Queen, Stuart A. and Carpenter, David B., *The American City* (New York: McGraw-Hill, 1953).

Riemer, Svend, *The Modern City* (New York: Prentice-Hall, 1952).

Sanderson, Ross W., *The Churches of Los Angeles, California* (New York: Committee on Cooperative Field Research, National Council of Churches, 1945) (mimeographed).

Sanderson, Ross W., *Toward a Church Strategy for Metropolitan Bridgeport* (New York: Board of Home Missions of the Congregational and Christian Churches, 1947).

Shippey, Frederick A., *Church Work in the City* (New York: Abingdon-Cokesbury Press, 1952).

Smith, Phillip M., "Protestant Comity in Metropolitan Pittsburgh," *American Sociological Review*, Vol. VIII (August, 1943), 425-32.

Smith, T. Lynn and McMahan, C. A., *The Sociology of Urban Life* (New York: The Dryden Press, 1951).

Tripp, Thomas A., *Slovak-American Congregational Churches in Pennsylvania* (New York: Congregational Church Extension Division, 1948) (mimeographed).

Villaume, William J., Church Planning and Adjustment (New York: The Committee for Cooperative Field Research, 1949).

Villaume, William J., *Protestantism in East Boston* (Boston: Department of Research and Planning, Massachusetts Council of Churches, 1947).

Villaume, William J., *South Boston* (Boston: Department of Research and Planning, Massachusetts Council of Churches, 1948).

Warner, W. Lloyd and Lunt, Paul S., *The Social Life of a Modern Community* (New Haven: Yale University Press, 1942).

Wilson, Logan and Kolb, William L., *Sociological Analysis* (New York: Harcourt, Brace & Co., 1949).

CHAPTER 19

Urban Planning and Development

By WILLIAM E. COLE

Planning as Concept. Planning is essentially the regulation and utilization of the physical resources of a city in accordance with a scheme or plan which considers not only the immediate needs of the city but also its future needs.

While the emphasis in the above concept is a physical emphasis the planner in no sense of the word can neglect the political, social and economic consequences of his actions. The expert in housing is concerned with more than a good structure at appropriate rental level, he is concerned with the development of a convenient unit and a good environment for people. The designer of streets is concerned with the safety and welfare of people who travel on them. The city planner is concerned with trying to develop an adequate city for people. Considerations of comfort, beauty, and economic adequacy and financial solvency have high priority in his objectives.

The Problems. The problem in planning is not so much that cities have never been planned but that planning has never been extensive enough or has not paced urban development in sufficient instances. Actually, the layout of ancient and medieval cities showed detailed attention not only to general layout but also to such details as design, the placement of public buildings, and the erection of monuments and other structures.[1] In America, the city of Philadelphia was laid out in 1682 on a checkerboard plan so characteristic of many American towns and cities. The plan for Washington, D. C., developed by Peter L'Enfant in 1791, was a classic in early American urban planning.

Another problem is that the term "planning," which was popularized in this country between 1930 and 1940 when because of the depression the leadership of the nation and the states had to embark upon new publicly supported enterprises such as public housing

---

[1] See Camillo Sitte, *The Art of Building Cities* (New York: Reinhard Publishing Corp., 1945). For more detailed accounts of the history of city planning see Robert Averill Walker's *Urban Planning* (Chicago: University of Chicago Press, 1949); or Thomas Adams, *Outline of Town and City Planning* (New York: Russell Sage Foundation, 1935).

[2] John Jewkes, *Ordeal by Planning* (New York: The Macmillan Co., 1948).

and regional planning, has fallen somewhat into disrepute and is classed by many people as a socialistic term.[2] Another problem is that the costs which the extensive physical adjustments and readjustments which are necessary to make cities more convenient and more livable are often high when considered for a short range period. A phase of the cost problem is the lack of public concern and support for urban improvements. This lack of support is due in large measure to the fact that the planners and the urban administrators have not developed adequate long range education programs to support planning activities. Planners have, upon occasion, "fumbled the ball" in their planning efforts and in their public relations. This, in turn, has encouraged opposition to planning. The wide range of vested interests, reflected in cities, which bring pressure upon planners, creates a situation in which it is difficult for a good job to be done unless there is the strongest type of planning support by the top administration in the cities.

Among the social, economic, and political problems to which planners must give attention the following inventory is at least suggestive:

1. Drastic inequalities of wealth and income in the urban community.
2. The lack of articulation among the various industries in urban communities.
3. Rapid obsolescence of the physical plant of many cities.
4. Competing forms of transportation which have left their disrupting imprint upon the national urban pattern.
5. The unparalleled growth of cities which has been accompanied by uncontrolled subdivision and speculative properties.
6. Urban housing, which has become one of the most burdensome problems the country now has to face.
7. The endangering of the public health in blighted areas and among low income families.
8. The religious, ethnic and cultural diversity of urban populations.
9. Lack of opportunity for higher education to a large percentage of urban youth.
10. Juvenile delinquency, organized crime, and commercial rackets in cities.
11. The mounting problem of inadequate urban finance.
12. The adjustment of the traditional scope of urban powers, especially lack of adequate home rule.
13. The overlapping of independent governmental units in metropolitan regions.
14. Inadequate urban civil service laws, and irresponsible and inadequate urban administrative and political leadership.[3]

[3] Adapted from National Resources Committee, *Our Cities: Their Role in the National Economy* (Washington, D. C.: Superintendent of Documents, 1937), pp. viii-x.

The planner knows, for instance, that unless the city has adequate institutions and services many of the ends he wishes to achieve are impossible.

In urban planning one notes varying mixtures of planning activity which are both remedial and preventive in measures. Much of the planning in old cities is remedial—the process of remodeling an old city—whereas in the design of new cities the work is designed as preventive. Much remedial planning may achieve a preventive purpose. For instance, when a bad traffic corner is engineered accident prevention may speedily follow. The rehousing of a slum—a remedial task—may also lead to the prevention of pathologies in the area because conditions and services will be improved for the people.

The Case for and against Planning. Some of the roots for the case for urban planning lie deep in social change. Urban growth has been so rapid and the nature of the urban culture changes so fast that only through the application of the best we know in planning technology may urban changes be predicted and the future needs of the people met. This means that planning itself is a continuous process.

The application of the principles and techniques of planning to public enterprise is no different from its application to private enterprise. It is simply good business if our cities, like our businesses, are to produce the best from their investment and if they, again like business, are to escape growing obsolescence.

Public urban planning is democratically correct in that, at its best, it represents all of the people of the urban community rather than a small segment of the population, and also that it tries to be above the interest of the few in favor of what is best for the majority.

The case against planning usually revolves around the problem of restriction and the use of restrictive measures. Here again the planner, in his best democratic tradition, tries to avoid extreme controls. Urban life is corporate life. What one does is closely related to what others also do. This makes controls inevitable. Indeed, there would be no freedom if controls were not in vogue. Human life would be unsafe without laws and their enforcement. Without zoning land values would be unstable and existing land values could not be preserved. Without subdivision control "shanty towns" would rise on sites needed for good housing. Without the power of eminent domain—again a control measure—cities could not obtain lands for public-use functions. Without building restrictions central business districts and individual property owners would be at the mercy of mass jerry-building because the unscrupulous would force the scrupulous to lower their building standards.

Public planning is entrusted to public servants. These servants are subject to recall and discipline. The methods they use in planning are, as a rule, subject to public hearing and review, thus quite within the framework of the best in the democratic tradition.

Planning Activities Cities Engage In. No very satisfactory, up-to-date, list of planning activities cities engage in has come to the attention of the writer. However, the listing in Table XLIV is suggestive.

As indicated from Table XLIV, the most common planning mechanism used by cities is zoning, followed in order by plot control, comprehensive planning, and street and park plans.

The Essential Elements of a City Plan. The essential elements of a city plan will depend in some degree upon the size and peculiar problems of a city. Usually, however, the plan will contain some combination of the following elements:

1. A complete land use plan for the city which incorporates a zoning plan.

TABLE XLIV

TYPES OF PLANNING ACTIVITY ENGAGED IN BY CITIES [a]

Type of Activity	Number of Cities
Zoning ordinance	1,322
Control of plots (mandatory)	275
Comprehensive plan	217
Thoroughfare plan	205
Park and parkway plan	168
Public building plan	99
Drainage and sewerage plan	97
School and library plan	97
Transit plan	86
Water supply plan	61
Transportation plan	29
Long-range financial plan	8

2. A system of streets and trafficways.
3. Parks and parkways.
4. Playgrounds and areas reserved for playgrounds.
5. Sites for schools and for other public buildings.
6. Railroad, bus and truck terminal sites.
7. Airport facilities.
8. Parking spaces.
9. Locations for utilities.
10. A financial plan, estimating the cost of the plan and how the costs may be met.

Beyond physical planning is city building which Black and Black call the "third dimension" in planning. They say:

City building involves more than the laying out of land, paving of streets, the creation of parks, and the laying of sewer and water mains. These are but servicing facilities for the effective use of buildings—houses, stores, offices, libraries, city halls and factories. This third dimensional element, architecture, largely makes the physical city. It is not a thing which can be directly

_____
[a] Compiled from Circular X, Appendix B, p. 11, by the National Resources Committee.

expressed in the city plan, but the economic and effective use of land for building purposes of all kinds to their proper places is by far the most important factor for consideration in plan making.[4]

The problem of control of architectural design in planning is a difficult one. The size and height of buildings in relation to space is controllable. The height and mass of buildings may be controlled through zoning.

U.S.AEC—Photo by Wescott

FIGURE 20.

Oak Ridge, Tennessee, Which Is Laid Out on a Neighborhood Basis with Roads and Streets Conforming to the Topography of the Land.

Imposed design may be made in publicly built and in publicly financed structures. Most urban structures are privately designed and privately built. Here there is no substitute for competency in the architectural fraternity and a friendly, cooperative relationship between the planning authorities and the architectural profession. In instances, a panel of architects who advise with the planning board will be helpful in many technical ways but also is a standard means of bringing about a liaison relationship between architects and plan-

[4] Russell Van Nest Black and Mary Hedges Black, *Planning for the Small American City* (Chicago: Public Administration Service, 1948).

ners. One can say that when private architects submit their preliminary plans to the planning boards for advice and scrutiny, this liaison relationship has reached satisfactory status.[5]

The Steps in Planning. Steps in urban planning may vary somewhat from city to city depending upon the necessary ground-work which has been developed. The following steps are, however, relatively inclusive:

1. The securing of a nucleus of local citizens and officials who are interested in planning and who are interested in promoting and guiding the necessary preliminary stages of the planning activity. This may well be the beginning of a larger citizens committee for the promotion of planning.

Courtesy of Department of City and Regional Planning, University of North Carolina

FIGURE 21. Land-use Plan for a Small City.

2. The securing of the necessary enabling legislation from the state. This may be in the nature of general permissive legislation or, if this is lacking, a special act for a specific city.
3. The passage of the necessary ordinance creating a planning board or committee.
4. The appointment of the board.
5. The selection of technical personnel together with whatever outside aid may be available.

---

[5] See Sir Patrick Abercrombie, "Discipline in Civic Design," *Town and Country Planning*, Vol. 19 (March, 1951), 118-124.

6. The assembling of basic maps, data and information available on the community.
7. The development of new studies or data.
8. The development of the plan.
9. The development of a financial plan to finance the plan.
10. Public hearings on the plan.
11. The official adoption of the plan.
12. The execution and timing of the various phases of the plan. This includes cooperating with other city, county, state and regional agencies in planning activities which may reach beyond the borders of the city.

Expectations of Urban Planning. Aside from specific situations one may only generalize upon the expectations of urban planning. What urban planning has accomplished and what it may accomplish was well summarized some years ago by the National Resources Committee:

1. Improvement of the standards of urban life and the raising of the level of living conditions. . . .
2. Elimination of urban blight and erosion; and above all, abolition of the slum. . . .
3. Better knowledge about the conditions of the cities in which over half our people now live. . . .
4. Better planned urban industrial location and development, made possible by a more intimate study of land use, industrial organization, fiscal policy, transportation policy, power policy. . . .
5. National-urban preparedness to meet insecurity and unemployment. . . .[6]

Beyond the individual city:

Urban planning is, of course, set in a framework of county and state governmental arrangements, and is closely tied up with the social programs and policies of the Nation. The city may contribute to the improvement and development of its own physical structure and to some extent of its political-economic structure and process. But the city cannot of itself solve the great national problems of contemporary industrial organization in a political democracy. The settlement of these larger questions requires the friendly cooperation of city and country alike; of national, state, and local governments, and of many other non-governmental associations as well.[7]

WORKSHOP AND PROBLEMS

1. What are some of the major problems in urban planning?
2. What is planning?

---

[6] National Resources Committee, *Our Cities: Their Role in the National Economy* (Washington, D. C.: Superintendent of Documents, 1937), pp. xii–xiii.
[7] *Ibid.*, p. xiii.

3. Develop a case for and against urban planning.

4. What are the more important types of planning activities cities engage in?

5. What are some of the expectations of urban planning?

6. Study what is being done in your state and community to develop better plans for cities.

BIBLIOGRAPHY

Anderson, William et al., *City Planning: A Selection of Readings in Its Theory and Practice* (Minneapolis: Burgess Publishing Co., 1950).

Black, Russell Van Nest, and Black, Mary Hedges, *Planning for the Small American City* (Chicago: Public Administration Service, 1948).

Bureau of Urban Research, *Urban Planning and Public Opinion* (Princeton, New Jersey: Bureau of Urban Research, Princeton University, 1942).

Churchill, Henry S., *The City Is the People* (New York: Reynal & Hitchcock, 1945).

Colean, Miles L., *American Housing Problems and Prospects. The Factual Findings* (New York: The Twentieth Century Fund, Inc., 1944).

Hilberseimer, Henry S., *The New City* (Chicago: Paul Theobald, 1944).

Lewis, Harold MacLean, *Planning the Modern City* (New York: John Wiley & Sons, 1949), 2 volumes.

Mumford, Lewis, *The Culture of Cities* (New York: Harcourt, Brace and Co., 1938).

National Resources Committee, *Our Cities: Their Role in the National Economy* (Washington. D. C.: Superintendent of Documents, 1937).

Riemer, Svend, *The Modern City* (New York: Prentice-Hall, Inc., 1952).

Saunders, S. E., and Rabuck, A. J., *New City Patterns* (New York: Reinhold Publishing Corporation, 1946).

Walker, Robert A., *The Planning Function in Urban Government* (Chicago: The University of Chicago Press, 1941).

————————————————, *Urban Planning* (Chicago: The University of Chicago Press, 1949).

CHAPTER 20

The Future of Urbanism

By WILLIAM E. COLE

The Question of Target Dates. It is perhaps best if we do not discuss the future of urbanism as an open end question. Rather, we will discuss some changes and outlooks for urban society as we see them up to the period around 1976, at which time we will be 200 years old as a nation. While we may make side excursions into the international outlook for urbanism, we shall limit our remarks largely to the United States.

Now, from 1954 to 1976 is only a little more than twenty years, but in a national culture that changes as rapidly as ours, and in an international world which can make rapid turns in one way or another, prediction for a twenty-year span is not easy. We face, frankly, a situation in which we have the tools and the know-how for our urban survival and salvation. On the other hand, we have the instruments for our destruction—a veritable garden variety of atomic bombs, airborne missles, and monitored planes. Added to these is great indifference to urban problems and situations among those living in cities, sitting on legislative benches at all levels of government, and otherwise occupying positions of leadership. While this indifference may not be our undoing, it helps.

Whither the Atom? Much depends upon the prospect of world peace, along with international control of the use of atomic bombs in war. War and the threat of war certainly will accelerate industrial decentralization as a government policy away from existing industrial areas, large centers of dense populations, and military installations. Such threats could bring rather revolutionary design in both urban structures—they being particularly built to withstand shock—and ground-plan developments of cities. Although there are other good reasons for designing cities along the so-called ribbon plan, such as elimination of congestion, better ecological harmony between worker and his work, minimizing air pollution and the like, their lessened vulnerability to destruction from air is an important reason for their design.[1]

---

[1] See L. Hilberseimer, *The New City* (Chicago: Paul Theobald, 1944).

325

(Official U. S. Air Force Photo.)

FIGURE 22. What Happens in the Use of the Atom and Airborne Weapons May Determine the Future of Cities.

Urbanism Will Continue. Urbanism will continue at perhaps an accelerated speed during the next twenty years. Now by urbanism we mean the urban dominance of the value systems, the activities and culture ways of the people, and the institutional controls of the people. There are two reasons why this statement is made. In the first place, urban interests control the major channels of the mass media of communication—the radio, the movie, television, the newspaper, advertising and magazine production. Through these mass media, hourly, the culture of the city bombards the people, and only or occasionally with farm and home hours, market reports, and broadcasts of hillbilly music, most of which originate in urban centers.

A second reason for saying that urbanism is likely to accelerate is that we seem to have lost, if we ever had, a courageous national program for developing and maintaining rural values and for building a type of rural education, at youth and adult levels, that might do for this country what has been done to preserve the folk culture and the rural idealism and values of some of the Scandinavian countries.

Progressively in late years, sociological research in rural areas and rural community leadership seems to have been more minimized in federal budgets. Agricultural education in the high schools is strongly vocational—too strongly. In some states agricultural extension services

do not have a single specialist in rural sociology or community organization and about all the attention some of the state colleges have given
to the culture of the folk is to exhume the bones of a few American
Indians. There is, in most education, an urban bias—education toward
the good things of the city—not toward rural values and occupations,
the absolute dependence upon the land and what it offers, and an emphasis upon better companionship between the two cultures. The emphasis here would seem to be urban.

Cities Will Grow. The outlook for increase in population in the world
and in the United States has been amply demonstrated. Urban growth
in this country is not likely to be as great between 1950 and 1960 as
it was between 1940 and 1950, but it will continue at a rapid pace,
particularly we believe in the fringe areas. There is considerable
evidence of industrial and commercial dispersion into the fringe areas
and over the boundaries into the rural hinterlands. Metropolitan areas
are likely to expand and to become more complex in their interrelationships. The automobile, the helicopter, and the roadable plane
are likely to be factors in this expansion. Limited access highways
will increasingly be built as connecting links between these cities,
making them more speedily accessible to each other. On these road-
ways, segregated travel for truck and automobile should aid in cur-
tailing congestion per unit of motor vehicles and miles driven.

Courageous measures are going to have to be used to solve some
of the tangled administrative and physical problems of metropolitan
areas. Planning boards and agencies of metropolitan scope, authorized
to engage in comprehensive metropolitan planning appear as one
solution, while metropolitan authorities formed by compact between
two or more states, as in the instance of the New York Port Authority,
is another solution. For the smaller metropolitan areas functional
consolidation of health, welfare, educational and other services, may
increase the efficiency of these services. In other areas annexation may
be the solution. We know also that regional development, such as that
in the Tennessee Valley area, will augment growth, development, and
economic stability.

The City as Environment. More and more the city is being considered
as not just a place but an environment for people. As this point of
view grows, attempts to make it a desirable place to live are likely
to be greater. This will call for more comprehensive master plan development than has heretofore existed. This scope of urban development will be so vast as to necessitate implementation, both in leadership and money, from federal and state levels and the companionship
interest and cooperation of both public and private enterprises, implemented through legislation like the national housing and redevelopment acts of 1949 and 1954 or the New Town Acts of England.

Physical plans have lagged in social features—such as construction along neighborhood lines, adequate facilities for community contacts, emphasis upon facilities which would improve the religious life of the people, and adequate space and facilities for schools and recreation. Only now are we beginning to build adequate safety features into our streets and traffic ways. While we are beginning to channelize and segregate traffic and build through traffic ways around residential areas, the results are too little. Entirely too little attention has been given to incorporating beauty as well as functionalism into urban ground plans and building design.

Along with planning the physical and social structures of the city, we will need to give more attention to atmospheric pollution and noise abatement as features of environment. To add to our critical problems of smog, smoke and ash in many cities, will be the problem of atomic residues when and if atomic energy becomes significant in industry. More research on noise, apart from the nuisances it creates, will need to be done before we can tie down its physical effects. The problems here are largely two—those of adequate ordinances and enforcement against noise and the problem of education of automobile and truck drivers.

The city, after all, is for the people. In fact, as Churchill puts it, the people are the city.[2] This recognition will implement decisions and measures to make it an adequate environment in which to live.

Lags in Administration. Many of the problems of cities are created by lags in leadership and administration—sometimes downright political graft and corruption.

Business men would not think of putting a 10 billion dollar business in incapable hands, but that is just what we do with our cities. We not only do this but we also hamstring cities with legislative ties and lack of home rule. The tide is turning. City managership has now become a professional field, with more and more managers being employed from outside the cities in which they are to work. Constitutional and charter changes are being made to give a greater element of home rule and to free cities from dominance by rural-minded legislatures. Municipal leagues are being formed to fight for what cities need and municipal advisory services are being set up by these leagues to aid cities with their many administrative, legal, and physical problems. These trends should change the complexion of municipal administration and government for the better.

Needed: a Generation of Urban Research. We have had too little research into what it is that motivates urban people; why urban people show lack of concern for their problems and conditions. We need more basic research on what urban people desire in their urban life. We need more basic research on urban groups, neighborhoods and in-

---

[2] Henry S. Churchill, *The City Is the People* (New York: Reynal and Hitchcock, 1945).

stitutions. We need better evaluation of the results of public housing, neighborhood planning and urban redevelopment measures. Urban building must be provided by more research and appraisal in order that we may know in which direction to build for the future. This future is still in our hands; we control the choices.

WORKSHOP AND PROBLEMS

1. Why would you say that 1976 is an importnat target date in the history of the United States?

2. Why do the form of cities and the future of the city depend, in part, upon the control of atomic weapons?

3. Why is control of mass media of communication likely to lead to the continued expansion of urbanism?

4. Why will courageous measures be necessary to solve the administrative and physical problems of large metropolitan areas?

5. Why is the recognition of the city as environment important?

6. What are likely to be some improvements in urban administration in the future?

7. Why is more basic urban research needed?

8. Prepare a report on "The Future of the City—1954-1976."

BIBLIOGRAPHY

Churchill, Henry S., *The City Is the People* (New York: Reynal and Hitchcock, 1945).

Dahir, James, *The Neighborhood Unit Plan: A Selected Bibliography with Interpretative Comments* (New York: Russell Sage Foundation, 1947).

Hilberseimer, L., *The New City* (Chicago: Paul Theobald, 1944).

Howard, Ebenezer, *Garden Cities of Tomorrow* (London: Faber and Faber, Ltd., 1946).

Le Corbusier, *Concerning Town Planning* (London: The Architectural Press, 1947).

Lewis, Harold MacLean, *Planning the Modern City* (2 vols.) (New York: John Wiley and Sons, 1949).

Sanders, S. E., and Rabuck, A. J., *New City Patterns* (New York: Reinhold Publishing Co., 1946).

Name Index

Ogburn, W. F., 76, 107

Panella, Pat M., 71
Park, Robert E., 53
Parker, Florence E., 169
Perry, Clarence, 236
Perry, Everett L., 302
Pfautz, Harold W., 108
Pirenne, Henri, 14
Plumley, Margaret L., 216
Pomeroy, W. B., 118, 125
Pope, Liston, 205, 297
Porterfield, Austin, 201, 202

Queen, Stuart A., 51, 71, 107, 195, 221

Raper, Arthur F., 108
Reckless, Walter C., 285, 286
Redfield, Robert, 93, 95
Redlich, Frederick C., 240
Reiss, Albert J., Jr., 24, 109
Riemer, Svend, 2, 310
Rogoff, Natalie, 109
Roterus, Victor, 247

Sanderson, Dwight, 98, 103
Sanderson, Ross W., 305, 306, 307, 310
Schacter, Stanley, 235
Scheel, Leonard A., 215
Schmid, Calvin F., 281
Schoolcraft, L. A., 239, 256
Sewell, William H., 109
Shaw, Clifford R., 239, 280
Shippey, Frederick A., 292
Shyne, Ann W., 214
Sitte, Camillo, 317
Sjoberg, Gideon, 135
Smith, T. Lynn, 13, 80, 291
Snell, Seward B., 249
Sorokin, P. A., 70
Spaulding, I. A., 106
Spiegelman, Mortimer, 25, 44
Spykman, N. J., 69
Stanbery, Van Buren, 247
Stone, Carol L., 136, 154

Stouffer, Samuel, 195
Strauss, Anselm L., 105
Sutherland, Edwin H., 285, 286

Taft, Donald R., 282
Taylor, Carl C., 69, 107, 108
Terman, Lewis M., 148, 151
Thomas, Dorothy Swaine, 65
Thomas, John L., 200
Thompson, Laura, 93
Thompson, Warren, 74, 75, 149
Thornthwaite, C. W., 46
Tomars, Adolph S., 101
Tonnies, Ferdinand, 95
Trever, Albert A., 2
Tripp, Thomas A., 305
Turner, Ralph, 2, 4

Vance, Rupert B., 42, 56, 63, 109
Villaume, William J., 307, 310
Vincent, M. J., 107

Walker, Robert Averill, 2, 317
Waller, Willard, 64
Wallerstein, James S., 285
Ware, Caroline F., 240
Warner, W. Lloyd, 108, 118, 296
Weber, A. F., 11, 14, 15, 20, 23, 42
Weidner, Edward W., 229
Weinberg, S. Kirson, 104, 105
Weston, Robert L., 211
Whelpton, P. K., 44, 45, 155
Whyte, William H., Jr., 234
Wilson, Logan, 101, 295, 297
Winch, Robert F., 125
Wirth, Louis, 69
Wyle, Clement J., 285

Yerushalmy, J., 76
Young, Kimball, 105
Young, Pauline V., 93

Zimmerman, Carle C., 70
Zorbaugh, Harvey W., 240

Subject Index

Administration, Lags in, 328
Agriculture, Decline of labor in, 244
Annexation, 59, 225; Arguments for, 60, 61
Annulment, 166
Area, Metropolitan, 51; Status, 54
Areas, Underdeveloped, Social programs, 267
Associations, Building and loan, 261; F.H.A., 262; YMCA, 273
Authority, Changing patterns, 151